feminism meets queer theory

books from

differences

series editors

NAOMI SCHOR

ELIZABETH WEED

feminism meets queer theory

edited by

ELIZABETH WEED
NAOMI SCHOR

Indiana University Press

Bloomington and Indianapolis

The editors wish to express
their gratitude to
Sheila Levrant de Bretteville
for her generous help with
the design of the
d i f f e r e n c e s *book series*
and to assistant editors
Steve Evans and
Mark Cooper.

This book is a publication of

Indiana University Press
601 North Morton Street
Bloomington, IN 47404-3797 USA

http://www.indiana.edu/~iupress

Telephone orders 800-842-6796
Fax orders 812-855-7931
Orders by e-mail iuporder@indiana.edu

Manufactured in the United States
of America

Library of Congress
Cataloging-in-Publication Data

Feminism meets queer theory / edited by
  Elizabeth Weed and Naomi Schor.
     p.   cm. — (Books from differences)
  This collection originally appeared in v. 6,
summer–fall 1994 of 'Differences: a journal
of feminist cultural studies'.
  Includes bibliographical references (p.   )
and index.
  ISBN 0-253-33278-8 (cloth : alk. paper).—
ISBN 0-253-21118-2 (pbk. : alk. paper)
  1. Feminist theory. 2. Homosexuality—
Philosophy. 3. Gays—Identity. I. Weed,
Elizabeth, date. II. Schor, Naomi. III. Series.
HQ1190.F442   1997
305.42'01—dc21   96-53416

  2   3   4   5   6   05   04   03   02   01   00

Contents

Introduction

*W*hen feminism meets queer theory, no introductions seem necessary. Both academic feminism and queer theory are connected, however directly or indirectly, to political movements outside the academy, in some cases to overlapping movements. Both are interdisciplinary modes of inquiry; both constitute themselves in critical relation to a set of hegemonic social and cultural formations. Indeed, the two are connected not only by commonalities but by affiliations. Queer theory, like lesbian and gay studies, has acknowledged its intellectual debts to feminist theory and women's studies, just as feminist theory has recognized the influence of queer theory. For many in the academy, feminism and queer theory are most easily understood as two branches of the same family tree of knowledge and politics, just as in most bookstores they are most easily found on shelves located side by side or back to back.

Since all this seems true enough, why entitle the volume "feminism *meets* queer theory"? If the purpose of the collection is to present some of the points of convergence and divergence between the two fields, why not give it the title of "the meeting of feminism and queer theory," or simply "feminism and queer theory"? Why a title that connotes a staging of strangeness or unpredictability?

The problem with the "and," of course, is that it too quickly renders its terms commensurable. To say that feminism and queer theory share commonalities and affiliations is not to say they are easily commensurable. In fact, they are clearly presented here as something of an unmatched pair: the unmodified "feminism" of the title would seem to be more properly paired with something like "queer politics" ("feminist politics meets queer politics"), just as "queer theory" would seem to be better matched with its counterpart, "feminist theory" ("feminist theory meets queer theory"). And yet, the solution is not to find a more proper couple, for if "feminism" and "queer theory" are an awkward pair, "feminist theory" and "queer theory" are no less so. Not only do the two bodies of theory have quite different historical formations, but because of these differences, the (various and complicated) relationships among feminist politics, women's studies, and feminist theory have no simple correspondence to the (various and complicated) relationships among queer politics, gay and lesbian studies, and queer theory.[1] Given the difficulty of finding a matched pair, the skewed coupling of the title remains unabashedly awry, suggesting, perhaps, a meeting that is not as straightforward as many academicians and bookstores might think.[2]

Still, why frame the collection of essays as a strange and even surprising meeting? The answer lies not so much in what queer theory represents, but in queer theory's representation of feminism—a representation that in the eyes of some feminist theorists renders feminism strangely unrecognizable. No matter how reluctant queer theory has been to pin itself down as a coherent set of theorizations,[3] it has been consistent about one aspect of its project: considerations of sex and sexuality cannot be contained by the category of gender. This is not, in itself, a controversial proposition. The problem, as Judith Butler shows in her argument "Against Proper Objects," is that in this formulation gender becomes the property of feminist inquiry while the proper study of sex and sexuality is located elsewhere.[4] This one move, the separation of gender from sex and sexuality, is by no means the only topic of conversation between feminism and queer theory—the essays in this volume address a number of other questions—but it is this move above all that makes the meeting of feminism and queer theory a strange one.

By rendering feminism unrecognizable—not to say illegible—to many feminist theorists, queer theory provokes a rethinking of earlier arguments that had seemed, if not resolved, at least displaced. That is, in engaging with queer theory, a number of the feminist theorists here are involved less in putting queer theory in its place—a place where many of the contributors also situate themselves—than in taking a close look at the odd sort of feminism queer theory presents them with. This means that one of the effects of the encounter is that "feminism" ineluctably, if unexpectedly, revisits itself. Running through the essays are debates about the sex/gender split, about whether gender or sexual difference is preferable as a category of analysis, about Freudian-Lacanian versus Foucauldian modes of theorizing. These debates evoke an earlier feminist period, in some cases a much earlier one. But like all "revisits," this one entails no simple reanimation of the past, no respectful return to former truths. The introduction of old arguments into the theoretical and political investments of the present serves, rather, to disturb the ground of both the old debates and the new, and this disturbance can only be enriching.

A more faithful, if less euphonious, title might be, then, "feminist theorists meet the feminism of queer theory." Queer theory's feminism is a strange feminism, stripped of its contentious elements, its internal contradictions, its multiplicity (see especially Butler; Braidotti; Rubin; Martin; and Hammonds). For example, the cordoning off of gender from the study of sexuality also means putting aside the considerable work done in recent years on the overlay and articulation of gendering and racialization. If, as Evelynn Hammonds says, black women are caught in the intersection of gender and sexuality, how much more difficult does "queerness" become for the black woman given the cleaving of the terms gender and sex/sexuality. To observe the whiteness of the gender/sex-sexuality split is not to say that queer theory has no place for theories of racialization. In a special 1994 issue of *Diacritics* entitled "Critical Crossings," Butler and Biddy Martin used the by then familiar thematics of "queer" to expand the discursive range of the field. Consider the opening comments of their introduction:

> Diacritics *graciously asked us to edit an issue on gay and lesbian studies, and we took the occasion to broaden the scope of that request to include work that interrogates the problem of cross-identification within and across race and postcolonial studies, gender theory, and theories of sexuality. We chose to expand our emphasis in order to avoid static conceptions of identity and political alignment. "Queer theory" has promised to complicate assumptions about routes of identification and desire. We wanted to test that promise by soliciting essays that analyze critical, even surprising, boundary crossings. (3)*

In an upcoming special edition of *College Literature* entitled "Queer Utilities: Textual/Theoretical/Pedagogical," Jean Walton, editor of the theoretical section, situates her effort as a continuation of the *Diacritics* project to expand the field of "queer." The first lines of her introduction echo those of Butler and Martin; the closing lines, cited below, make explicit the risks of not expanding the field:

Emerging from the collection as a whole is the recognition that what has been termed the "presumption of heterosexuality" by U.S. queer theory is, to be precise, a presumption of white heterosexuality; if it is felt as an imposition, a stricture, or even an unwittingly productive construct, it is felt as such by virtue of its whiteness as much as by its heteronormativity. Indeed, these essays join with much recent work to show the extent to which heteronormativity is propped up by its unmarked whiteness, and thus how it is experienced differently by queers of color than by their white compatriots. One of the prime strategies of lesbian and gay studies has been to "queer" what had otherwise seemed to be "straight": mainstream cinema, pop music, novels, indeed, the "nation" itself. But more recently, it seems imperative to ask: does "queering" a primarily white heteronormative hegemony necessarily *throw its previously unmarked whiteness into relief? Or is the political act of "queering" itself rooted in, and therefore reproductive of, a racial whiteness oblivious to its own conditions of privilege?*[5]

The choices made in collecting essays for a special issue of *differences* in 1994 were different from those made by Butler and Martin, and recently by Walton. Our purpose was not to enlarge queer theory, to bring feminist theoretical insights about racialization, or class formations, or economic exploitation to the meeting of the two fields, *but rather to look squarely at the way the intersection of feminism and queer theory has been rendered by queer theory.* On the one hand, there are queer thematics (such as the rich elaboration of the workings of normativity or the disruption of identity), which seem to invite an obvious interplay between the two fields; on the other, there is an exclusionary logic that all but precludes such interplay. This move, which renders feminism's relationship to queer theory simultaneously inevitable and impossible, makes the encounter with queer theory different from many of feminism's other encounters. The field of academic feminism is, of course, constituted by multiple feminisms, and its history is that of numerous contestations, from lesbian theorists, from African American and other theorists of color, from those concerned with theories of class and with third world and postcolonial positionalities. In each of these historical encounters, the theoretical interest in question has produced a representation of a feminism from which it has distinguished itself and, in doing so, has shifted the terms of debate. Queer theory's representation of feminism has seemed qualitatively different from those encounters. The feminism against which queer theory defines itself is a feminism reduced almost to caricature: a feminism tied to a concern for gender, bound to a regressive and monotonous binary opposition. That reduction of feminist critique calls for analysis.

The volume succeeds in bringing about not one but many meetings: of feminist theorists and queer theorists, of queer feminist theorists and feminist queer theorists. There are interviews: in two illuminating interviews Butler engages Rosi Braidotti and Gayle Rubin in discussion. The first focuses on Butler's and Braidotti's very different theoretical views of gender and sexual difference and on Braidotti's views of the differences between European and U.S. feminism; the second looks at Butler's and Rubin's understandings of the latter's formative role in the development of feminist and then queer theories. There are critical exchanges: Braidotti and Trevor Hope exchange comments on his reading of the way feminists, including Braidotti, reinscribe an archaic and foundational homosexuality at the origin of Western civilization; and Teresa de Lauretis responds to Elizabeth Grosz's review of her book *The Practice of Love*. In that exchange, Grosz sees de Lauretis pushing the limits of psychoanalysis to account for lesbian desire and ventures that even in as exceptional a study as *The Practice of Love* psychoanalysis may have reached its limit. De Lauretis, for her part, takes her distance from both feminist theory and queer theory (which she proposed "as a working hypothesis for lesbian and gay studies in this very journal [*differences* 3.2]" [297; 316 in this volume]) to forge a theory of lesbian sexuality and desire.

The individual essays also represent encounters: Butler confronts queer theory with its splitting of gender from sex/sexuality and sets out the terms for the interviews with Braidotti and Rubin; Biddy Martin brings two texts from turn-of-the-century Germany to bear on the current theoretical bind of gender, sexuality, and psychic life. Evelynn Hammonds confronts queer theory with the question of silence regarding black women's sexuality: not only the thematic "silence" in writings by and about black women, or the "politics of silence" historically practiced by black women, but also the constitutive silence of "canonical" theories of sexuality. Kim Michasiw puts psychoanalysis, femininity, and masculinity to work in his discussion of queer readings of camp; Carole-Anne Tyler confronts those who denigrate passing with an argument that we are all only always passing; and I look at the ways the cleaving of gender from sex and sexuality effects critical reading.

In the end, no theoretical consensus, no deft resolution emerges from all the encounters. But the essays do put some current critical debates into relief. They enable us to ask, for example, about the importance of theoretical style. Even if the division is not neatly drawn (see Braidotti) between a queer thematics of Foucauldian and Deleuzian flow and a feminist thematics more dependent on the concept and its deconstruction, what can be said about this growing stylistic rift? The essays also lead us to ask what difference there might be between feminism's historical concern with essentialism and antiessentialism as against queer theory's interest in essentialism and constructionism. Finally, the essays might indicate a way of approaching feminism's relationship to today's rapidly shifting and often impatient field of critical theory. It is telling, perhaps, that both de Lauretis (306; 325 in this volume) and Braidotti appeal at one point to the notion of "working through." In Braidotti's words:

> *Repetitions are ways of revisiting sites and positions in order to disengage ourselves from the hold they may still have on us. It is a process of working through, for which the psychoanalytic process of remembrance is one adequate model (though by no means the only one). Working through is a way of walking backwards through what we have been. . . . (220, this volume)*

Notes

1   For example, none of the undecidability of the term "women's studies" (see Gallop 13–21) is present in "gay and lesbian studies"; by the same token, none of the provocation of "queer theory" can be found in "feminist theory." Queer politics enact a split with gay and lesbian politics that overlaps but does not duplicate splits between "mainstream" feminist politics and lesbian politics or between feminist sexual liberationists and feminists against pornography. And so on.

2   One might ask why not call it a "queer" meeting, since the term "queer" sees itself as

effecting essentially productive displacements or defamiliarizations. The question here would be through what route this particular encounter becomes productive.

3   As Lauren Berlant and Michael Warner say, queer theory has a very short history and "cannot be assimilated to a single discourse, let alone a propositional program. . . . Queer commentary takes on various shapes, risks, ambitions, and ambivalences in various contexts. . . . The danger of the label q*ueer theory* is that it makes its queer and nonqueer audiences forget these differences and imagine a context (theory) in which *queer* has a stable referential content and pragmatic force" (343–44).

4   Butler's argument engages with the introduction to *The Lesbian and Gay Studies Reader*, but it applies as well to queer theory. The latter breaks in some ways with lesbian and gay studies, but not with regard to the gender/sex-sexuality split.

5   Butler and Martin have a related, if different, ending: "These are some of the cross-purposes to which we have subjected this issue with the hope of providing a more precise account of how various kinds of writing within minority studies generally cross with—and require—each other. Rather than offer a pluralist panoply of "difference," we aim to offer a set of intersecting analyses that work in concert, though not in unison, to reconsider cross-identification as a critical point of departure and to explore the way in which these fields are mutually implicated in each other" (3).

Works Cited

Abelove, Henry, Michèle Aina Barale, and David M. Halperin, eds. *The Lesbian and Gay Studies Reader*. New York: Routledge, 1993.

Berlant, Lauren, and Michael Warner. "What Does Queer Theory Teach Us about X?" Guest Column. *PMLA* 110.3 (1995): 343–49.

Butler, Judith, and Biddy Martin. "Cross-Identifications." *Diacritics* [Special issue on "Critical Crossings"]. Ed. Judith Butler and Biddy Martin. 24.2–3 (1994): 3.

Gallop, Jane. *Reading Lacan*. Ithaca: Cornell UP, 1985.

Walton, Jean. "Racialized Lesbian Desire on the Transnational Scene." *College Literature* [Special issue on "Queer Utilities: Textual/Theoretical/Pedagogical"]. Ed. Donald Hall, Garry Leonard, Jean Walton. 24.1 (1997).

feminism meets queer theory

Against Proper Objects[1]

*W*hen this essay was originally published in *differences*, it was billed as an "introduction," and that produced a certain ambiguity. The essay was not meant as an introduction to the volume, but simply to the two interviews that I had conducted for the special issue. That volume's editors are Naomi Schor and Elizabeth Weed, and they decided which essays to include. Indeed, I had not seen the essays prior to publication.

At the time the volume was proposed to me, it seemed that an exploration of the "encounter" between feminist and queer theory was timely and potentially productive, but I forgot at that moment how quickly a critical encounter becomes misconstrued as a war. For those of us who work in the interstices of the relation between queer theory and feminism (as well as other contemporary critical discourses), and who insist on continuing the important intellectual tradition of immanent critique, the risk will always take the following form: if one analyzes the heterosexist assumptions of feminist theory, one will be construed as "anti-" or "post-" feminist; if one analyzes the anti-feminism of some gay and lesbian theory, one will be construed as hostile to that lesbian and gay theory. What conditions such a logic of non-contradiction, pitting minority communities against one another at an historical moment in which the struggles between them need to be put into a dynamic and empowering interplay?

For either set of intellectual movements to remain vital, expansive, and self-critical, room must be made for the kind of immanent critique which shows how the presuppositions of one critical enterprise can operate to forestall the work of another. In many ways, the resistance to sympathetic or, indeed, immanent critique, symptomatizes the academic residue of an identity politics that thinks that critique only and always weakens a movement rather than understanding that the democratic and non-dogmatic future of any such movement depends precisely on its ability to incorporate, without domesticating, challenges from its own alterities. If to wage such a critique is to be construed as having "broken" with the movement in question, then it seems that lines of loyalty become indistinguishable from positions of dogmatic refusal. It is, I am sure, the dogmatic refusal of such challenges that weakens feminism as well as gay and lesbian studies, putting both at risk at the moment in which they refuse one another. There can be no viable feminism that fails to account for its complicity in forms of oppression, whether they be colonial, class-based, racist, or homophobic. And there can be no viable lesbian and gay studies paradigm that does not examine its own complicitous investments in misogyny and other forms of oppression.

My own contribution to this debate has perhaps not been as constructive as it could have been, and so I offer the following words to recontextualize the critique I have offered. My own history within feminism has always been an uneasy one, and I found myself increasingly enraged as a graduate student and young faculty member as countless feminist frameworks seemed either to elide or pathologize the challenge to gender normativity posed by queer practices. The writing of *Gender Trouble* was perhaps the acerbic culmination of that history of unease and anger within feminism. The binary between "men" and "women" seemed not only to be a constant presupposition within feminist work, but was elevated to the theological status of the "irrefutable" within some French Feminism. The implicit and compulsory presumption of heterosexuality supported the normativity and irreversibility of that binary and posited relations of complementarity or asymmetry between its terms in ways that only shored up, without marking, the heterosexist assumptions of the paradigm. As I wrote against such moves, I meant to open up another possibility for feminist thought, one that would overcome its complicity in heterosexist presuppositions, and mark an alliance with lesbian and gay struggles. That the work was taken as a queer departure from feminism signaled to me how deeply identified feminism is with those very heterosexist assumptions.

The question, of course, is: does it have to be? Partly in opposition to a feminist reduction of sexuality to a heterosexist frame for thinking sexual difference, "sexuality" has emerged, through the use of Foucault, as a point of departure that suspends the question of sexual difference or, indeed, of gender. The lesbian and gay opposition to the heterosexism of feminism thus culminates in a certain elision of sexual difference and, indeed, a certain indifference to the debates that continue between "gender" and "sexual difference" paradigms. To mark sexuality off as a domain separable from gender seemed to many of us, especially of the queer persuasion, to emphasize sexual practices rather than either gender or sexual identity and to allow for forms of "dissonance" to emerge between gendered self-understandings and forms of sexual engagement.

The opening up of such "dissonant" configurations is quite in line with the kind of gender trouble that I promote, and yet I want to persist in asking some critical questions about the language we use to describe such important terrain. Can sexual practices ever fully be divorced from questions of gender, or do questions of gender persist as the "unconscious" of sexual play? Such a question is not meant to return us to the pathos of an irrefutable "sexual difference," but to suggest that the "break" with gender always comes at a cost and, perhaps also, with its spectral return. The normative weight of gender is not suddenly thrown off at the moment in which we imagine ourselves to be fully identified with what we do. On the contrary, it is precisely our sense of gender that is disoriented through such practices: the possibility of reworking normative gender categories is part of the pleasure and danger of such acts. Although we may posit the heuristic possibility of a world in which acts and identities would be fully separable, it still remains for us to describe what it might mean to live that very separation.

The revised version of my essay is meant to precipitate such a discussion.

A set of paradoxes has emerged within recent debates in feminist and queer theory that complicates any effort to stage a simple standoff between the two domains. Within queer studies generally, a methodological distinction has been offered which would distinguish theories of sexuality from theories of gender and, further, allocate the theoretical investigation of sexuality to queer studies and the analysis of gender to feminism. Consider the introduction to *The Lesbian and Gay Studies Reader* in which an "analogy" (xv) with women's studies is offered as a way of understanding the range of issues pertaining to lesbian and gay studies. Citing a 1975 essay by feminist historian Joan Kelly-Gadol, the editors write that "women's history is not meant to be additive . . . rather, women's history seeks to establish the centrality of *gender* as a fundamental category of historical analysis and understanding—a category central, in other words, to each of those previously existing sub-departments of history" (xv). Applauding the feminist effort to make gender into "a central category of analysis," the editors seek to make the same kind of claim for the objects of research proper to lesbian and gay studies: "Lesbian/gay studies does for *sex* and *sexuality* approximately what women's studies does for gender" (xv).

Against Methodology

In laying out the "proper" domain for feminist analysis, the editors of *The Lesbian and Gay Studies Reader* formulate the methodological domain of women's studies as that which "includes any research that treats gender (whether female or male) as a central category of analysis." The parenthetical reference to "female or male" suggests that these terms are interchangeable with the notion of gender, although conventional formulations of the sex/gender distinction associated "sex" with female or male—or with the problematic of a continuum between them—and "gender" with the social categories of men and women. This brief and parenthetical suggestion that gender might be understood as equivalent to "female or male" thus appears to rest on a conflation of sex with gender.

Significantly, though "female or male" appear in this formulation of feminism, the term "sex" does not; gender appears to be reduced to sex in this sentence at the same time that the term "sex" remains merely implied. One might think this is a small point. Note, however, that the term "sex" does become explicit in the next sentence, but only as one of the two proper objects of lesbian and gay studies: "sex and sexuality." In this second context, "sex" appears to mean "sexual desire and practice" but also the Foucauldian sense of "sex" as a regime of identity or a fictional ideal by which sex as anatomy, sensation, acts, and practice are arbitrarily unified.[2] If, as appears likely, the Foucauldian meaning of "sex" is implied by its mention in this context, then "sex" would include the matter of "female or male" mentioned above. Thus, the editors lead us through analogy from a feminism in which gender and sex are conflated to a notion of lesbian and gay studies in which "sex" encompasses and exceeds the purview of feminism: "sex" in this second instance would include not only questions of identity and attribute (female or male) but discourses of sensation, acts, and sexual practice as well.

To the extent that the analogy "works" through reference to a term—"sex"—which commonly concerns both feminism and lesbian/gay studies, that commonality must be denied, through elision or through the semantic splitting and redistribution of its constitutive parts. Whereas "sex" in the elided sense attributed to feminism will mean only identity and attribute, "sex" in the explicit and lesbian/gay sense will include and supersede the feminist sense: identity, attribute, sensation, pleasures, acts, and practices. Thus "sex" in the sense deployed by lesbian and gay studies is understood to include the putative feminist binary (female or male) but also to imply the second proper object of lesbian and gay studies: "sexuality."

I belabor the structure of this analogy because the terms that the analogy seeks to compare are not as separate as they may at first appear. And if the terms are separated in arbitrary or illegible ways (as in the case of "gender [female or male]") it is because such a separation, however falsifying or arbitrary, assists in making the methodological claim that is supposed to ground lesbian and gay studies as an "autonomous" enterprise.

As the analogy is now set up, feminism is figured as concerned not only with one aspect of "sex"—putative anatomical identity—but with no aspects of sexuality. Is this a description of feminist practice, one which follows feminism's own self-restriction of its own methodological concerns to that of "gender" (reduced to "sex" in its biological formulations)? Where would the feminist traditions in favor of enhancing sexual freedom fit in such a scheme, much less those that analyze the interrelation of gender and sexuality? Or is it that, whenever feminism engages in such claims it can now be said no longer to be feminism but rather to belong to the methodology of lesbian and gay studies? Perhaps the restriction of feminism to gender, construed as biological binary, is nothing other than a prescribed restriction of feminist practice to terms illegible to feminist criticism performed in the service of augmenting claims made by lesbian and gay studies for methodological autonomy?

Even if we accept Foucault's proposal to consider "sex" as a fictional unity, a speculative ideal, which compounds the semantic senses of sex as identity, sensation, and practice, to name a few, are we to accept Foucault's presumption that "sex" is as monolithic and unified a category as it seems? Does "sex" not gain that appearance of a monolithic unity, a speculative ideal, to the extent that it covers over "sexual difference" or, rather, assimilates sexual difference to the category of "sex"? Insofar as lesbian and gay studies relies on *this* notion of sex it appears to take as one of its grounds, its founding methodological claims, a refusal of sexual difference in the theoretical constitution of "sex" as a proper object of study.

The terms of the analogy suggest as much once we consider that the

theoretical distinction between feminist and lesbian/gay studies effects a refusal of the first term, "gender," through an assimilation of its elided sense,
"sex," to the second set of terms: "sex and sexuality." Indeed, only by reducing
feminism to "gender," then implicitly conflating gender with sex, i.e. "female
or male," and then explicitly declaring "sex" to be one of its two proper objects, can lesbian and gay studies establish itself as the proper successor to
feminism. This place, however, is established in part through assimilating
sexual difference to sex in such a way that sexual difference itself is refused
through the trajectory of the sublation. Sexual difference, irreducible to "gender" or to the putative biological disjunction of "female or male," is rhetorically
refused through the substitution by which a unitary "sex" is installed as the
proper object of inquiry.

Here we begin to see the difficulty of establishing a point of departure
that does not itself perform a certain significant exclusion. The editors of *The
Lesbian and Gay Studies Reader* mean only to make a distinction between
feminist frameworks that cannot capture the complexity of analysis that takes
place within lesbian and gay studies, the importance of keeping a "dissonant"
relation open between gender and sexuality, and the necessity of considering
sexuality as having a distinct character as a regulatory regime, one that cannot
be accounted for through a gender-based analysis. All this seems true and right,
and despite the best intentions of these editors, all of whom have been active in
feminist scholarship, a quandary besets the analysis that could not have been
anticipated.

The analogy which opens the discussion of "proper objects" is hardly
benign in that the "ground" is established through an elision of the significance
of sexual difference. The distinction between the two domains works in at least
two ways. The second term (gay and lesbian studies) is distinguished from the
first (feminist studies) through a separation of the *kinds* of objects they pursue.
To the extent, however, that the second pursues a kind of object ("sex") that
both refuses and includes the object of the first ("female or male"), that
distinction becomes the rhetorical means by which an elision is performed.
This erasure begins with the reduction of gender to sex—a caricature of
feminist theoretical work of the last twenty years—which then stages the
possibility of an assimilation of that caricatured version of feminism to the
putatively more expansive terrain of lesbian and gay studies. That assimilation
takes place through elision but also as a chiasmic effect. Considered as analogy,

the terms are discrete; considered as an historical account encoded in the terms of analogy, lesbian and gay studies improves upon the terms of feminism; considered as chiasm, the analogy breaks down, and the terms which appear to be parallel (gender and sex/sexuality) or the same ("sex" in the elided sense and "sex" in the explicit sense) are neither, and the narrative of supersession loses its plausibility.

If the "sex" which feminism is said to study constitutes one dimension of the multidimensional "sex" that lesbian and gay research is said to study, then the implicit argument is that lesbian and gay studies does precisely what feminism is said to do but does it in a more expansive and complex way. This distinction between "sex" as anatomical identity and "sex" as regime or practice will become quite crucial to the formulation of lesbian/gay studies as the analysis of sex and sexuality, for the ambiguity of sex as act and identity will be split into univocal dimensions in order to make the claim that the kind of sex that one *is* and the kind of sex that one *does* belong to two separate kinds of analysis: feminist and lesbian/gay, respectively.

And yet, "sex" carries different valences in each context. The terms of the analogy are falsifying to the extent that the object of feminism cannot be reduced to "gender (female or male)," and the "sex" whereof lesbian and gay studies speaks—*to the extent that it defines itself against feminism*—is constituted through a repudiation of sexual difference, a move which many lesbian and gay scholars would surely refuse, including no doubt the editors of the volume in question. Indeed, what is at issue is clearly *not* a question of what the editors of the volume intend, given that all three have made strong contributions to feminist scholarship, but rather with a set of political and historical implications of the analogy between feminism and lesbian/gay studies which have been difficult to discern for many of us who work within and between these domains of study.[3]

The problem here is not just the fairly obvious one that there is little, if any, feminist research that would make use of the oxymoron "gender (male or female)" as a methodological point of departure. Even Joan Kelly-Gadol's cited article construes the notion of "sex" as a fully social category and, though published in 1975, a year after the publication of Gayle Rubin's "The Traffic in Women," it does not pursue the implications of the sex/gender distinction as is done in the subsequent work of Sherry Ortner, Harriet Whitehead, Moira Gaetens, Evelyn Fox Keller, and Joan W. Scott.[4] Perhaps more salient here is that "gender" has denoted not a set of attributes or identities, but a framework of differential analysis and "a primary way of signifying relationships of power" (Scott, "Gender" 44). Feminist efforts to refuse the reduction of gender to a disjunctive and biological binarism have been quite central to several disciplines for several decades: a) the work on the biological sciences of Ruth Hubbard, Anne Fausto-Sterling, Monique Wittig, Donna Haraway, Helen Longino, to name but a few; b) the massive literature within feminism that not only explores the links among gender, race, and sexuality, but shows how "gender" is produced through these overlapping articulations of power. This scholarship in the fields of Third World and postcolonial feminism has called into question in different ways not only the exclusive focus of feminism on gender, but the centrality of racial and class formations in the constitution of gender itself. Feminists posing these kinds of questions include Norma Alarcón, Cherríe Moraga, Chandra Mohanty, Valerie Smith, Hortense Spillers, Gayatri Chakravorty Spivak, among scores of others.

Although the problems associated with the sex/gender distinction are many, it seems clear that the more general question of the relation of the biological and the cultural—which includes scholarly reflection on the production of the very distinction between the two categories—has commanded feminist intellectual attention from the beginning of the Second Wave. That there are competing feminist views on how that tension ought to be formulated is clear, but few, if any, feminist texts proceed with a simple parenthetical conflation of the two. In fact, what is incisive and valuable in feminist work is precisely the kind of thinking that calls into question the settled grounds of analysis. And even the recourse to sexual difference within feminist theory is at its most productive when it is taken not as a ground, foundation, or methodology, but as a *question* posed but not resolved.

What separates the putative object of feminism—gender, construed as sex—from the putative object of lesbian and gay studies—sex, construed as sexuality—is a chiasmic confusion in which the constitutive ambiguity of "sex" is denied in order to make arbitrary territorial claims. And though the language of the editorial introduction to the volume appears to appreciate the feminist precedent, this is an idealization which is perhaps not without its aggression. Indeed, lesbian and gay studies in this form cannot articulate its own "proper object" outside the terms of this analogy with feminism, an analogy that relegates feminism to an analysis of "gender" reduced to a biological frame and evacuated of all sexuality. In this sense, the very formulation of lesbian and gay studies depends upon the evacuation of a sexual discourse from feminism. And what passes as a benign, even respectful, analogy with feminism is the means by which the fields are separated, where that separation requires the desexualization of the feminist project and the appropriation of sexuality as the "proper" object of lesbian/gay studies.

The institution of the "proper object" takes place, as usual, through a mundane sort of violence. Indeed, we might read moments of methodological founding as pervasively anti-historical acts, beginnings which fabricate their legitimating histories through a retroactive narrative, burying complicity and division in and through the funereal figure of the "ground."

The use of the analogy between feminist and lesbian/gay also presumes that the problem of precedent might be adequately addressed through recourse to a binary frame. Lesbian and gay studies will be derived from feminism, and yet, the editors argue, there will continue to be important communication between the two domains.[5] But what constitutes these domains as sequential and distinct, framed by analogy and its binary presumption? How is it that this framing of lesbian/gay in relation to feminism forecloses the field of social differences from which both projects emerge? In particular, terms such as "race" and "class" are ruled out from having a constitutive history in determining the parameters of either field. Whether the position is for or against the centrality of gender to sexuality, it is gender and sexuality alone that remain the common objects of contention. The presumption is that they can be compared and contrasted but that the binary frame presumed and instituted through the analogy is itself self-evidently "proper."

Against the Anti-Pornography Paradigm

The anti-pornography movement through the 80s and, more recently, the assimilation of feminist politics to the discourse on victimization, have succeeded in rendering popular a view of feminism in which positions of gender are strictly correlated with positions of domination or subordination within sexuality. Feminist arguments such as Catharine MacKinnon's offer an analysis of sexual relations as structured by relations of coerced subordination and argue that acts of sexual domination constitute the social meaning of being a "man," as the condition of coerced subordination constitutes the social meaning of being a "woman." Such a rigid determinism assimilates any account of sexuality to rigid positions of domination and subordination and assimilates those positions to the social gender of man and woman. But that deterministic account has come under continuous criticism from feminists not only for an untenable account of female sexuality as coerced subordination, but for the totalizing view of heterosexuality as well—one in which all power relations are reduced to relations of domination—and for the failure to distinguish the presence of coerced domination in sexuality from pleasurable and wanted dynamics of power. The Barnard Conference in 1983 entitled "The Scholar and the Feminist IX" publicly staged the debate between feminists who would elevate their readings of pornographic "victimization" to the model for all gender relations, and those who drew on strong feminist traditions of promoting sexual freedom for women to counter the pornography paradigm for thinking sexuality. These latter feminists consistently refused the assimilation of all sexuality to coercive models of domination and refused as well the assimilation of models of domination to socially fixed positions of gender within a totalizing map of patriarchal domination.

The feminist tradition in favor of sexual freedom,[6] with strong ties to radical sexual theory and activism, has been clearly voiced by numerous scholars, some of whom, such as Ellen Dubois and Judith Walkowitz, have explicitly argued for the historical links between a progressive sexual politics and feminist aims.[7] This tradition has continued in the writings of Dorothy Allison, bell hooks, Cherríe Moraga, Joan Nestle, Esther Newton, Sarah Schulman, and others. Central to Carole Vance's reformulation of this position is a consideration of both the pleasure and the danger of women's sexual freedom, where danger carries both the anti-erotic threat of coerced sexuality, as in rape, battery, and the mundane masculinist rituals of intimidation, and the highly erotic promise of transgressing traditional restrictions on women's sexuality. The purposefully ambiguous agenda thus offered and continues to offer an important alternative to the anti-pornography framework in which every instance of the sexual ambiguity of power is quickly resolved into univocal positions of coercive domination.

Significantly, this very feminist tradition in which both pleasure and danger govern the discourse on sexuality is elided in the articulation of lesbian/ gay from feminist in the founding methodology of queer studies. Those radical sexual positions within feminism offered an alternative to the MacKinnon framework and made it possible for many women to remain feminists in spite of the rising popularity of the feminist framework of female victimization. To restrict the proper object of feminism to gender, and to appropriate sexuality as the proper object of lesbian/gay studies, is either to deny this important feminist contribution to the very sexual discourse in which lesbian and gay studies emerged or to argue, implicitly, that the feminist contributions to thinking sexuality culminate in the supersession of feminism by lesbian and gay studies.

The appropriation of Gayle Rubin's influential essay, "Thinking Sex" (1983), as a founding piece in gay and lesbian studies is especially important in understanding the way in which this act of methodological founding depends upon—and enacts—a restriction of the scope of feminist scholarship and activism. Important to underscore is the above-mentioned feminist context in which Rubin's essay was published and the criticisms of some feminist paradigms she offered. Rubin clearly argued that feminism ought not to be the only or the primary theoretical model for understanding sexuality, but her call was not for a lesbian/gay theoretical frame but for an analysis that might account for the regulation of a wide range of sexual minorities.[8]

Whereas the editors of *The Lesbian and Gay Studies Reader* are right to claim in the introduction to their reprinting of "Thinking Sex" that "[feminism] does not and cannot provide by itself a full explanation for the oppression of sexual minorities," they do not supply any grounds for the claim that lesbian and gay studies can provide by itself a more appropriate framework for the analysis of sexual minorities. A close reading of Rubin's essay suggests indeed that it would be as much a mistake to hand over the thinking of sexuality to feminism—as its proper object—as it would be to hand it over to lesbian and gay studies—as its proper object.

In the final two pages of the essay, Rubin effects a number of controversial moves which have set the stage for conceptualizing gender and sexuality as two separable domains of analysis. She opposes reductive monocausal accounts in which either all of sexuality is attributable to gender or all of gender is construed as the causal effect of regimes of sexuality. If sexual relations cannot be reduced to gender positions, which seems true enough, it does not follow that an analysis of sexual relations apart from an analysis of gender relations is possible. Their interrelation may have a necessity that is neither causal nor fixed for all time. Indeed, in the place of a methodological separation of lesbian/gay and feminist studies, it may be that non-reductive and non-causal accounts of the relation of gender and sexuality are in order. The separation of the two domains by Rubin is meant to contest those feminist efforts "which treat sexuality as a derivation of gender" (308). Understood this way, the separation of the two domains is to be contextualized within the effort to dispute those feminist frameworks which seek to establish sexuality, and sexual domination in particular, as the scene by which gender positions are installed and consolidated along an axis of domination and submission.

Rubin's critique of the causal reduction of sexuality to gender in "Thinking Sex" signaled an important departure from her earlier work. Whereas in "The Traffic in Women: Towards a 'Political Economy' of Sex," gender was construed as the instrument and effect of sexual regimes, in "Thinking Sex" Rubin refers to sexuality as an "autonomous" (309) domain. This separation of gender and sexuality suggests that feminism, considered as an analysis of gender, is not necessarily the most appropriate discourse for considering the kinds of power relations within which sexuality is formed and regulated. Rubin refers to the fusion of two different meanings of "sex" whereby to be a sex implies having sex in a given way, that is, that "sexuality is reducible to sexual intercourse and that it is a function of the relations between women and men" (307). Where and when a feminist analysis accepts this cultural presumption, feminism actively recapitulates heterosexist hegemony. For example, Mac-Kinnon's view of feminism is one which makes free use of the copula in which causal relations are elliptically asserted through the postulation of equivalences, i.e. within the structures of male dominance, conceived exclusively as heterosexual, sex is gender is sexual positionality. Although MacKinnon seeks to explain this hegemony, the terms by which the explanation proceeds tend to freeze the relations described, thus recapitulating the very cultural presumption of a heterosexually framed scene of sexual domination. *But when and where feminism refuses to derive gender from sex or from sexuality, feminism appears to be part of the very critical practice that contests the heterosexual matrix, pursuing the specific social organization of each of these relations as well as their capacity for social transformation.*

Significantly, Rubin situates her own position historically. She begins the argument by claiming quite clearly that a "rich discussion [on sexuality] is evidence that the feminist movement will always be a source of interesting thought about sex," and then proceeds to question whether "feminism is or ought to be the privileged site of a theory of sexuality." This sentence is then followed by another in which feminism is given definition: "Feminism is the theory of gender oppression," and then, "it does not follow that a theory of gender oppression, that is, an analysis of oppression on the basis of gender, will offer up an adequate theory of sexual oppression, oppression on the basis of sexual practice" (307).

Toward the end of this short theoretical conclusion of the "Thinking Sex" essay, Rubin returns to feminism in a gestural way, suggesting that "in the long run, feminism's critique of gender hierarchy must be incorporated into a radical theory of sex, and the critique of sexual oppression should enrich feminism. But an autonomous theory and politics specific to sexuality must be developed" (309). Hence, for Rubin, a separate account of sexual oppression, one which accounts for sexual minorities, including queers, sadomasochists, transvestites, inter-generational partners, and prostitutes is an historical necessity in 1984. The contemporary appropriation of this position for founding lesbian and gay studies thus reduces the expansive category of sexual minorities to the representation of one group of members on the list.

According to the logic of Rubin's argument, it would be as wrong to claim that gender can only or best be understood in the context of class (as some Marxists have argued) as it would be to claim that sexuality can only or best be understood in the context of gender (as some feminists have argued). By extension, it would be equally fallacious to claim that sexuality is only or best understood in the context of lesbian and gay studies. Indeed, according to Rubin's logic, sexuality is no more likely to receive a thorough analysis under the rubric of lesbian and gay studies than it is under that of feminist studies. Not only do central notions like the racialization of sexuality get dropped or domesticated as "instances" of either feminism or lesbian and gay studies, but the notion of sexual minorities, which include sex workers, transsexuals, and cross-generational partners, cannot be adequately approached through a framework of lesbian and gay studies. One need only consider the absurdity of the claim that the history and politics of prostitution is best served within the framework of lesbian and gay studies. Similarly, the important dissonance between transsexuality and homosexuality is lost when and if the claim is made that the analysis of transsexuality is best served within the frame of lesbian and gay studies. Indeed, to the extent that lesbian and gay studies refuses the domain of gender, it disqualifies itself from the analysis of transgendered sexuality altogether. And though it is clear that lesbian and gay studies may have some interesting perspectives to contribute to the analysis of heterosexuality, it would be quite a leap to claim that heterosexuality ought now to become the exclusive or proper object of lesbian and gay studies. Yet, all of these improbable claims are invited by the methodological announcement that "sex and sexuality" constitute the proper object of inquiry for lesbian and gay studies and, by implication, *not* the proper object for other kinds of inquiry.

Rubin's essay called for political attention to be paid to "sexual minorities" who are not always women and who constitute a class of sexual actors whose behavior is categorized and regulated by the state in invasive and pathologizing ways. The expansive and coalitional sense of "sexual minorities" cannot be rendered interchangeable with "lesbian and gay," and it remains an open question whether "queer" can achieve these same goals of inclusiveness.

Has "the Long Run" Arrived?

It is important to appreciate the way in which Rubin's revision of the early essay is simultaneous with her effort to separate a theory and politics of sexuality from one of feminism. In some ways, it is the figure of MacKinnon against whom Rubin's own position is articulated. It is, after all, MacKinnon who in Rubin's terms "attempt[s] to subsume sexuality under feminist thought." She does this by arguing that genders are the direct consequence of the social constitution of sexuality. In MacKinnon's terms, "the molding, direction, and expression of sexuality organizes society into two sexes, women and men" ("Traffic" 182).

As important as it is to oppose the theory and politics of MacKinnon's version of gender oppression, Rubin's tactic of separating sexuality from the sphere of feminist critique has taken on implications that could not have been foreseen when the essay was written. With the recent media success of anti-pornography feminists, and the veritable identification of feminism with a MacKinnon-style agenda, feminism has become identified with state-allied regulatory power over sexuality. This shift in public discourse has back-grounded those *feminist* positions strongly opposed to MacKinnon's theory and politics, including Rubin's own.[9] As a result, those feminist positions which have insisted on strong alliances with sexual minorities and which are skeptical of the consolidation of the regulatory power of the state have become barely legible as "feminist." A further expropriation of the tradition of sexual freedom from the domain of feminism has taken place, then, through the odd twist by which feminism is said no longer to have "sexuality" as one of its objects of inquiry.

Rubin's own essay, however, works along slightly different lines. In "Thinking Sex," Rubin seeks recourse to Foucault to put into question the very relation between kinship relations and gender that had been at the center of "The Traffic in Women." She writes,

> It appeared to me at that time that gender and desire were systemati-
> cally intertwined in such social formations. This may or may not be
> an accurate assessment of the relationship between sex and gender in
> tribal organizations. But it is surely not an adequate formulation for
> sexuality in Western industrial societies. As Foucault has pointed out,
> a system of sexuality has emerged out of earlier kinship forms and
> has acquired significant autonomy. (307)

In *The History of Sexuality* Foucault claims that from the eighteenth century onward, there is a new apparatus superimposed on the system of kinship, the emergence of and deployment of "sexuality."[10] He then proceeds to make a distinction which seems to have central importance for Rubin in "Thinking Sex": with respect to kinship, he argues, "what is pertinent is the link between partners and definite statutes," and in sexuality, what is pertinent is "the sensations of the body, the quality of pleasures, and the nature of impres-sions" (106). Whereas kinship appears to be regulated by juridical strictures pertaining to persons and their appropriate social functions, sexuality takes impressions and sensations as the field to be regulated.

Rubin's own essay in which this citation appears is primarily con-cerned with juridical efforts in the early 1980s to restrict sexual acts and practices, to narrow the notion of juridical consent, and to banish sexual activity from public spaces. In support of the claim that sexuality constitutes a new domain of regulation, and that sexual oppression is distinct from gender oppression, she offers an historical argument that sexuality is no longer formed or constrained by kinship. The presumption here is that gender oppression can be understood through the regulation of kinship, and that kinship no longer operates as it once did to install and perpetuate gender relations through the regulation of sexuality within specific constraints of kinship, that is, through the workings of sanction and prohibition. Kinship formed the focus of Rubin's "Traffic" essay, and the effect of the historical distinction that she makes here between kinship and sexuality is to claim that the latter essay supersedes the former.

But is this supersession possible? Is the historical and analytic distinction between kinship and sexuality finally tenable? Rubin's focus in "Traffic" on kinship as a way of regulating sexuality implied that in the absence of explicit rules and institutions, kinship survives psychically as the force of prohibition and guilt in sexual life. Hence, the feminist justification for the turn to psychoanalysis was grounded precisely in this requirement to read the traces of kinship in psychic life. The putatively historical shift from kinship to sexuality, associated with the methodological shift from gender to sexuality, necessitates a turn from psychoanalysis to Foucault. But can the latter term (of any of these pairs) be fully or meaningfully separated from the former?[11]

The argument in "Thinking Sex" that posits the anachronism of kinship is supported by a Foucauldian historiography in which state-sponsored efforts at population control and the heightened medicalization of sexuality are figured as replacing kinship as the organizing structure of sexuality. This new deployment, argues Foucault, proceeds through diagnosis and normalization rather than through taboos and sanctions. And yet, the limiting presumption of a European history constrains the plausibility of the narration of such a "shift." How do the geopolitical constraints of that history restrict the generalizability of the argument in whose service it is invoked? And even if certain forms of kinship within certain European contexts lose the power to organize sexuality unilaterally, and public discourses on sexuality become more central, are there reconfigured forms of kinship that result from this very shift and which exert an organizational force on sexuality?

In following Foucault's scheme, Rubin severs the newer deployment of sexuality from the older regime of kinship, dropping the psychoanalytic analysis offered in "Traffic" and offering in its place a regime-theory of sexuality, which would include psychoanalysis itself as one of its regulatory modes. The credibility of this argument rests on the proposition that the modern, medicalized regime by which sensation and pleasure are normalized is not in the service of "family values" or a given normative view of kinship relations. That it is sometimes in precisely that service suggests that whereas it would be a mistake to argue that kinship relations uniformly govern the regulation of sexuality, it would be equally mistaken to claim their radical separability. In fact, the analysis of sexual minorities, offered as a separate class, requires to be thought in relation to an analysis of normative kinship. Consider the various juridical efforts to control inter-generational sexuality in which the figure of the sexually endangered child is almost always positioned outside the home, thus veiling the sexual abuse of children within the home in the service of an idealized view of the family as a desexualized safe haven for children. Consider as well the prohibitions on public sex which redraw the public/private distinction, and reprivatize sexual relations, where notions of "privacy" apply almost exclusively to the state-sanctioned forms of heterosexual conjugality (cf. Bowers v. Hardwick). Consider as well the sequestration of HIV positive prostitutes and gay men, and the construction of both venues for sexuality as causally—rather than conditionally—linked to the disease; the moralizing against those at risk for AIDS by virtue of their sexual practices directly supports the ideological fiction of marriage and the family as the normalized and privileged domain of sexuality.

We might read the desire for a sexuality beyond kinship as a sign of a certain utopian strain in sexual thinking which is bound to fail, and which requires that our conceptions of kinship remain frozen in their most highly normative and oppressive modes. Those who imagine themselves to be "beyond" kinship will nevertheless find terms to describe those supporting social arrangements which constitute kinship. Kinship in this sense is not to be identified with any of its positive forms, but rather as a site of redefinition which can move beyond patrilineality, compulsory heterosexuality, and the symbolic overdetermination of biology. Examples of the convergence of queer and kinship concerns include the "buddy" system set up by Gay Men's Health Crisis and other AIDS service organizations to fulfill the social and medical support needs of its patients, laws legitimating lesbian and gay parenting and adoption, legal claims of guardianship, the rights to make medical decisions for incapacitated lovers, the right to receive and dispose of the body of a deceased lover, to receive property, to execute the will. And in lesbian and gay human rights work, it is common to find that lesbian and gay rights are not recognized as "human" rights precisely because lesbians and gay men, along with other sexual minorities, are not perceived as sufficiently "human" given their estrangement or opposition to the normative kinship configurations by which the "human" becomes recognizable.

The effort to think sexuality outside of its relation to kinship is, thus, not the same as thinking sexuality apart from reproduction, for reproductive relations constitute only one dimension of kinship relations. To claim that the two domains ought to be thought in relation to one another is not to claim that sexuality ought to remain restricted within the terms of kinship; on the contrary, it is only to claim that the attempt to contain sexuality within the domain of legitimate kinship is supported by moralizing and pathologizing discourses and institutions. It is that complicity—and the risks of breaking with that complicity—that requires us to understand the two domains in relation to each other.

Apart from these explicit demands and difficulties of kinship, and their clear relation to the regulation of sexual life, there is perhaps a less tangible desire to be discerned in the theoretical effort to separate the analysis of sexuality from the study of kinship, namely, the desire to desire beyond the psyche, beyond the traces of kinship that psyches bear. These include the formative and consequential markings of culturally specific familial organizations, powerful and shaping experiences of sexual prohibition, degradation, excitation, and betrayal.

Politically, the costs are too great to choose between feminism, on the one hand, and radical sexual theory, on the other. Indeed, it may be precisely the time to take part in what Rubin in 1984 foresaw as the necessity, "in the long run," for feminism to offer a critique of gender hierarchy that might be incorporated into a radical theory of sex, and for radical sexual theory to challenge and enrich feminism. Both sets of movements might also strengthen the feminist effort to displace MacKinnon's structurally static account of gender, its pro-censorship position, and its falsifying cultural generalizations about the eternally victimized position of women.[12]

The Trouble with Gender

A characterization of feminism as an exclusive focus on gender thus misrepresents the recent history of feminism in several significant ways: 1) the history of radical feminist sexual politics is erased from the proper characterization of feminism; 2) the various anti-racist positions developed within feminist frameworks for which gender is no more central than race, or for which gender is no more central than colonial positionality or class—the domains of socialist feminism, postcolonial feminism, Third World feminism— are no longer part of the central or proper focus of feminism; 3) the MacKinnon account of gender and sexuality is taken as paradigmatic of feminism, and the strong feminist opposition to her work is excluded from the parameters of feminism; 4) gender is reduced to sex (and sometimes to sex-assignment), rendered fixed or "given," and the contested history of the sex/gender distinction is displaced from view; 5) the normative operation of gender in the regulation of sexuality is denied. The result is that the sexual contestation of gender norms is no longer an "object" of analysis within either frame, as it crosses the very domains of analysis that this methodological claim for lesbian and gay studies strains to keep apart.

Finally, the significant differences between feminists who make use of the category of gender and those who work within the framework of sexual difference is erased from view by this simplistic formulation of feminism. In Rosi Braidotti's feminist theoretical work, sexual difference can be reduced neither to a biological difference nor to a sociological notion of gender. In her view, the sex-gender distinction makes little sense within the framework of sexual difference. Whereas for her sexual difference has a discursive life, it is irreducible to discourse. Along with Elizabeth Grosz, Braidotti seeks to rethink corporeality in semiotic and symbolic terms that articulate sexual difference in ways that defy biologism and culturalism at once. Indeed, within such theories the notion of sexual difference is irreducible to gender and both of those notions are irreducible to sex or sex-assignment. In fact, those who work within the framework of sexual difference argue against "gender" on the grounds that it presupposes a notion of cultural construction in which the subject is taken as a given and gender then acquires a supplementary meaning or role. Some would argue that such a view can recognize neither the way in which the workings of sexual difference in language establish the subject nor the masculinity of that subject—and the exclusion of the feminine from subject formation that that subject requires. Others would claim that there may well be a feminine subject, but that an understanding of the formation of the subject is still *an effect* of sexual difference. Gender theory misunderstands the ways in which that asymmetrical relation between the sexes is installed through the primary workings of language, which presuppose the production of the unconscious. The turn to gender, for those who emerge from a Lacanian or post-Lacanian tradition, signals a papering over of this more fundamental structuring of language, intelligibility, and the production of the subject along the axis of a split which also produces the unconscious.

In some contemporary European contexts, the turn to gender and gender studies is explicitly taken to be a turn away from a feminist analysis which insists on the fundamental or persistent character of this sexual asymmetry. According to Braidotti, some versions of the gender studies model consider the cultural construction of femininity and masculinity as homologous kinds of constructions, which suggests that the study of gender directly contradicts the political impetus of feminist analysis—to mark the constitutive asymmetry of sexed positions by which language and the unconscious emerge.

Oddly, then, within the U.S., feminism is under criticism from lesbian and gay studies for its ostensibly exclusive emphasis on gender, whereas in some European contexts, the turn to gender is understood as an anti-feminist move and a deradicalization of the feminist political agenda. Paradoxically, this construal of feminism as exclusively focused on gender not only denies the history of U.S. feminist claims for radical sexual freedom, but also denies the emergence of a feminism specific to women of color in the U.S. who have sought to complicate the feminist framework to take account of relations of power that help to constitute and yet exceed gender, including race and racialization, as well as geopolitical positionality in colonial and postcolonial contexts. Whereas the turn to gender was for some U.S. feminists, then, a way to move beyond sexual difference as a framework which appeared to give priority to "masculine" and "feminine" at the expense of other kinds of differences, relations, institutions, and contexts, gender has become, in some European contexts, a sign of a politically defused feminism, a framework which assumes the symmetrical positioning of men and women along with the homologous means of their construction.

Within the course of several months I have heard feminist scholars in the U.S. worry that gender has been "destroyed" through the recent criticisms of feminism's presumptive heterosexuality. On the other hand, I have heard feminists who work within structuralist and poststructuralist accounts of sexual difference lament the reduction of a psychoanalytically complicated notion of sexual difference to an apparently sociological notion of gender. "Death to gender!" recently remarked a feminist friend objecting to the replacement of a feminist perspective on sexual difference by a theory of the cultural or social construction of gender. From what feminist position does this call for the destruction of gender come, and from what concerns does the feminist worry over its dissolution emerge? Is it too alive or too moribund, and is "it" the selfsame gender?

A feminist analysis that takes sexual difference as a point of departure tends to ask how it is that masculine and feminine are constituted differentially and to insist that this differential is non-dialectical and asymmetrical in character. The recourse to a symbolic domain is one in which those positionalities are established and which, in turn, set the parameters for notions of the social. The analysis of gender, on the other hand, tends toward a sociologism, neglecting the symbolic or psychoanalytic account by which masculine and feminine are established in language prior to any given social configuration. Recourse to sexual difference, then, tends to be concerned with the status of the asymmetrical relation or, in Lacanian terms, "non-relation" between the sexes as well as the separability of the symbolic and social domains whereby the symbolic is understood to precede and orchestrate the parameters of the social.

Whereas some cultural constructionists might claim that gender is equivalent to its construction, those who work within—and in a productively critical relation to—the Lacanian frame of sexual difference would insist on the radical *incommensurability* of the feminine with any of its given articulations. Irigaray, for instance, maintains that the feminine is necessarily redoubled, that it exists first as a signifier within a masculinist economy, but then it "exists" outside that economy (where nothing may exist), as precisely what that economy must repudiate in order to simulate its own representation of the feminine as the feminine itself. This lays the groundwork for Naomi Schor's insistence that recourse to the feminine involves a "double mimesis" (48). *Gender theory, according to this framework, would misidentify the construction of the feminine within a masculinist economy with the feminine itself*, thereby effecting a complicity with the socially given modes of masculine and feminine and forfeiting the critical distance required for a feminist contestation of these constructions.[15]

When Irigaray claims that the feminine is always elsewhere, she is marking out a space for the feminine that exceeds and defies any of its given or positive articulations. This becomes a necessity on the presumption that the existing field of articulability is governed and constrained by phallogocentrism. Thus, when Gayatri Chakravorty Spivak argues that the feminine is produced and erased at the same time, she means that the effect of that very discursive production (within masculinism) accomplishes the repudiation and refusal of the feminine. This second reference to the feminine resists representation because representation is predicated on the resistance and repudiation of the feminine. Something similar is argued by Drucilla Cornell when she insists that the feminine has no place in reality (16–20). The feminine marks that limit of representability which would undo the presuppositions of representation itself (and in Cornell's work is thus associated with the sublime). For each of these views, the cultural construction of "women" constitutes the effacement of women, and those who take the construction of women to be the "truth" of women close the critical gap that it is feminism's task to keep open.

From this perspective on the incommensurability of the "feminine" or "woman" with any living being, a set of critical questions emerge that take issue with gender theory and its tendency to conflate the symbolic and the social: what is the system or, less rigidly, the field of representation in which feminism seeks to make its claims, and how do we understand the persistent failure of representing women within that field as marking the limit of representability as such? If the representations that do exist are normative phantasms, then how are we to reverse or contest the force of those representations? In what manner of double-speak must feminism proceed when it is understood as the unrepresentable in its paradoxical effort to represent itself?[14]

A symbolic status is often attributed to this founding scene by which the feminine is repudiated and assumes its ambiguous status as the limit of representability. To be more precise, this repudiation or exile is understood as what enables and structures the articulation of the symbolic itself. The symbolic is understood as a field of normativity that exceeds and structures the domain of the socially given. And yet, how are we to think the relation between the symbolic and the social? Is this structure of feminine repudiation not *reenforced* by the very theory which claims that the structure is somehow prior to any given social organization, and as such resists social transformation? The heterosexual pathos of the founding scene of psychoanalysis is reenforced precisely by those descriptions in which the phallus emerges as primary signifier and the feminine as the always already repudiated. The claim that masculine and feminine are forever constituted in this particular asymmetry appears to reconsolidate the cultural presumption of heterosexist hegemony.

If, then, what is called "the symbolic" encodes a socially sedimented heterosexual pathos, how ought the relation between the social and the symbolic to be reconfigured? If the symbolic is subject to rearticulation under the pressure of social arrangements how might that be described, and will such descriptions trouble any effort to draw a clear distinction between the social and the symbolic? Has the social—within postmarxism—become equated with the descriptively given, and how might ideality (possibility, transformability) be reintroduced into feminist accounts of the social? Such a project would refuse the simple conflation of the domain of the social with what is socially given or already constituted, and reformulate a Marxian account of social transformation outside of implausible historical teleologies. To the extent that views of social transformation have relied on such teleological accounts of history, it seems imperative to separate the question of transformation from teleology. Otherwise, the site of political expectation becomes precisely the incommensurability between a symbolic and a social domain, one in which the symbolic now encodes precisely the ideality evacuated, after Marxism, from the domain of the social.

Finally, how would a troubling of the distinction between the symbolic and the social diffuse the current tension between the frameworks of sexual difference and gender? In other words, if gender designates a cultural or social sphere of acquired and variable meanings, then how is this sphere to be thought in dynamic relation to reigning schemes of sexual normativity?

In my view, the hetero-pathos that pervades the legacy of Lacanian psychoanalysis and some of its feminist reformulations can be countered only by rendering the symbolic increasingly dynamic, that is, by considering the conditions and limits of representation and representability as open to significant rearticulations and transformations under the pressure of social practices of various kinds. On the other hand, it seems clear that the methodological separation of questions of sexuality from questions either of sexual difference or of gender within lesbian and gay studies reintroduces the problem of the feminine—and feminism—as the site of the unrepresentable. If gender is said to belong to feminism, and sexuality in the hands of lesbian and gay studies, then those who wish to enact a separation between the two will seize upon the methodology in ways that the editors of *The Lesbian and Gay Studies Reader* would clearly not condone. If sexuality is conceived as liberated from gender, then the sexuality that is "liberated" from feminism will be one which suspends the reference to masculine and feminine, reenforcing the refusal to mark that difference, which is the conventional way in which the masculine has achieved the status of the "sex" which is one. Such a "liberation" dovetails with mainstream conservatism and with male dominance in its many and various forms, thus to a large extent calling into question the assumed symmetry of "lesbian and gay"—a symmetry grounded in the separation of lesbian from feminist, of "sex" from sexual difference, a ground constituted through the enactment and covering of a split.

In a recent article in *The Village Voice*, Richard Goldstein warns against the anti-feminism accompanying the rise of gay conservatives to power positions within the queer movement.

> *The biggest blunder of gay conservatives is to ignore the most important alliance gay people can make. That is the bond between queers and feminists. It's no surprise that the gay right overlooks this possibility. Their frat is not just male, but masculinist. Though they'd never be caught in leather, gayocons worship the sexual hierarchy that affirms male power. (28)*

It is no surprise, then, that the "gayocon" sensibility has arrived in queer studies, where methodological distinctions perform the academic version of breaking coalition.

Although my own abbreviated formulations of these debates are surely contestable, they are offered here as provocations for further contestation among feminist scholars of various persuasions who are open to a consideration of how heterosexual presumption structures some of the founding scenes of feminist inquiry, but also to queer scholars who seek to sustain connections to a more expansive conception of critique and who are suspicious of the amnesias supporting the progressive historical claims of the avant-garde. I would insist that both feminist and queer studies need to move beyond and against those methodological demands which force separations in the interests of canonization and provisional institutional legitimation. For the analysis of racialization and class is at least equally important in the thinking of sexuality as either gender or homosexuality, and these last two are not separable from more complex and complicitous formations of power. Indeed, it is that complexity and complicity that call to be thought most urgently, which means thinking against the institutional separatisms which work effectively to keep thought narrow, sectarian, and self-serving. The critique of the conservative force of institutionalization ought to be kept alive as a crucial mode of self-interrogation in the rush to acquire new legitimacy. Perhaps the time has arrived to encourage the kinds of conversations that resist the urge to stake territorial claims through the reduction or caricature of the positions from which they are differentiated. The "grounds" of autonomy are precisely these sites of differentiation, which are not grounds in any conventional sense. These are rifted grounds, a series of constituting differentiations which at once contest the claim to autonomy and offer in its place a more expansive, mobile mapping of power. There is more to learn from upsetting such grounds, reversing the exclusions by which they are instated, and resisting the institutional domestication of queer thinking. For normalizing the queer would be, after all, its sad finish.

I have pursued two interviews in an effort to provoke a remapping of the terms of debate and to encourage a kind of intellectual trespass which values the expansive possibilities of such confrontations over the retreat into intellectual territory.

Notes

1 Throughout this essay I draw upon Biddy Martin's conceptualization of the problematic relation between gender and sexuality in contemporary feminist and queer studies. Not only in conversation, but in her written work as well, she has insisted on theory as a "moving between" what have become, for some, polarized or separate positions. She deftly argues in "Sexuality without Genders and Other Queer Utopias" against certain trends within contemporary theory on the construction of social identities. Bodies, she writes, ought not to be described as simple effects of discourse or as the malleable surface of social inscription, but considered in a more complex and intimate relation with psychic reality. She claims as well that there are problems with theories that tend to foreground gender at the expense of sexuality and race, sexuality at the expense of gender and race, and race at the expense of sexuality and gender. Her analysis offers a set of trenchant critiques which show that certain political agendas are served through the foregrounding of one determinant of the body over others but also that those very theories are weakened by their failure to broach the complex interrelations of these terms.

2 Foucault himself argues against the use of sex as "fictitious unity . . . [and] causal principle": "[T]he notion of 'sex' made it possible to group together, in an artificial unity, anatomical elements, biological functions, conducts, sensations, and pleasures, and it enabled one to make use of this fictitious unity as a causal principle, an omnipresent meaning: sex was thus able to function as a unique signifier and as a universal signified" (*History* 154).

3 My argument here is with the implicit reasoning whereby a grounding of lesbian and gay studies takes place, a form of argumentation which has been reiterated in a variety of

contexts and which the editors of the volume cite implicitly from those sources. In fact, I would argue that much of the scholarship of Abelove, Barale, and Halperin has important feminist dimensions and that they have marked several essays in the volume they edited as contributing to a dialogue between feminism and queer studies. Indeed, I think it would be a mistake, finally uninteresting and unproductive, to hold any of these authors—or any others—responsible for the analogy in question. The analogy is much more important as a theoretical development with cultural currency that exceeds the particular articulations it receives in the works of specific authors.

4   The editors cite both the late Joan Kelly-Gadol and Joan W. Scott as examples of feminists who have made gender into a central focus for women's history. Yet both of these writers have insisted that the turn to gender opens up the question of how a monolithic history might be retold in which the presumption of symmetry between men and women is contested. Interestingly, the framework for lesbian and gay studies that is founded through this analogy with their work assumes a symmetry that their work contests.

5   The editors write "Lesbian/gay studies does for *sex* and *sexuality* approximately what women's studies does for gender. That does not mean that sexuality and gender must be strictly partitioned. On the contrary, the problem of how to understand the connections between sexuality and gender continues to furnish an illuminating topic of discussion in both women's studies and lesbian/gay studies; hence, the degree of overlap or of distinctness between the fields of lesbian/gay studies and women's studies is a matter of lively debate and ongoing negotiation" (xv–xvi).

6   The feminist tradition of sexual freedom appears most recently to be identified with a strong defense of civil liberties and, on occasion, an affiliation with civil libertarianism. But nineteenth-century socialist traditions of sexual freedom were centrally concerned with a critique of the family and with state institutions. A contemporary articulation of a feminist theory of freedom needs to be developed in relation to a critique of individualism, of centralized state power in its regulatory dimensions, and the interrelation between the two.

7   The volumes *Pleasure and Danger* edited by Carole S. Vance and *Powers of Desire: The Politics of Sexuality* edited by Ann Snitow, Christine Stansell, and Sharon Thompson were centrally important in waging this critique of the anti-pornography paradigm.

8   In *Epistemology of the Closet*, Eve Kosofsky Sedgwick makes use of Rubin's distinction between gender and sexuality to argue that sexuality has a kind of ambiguity that gender does not. Sedgwick claims that "virtually all people are publically and unalterably assigned to one or the other gender, and from birth. . . . " On the other hand, "sexual orientation, with its far greater potential for rearrangement, ambiguity, and representational doubleness . . . offer(s) the apter deconstructive object" (34). Sedgwick thus

identifies the question of gender with the question of sex-assignment and then appears to make the presumption that the assignment of sex "works"—a presumption that psycho-analytic theory, which retains an emphasis on unconscious fantasy, would call into question. Even if one were to accept the reduction of gender with its complex social variability to the notion of sex-assignment (a pre-feminist construal of "gender"), it seems that "assignment" might be reconsidered in terms of the complex dynamic of social interpellation, whereby being called "a girl" is simply not enough to make it so. The problem of assuming an assignment can be understood only through a consideration of psychic resistance and ambivalence proper to a theory of identification, processes which collectively call into question the efficacy of "assignment" both as a social performative and as the basis for a theory of gender.

For an extended analysis of Sedgwick's account of gender, see Biddy Martin's excellent essay, "Sexualities Without Genders and Other Queer Utopias." Martin considers those passages in which Sedgwick understands feminism to be exclusively concerned with "the question of who is to have control of women's (biologically) distinctive reproductive capability" (*Epistemology* 28). Such a restriction of feminist work to this particular question miscontrues the range of feminist engagements with questions of reproduction, but also with non-reproductive sexuality. If we consider those feminist questions not as who controls women's reproductive capacities, but rather, as whether women may lay claim to sexual freedom outside the domain of reproduction, then the question of *sexuality* proves as central to the feminist project as the question of *gender*.

By separating sexuality from gender in this way, Sedgwick also restricts the scope of Rubin's coalitional understanding of "sexual minorities." Whereas Rubin saw the turn to sexuality as a way to provide a framework which would include and link queers, transgendered people, cross-generational partners, and prostitutes, Sedgwick under-stands sexuality as the proper domain of lesbian and gay studies or, rather, of "an antihomophobic inquiry" (15). By separating the notion of gender from sexuality, Sedgwick narrows the notion of sexual minorities offered by Rubin, distancing queer studies from the consideration of transgendered persons, transgendered sexualities, transsexuality, transvestism, cross-dressing, and cross-gendered identification. Although Sedgwick appears to defend this methodological separation, her own readings often make rich and brilliant use of the problematic of cross-gendered identification and cross-sexual identification. See, for instance, "White Glasses" in *Tendencies*.

Finally, it seems that we might accept the irreducibility of sexuality to gender or gender to sexuality, but still insist on the necessity of their interrelationship. If gender is more than a "stigmata," a "tag" that one wears, but is, rather, a normative institution which seeks to regulate those expressions of sexuality that contest the normative boundaries of gender, then gender is one of the normative means by which the regulation of sexuality takes place. The threat of homosexuality thus takes the form of a threat to established masculinity or established femininity, although we know that those threats can reverse their direction, enabling precisely the occasions for the proliferation of what is to be prohibited.

9   See the work of Wendy Brown, Carol Clover, Drucilla Cornell, Lisa Duggan, bell hooks, Nan Hunter, Molly Ladd-Taylor, Anne McClintock, Mandy Merck, Carole Vance, and Linda Williams, to name a few.

10   For a fuller elaboration, see my "Sexual Inversions."

11   Teresa de Lauretis's recent *The Practice of Love* crosses feminist with gay and lesbian studies in such a way that sexuality is not reducible to gender and neither is Foucault fully incompatible with psychoanalysis.

12   See Chandra Mohanty's "Under Western Eyes" not for a critique of MacKinnon per se, but for the colonialist consequences of the universalization of women's subordination implied by Western versions of feminism which disassociate gender oppression from racial, cultural, and geopolitical specificities.

13   In my own work I have tried to establish that incommensurability within gender theory by insisting on the incommensurability between gender norms and any lived effort to approximate its terms. In this sense, I have imported a Lacanian scheme into gender theory, although I have sought to retain something of the transformative possibilities associated with gender as a social category, thus distancing myself from a Lacanian notion of the symbolic.

14   This appears to be a central concern of Joan W. Scott's recent book, *Only Paradoxes to Offer*, in which she charts both the impossibility and necessity of women's claims to citizenship in the French Revolution and its aftermath.

Works Cited

Abelove, Henry, Michèle Aina Barale, and David M. Halperin, eds. *The Lesbian and Gay Studies Reader*. New York: Routledge, 1993.

Assiter, Allison, and Carol Avedon. *Bad Girls and Dirty Pictures: The Challenge to Reclaim Feminism*. London: Pluto, 1993.

Brown, Wendy. "The Mirror of Pornography." *States of Injury: Essays on Power and Freedom in Late Modernity*. Princeton: Princeton UP, 1995. 77–95.

Butler, Judith. "Sexual Inversions." *Discourses of Sexuality: From Aristotle to AIDS*. Ed. Domna Stanton. Ann Arbor: U of Michigan P, 1992. 344–61.

Clover, Carol. *Men, Women, and Chain Saws*. Princeton: Princeton UP, 1993.

Cornell, Drucilla. *Beyond Accommodation*. New York: Routledge, 1991.

de Lauretis, Teresa. *The Practice of Love: Lesbian Sexuality and Perverse Desire*. Bloomington: Indiana UP, 1994.

F.A.C.T. Book Committee. *Caught Looking: Feminism, Pornography, and Censorship*. New York: Caught Looking, Inc., 1986.

Foucault, Michel. *The History of Sexuality. An Introduction*. Trans. Robert Hurley. New York: Random House, 1978. Vol. 1 of *The History of Sexuality*. 3 vols. 1978–86.

Goldstein, Richard. "The Coming Crisis of Gay Rights." *The Village Voice* 28 June 1994: 25–29.

Grosz, Elizabeth. *Volatile Bodies*. Bloomington: Indiana UP, 1994.

Martin, Biddy. "Sexualities Without Genders and Other Queer Utopias." *Diacritics* [Special issue on "Critical Crossings"]. Ed. Judith Butler and Biddy Martin. 24.2–3 (1994): 104–21.

Merck, Mandy. *Perversions*. London: Routledge, 1993.

Mohanty, Chandra Talpade. "Under Western Eyes: Feminist Scholarship and Colonial Discourses." *Third World Women and the Politics of Feminism*. Ed. Chandra Talpade Mohanty, Ann Russo, and Lourdes Torres. Bloomington: U of Indiana P, 1991. 51–80.

Rubin, Gayle. "Thinking Sex: Notes for a Radical Theory of the Politics of Sexuality." Vance 267–319. Rpt. in Abelove, Barale, and Halperin 3–44.

——. "The Traffic in Women: Notes on the 'Political Economy' of Sex." *Toward an Anthropology of Women*. Ed. Rayna R. Reiter. New York: Monthly Review, 1975. 157–210.

Schor, Naomi. "This Essentialism Which is Not One." *differences: A Journal of Feminist Cultural Studies* 1.2 (1989): 38–58.

Scott, Joan W. "Gender as a Useful Category of Analysis." *Gender and The Politics of History*. New York: Columbia UP, 1988. 28–52.

——. *Only Paradoxes to Offer: French Feminists and the Rights of Man.* Cambridge: Harvard UP, 1996.

Sedgwick, Eve Kosofsky. *Epistemology of the Closet.* Berkeley: U of California P, 1991.

——. *Tendencies.* Berkeley: U of California P, 1993.

Snitow, Ann, Christine Stansell, and Sharon Thompson, eds. *Powers of Desire: The Politics of Sexuality.* New York: Monthly Review, 1983.

Spivak, Gayatri Chakravorty. "Subaltern Studies: Deconstructing Historiography." *In Other Worlds: Essays in Cultural Politics.* New York: Methuen, 1987. 197–221.

Vance, Carole S., ed. *Pleasure and Danger: Exploring Female Sexuality.* London: Routledge, 1984.

Walkowitz, Judith. *City of Dreadful Delight: Narratives of Sexual Danger in Late-Victorian London.* Chicago: U of Chicago P, 1992.

Williams, Linda. *Hard Core.* Berkeley: U of California P, 1989.

ROSI BRAIDOTTI
WITH JUDITH BUTLER

Feminism by Any Other Name. *Interview*

*R*osi Braidotti is Professor and Chair of Women's Studies at the University of Utrecht in the Netherlands. She received her doctorate in Philosophy from the Sorbonne in Paris, and has worked extensively in the intersections of feminist theory and philosophy. Her books include Nomadic Subjects: Embodiment and Sexual Difference in Contemporary Feminist Theory *(Columbia University Press, 1994);* Patterns of Dissonance: An Essay on Women in Contemporary French Philosophy *(Polity and Routledge, 1991); and* Women, the Environment, and Sustainable Development *(Zed Books, 1994), co-authored with Ewa Charkiewicz, Sabine Häusler, and Saskia Wieringa. She has published widely in Dutch, French, Italian, and English, and she works with feminist scholars in a range of countries. She is one of the central coordinators for the Network of Interdisciplinary Women's Studies in Europe (NOI♀SE) and for* ERASMUS, *the interdisciplinary exchange program set up among European NOI♀SE affiliates supported by the European Community.*

The interview here pertains centrally to the theoretical and political implications of formulating feminist theory in Europe, and to debates emerging from the paradigms of sexual difference and gender. At the time of this transcription Rosi Braidotti and I have never met in person, but we appear to be part of a post-topical feminist community. She has described our interview as taking place in "cyberspace": we sent queries and responses back and forth across the Atlantic at odd hours with the aid of various fax machines. The following is a result of our efforts:

JB: How would you describe the difference, both institutionally and theoretically, between gender and women's studies in Europe right now?

RB: Don't forget that you are talking to a nomadic subject. I was born on that northeastern corner of Italy that changed hands several times before becoming Italian after World War I. My family emigrated to Melbourne, Australia, alongside millions of our country(wo)men. I grew up in the polycultural metropolises of down-under, just as the "white Australia" policy was coming to an end, to be replaced by the antipodean version of multiculturalism. The great common denominator for all European migrants was a negative identity; i.e. our *not* being British. This is the context in which I discovered that I was, after all, European—which was far from a single, let alone a steady, identity.

Insofar as "European" could be taken as "continental"—as opposed to British—it was an act of resistance to the dominant colonial mode. Calling myself European was a way of claiming an identity they taught me to despise. But I knew enough about Europe not to believe that it was *one*. The sheer evidence of the innumerable migrant ghettos would testify to its diverse and divisive nature. Thus, discovering my "European-ness" was an external and oppositional move, which far from giving me the assurance of a sovereign identity, cured me once and for all of any belief in sovereignty. Reading and recognizing Foucault's critique of sovereignty became later on the mere icing on a cake whose ingredients had already been carefully selected, mixed, and pre-baked.

The Europe I feel attached to is that site of possible forms of resistance that I've just described. My support for the highly risky business of European integration into a "common house" (the European Community, also referred to as "The European Union" in what follows) rests on the hope, formulated by Delors and Mitterand—that this "new" Europe can be constructed as a collective project. The Europe of the European Union is *virtual* reality: it's a project that requires hard work and commitment. I am perfectly aware of the fact that, so far, the results are not splendid, if you consider the debacle in Bosnia-Herzegovina and the increasing waves of xenophobia and racism that are sweeping across this region.

Nonetheless I believe that without the project of the European Union, this wave is here to stay. The resurgence of xenophobia and racism is the negative side of the process of globalization that we are going through at the moment. I share the hope that we shall grow out of it and confront the new, wider European space without paranoia or hatred for the other. I am deeply and sincerely convinced that European integration is the only way for this continent to avoid the hopeless repetition of the darker sides of our dark past. The anti-

Europeans in Europe today are: the conservative and the extreme right, as well as the extreme fringe of the nostalgic left, including the many "green parties" and other well-meaning but often ineffectual intellectuals. Shall we ever get over the Weimar syndrome?

With these qualifications in mind, I'd like to point out two initiatives in which I am involved, which in my opinion have the potential to influence the international debate. Firstly, the making of the *European Journal of Women's Studies*. Secondly, the growing number of ERASMUS (intra-European) networks for women's studies, of which the Utrecht-run one, significantly called NOI♀SE, is the best example. A great many of my observations about gender and its institutional perspectives come from my experience in NOI♀SE.[1]

Having said this, would you really be surprised if I told you that it is impossible to speak of "European" women's studies in any systematic or coherent manner? Each region has its own political and cultural traditions of feminism, which need to be compared carefully. As a matter of fact, there is already quite a rich bibliography of comparative studies on the question of how to institutionalize women's studies in Europe today.[2] Based on the experience of the initiatives listed above, I would raise the following points:

1.　Only northern European universities enjoy some degree of visibility for positions that can be identified as women's studies and feminist studies. The term "women's studies" is preferred as it stresses the link with the social and political women's movements. Only research institutions or centers that are not tied to teaching programs at the undergraduate level can afford the denominator "feminist." Generally, however, "feminist" is perceived as too threatening by the established disciplines, especially by sympathetic, non-feminist women within them—so it tends to be avoided.

2.　Many women's studies courses are integrated. An alarming proportion of them are "integrated" into departments of American Literature or American Studies, especially in southern and eastern European countries. The reason for this is obvious: as feminism is strong in the U.S.A., its presence in an American Studies curriculum requires no additional legitimation. The paradox here is that these courses never reflect local feminist work, initiatives, or practices.

3. We have very little teaching material in women's studies that is conceptualized and produced in Europe. The U.K. is active, but they still tend to look at their privileged North Atlantic connections more favorably than they do their European partners. On the continent, there's not even one publisher that has the capacity to attract and monitor the feminist intellectual production in a truly trans-European manner. The quasi-monopoly exercised on the feminist market by the Routledge giant is in this respect very problematic for us continental feminists because it concentrates the agenda-setting in the hands of that one company.

All of this makes us *dependent* upon the commercial, financial, and discursive power of American feminists. This dependency is a problem when it comes to setting the feminist agenda. It also means that there's no effective feedback between local feminist political cultures and local university programs in women's studies. A sort of schizophrenia is written into this, as in all colonial situations. I think Europe is a bit of a colony in the realm of women's studies.

Special mention must be made, in this respect, of the work of the feminist historians who are among the few groups that have managed to bridge the gap between university programs and local feminist practices and traditions. See, for example, the multi-lingual and polyvocal collection of volumes on Women's History, edited by Michelle Perrot and Georges Duby and translated into every major European language. In both Italy and the Netherlands the historians have gotten themselves organized in strong national associations that produce enlightening publications. I also have the impression that the historians have more systematic professional exchanges with their American colleagues than any of the other disciplines—judging by the fact that Gianna Pomata and Luisa Passerini, for instance, were well received in the United States.

JB: As you no doubt know, there has emerged an important and thoroughgoing critique of Eurocentrism within feminism and within cultural studies more generally right now. But I wonder whether this has culminated in an intellectual impasse such that a critical understanding of Europe, of the volatility of the very category, and of the notions of nation and citizenship in crisis there, have become difficult to address.

In that context, (a) How has the postcolonial critique of Eurocentrism—and the reappropriation of the "European" within that critique—registered with feminist domains? (b) Has your network of feminist institutions in Europe addressed the question of the current parameters of Europe as a feminist question? Do you know some of the feminist philosophers in Belgrade or the lesbian group, Arkadia? They seem to be drawing some important critical linkages between nation-building, heterosexual reproduction, the violent subordination of women, and homophobia.

RB: I think that the impact of the critiques of Eurocentrism upon women's studies has been fundamental. I am thinking not only of work done in cultural studies such as that of Stuart Hall, Homi Bhabha, Paul Gilroy, bell hooks, Gayatri Chakravorty Spivak and many others, but also of critiques that take place within more traditional disciplines, such as those of Julia Kristeva (psychoanalyst), Edgar Morin (historian of the philosophy of science), Bernard Henry-Levy (philosopher), Massimo Cacciari (philosopher), and others. All of these share a deep distrust of any essentialist definition of Europe, although for quite different reasons.

I would not describe this situation as an impasse, but rather as a clearcut political divide between, on the one hand, those on the right who uphold a nostalgic, romanticized ideal of a quintessential Europe as the bastion of civilization and human rights and, on the other hand, the progressive left for whom Europe is a project yet to be constructed by overcoming the hegemonic nationalist and exclusionary tendencies that have marked our history. In between these two great camps are the individualist libertarians who fear and oppose the power of the Brussels bureaucracy in the name of "freedom": a great many in the ecological or "green" parties are in this position. The right as well as this last group oppose the Maastricht Treaty which includes provisions for a social charter of workers' rights, a common currency, and an enhanced federalism; the left see federalism as a necessary, however painful, process.

These divisions are also present within the women's movements in Europe. The clearest evidence of this is the huge numbers of women who participated in the anti-Maastricht referenda recently held in the community.

Take the case of Denmark: in the first referendum, it was definitely the women who defeated the Treaty; their arguments were based in a critique of Eurocentrism, but in the libertarian mode I mentioned above. They feared both the centralization of decision-making in Brussels and the loss of social welfare privileges that the Maastricht Treaty would entail for them. Because the Treaty is an attempt to find a compromise among all the member states, some of the social provisions in the Treaty which may appear progressive from a Greek or Italian perspective tend to look rather disappointing from a Scandinavian one. For instance, the Danish women stressed that the European Union takes the family as the basic social unit. They thought, quite rightly, that European legislation would have negative consequences for single women and lesbians.

Other examples of feminist critiques of Eurocentrism can be found in the work done by black and migrant women commissioned by Brussels. These women include prominent academics such as Helma Lutz, Philomena Essed, and Nira Yural-Davis, who wrote books and official reports denouncing the "Fortress Europe," sponsored by Brussels.

I think there is a consensus that racism and xenophobia are the largest problems in the European Community at the moment. What I want to emphasize is that these problems can be solved only at an intra-European level and cannot be left to single nation-states, which are generally far more conservative and nationalistic than the European commission in Brussels.

JB: I take it that for you the European Union constitutes a hyper-federalism that thwarts the nationalist tendencies at work in various European nation-states?

RB: Yes, but I want to add that this is a *hope* and a political choice. I take it that by "hyper-federalism" you do not mean something abstract: the European project is powerfully real in its economic and material realities.

Let me give you concrete examples: no sooner had the first issue of the *European Journal of Women's Studies* come out last week than the United Kingdom Women's Studies Association accused it of being Eurocentric. They obviously had not read the editorial, which states quite clearly our political determination to undo the hegemonic and imperialist view of Europe by stressing the discrepancies and differences internal to women's studies. How often and how clearly must we say that we need to deconstruct the essentialist and dominant view of Europe by starting a social and intellectual process of federalism, i.e. anti-nationalism?

JB: I take it that federalism can be an instrument of nationalism, though, and that it may not be enough for a women's studies journal to declare, however clearly, its anti-Eurocentrism if the substance of its articles tend to underscore an opposing intellectual disposition. I haven't seen the journal in question, so I can't make a judgement. But I would suggest that an anti-Eurocentric stance probably has to do more than mark differences, that is, those markings have to become a point of departure for a critique of nationalism in both its federalist and anti-federalist forms. But as I understand it, your point is that right now to center a progressive politics on Europe is not the same as Eurocentrism, and that Eurocentrism is not the same as nationalism. I take it that part of what will make good this last claim is to be sure the boundaries of what is accepted as "Europe" contest rather than reinscribe the map of colonial territorialities.

RB: Yes, but that can only be achieved through political action. Let me give you a different example of what I mean. This year the Europride week took place in Amsterdam and gay people and various associations gathered to talk and celebrate. Some complained that a Europride week was too Eurocentric. They either did not know or chose to ignore the points of view expressed by Italian, Spanish, Greek and other European gay rights activists who clearly stated that European legislation on gay rights is far more advanced than legislation existing at national levels. As a consequence, we need to appeal to Europe in order to oppose national governments; the Irish feminists worked this tactic in the case of abortion legislation. Many lesbian organizations have also pointed out that, with the exception of Holland and Denmark, there are no lesbian rights at all in the nations comprising the European Community today. Take the case of the Italian lesbian couple who recently gave birth to a child through donor insemination. The Vatican *excommunicated* them. Whereas at some level I find it quite hilarious to be officially condemned to eternal damnation, it is also important to remember how enormous is the social ostracism of these women.

In such a context, opposing European federalism in the name of anti-Eurocentrism ends up confirming the hegemonic and fascistic view of Europe which we are all fighting against. It is quite analogous to opposing special actions for women in the name of antiessentialism. I think we need to approach these questions strategically.

JB: So how is it that the kind of feminist scholarship and activism in which you are involved calls into question the given parameters of "Europe"?

RB: The ERASMUS NOIȘSE network has placed the critical evaluation of European multiculturalism at the center of our interests. The joint curriculum that we have been developing focuses entirely on cultural diversity, European multiculturalism, and anti-racism. Significantly, we (Christine Rammrath and all the participating partners) spent about three years in preliminary research for this new curriculum. The bibliographic search confirmed the points I made before about the domination of American sources on the theme of multiculturalism.

It seems quite obvious that we Europeans have been slower to face these issues, partly because intra-European cultural and ethnic divisions are so huge that they seem threatening. The first time we opened a discussion on the theme of racism in Europe, many of the southern European participants in our network felt very strongly that they have been the oppressed in the Community today, that they have suffered from racism in the course of the mass migrations (to northern and western Europe) from countries such as Greece, Spain, and Italy. They also acknowledged how difficult it is for countries or peoples who are accustomed to economic and social marginality, such as southern European emigrants, to realize that, at this point in history in the European Community they are actually discriminating against peoples from even further south or from Eastern Europe: the Turks, the Moroccans, the peoples from the former Yugoslavia, the African migrants who enter the Community legally or not. I think that the process by which this realization is made is both painful and necessary.

If you look at how these concerns are reflected in the university curricula in women's studies, you will be struck by omissions and silences. In her background preliminary study on this theme, Marischka Verbeek argues that whereas U.S.-style black feminism is well represented in most European courses, issues closer to local realities are more often omitted. I think that there is a tendency to defer confrontation with the more immediate "Other."

JB: What I found recently in Germany was a revival of interest in Jewish culture, and a strong show against anti-semitism in public discourse, but that form of anti-racism did not appear to translate into a more systematic and wide-ranging public examination of racism against the Turks and other domestic minorities. It was as if the work of culturally rehabilitating Jewish culture within Germany—an important and necessary project in its own right—works in part to displace public attention away from of the most vehement forms of contemporary racism.

RB: I think that the concern about anti-semitism is perfectly justified, but anti-racism needs to cover a broader spectrum. In the context I am referring to above, this deferral takes a spatial and temporal dimension. You will find women's studies courses in history throughout Europe that deal with issues of colonialism and imperialism in the last century, including American slavery as well as anti-semitism and the holocaust in Nazi Europe. It is much more difficult, however, to find material related to recent events, such as the growing persecution of immigrant workers, the killing of gypsies and other nomads, the resurgence of Nazi-skinheads, anti-semitism, and the growth of the "Fortress Europe" mentality. This difficulty is the result of the inherent conservatism of European universities which are still monopolized by rigid disciplinary boundaries and of the delayed relation of theory to practice. As you know, thinking the present is always the most difficult task. In our European network, we have taken this task as our focus. We plan to start producing research and a book series in the next few years.

JB: Can you say more about feminist critiques of nationalism in the contemporary context?

RB: I think that the former Yugoslavia is the nightmare case that illustrates everything the European Union is trying to fight against. Paradoxically, it has also demonstrated the inefficiency and powerlessness of the European Community which simply has no military way of enforcing its policies and has shown pathetic diplomatic skills.

You asked before about the work of the Yugoslav philosophers. I think you mean Dasa Duhacek and Zarana Papic whose work is well-known and very well received at the moment. I think that the analyses Papic proposes of nationalism, patriarchy, and war are important, courageous, and necessary. I am especially impressed by her reading of the current war as a "tribalist patriarchalism" which seeks to erase sexual difference through the rule of war-oriented nationalist masculinism. One cannot be a woman in the former Yugoslavia: one must be a Serbian, a Croatian, or a Bosnian woman. Sexual difference is killed by nationalism.

In this respect, Papic's work is not unique. There are several interesting analyses of the intersection between nationalism, war, and masculinity in Europe. There is the work of Maria Antoinetta Macciocchi, former Communist and now Euro-parliamentarian. Already in her study of Italian fascism, *La Donna Nera* published in the seventies, she broke the taboo against linking nationalist masculinity with the subordination of women. Her later work, published in French, *Les femmes et leurs maîtres*, is also of great interest. I think also of Gisela Bock's research on women in Nazi Germany and the literature by migrant and postcolonial women who are either citizens or residents in the European Community, from Buchi Emecheta to the Algerian-Jewish Hélène Cixous. Interesting also is the work of Italian women who were caught in the armed rebellion of the 70s against the nation-state (the so-called "terrorists").

JB: What are the intellectual reasons for preferring the term Feminist Studies over Gender or Women's Studies?

RB: This question has been at the center of a hot debate in *The Dutch Journal of Women's Studies* and I think it will continue in the pages of the new *European Journal of Women's Studies*.

Let me start with this formulation: I think that the notion of "gender" is at a crisis-point in feminist theory and practice, that it is undergoing intense criticism from all sides both for its theoretical inadequacy and for its politically amorphous and unfocused nature. Italian feminist Liana Borghi calls gender "a cookie cutter," which can take just about any shape you want.[5] The areas from which the most pertinent criticism of "gender" has emerged are: the European sexual difference theorists, the postcolonial and black feminist theorists (my colleague Gloria Wekker explains that in our practice here in Europe we use the term "black feminist theory" as a political category, and we refer to black and migrant women. In the U.S., on the other hand, you seem to use the term "black" as synonymous with "African-American" and you refer to "women of

color" to cover other ethnic denominators), the feminist epistemologists working in the natural sciences, postmodernist cyborg feminism, and the lesbian
thinkers. I think your work has been very influential in arousing healthy
suspicion about the notion of gender, too.

A second remark: the crisis of gender as a useful category in feminist
analysis is simultaneous with a reshuffling of theoretical positions which had
become fixed and stalemated in feminist theory, most notably the opposition
between, on the one hand, "gender theorists" in the Anglo-American tradition
and on the other, "sexual difference theorists" in the French and continental
tradition.[4] The debate between Anglo-American "gender" theory and Continental sexual difference theorists became stuck in the 80s in a fairly sterile
polemic between opposing cultural and theoretical frameworks which rest on
different assumptions about political practice.[5] This polarized climate was re-
shuffled partly because of the increasing awareness of the culturally specific
forms assumed by feminist theory and this has resulted in a new and more
productive approach to differences in feminist positions.

A third related phenomenon in this respect is the recent emergence of
the international debate of Italian, Australian, and Dutch feminist thought, as
well as others; these alternatives have helped to displace the too comfortable
binary opposition between French Continental and Anglo-American positions.[6]
These publications have helped not only to put another, however "minor,"
European feminist culture on the map, but also to stress the extent to which the
notion of "gender" is a vicissitude of the *English language*, one which bears
little or no relevance to theoretical traditions in the Romance languages.[7] This
is why gender has found no successful echo in the French, Spanish or Italian
feminist movements. When you consider that in French "le genre" can be used
to refer to humanity as a whole ("le genre humain") you can get a sense of the
culturally specific nature of the term and, consequently, of its untranslatability
as well.

JB: But what do you make of the German Movement? How is it that the
term which has no theoretical tradition in that language nevertheless can take
hold there, precisely as a disruption of that tradition?

RB: My impression from working with groups in Berlin, Kassel,
Bielefeld and Frankfurt is that the process of institutionalizing feminism has

been slow and not very successful. Even Habermas has not appointed a single feminist philosopher in his department! The feminist wave of the 70s did not survive the long march through the institutions. "Gender" is coming in as a later, compromise solution in the place of the more radical options that have emerged from local traditions and practices.

The imported nature of the notion of gender also means that the sex/gender distinction, which is one of the pillars on which English-speaking feminist theory is built, makes neither epistemological nor political sense in many non-English, western European contexts, where the notions of "sexuality" and "sexual difference" are currently used instead. Although much ink has been spilled over the question of whether to praise or attack theories of sexual difference, little effort has been made to try and situate these debates in their cultural contexts.

I think that one of the reasons for the huge impact of your *Gender Trouble* in the German context is that it brings in with a vengeance a long overdue discussion. What is special about the German context, and potentially very explosive, is that their debate on feminist gender theory is simultaneous with a radical deconstruction of that notion. Many rather conventional German feminists are very worried about it.

More generally, though, the focus on gender rather than sexual difference presumes that men and women are constituted in symmetrical ways. But this misses the feminist point about masculine dominance. In such a system, the masculine and the feminine are in a structurally dissymmetrical position: men, as the empirical referent of the masculine, cannot be said to have a gender; rather, they are expected to carry the Phallus—which is something different. They are expected to exemplify abstract virility, which is hardly an easy task.[8] Simone de Beauvoir observed fifty years ago that the price men pay for representing the universal is a loss of embodiment; the price women pay, on the other hand, is at once a loss of subjectivity and a confinement to the body. Men become disembodied and, through this process, gain entitlement to transcendence and subjectivity; women become over-embodied and thereby consigned to immanence. This results in two dissymmetrical positions and to opposing kinds of problems.

JB: Your point that gender studies presumes and institutionalizes a false "symmetry" between men and women is very provocative. It seems to me, though, that the turn to "gender" has also marked an effort to counter a perhaps too rigid notion of gender asymmetry. How do you respond to the following kind of critique of "sexual difference": when sexual difference is understood as a linguistic and conceptual presupposition or, for that matter, an inevitable condition of all writing, it falsely universalizes a social asymmetry, thereby reifying social relations of gender asymmetry in a linguistic or symbolic realm, maintained problematically at a distance from socio-historical practice?

As a second question, is there a way to affirm the political concerns implicit in this critique and at the same time to insist on the continuing value of the "sexual difference" framework?

RB: I don't see sexual difference as a monolithic or ahistorical theory. Quite to the contrary. In *Nomadic Subjects* I have tried to work out a three-level scheme for understanding sexual difference. On the first level, the focus is on the differences between men and women. Here the aim is descriptive and diagnostic. The approach to sexual difference involves both the description and denunciation of the false universalism of the male symbolic, in which one finds the notion of the subject as a self-regulating masculine agency and the notion of the "Other" as a site of devaluation. What comes into focus in the second level is that the relation between Subject and Other is not one of reversibility. As Irigaray points out, women's "otherness" remains unrepresentable within this scene of representation. The two poles of opposition exist in an asymmetrical relationship. Under the heading of "the double syntax" Irigaray defends this irreducible and irreversible difference not only of Woman from man, but also of real-life women from the reified image of Woman-as-Other. This is proposed as the foundation for a new phase of feminist politics.

JB: But what does it mean to establish that asymmetry as irreducible and irreversible, and then to claim that it ought to serve as a foundation for feminist politics? Doesn't that simply reify a social asymmetry as an eternal necessity, thus installing the pathos of exclusion as the "ground" of feminism?

RB: You must not confuse the diagnostic function of sexual difference with its strategic or programmatic aims. The emphasis, for me, is on the implications of the recognition of the asymmetrical position between the sexes, namely that reversibility is *not* an option, either conceptually or politically. The point is to overcome the dialectics of domination, not to turn the previous slaves into new masters. Emancipationism tries to push women in that direction, thereby introducing homology into a male-dominated system. Just slotting women *in*, without changing the rules of the game, would indeed be mere reification of existing social conditions of inequality. Sexual difference feminists are opposed to that and want to criticize the political bankruptcy of that move. We should bank instead on the margin of ex-centricity from the phallic system that women "enjoy" as part of the patriarchal socio-symbolic deal. It's *that margin of non-belonging* that serves as foundation for feminist politics. Whereas Derrida-style feminists are happy to let this margin float in a disseminating vortex, sexual difference feminists are determined to anchor it in women's lived experience.

The central issue at stake in this project is how to create, legitimate, and represent a multiplicity of alternative forms of feminist subjectivity without falling into either a new essentialism or a new relativism. The starting point for the project of sexual difference is the political will to assert the specificity of the lived, female bodily experience. This involves the refusal to disembody sexual difference through the valorization of a new allegedly "postmodern" and "antiessentialist" subject; in other words, the project of sexual difference engages a will to reconnect the whole debate on difference to the bodily existence and experience of women.

I think it is a factor of our historical condition that feminists identify feminism as a political site of experimentation and that they are reconsidering the notion of Woman (the patriarchal representation of women, as cultural imago) at the exact period in history when this notion is deconstructed and challenged in social as well as discursive practice. Modernity makes available to feminists the essence of femininity as an historical construct that needs to be worked upon. The real-life women who undertake the feminist subject-position as a part of the social and symbolic reconstruction of what I call female subjectivity are a multiplicity in themselves: split, fractured, and constituted across intersecting levels of experience.

This third level, which I call "the differences within," is approached through an analytic of subjectivity. It highlights the complexity of the embodied structure of the subject: the body refers to a layer of corporeal materiality, a substratum of living matter endowed with memory. The Deleuzian view of the corporeal subject that I work with implies that the body cannot be fully apprehended or represented: it exceeds representation. I stress this because far too often in feminist theory the level of "identity" gets merrily confused

with issues of political subjectivity. Identity bears a privileged bond to unconscious processes—which are imbricated with the corporeal—whereas political
subjectivity is a conscious and willful position. Unconscious desire and willful
choice are of different registers. My emphasis falls on the positivity of desire, on
its productive force. I would like to understand feminism not only in terms of
willful commitment to a set of values or political beliefs, but also in terms of the
ethical passions and the desire that sustain it.

What feminism liberates in women is their desire for freedom, light-
ness, justness and self-accomplishment. These values are not only rational
political beliefs, but also objects of intense desire. This merry spirit was quite
manifest in the earlier days of the women's movement, when it was clear that
joy and laughter were profound political emotions and statements. Not much of
this joyful beat survives in these days of postmodernist gloom, and yet we would
do well to remember the subversive force of Dionysian laughter. A healthy dose
of hermeneutics of suspicion towards one's political beliefs is no form of
cynicism, or nihilism, but rather a way of returning politics to the fullness, the
embodiedness, and consequently the partiality of lived experience. I wish
feminism would shed its saddening, dogmatic mode to rediscover the joy of a
movement that aims to change the form of life.

JB: I wonder whether the notion of the bodily specificity of women is
compatible with the notion of difference that you also want to applaud, for the
claim to specificity may well be disrupted by difference. It seems important not
to reduce the one term to the other. I think part of the suspicion toward the
"sexual difference" framework is precisely that it tends to make sexual difference more hallowed, more fundamental, as a constituting difference of social
life more important than other kinds of differences. In your view, is the
symbolic division of labor between the sexes more fundamental than racial or
national divisions, and would you argue for the priority of sexual difference
over other kinds of differences? If so, doesn't this presume that feminism is
somehow more fundamental and has greater explanatory power and political
salience than other kinds of critical intellectual movements?

RB: Your question tends to re-essentialize the issue of female subjectivity, whereas everything I am saying rests on a de-essentialized, complex, and
multi-layered understanding of the female subject. Woman is a complex entity

which, as Kristeva puts it, pertains *both* to the longer, linear time of history and to a deeper, more discontinuous sense of time: this is the time of cyclical transformation, of counter-genealogies, of becoming and resistance. Although I am aware of how irritated a postcolonial thinker such as Spivak is with Kristeva's "sacralization" of sexual difference, I prefer to approach Kristeva's analysis as a description—and, for me, a very adequate one—of how Western culture has historically organized a very effective dichotomy between, on the one hand, the teleological time of historical agency—colonized by men—and, on the other, the time of cyclical becoming, of unconscious processes, of repetitions, and internal contradictions to which women have not only access but also a privileged relationship. To understand the latter, I proposed that we interpret the notion of "situated" knowledge, or the "politics of location," not only in spatial terms (class, ethnicity, etc.), but also as a temporal notion. It has to do with counter-memory, the emergence of alternative patterns of identification, of remembrance: memory and the sense of time are closely linked to sexual difference.

My position is that we need to fight on all levels, but to assert that the starting point is the recognition of a common symbolic position does not imply that women are in any way the same. I won't deny the real tensions that exist between the critique of the priority traditionally granted to the variable "sexuality" in Western discourses of subjectivity and my stated intention of redefining feminist subjects as embodied genealogies and counter-memories. The question is how to resituate subjectivity in a network of inter-related variables of which sexuality is only one, set alongside powerful axes of subjectification such as race, culture, nationality, class, life-choices, and sexual orientation. No wonder that this project has led some to reject the entire idea of sexual difference and to dispose with the signifier "woman" altogether.

These tensions form an historical contradiction: that the signifier "woman" be both the concept around which feminists have gathered in a political movement where the politics of identity are central, and that it be also the very concept that needs to be analyzed critically. I think that the feminist emphasis on sexual difference challenges the centrality granted to phallocentric sexuality in Western culture, even though by naming it as one of the pillars of this system, it appears to be endorsing it. As I said earlier, the real-life women who undertake the process of social and symbolic reconstruction of female subjectivity are not a new version of Cartesian consciousness, but rather a deconstructed, multiple entity in themselves: split, fractured, and constituted over intersecting levels of experience. This multiple identity is relational, in that it requires a bond to the "Other"; it is retrospective, in that it rests on a set of imaginary identifications, that is to say unconscious internalized images which escape rational control. This fundamental *non-coincidence* of identity with the conventional Cartesian idea of consciousness is the crucial starting point. Because of it, one's imaginary relations to one's real-life conditions, including one's history, social conditions, and gender relations, become available as material for political and other types of analysis.

Now, we all know—with Foucault—that Western culture has given high priority to sexuality as a matrix of subjectivity. By taking up issues with the institution of sexuality, sexual difference feminists point out that the normative effects of the web of power that takes the sexed body as target are not equally distributed between the sexes, but rather implement the lack of symmetry between them, which is the trademark of patriarchy. Hence, feminists go beyond Foucault and in so doing challenge the whole institution of sexuality. For one thing, Irigaray and others challenge it by redefining the body in a form of corporeal materialism that goes beyond the sacralized conception upheld in the west; the mimetic repetition is a strategy to engender the new, as you well know.

As a consequence, the best strategy for moving out of this contradiction is radical embodiment and strategic mimesis, that is, the working through of the contradictions: *working backwards through*, like Benjamin's angel of history, a strategy of deconstruction that also allows for temporary redefinitions, combining the fluidity and dangers of a process of change with a minimum of stability or anchoring. This is why I relate strongly to your "Contingent Foundations" piece. The process is forward-looking, not nostalgic. It does not aim at recovering a lost origin, but rather at bringing about modes of representation that take into account the sort of women *we have already become*. In this respect, I suppose you are right in stating that I grant to feminism a greater explanatory power than other critical theories.

JB: It seems we are in an odd position, since for you the turn to "gender" depoliticizes feminism, but for some, the turn to gender is a way of insisting that feminism expand its political concerns beyond gender asymmetry, to underscore the cultural specificity of its constitution as well as its interrelations with other politically invested categories, such as nation and race. Is this political aim in the turn to gender legible to you?

RB: The opposition to gender is based on the realization of its politically disastrous institutional consequences. For instance, in their contribution to the first issue of the *European Journal of Women's Studies*, Diane Richardson and Victoria Robinson review the ongoing controversy concerning the naming of feminist programs in the institutions. They signal especially the take-over of the feminist agenda by studies on masculinity, which results in transferring funding from feminist faculty positions to other kinds of positions. There have been cases here in the Netherlands, too, of positions advertised as "gender studies" being given away to the "bright boys." Some of the competitive take-over has to do with gay studies. Of special significance in this discussion is the role of the mainstream publisher Routledge who, in our opinion, is responsible for promoting gender as a way of de-radicalizing the feminist agenda, re-marketing masculinity and gay male identity instead.

On the other hand, I remember conversations with people in eastern European countries who argued that gender allowed them to bring to visibility very basic problems linked to the status of women after the paralysis of the Communist regime. Still, there are many feminists, especially in Asia, who refuse our own definition of gender equality because they see it as an imitation of masculine norms and forms of behavior.

JB: Yes, I found in Prague that the Gender Studies group found it necessary to distance themselves from the term "feminism" since that latter term had been explicitly used by the Communist state to persuade women that their interests were best served by the state.

RB: I can see their point and have absolutely no objection to it as a first step toward setting up a feminist project—as long as it does not stop there.

The other relevant use of gender occurs, of course, in development work and in the sort of work done by U.N. agencies. It is clear that in a context where physical survival, clean air and water, and basic necessities are at stake, you need to allow for a more global term than sexual difference. Also, as the emphasis on sexuality is so central to the Western mind set, it may not apply widely outside it.

JB: But what do you think of this association of "gender" with equality in opposition to difference?

RB: All I can say is that I believe firmly that a feminist working in Europe today simply has to come to terms with the knot of contradictions surrounding the question of difference. I remember the first time I attempted such a conversation with an American colleague was when Donna Haraway came to Utrecht. Donna asked how it is I believe that difference is *the* question. I replied that it has to do with European history and with my being situated as a European feminist.

As I told you before, I think that the notion and the historical problems related to difference in general and "sexual difference" in particular are extremely relevant *politically* in the European Community today. The renewed emphasis on a common European identity, which accompanies the project of the unification of the old continent, is resulting in "difference" becoming more than ever a divisive and antagonistic notion. According to the paradox of simultaneous globalization and fragmentation, which marks the socio-economic structure of these post-industrial times, what we are witnessing in Europe these days is a nationalistic and racist regression that goes hand in hand with the project of European federalism.

It is actually quite an explosion of vested interests that claim their respective differences in the sense of regionalisms, localisms, ethnic wars, and relativisms of all kinds. "Difference," in the age of the disintegration of the Eastern block, is a lethally relevant term, as several feminist Yugoslav philosophers put it. Fragmentation and the reappraisal of difference in a post-structuralist mode can only be perceived at best ironically and at worst tragically, by somebody living in Zagreb, not to speak of Dubrovnik or Sarajevo.

I think the notion of "difference" is a concept rooted in European fascism, having been colonized and taken over by hierarchical and exclusionary ways of thinking. Fascism, however, does not come from nothing. In the European history of philosophy, "difference" is central insofar as it has *always* functioned by dualistic oppositions, which create sub-categories of otherness, or "difference-from." Because in this history, "difference" has been predicated on relations of domination and exclusion, to be "different-from" came to mean "less than," to be *worth* less than. Historically, difference has consequently acquired essentialistic and lethal connotations, which in turn have made entire categories of beings disposable, that is to say: just as human, but slightly more mortal than those who are not marked off as "different."

What I was trying to say earlier is that, as a critical thinker, an intellectual raised in the baby-boom era of the new Europe, as a feminist committed to enacting empowering alternatives, I choose to make myself *accountable* for this aspect of my culture and my history. I consequently want to think through difference, through the knots of power and violence that have accompanied its rise to supremacy in the European mind. This notion is far too important and rich to be left to fascist and hegemonic interpretations.

What I hope to do, to achieve through accountability, is to reclaim and repossess this notion so that through a strategy of creative mimetic repetition it can be cleansed of its links with power, domination, and exclusion. Difference becomes a project, a process. Moreover, within Western feminist practice and the history of ideas, the notion of difference has enjoyed a long and eventful existence. I cannot think of a notion that has been more contradictory, polemical, and important. "Difference," within feminist thinking, is a site of intense conceptual tension. At the same time, my firm defense of the project of sexual difference as an epistemological and political process also expresses my concern for the ways in which many "radical" feminists have rejected difference, dismissing it as a hopelessly "essentialistic" notion, relying instead on the notion of "gender," with the implicit sex/gender divide.

The poststructuralist feminists in the mid-seventies challenged Beauvoir's emphasis on the politics of egalitarian rationality and emphasized instead the politics of difference. As Marguerite Duras puts it, women who continue to measure themselves against the yardstick of masculine values, women who feel they have to correct male mistakes will certainly waste a lot of time and energy. In the same vein, in her polemical article called "Equal to Whom?" Luce Irigaray recommends a shift of political emphasis away from reactive criticism onto the affirmation of positive counter-values.

In a revision of Beauvoir's work, poststructuralist feminist theories such as your own work have reconsidered difference and asked whether its association with domination and hierarchy is as intrinsic as the existentialist generation would have it and therefore as historically inevitable. On the other hand, Nietzsche, Freud, and Marx—the apocalyptic trinity of modernity—introduce another provocative innovation: the idea that subjectivity does not coincide with consciousness. The subject is ex-centric with his/her conscious self because of the importance of structures such as unconscious desire, the impact of historical circumstances, and social conditions of production. This represents a major point of disagreement with equality-minded gender theorists.

JB: Can you explain a bit more why it is that the sex/gender distinction makes no sense to those working within the sexual difference model? Is it that the sexual difference model accommodates the theoretical contribution of the sex/gender model, i.e. that it is not reducible to a biologism? Is it that English language users tend to biologize sexual difference?

RB: Sexual difference rests on a post-phenomenological notion of sexuality as reducible neither to biologism or sociologism. To really make sense of this, you would have to look more closely at the respective definitions of "the body" which each of these frameworks entails. The sex-gender distinction re-essentializes sex: that English speakers should tend to biologize sexual difference is a clear reflection of this mind-set. It is no wonder, then, that throughout the feminist 80s, a polemic divided the "difference-inspired" feminists, especially the spokeswomen of the "écriture feminine" movement, from the "Anglo-American" "gender" opposition. This polemic fed into the debate on essentialism and resulted in a political and intellectual stalemate from which we are just beginning to emerge.

JB: Perhaps it isn't so much that sexual difference appears biologistic, but that even when it is affirmed as linguistic, in the sense that structuralist linguistics produced, it still appears fixed. Isn't it also the case that some feminists who work within the framework of sexual difference maintain a strong distinction between linguistic and social relations of sex?

RB: I do not recognize this reading of sexual difference except as a caricature, and there have been many of those going around of late. The whole point of taking the trouble to define, analyze, and act on sexual difference as a project aiming at the symbolic empowerment of the feminine (defined as "the other of the other") is to turn it into a platform of political action for and by women. The reading you suggest seems to me to be the classical anti-sexual difference line first formulated by Monique Plaza and then repeated by Monique Wittig, Christine Delphy, and the whole editorial board of *Questions féministes*. According to them, sexual difference is psychically essentialist, ahistorical and apolitical. I read it as exactly the opposite, and I am so sick and tired of the Marxist hangover that prevents people from seeing the deep interrelation between the linguistic and the social.

I think that the sexual difference theorists[9] transformed the feminist debate by drawing attention to the social relevance of the theoretical and linguistic structures of the differences between the sexes. They claimed that the social field is coextensive with relations of power and knowledge, that it is an intersecting web of symbolic and material structures.[10] This school of feminist thought argues that an adequate analysis of women's oppression must take into account both language and materialism[11] and not be reduced to either one. It is very critical of the notion of "gender" as being unduly focused on social and material factors to the detriment of the semiotic and symbolic aspects.

I think we are confronted with opposing claims which rest on different conceptual frameworks: the emphasis on empowering a female feminist sub-ject, which is reiterated by sexual difference theorists, clashes with the claim of gender theorists, that the feminine is a morass of metaphysical nonsense and that one is better off rejecting it altogether. From a sexual difference perspec-tive, the sex/gender distinction perpetuates a nature/culture, mind/body di-vide which constitutes the worst aspect of the Cartesian legacy of Simone de Beauvoir. We have an odd set of opposing critiques here—which almost mirror each other in a strange way. What I do find interesting for the purpose of our discussion, however, is that these opposing claims constitute a divide which is not one between heterosexuality and lesbian theory—i.e., a sexual difference bound by heterosexuality and gender displaced onto lesbian theory—but rather a disagreement *within* theories and practices of female homosexuality.[12] Sexual difference theorists like Cixous and Irigaray posit lesbian desire in a con-tinuum with female sexuality, especially the attachment to the mother. They also refer back to the anti-Freudian tradition within psychoanalysis to defend both the specificity of women's libido and the continuity between lesbian desire and love for the mother.[13]

Of course, the consequences of their analyses differ: whereas Cixous then argues for a female homosexual aesthetics and ethics capable of universal appeal, Irigaray pleads for a radical version of heterosexuality based on the mutual recognition of each sex by the other, i.e. a new feminist humanity. They both reject the notion of lesbianism not only as a separate identity, but as a political subjectivity. In a very different vein, Wittig argues for the specificity of lesbian desire but disengages that desire from the accounts of female sexuality, infantile homosexuality, and the attachment to the mother.

As you rightly point out, the two positions—Cixous and Irigaray on the one hand, Wittig on the other—situate language and, especially, literary language quite differently. That is why it is important to analyze the conceptual frameworks within which they operate. I think Wittig has a nonpoststructuralist understanding of language and, consequently, of identity. Although her actual creative work suggests the opposite. One would need to compare her theory with the effect of her fiction to see how contradictory her position appears.

Nowadays, the anti-sexual difference feminist line has evolved into an argument for a "beyond gender" or a "post-gender" kind of subjectivity. This line of thought argues for the overcoming of sexual dualism and gender polarities in favor of a new sexually undifferentiated subjectivity. Thinkers such as Wittig go so far as to dismiss the emphasis on sexual difference as leading to a revival of the metaphysics of the "eternal feminine."

As opposed to what I see as the hasty dismissal of sexual difference, in the name of a polemical form of "antiessentialism," or of a utopian longing for a position "beyond gender," I want to valorize sexual difference as aiming at the symbolic empowerment of the feminine understood as "the other of the other": as a political project.

JB: Wasn't part of Wittig's important theoretical point precisely that the version of sexual difference circulating within *écriture féminine* at the time, and derived largely from Lévi-Strauss's notion of exchange, was the institutionalization of heterosexuality? In affirming sexual difference as a function of language and signification, there was an affirmation of heterosexuality as the basis of linguistic intelligibility! Her point was that language was not as fixed as that, and certainly not as tied to a binding heterosexual presumption. I take it that lesbian authorship in her view enacted linguistically a challenge to that theoretical presumption. What I find interesting there is that she did not mobilize literature as a "Trojan horse" to establish a lesbian subjectivity, but to inaugurate a more expansive conception of universality. Indeed, the lesbian for her, with its tenuous relation to gender, becomes a figure for this universality. I take this to be, quite literally, a form of *post*structuralism to the extent that Wittig, more than any other inheritor of that theory, calls into question the heterosexual presumption.

I also think that it would be a mistake to locate the discourse on lesbian desire within the available conception of female sexuality or femininity in the psychoanalytically established sense. It seems clear to me that there are important cross-identifications with masculine norms and figures within lesbian desire for which an emphasis on feminine specificity cannot suffice. I also think that those very terms, masculine and feminine, are destabilized in part through their very reappropriation in lesbian sexuality. I take it that this is one reason why sexual difference theorists resist queer theory.

Although it may be true that the turn to gender obfuscates or denies the asymmetrical relation of sexual difference, it seems equally true that the exclusive or primary focus on sexual difference obfuscates or denies the asymmetry of the hetero/homo divide. And that dynamic has, of course, the power to work in reverse, whereby the exclusive emphasis on the hetero/homo divide works to obfuscate the asymmetry of sexual difference. These are, of course, not the only matrices of power in which these displacements occur. In fact, they are bound to occur, in my view, *wherever* one matrix becomes distilled from the others and asserted as primary.

RB: I will agree on one thing: you do remain very much under Wittig's influence. Let me focus on a few points: your suggestion that sexual difference theorists "resist" queer theory. I think the verb "resist" suggests a more active and purposeful denial of this theory than is actually the case. What is true is that queer theory has had little impact on European feminism so far, but that is mostly due to the fact that a great deal of uncertainty still surrounds the term. Most of us have read the issue of *differences* on "Queer Theory" (3.2 [1991]), but the positions expressed there and elsewhere seem to be quite diverse. For instance, you seem to claim a "queer" identity as a practice of resignification and resistance, rather than as a lesbian counter-identity. In this respect, there is an interesting dialogue to be had between you and Teresa de Lauretis, who is more concerned with issues of lesbian epistemology, desire, and subjectivity.

Moreover, in countries like Holland, where gay and lesbian studies are institutionalized and the social and legal position of gays and lesbians is comparatively quite advanced, the emphasis at the moment does not seem to be so much on claiming an identity they taught us to despise, as on a sort of epistemological anarchy, a psychic and social guerilla warfare against the kingdom of identity per se. The term "queer" sounds strangely old-fashioned in this context. I think that to really understand why sexual difference theorists do not care for queer theory you need to address the very real conceptual differences between the two schools of thought.

And here let me move on to another point you make, concerning Wittig's practice of lesbian authorship. If the issue is the analysis of the limitations of the social/sexual contract such as Lévi-Strauss proposes, let me say that Wittig was neither the first nor the only one to raise questions about it. In her early 70s essay called "Des marchandises entr'elles," Irigaray opens fire on the whole theory of exogamy and diagnoses the heterosexual contract as confining women to a reified position in the realm of desire, as well as in the socio-economic spheres. As I said earlier, however, she then goes on to propose another line of attack, quite different from Wittig's, but equally aware of the hold that heterosexual desire has on women.

I guess part of my cross-questioning has to do with the fact that I do not recognize Wittig in the reading you are proposing of her. I think there's more of you in it than Wittig herself, though I am sure you would say the same of my readings of Irigaray—with which I would have to agree. Let me focus on only one point, however: I do not see how the kind of lesbian subjectivity Wittig defends can be taken as a more universal conception of subjectivity. All I see is the affirmation of a lesbian identity which rests on the *dissolution* of the signifier "woman" and the dismissal of all that which, historically and psychically—following the multi-layered scheme I suggested earlier—we have learned to recognize as "female desire." I object to that because I see it as a contradictory claim which aims to hold together simultaneously a notion of a specific, object-oriented practice of lesbian desire *and* a concept of sexually undifferentiated, "post-gender" subjectivity. I just do not see how that would work. You know from my first book how critical I am of any attempt to "dissolve" women into "post-something" categories; I think it is one of the most pernicious aspects of both postmodern and other theories.

I also have a conceptual objection: Wittig speaks as if we could dispose of "woman," shedding her like an old skin, ascending onto a third subject position. This strikes me as a voluntaristic attempt to tear women away from the crucial paradox of our identity. Paradoxes need to be handled with more care than that. As I said earlier, the paradox of female identity for feminists is that it needs to be both claimed and deconstructed. Such a paradox is therefore the site of a powerful set of historical contradictions, which must be worked through fully and collectively before they can be overcome. It is not by willful self-naming that we shall find the exit from the prison-house of phallogocentric language.

Wittig may appear to have a more optimistic approach to language, believing in the plasticity and changeability of the linguistic chain. Without giving into some of the linguistic euphoria which marks the more exalted moments of *écriture féminine*, especially in Cixous, I do think nonetheless that changes in the deep structures of identity require socio-symbolic interventions that go beyond willful self-naming and that these call for concerted action by men and women. The famous statement that the unconscious processes are trans-historical and consequently require *time* to be changed was not supposed to mean that we can step outside or beside the unconscious by making a counter-move towards "historical or social reality." It rather means that to make effective political choices we must come to terms with the specific temporality of the unconscious. Hence the points I made earlier about women and time. It seems to me that Wittig wants none of this. Insofar as her theoretical work—as opposed to her fictional work—rests on the assumption of a nature/culture, sex/gender divide which springs from Beauvoir's Cartesian legacy, she's vehemently opposed to the practice of the unconscious, be it in the literary texts or through psychoanalysis. If the optimistic side of this is that she believes that we can change the world by renaming it, the negative one is that she neglects the issue of the split nature of the subject, the loss and pain that mark her/his entry into the signifying order. Wittig makes no allowance for this specific pain and prefers simply to declare that the phallicity of language is not at issue.

Thus, I find her deeply antithetical to the basic assumptions of post-structuralism, especially the idea of the non-coincidence of identity with consciousness. Contrary to you, I think we need more than ever to work through the psychoanalytic scheme of desire, because it offers a set of multiple points of entry into the complexity of subjectivity. Besides, historically, psycho-analysis has evolved into the most thorough account of the construction of desire in the West, and you know how I feel about historical accountability!

JB: To me it is less interesting to establish Wittig's poststructuralist credentials than to consider the way in which she rewrites the imaginary and originary drama of the splitting of the subject. The subject comes into "sex" from a unitary being, split on the occasion of its sexing. You are quite right that she underestimates the usefulness of psychoanalysis for her project, but she does give us a quite trenchant critique of the sexual contract as it is presupposed and reinstituted through structuralism. I also think that she understands the pain and agony involved in the process of remaking oneself: *The Lesbian Body* is precisely a painful, collective, and erotic effort to substitute (metaphorize) an older body with a newer one, and the struggle involved is quite graphically difficult and in no simple sense voluntaristic. I think as well that there is no way to read what Wittig has to say about Proust, about the "Trojan horse" of literature, without realizing that what she seeks is a medium of universality that does not dissimulate sexual difference. I think, at her best, she recasts writing as a complex action of materialism.

RB: I do think there are discrepancies between her theoretical positions and her fictional work; I do prefer the latter by far. One last point—about the asymmetrical relation between hetero/homo and the issues related to the power of each position. If at the level of diagnosis sexual difference theory clearly identifies heterosexuality as the location of power and domination, at the programmatic level, it challenges the idea of heterosexuality as the center and lesbianism as the periphery. Resting on psychoanalysis and on political determination alike, a sexual difference approach posits the center in terms of women's own homosexual desire for each other, whereas heterosexuality is seen as a further horizon towards which one could move, if one felt so inclined. It happens that Irigaray feels very much that way inclined, and Cixous, not a tiny bit—but the frame of reference is similar. And this is the reason why sexual difference theorists do *not* believe in radical lesbian claims. Not believing in them is quite another position than denying them.

I am quite struck by your final remark about clashes which occur between opposing claims as to which matrix of power really matters: is it man/woman, hetero/homo, white/black, etc.? I think this approach is inadequate because if feminism and poststructuralism—each in its specific way—have taught us anything it is the need to recognize complexity; i.e., the simultaneous yet discontinuous presence of potentially contradictory aspects of diverse axes of subjectivity. In other words, I take it as a fundamental point to resist belief in the almighty potency of *one* power location; one is never fully contained by any one matrix of power, except in conditions of totalitarianism, which is the ultimate denial of complexity in that it reduces one to the most basic and most ruthlessly available matrix. For instance, as we said earlier, women in the former Yugoslavia are stuck with an ethnic identity which becomes the sole definer of who they are. The fact of being women, or lesbians, only exposes them to more brutal carnal violation than the same ethnic entities who happen *not* to be women. You can say the same for conditions of slavery—but these are extreme, and extremely revealing, cases. Everyday oppression tends to work through a network of constant checks and systems of surveillance, so that one cannot make a priority as to which matrix matters at all times. The temporal scale is very important. What matters especially to me is that we feminists find a way of accounting for the different matrices which we inhabit at different points in time—that we compare notes about them, identify points of resistance to them. There's no denying that sexual difference theorists and radical lesbian theorists will identify different points of resistance and different strategies to activate them. But why would that be a problem? Do we have to have only one point of exit from the kingdom of the phallus? I think, on the contrary: the more, the merrier. Let us turn our differences into objects of discursive exchange among us.

JB: I think a further problem with the notion of sexual difference has been its assumption of the separability of the symbolic organization of sexual difference—i.e. the Subject and (erased) Other—the Phallus and Lack, from any given social organization. It may be a Marxist hangover—I don't know—but it seems to me a yet unanswered question whether sexual difference, considered as symbolic, isn't a reification of a social formation, one which in making a claim to a status beyond the social offers the social one of its most insidious legitimating ruses. At worst, it reifies a given organization of compulsory heterosexuality as the symbolic, vacating (yet rarifying) the domain of the social and the political project of social transformation.

RB: I disagree with this account of sexual difference and I find this to be one of the most fruitful points of divergence between us. Working with the multi-layered project of sexual difference, I distinguish between its descriptive and programmatic aspects. I would thus say that the separation of the symbolic from the material, as well as the separability—i.e. the thinkability—of the separation, are an effect of the patriarchal system of domination. By providing a description of this symbolic as an historically sedimented system, sexual difference theory highlights *the violence of the separation* between the linguistic and the social.

This description, however, must not to be taken as an endorsement of this symbolic. Following the strategy of mimetic repetition, the perspective of sexual difference simultaneously exposes and offers a critique of the phallogocentric reification of social inequalities into an allegedly distinct and discursively superior symbolic structure. For instance, Irigaray states time and again that the phallogocentric regime cannot be separated from a material process of the male colonization of social space, starting from the woman's body and then spreading across the basic "symbolic" functions in the West (according to the scheme proposed by Dumézil): the educational, the religious, the military, and the political. The separability of the symbolic from the material presupposes a patriarchal power that enforces the conditions under which such a separation is produced. In this sense, the symbolic is a slab of frozen history.

But if you read Irigaray closely, you will see that her aim is to recombine that which patriarchal power has separated. Irigaray calls for the meltdown of the male symbolic in order to provide for the radical re-enfleshing of both men and women. She has always been explicit on the point that the production of new subjects of desire requires a massive social reorganization and transformation of the material conditions of life. This is no Marxist hangover, just radical materialism in the poststructuralist mode.

JB: To claim that the social and the symbolic must both be taken into account is still to assume their separability. How do you, then, distinguish between social and material, on the one hand, and semiotic and symbolic, on the other?

RB: Let us not confuse the thinkability of an issue with its reaffirmation. To think is a way of exposing and offering a critique, not necessarily an endorsing of certain conditions.

Thus, your question comes from a very uncomfortable place, which I want to challenge. I would like to historicize your question and not let it hang in a conceptual void. Let me turn it right around and ask you how you hope to keep up a distinction between the socio-material and the linguistic or symbolic? I think we are living through a major transition: the sort of world that is being constructed for us is one where "bio-power" as thought by Foucault has been replaced by the informatics of domination and the hypnosis of techno-babble. As Deleuze rightly puts it in *Capitalism and Schizophrenia*, and as many black and postcolonial feminists have noted: in the new age of transnational capital flow and world migration and, I would add, of the internet and computer pornography, of off-shore production plants and narco-dollars, the material and symbolic conditions are totally intertwined. I think we need new theories that encompass the simultaneity of semiotic and material effects, not those that perpetuate their disconnection.

JB: I agree, though. You mention here the intertwining of the symbolic and the material, but I am not sure where terms like the social and the historical fit into this scheme. I meant only to point out that those who separate the symbolic from the social tend to include under the rubric of the "symbolic" a highly idealized version of the social, a "structure" stripped of its sociality and, hence, an idealization of a social organization of sex under the rubric of the symbolic. Your reference to "the patriarchal system of domination" impresses me in a way. I think that the phrase has become permanently disabled in the course of recent critiques of (a) the systematic or putative universality of patriarchy, (b) the use of patriarchy to describe the power relations relating to male dominance in their culturally variable forms, and (c) the use of domination as the central way in which feminists approach the question of power.

I also think that to call for the simultaneity of the social and the symbolic or to claim that they are interrelated is still to claim the separability of those domains. Just before this last remark, you called that "separation" a violent one, thus marking an insuperability to the distinction. I understand that you take the symbolic to be historically sedimented, but you then go on to distinguish the symbolic from both the social and the material. These two terms remain unclear to me: are they the same? When does history become "the historically sedimented" and are all things historically sedimented the same as "the symbolic"? If the symbolic is also dynamic, as you argue in relation to Deleuze, what does this do to the definition?

RB: I do not see sexual difference as postulating a symbolic beyond the social—quite the contrary. You know, I am beginning to think that where we differ the most is on how we understand the theoretical speaking stance and the activity of thinking. I do not think that to emphasize the simultaneity of the social and the symbolic is the same as endorsing the separability of these domains. The conditions of the thinkability of a notion need to be analyzed in a more complex manner. Let me put it this way: there is more to an utterance than its propositional content. One also needs to take into account the pre-conceptual component, i.e. affectivity, forces, the flows of intensity that under-lay each utterance. With respect to "the separability of the social from the symbolic," I would distinguish among different possible topologies:

1. a cartographic urge: the description and the assessment of the effects of a patriarchal symbolic;

2. a utopian drive: the feminist political project to overthrow the afore-mentioned system and set up an alternative one;

3. a polemical touch: the desire to set everybody talking about it.

Where I do agree with Deleuze is in approaching the theoretical process as a dynamic, forward-looking, nomadic activity. The process of mak-ing sense, therefore, rests on non-conceptual material and on more fluid transitions than you seem to allow for. The point remains, however: we need to construct new desiring subjects on the ruins of the phallogocentrically en-forced gender dualism. New subjects also require new social and symbolic structures that allow for changes in identity and structures of desire to be enacted socially and registered collectively. To achieve this, we need a quiet, molecular, viral, and therefore unstoppable revolution within the self, multi-plied over a multitude of different selves acting as historical agents of change.

Of course, history is the process of multi-layered sedimentations of events, activities, discourses, on the model of the archive which both Foucault and Deleuze propose, though in different modes (the latter more radically than the former). The symbolic system is linked to this historical sedimentation, though not always positively: I mean, it would be really too naive to think that the symbolic would automatically register the kind of social changes and in depth transformations brought about by movements such as feminism. I think the process of symbolic change is more like a dual feedback mechanism, which requires the sort of diversified and complex intervention that Kristeva talks about. I also think you need to make a distinction between Lacan's ideas on the symbolic and its link to historical processes and Irigaray's and Deleuze's ideas on the matter: they are quite different. I prefer Deleuze's definition of the symbolic as a programmatic model because he sees it as the dynamic process of production of signifying practices in a manner which interlocks the linguistic and social conditions of this production. The problem is, however, that Deleuze denies—or rather, hesitates about—the specificity of sexual difference. Irigaray is clearer about the latter, on the other hand, but she still remains attached to the Lacanian scheme of the symbolic/imaginary link-up, which opens up a whole set of other problems, not the least of which is the issue of the female death drive. This results in a less dynamic scheme of operation.

JB: But here, Rosi, it seems that you pick and choose those definitions of the symbolic that appear to suit your purposes, and if Deleuze is more dynamic, then Deleuze wins the contest. I wonder whether the symbolic is meant to operate in that way, that is, as a set of regulating structures and dynamics which might be elected over others. My sense is that symbolic is taken to mean a set of structures and dynamics which set the limit to what can and cannot be elected. Who, for instance, is the author who decides these questions, and how is it that authorship itself is decided in advance by precisely this symbolic functioning? I think that the symbolic designates the ideality of regulatory power and that that power must finally be situated and criticized within an enhanced conception of the social. This is clearly a difference between us. In what directions do you intend to go?

RB: Surely, by the mid-90s, we can say that there are *theories of the symbolic* which feminists need to analyze and assess comparatively, and yes, I definitely believe that, at this point in time, feminists must choose among them. You seem to have a more static idea of how the symbolic works than I do; thus, my preference for Deleuze is not merely instrumental. I just think that his definition of the symbolic is more useful for feminist politics because it breaks from Lacan's psychic essentialism. I am also surprised that you seem to attribute all the regulatory power to the symbolic function alone. I see that function only as *a term in a relation*—for Lacan, the symbolic/imaginary/real relation, for Irigaray, the symbolic/imaginary/political relation, and for Foucault, the process of subjectification through truth, knowledge, and discursive practice. I am much more interested in the process, the relation, than any of its terms—hence my emphasis on nomadic shifts.

At the moment, I'm working on this tension between Deleuze's *explicit* hesitation on sexual difference, as opposed to what I see as Irigaray's implicit inability to really move beyond it. I tell you, there are days when I am attracted to Haraway's "cyborg" theory, just because it postulates the demise of the vision of the subject as split and resting on the unconscious. But, of course, I cannot follow that road. So I pursue my nomadic journey in between different processes, terms of relation, and theories, hoping to be able to resist the two greatest temptations facing feminists: firstly, losing sight of the practical, political implications of both this journey and the theories that sustain it; secondly, believing that any one theory can ever bring salvation.

In this respect, the theoretical overload that marks our exchange may have at least one positive effect on the readers. By reaction, it may make them want to practice a merrier brand of idiosyncratic and hybrid thinking, something that is neither conceptually pure nor politically correct: a joyful kind of feminist "dirty-minded" thinking.

July 1994

Notes

1 NOI♀SE (Network Of Interdisciplinary Women's Studies in Europe) takes place within the ERASMUS exchange scheme of the European Union. It's an intra-university students and teachers exchange program fully sponsored by the commissions of the European Union. We have partners from ten European countries and we have around 40 students every academic year.

The central theme of our NOI♀SE network is the development of European women's studies from a multicultural perspective. Christine Rammrath and I have years of work behind us, to construct a joint European curriculum in women's studies. And I can tell you that the curriculum looks amazing. It is being tested in Bologna this summer, Denmark next summer and then it gets rolling in 1996.

2   a) GRACE, European Women's Studies Databank, Power, Empowerment and Politics, Feminist Research, Women and Work, Inequalities and Opportunities.

   b) Steering group for women's studies, coordinated by Jalna Hanmer: Women's Studies and European Integration with Reference to Current and Future Action Programmes for Equal Opportunities between Women and Men.

   c) Margo Brouns, "The Development of Women's Studies: A Report from the Netherlands."

   d) ENWS, Establishing gender studies in Central and Eastern European countries.

3   In the seminars of the research group "Gender and Genre" held in Utrecht in 1992 and 1993.

4   See Duchen.

5   For an attempt to bypass the polemics and highlight the theoretical differences, allow me to refer you to my study *Patterns of Dissonance*.

6   See *Sexual Difference: A Theory of Political Practice*, by the Milan Women's Bookshop. See also the volumes edited by Bono and Kemp, and by Hermsen and van Lemming.

7   This point is made strongly by de Lauretis. See also "Savoir et difference des sexes," a special issue of *Les cahiers du grif* (45 [1980]) devoted to women's studies, where a similar point is raised in a French context.

8   One of the classics here is Rubin. See also Hartsock.

9   See Irigaray, *Speculum, Ce sexe qui n'en est pas un*, and *Ethique de la différence sexuelle*. See also Cixous, "Le rire de la Meduse," *La jeune née, Entre l'écriture*, and *Le livre de Promethea*.

10   As Foucault argued in his *L'Ordre du discours*.

11   See Coward and Ellis.

12   To appreciate the difference, one has only to compare the vision of female homosexuality in Cixous's *Le livre de Promothea* with Wittig's in *Le corps lesbien*.

13   See the debate within the psychoanalytic society which, from the very start, opposed the male-centered theories of Freud on female sexuality to the woman-centered ones defended by Ernst Jones and Melanie Klein. Irigaray gives a full overview of this debate in *Ce Sexe*.

Works Cited

Beauvoir, Simone de. *Le deuxième sexe.* Paris: Gallimard, 1949. Trans. as *The Second Sex.* Trans. and ed. H. M. Parshley. New York: Vintage, 1974.

Benjamin, Walter. *Illuminations.* Ed. and introd. Hannah Arendt. Trans. Harry Zohn. New York: Schocken, 1968.

Bock, Gisela. *Storia, storia delle donne, storia di genere.* Firenze: Estro strumenti, 1988.

Bono, Paola, and Sandra Kemp, eds. *Italian Feminist Thought.* Oxford: Blackwell, 1991.

———. *The Lonely Mirror.* New York: Routledge, 1993.

Braidotti, Rosi. *Patterns of Dissonance.* New York, Routledge, 1991.

———. "Towards a New Nomadism: Feminist Deleuzian Tracks, or Metaphysics and Metabolism." *Gilles Deleuze and The Theater of Philosophy.* Ed. Constantin Boundas and Dorothea Olkowski. New York: Routledge, 1994.

Brouns, Margo. "The Development of Women's Studies: A Report from the Netherlands." The Hague: STEO, 1989.

Cixous, Hélène. *Entre l'écriture.* Paris: Des Femmes, 1986.

———. *Le livre de Promethea.* Paris: Gallimard, 1987. Trans. as *The Book of Promethea.* Trans. Betsy Wing. Lincoln: U of Nebraska P, 1991.

———. "Le rire de la Meduse." *L'Arc* 61 (1974): 39–54. Trans. as "The Laugh of the Medusa." *Signs* 1 (1976): 875–93.

Cixous, Hélène, and Catherine Clément. *La jeune née.* Paris: Union Générale d'Éditions, 1975. Trans. as *The Newly Born Woman.* Trans. Betsy Wing. Minneapolis: U of Minnesota P, 1986.

Coward, Rosalind, and John Ellis, eds. *Language and Materialism: Developments in Semiology and the Theory of the Subject.* Boston: Routledge, 1977.

de Lauretis, Teresa. "The Essence of the Triangle, or Taking the Risk of Essentialism Seriously." *differences: A Journal of Feminist Cultural Studies* 1.2 (1988): 3–37.

Deleuze, Gilles, and Guattari, Félix. *Milles plateaux: Capitalisme et schizophrenie.* Paris:

Minuit, 1980. Trans. as *A Thousand Plateaus: Capitalism and Schizophrenia*. Trans. Brian Massumi. Minneapolis: U of Minnesota P, 1987.

Duby, Georges, and Michelle Perrot, eds. *A History of Women in the West*. 10 vols. to date. Cambridge: Belknap, 1992– .

Duchen, Claire. *Feminism in France*. London: Routledge, 1986.

Duhacek, Dasa. "Proposal for the Experimental Women's Studies in Belgrade." Unpublished essay, 1992.

Dumézil, Georges. *Mythes et Épopée*. Paris: Gallimard, 1968.

Duras, Marguerite. Interview. *Shifting Scenes: Interviews on Women, Writing, and Politics in Post 1968 France*. Ed. Alice Jardine and Anne Menke. New York: Columbia UP, 1991. 71–78.

Essed, Philomena. *Understanding Everyday Racism: An Interdisciplinary Theory*. London: Sage, 1991.

"Establishing Gender Studies in Central and Eastern European Countries." *Bulletin of ENWS*. Mar. 1993.

Faré, Ida. *Mara e le altre: le donne e la lotta armata*. Milano: Feltrinelli, 1979.

Foucault, Michel. *L'Ordre du discours*. Paris: Gallimard, 1971. Trans. as "The Discourse on Language." Trans. Rupert Swyer. *The Archaeology of Knowledge and The Discourse on Language*. New York: Pantheon, 1972.

Hartsock, Nancy. "The Feminist Standpoint: Developing the Ground for a Specifically Feminist Historical Materialism." *Discovering Reality: Feminist Perspectives on Epistemology, Metaphysics, Methodology, and Philosophy of Science*. Ed. Sandra Harding and Merrill B. Hintikka. Boston: Reidel, 1983.

Hermsen, Joke, and Alkeline van Lemming, eds. *Sharing the Difference: Feminist Debates in Holland*. New York: Routledge, 1991.

Irigaray, Luce. *Ce sexe qui n'en est pas un*. Paris: Minuit, 1977. Trans. as *This Sex Which is Not One*. Trans. Catherine Porter. Ithaca: Cornell UP, 1985.

——. "Egales à qui?" *Critique* 480 (1987): 420–37. Trans. as "Equal to Whom?" *differences: A Journal of Feminist Cultural Studies* 1.2 (1988): 59–76.

———. *Ethique de la différence sexuelle.* Paris: Minuit, 1984. Trans. as *An Ethics of Sexual Difference.* Trans. Carolyn Burke and Gillian C. Gill. Ithaca: Cornell UP, 1993.

———. *Speculum de l'autre femme.* Paris: Minuit, 1974. Trans. as *Speculum of the Other Woman.* Trans. Gillian C. Gill. Ithaca: Cornell UP, 1985.

Kristeva, Julia. "Women's Time." *Signs* 7.1 (1981): 31–53.

Lutz, Helma. "Feminist Theory and Practice: An Interview with bell hooks." *Women's Studies International Forum* 16.4 (1993): 419–25.

Macciocchi, Maria Antonietta. *La donna nera: consenso femminile e fascismo.* Milano: Feltrinelli, 1976.

———. *Les femmes et leurs maîtres.* Paris: Bourgois, 1978.

Milan Women's Bookshop. *Sexual Difference: A Theory of Political Practice.* Bloomington: Indiana UP, 1990.

Papic, Zarana. "Nationalism, Patriarchy, and War." Conference of the European Association of Women Philosophers. Amsterdam, 1992.

Richardson, Diane, and Victoria Robinson. "Theorizing Women's Studies, Gender Studies, and Masculinity: The Politics of Naming." *The European Journal of Women's Studies* 1.1 (1994): 11–27.

Rubin, Gayle. "The Traffic in Women: Notes on the 'Political Economy' of Sex." *Towards an Anthropology of Women.* Ed. Rayna Reiter Rapp. New York: Monthly Review, 1975. 157–210.

Verbeek, Marischka. "The Erasmus Video Document on Race, Ethnicity, and Gender." NOI♀SE Conference on Multicultural Women's Studies in Europe. Driebergen, The Netherlands, 18–22 June 1993.

Wittig, Monique. *Le corps lesbien.* Paris: Minuit, 1973. Trans. as *The Lesbian Body.* Trans. David Le Vay. Boston: Beacon, 1975.

Yural-Davis, Nira, and Floya Anthias. *Racialized Boundaries: Race, Nation, Gender, Colour, and Class and the Anti-Racist Struggle.* New York: Routledge, 1992.

GAYLE RUBIN

WITH JUDITH BUTLER

Sexual Traffic. *Interview*

*G*ayle Rubin is an anthropologist who has written a number of highly influential articles, including "The Traffic in Women: Notes on the 'Political Economy' of Sex," "Thinking Sex," "The Leather Menace," and "Misguided, Dangerous and Wrong: An Analysis of Anti-Pornography Politics." A collection of her essays will soon be published by the University of California Press. She is currently working on a book based on ethnographic and historical research on the gay male leather community in San Francisco.

Rubin has been a feminist activist and writer since the late 1960s, and has been active in gay and lesbian politics for over two decades. She has been an ardent critic of the anti-pornography movement and of the mistreatment of sexual minorities.

Her work has offered a series of methodological suggestions for feminism and queer studies which have significantly shaped the emergence of both fields of study.

JB: The reason I wanted to do this interview is that some people would say that you set the methodology for feminist theory, then the methodology for lesbian and gay studies. And I think it would be interesting as a way to understand the relation between these two fields for people to understand how you moved from your position in "The Traffic in Women" to your position in "Thinking Sex." But then also it would be interesting to hear a bit about the kind of work you are doing now. So, I thought I might begin at one of the beginnings, namely "The Traffic in Women," and ask you to elaborate a little bit on the context in which you wrote it, and also to ask you when you began to take distance from the position you elaborated there.

GR: Well, I guess I have a different sense of the relationship of those papers to feminist thought and lesbian and gay studies. Each was part of an ongoing process, a field of inquiry developing at the time. "Traffic in Women" had its origins in early second wave feminism when many of us who were involved in the late 1960s were trying to figure out how to think about and articulate the oppression of women. The dominant political context at that time was the New Left, particularly the anti-war movement and the opposition to militarized U.S. imperialism. The dominant paradigm among progressive intellectuals was Marxism, in various forms. Many of the early second wave feminists came out of the New Left and were Marxists of one sort or another. I don't think one can fully comprehend early second wave feminism without understanding its intimate yet conflicted relationship to New Left politics and Marxist intellectual frameworks. There is an immense Marxist legacy within feminism, and feminist thought is greatly indebted to Marxism. In a sense, Marxism enabled people to pose a whole set of questions that Marxism could not satisfactorily answer.

Marxism, no matter how modified, seemed unable to fully grasp the issues of gender difference and the oppression of women. Many of us were struggling with—or within—that dominant framework to make it work or figure out why it didn't. I was one of many who finally concluded that one could only go so far within a Marxist paradigm and that while it was useful, it had limitations with regard to gender and sex.

I should add that there were different kinds of Marxist approaches. There were some pretty reductive formulations about the "woman question," and some especially simplistic strategies for women's liberation. I remember one group in Ann Arbor, which I think was called the Red Star Sisters. Their idea of women's liberation was to mobilize women's groups to fight imperialism. There was no room in their approach to specifically address gender oppression; it was only a precipitate of class oppression and imperialism, and presumably would wither away after the workers' revolution.

There were a lot of people working over Engels's *The Origin of the Family, Private Property, and the State*. Engels was part of the Marxian canon, and he *did* talk about women, so his work was granted special status. There were dozens of little schemas about the ostensible overthrow of the supposed early Matriarchy and the invention of private property as the source of women's oppression. In retrospect some of this literature seems quaint, but at the time it was taken very seriously. I doubt people who weren't there could begin to imagine the intensity with which people fought over whether or not there was an original Matriarchy, and whether its demise accounted for class differences and the oppression of women.

Even the best of Marxist work at that time tended to focus on issues that were closer to the central concerns of Marxism, such as class, work, relations of production, and even some very creative thinking about the social relations of reproduction. There was a wonderful, very interesting literature that came up around housework, for example. There was good work on the sexual division of labor, on the place of women in the labor market, on the role of women in the reproduction of labor. Some of this literature was very interesting and very useful, but it could not get at some core issues which concerned feminists: gender difference, gender oppression, and sexuality. So there was a general effort to differentiate feminism from that political context and its dominant preoccupations. There were a lot of people looking for leverage on the problem of women's oppression, and searching for tools with which one could get different angles of vision on it. "Traffic in Women" was a part of that effort and is an artifact of that set of problems. There were many other articles dealing with similar issues; one of my favorites was "The Unhappy Marriage of Marxism and Feminism," by Heidi Hartman.

The immediate precipitating factor of "Traffic" was a course on tribal economics given by Marshall Sahlins at the University of Michigan, about 1970. That course changed my life. I had already been involved with feminism, but this was my first experience of anthropology, and I was smitten. I was utterly seduced by Sahlins's theoretical approach, as well as the descriptive richness of the ethnographic literature.

I was co-writing with two friends a term paper for the course, and our topic was the status of women in tribal societies. Sahlins suggested that I read Lévi-Strauss's *The Elementary Structures of Kinship*. To use the vernacular of the time, "it completely blew my mind." So did some of the other literature of French structuralism. I read the Althusser article on Freud and Lacan from *New Left Review* right around the time I was reading *The Elementary Structures of Kinship* and there was just some moment of revelation that these approaches had a relationship. Then I went and read most of the classic psychoanalytic essays on "femininity." The confluence of those things was where "The Traffic in Women" came from. I was very excited about all these connections and wanted to incorporate them into the term paper for Sahlins's class. One of my co-authors was reluctant to include this wild stuff in the body of the paper, so I wrote the first version of "Traffic" as an appendix for the paper. Then I kept reading and thinking about it.

At that time, the University of Michigan allowed students to declare an independent major through the honors program. I had taken advantage of the program to construct a major in Women's Studies in 1969. There was no Women's Studies program at Michigan then, so I was the first Women's Studies major there. The independent major required a senior honors thesis, so I did half on lesbian literature and history, and half on this analysis of psychoanalysis and kinship. I finished the senior thesis in 1972 and kept reworking the "Traffic" part until Rayna Rapp (then Reiter) extracted the final version for *Toward an Anthropology of Women*. A penultimate version was published in an obscure Ann Arbor journal called *Dissemination* in 1974.

Something that people now probably forget is how little of the French structuralist and poststructuralist literature was available then in English. While Lévi-Strauss, Althusser, and Foucault were very well translated by 1970, Lacan was not readily available. Besides the Althusser essay on him, Lacan was mostly represented in English by one or two articles, *The Language of the Self* (translated with extensive commentary by Anthony Wilden), and a book by Maud Mannoni. I remember seeing maybe one or two articles by Derrida. Most of Derrida, as well as Lyotard, Kristeva, Irigaray, and Bourdieu were still pretty much restricted to those fluent in French. This kind of thinking was virtually unknown in the United States. When I wrote the version of "Traffic" that was finally published, one of my friends edited it. She thought only ten people would read it. I thought maybe two hundred would read it, and I think we agreed on fifty.

JB: You were saying that in some ways you wanted to make an intervention in Marxist feminism, and make feminism something other than a kind of subsidiary movement in Marxism. Would you elaborate on that?

GR: I felt that if people privileged Marxism as the theory with which to approach the oppression of women, then they were going to miss a lot, and they did. I think of "Traffic" as a neo-Marxist, proto-pomo exercise. It was written on the cusp of a transition between dominant paradigms, both in progressive intellectual thought in general, and feminist thought in particular. But the basic problem was that Marxism had a weak grasp of sex and gender, and had intrinsic limitations as a theoretical framework for feminism. There were other issues, such as the whole problem of trying to find some theoretical basis for lesbianism.

JB: It seemed to me that you based much of what you say about sexuality and gender in "The Traffic in Women" in an understanding of kinship that you were taking from Lévi-Strauss. To the extent that you could show that kinship relations were in the service of compulsory heterosexuality you could also show that gender identities were in some sense derived from kinship relations. You then speculated that it might be possible to get beyond gender— maybe "gender identity" is the better word—if one also could do something like overthrow kinship. . . .

GR: Right, and the cultural residue and the symbolic manifestations and all of the other aspects of that system, and the inscription and installation of those structures and categories within people.

JB: It was a utopian vision of sorts.

GR: Well, we were all pretty utopian in those days. I mean this was about 1969 to 1974. I was young and optimistic about social change. In those days there was a common expectation that utopia was around the corner. I feel very differently now. I worry instead that fascism in our time is around the corner. I am almost as pessimistic now as I was optimistic then.

JB: Yes. So could you narrate something about the distance you took from that particular vision and what prompted the writing of "Thinking Sex"?

GR: There was a different set of concerns that generated "Thinking Sex." I suppose the most basic differences were that, theoretically, I felt that feminism dealt inadequately with sexual practice, particularly diverse sexual conduct; and practically, the political situation was changing. "Thinking Sex" came from the late 1970s, when the New Right was beginning to be ascendant in U.S. politics, and when stigmatized sexual practices were drawing a lot of repressive attention. 1977 was the year of Anita Bryant and the campaign to repeal the Dade County gay rights ordinance. Such campaigns are now, unfortunately, the common stuff of gay politics, but at that time the bigotry and homophobia that emerged in that fight were shocking. This period was when Richard Viguerie's direct mail fund-raising operation was underwriting a new era of radical right wing political organizing. By 1980 Reagan was in office. This shifted the status, safety, and legal positions of homosexuality, sex work, sexually explicit media, and many other forms of sexual practice.

"Thinking Sex" wasn't conceived in a direct line or as a direct departure from the concerns of "Traffic." I was trying to get at something different, which had some implications for my previous formulations. But I think those last few pages have been overinterpreted as some huge rejection or turn-about on my part. I saw them more as a corrective, and as a way to get a handle on another group of issues. I wasn't looking to get away from "Traffic in Women." I was trying to deal with issues of sexual difference and sexual variety. And when I use "sexual difference" I realize from reading your paper "Against Proper Objects" that you are using it in a very different way than I am. I am using the term to refer to different sexual practices. You seem to be using it to refer to gender.

JB: You mean, I am using "sexual difference" in the way that you were using "gender" in "Traffic in Women"?

GR: Well I'm not sure. Tell me how you are using "sexual difference," because I'm not clear on it.

JB: Yes, well, I think that for the most part people who work in a "sexual difference" framework actually believe in some kind of symbolic position of the masculine and the feminine, or believe there is something persistent about sexual difference understood in terms of masculine and feminine. At the same time they tend to engage psychoanalysis or some theory of the symbolic. And what I always found interesting in "The Traffic in Women" was that you used the term gender to track that same kind of problem that came out of Lacan and Lévi-Strauss, but that you actually took a very different direction than most of the—what I would call—sexual difference feminists who now work almost exclusively within psychoanalytic domains. And what interested me in "The Traffic in Women" was that you, by using a term that comes from American sociological discourse—"gender"—by using that term, you actually made gender less fixed, and you imagined a kind of mobility to it which I think would be quite impossible in the Lacanian framework. So I think that what you produced was an amalgamation of positions which I very much appreciated, and it became one of the reasons I went with gender myself in *Gender Trouble*.

GR: Well, I didn't want to get stuck in the Lacanian trap. It seemed to me, and with all due respect to those who are very skilled at evading or manipulating the snares, that Lacan's work came with a dangerous tendency to create a kind of deep crevasse from which it would be hard to escape. I kept wanting to find ways not to get caught in the demands of certain systems, and Lacanian psychoanalysis both provided leverage and posed new challenges. Lacanian psychoanalysis is very useful in dealing with structures of gender and desire, but it comes with a price. I was concerned with the totalizing tendencies in Lacan, and the non-social qualities of his concept of the symbolic.

JB: Yes. This is actually an interesting problem. My sense is that in British feminism, for instance, in the seventies, there was a belief that if you could reconfigure and change your kinship arrangements that you could also reconfigure your sexuality and your psyche, and that psychic transformation really followed directly from the social transformation of kinship arrange- ments. And then when everybody had done that and found out that their psyches were still in the same old pits that they had always been in, I think that the Lacanian position became very popular. I guess the problem became how to describe those constraints on sexuality which seem more persistent than what we can change through the transformation of social and kinship relations. Maybe there is something intractable, maybe there is something more persistent. . . .

GR: Leaving aside such issues as how much these social and kinship relations have actually been transformed at this point, the magnitude of such changes and the time spans required to make them, and the fact that most of our psyches were long since formed and are resistant to such swift reeducation, what is the something that is *intractable*? One of the nifty things about psycho- analytic approaches is that they explain both change and intractability. But there is something about the particular intractability of what is called the symbolic that I don't understand. Is there supposed to be something in the very nature of the structure of the brain and the way it creates language?

JB: I would say the structure of language, the emergence of the speaking subject through sexual differentiation, and how language subsequently creates intelligibility.

GR: That makes it somehow necessary to have a masculine and a feminine?

JB: As you know from some of the reading of Lacan that you have done, there is a tendency to understand sexual difference as coextensive with language itself. And that there is no possibility of speaking, of taking a position in language outside of differentiating moves, not only through a differentiation from the maternal which is said to install a speaker in language for the first time, but then further differentiations among speakers positioned within kinship, which includes the prohibition on incest. To the extent that is done within the constellation of, say, Mother/Father as symbolic positions . . .

GR: There is something intrinsically problematic about any notion that somehow language itself or the capacity for acquiring it requires a sexual differentiation as a primary differentiation. If humans were hermaphroditic or reproduced asexually, I can imagine we would still be capable of speech. A specific symbolic relation that precedes any social life whatsoever—I have a problem with that. One of the problems I have with Lacan was that his system didn't seem to allow quite enough latitude for the social structuring of the symbolic.

JB: Right. I agree with you on this. But I think that it is one of the reasons why the social doesn't have such a great name and is really not of interest for many who work in the Lacanian domain. I guess what I always found really great about "The Traffic in Women" is that it actually did give us a way to understand psychic structures in relationship to social structures.

GR: Well that is what I wanted to do, and I didn't want to get entangled in a symbolic that couldn't be socially accessed in some way. People often assume that if something is social it is also somehow fragile and can be changed quickly. For example, some right wing anti-gay literature now argues that since homosexuality is socially constructed, people can (and should) easily change their sexual orientation. And as you were saying earlier, frustration with the enduring quality of certain things sometimes leads people to think that they can't be socially generated. But the kind of social change we are talking about takes a long time, and the time frame in which we have been undertaking such change is incredibly tiny.

Besides, the imprint of kinship arrangements on individual psyches is very durable. The acquisition of our sexual and gender programming is much like the learning of our native cultural system or language. It is much harder to learn new languages, or to be as facile in them as in our first language. As Carole Vance has argued, this same model can be useful for thinking about gender and sexual preferences ("Social"). As with languages, some people have more gender and erotic flexibility than others. Some can acquire secondary sexual or gender languages, and even fewer will be completely fluent in more than one position. But most people have a home language, and home sexual or gender comfort zones that will not change much. This doesn't mean these things are not social, any more than the difficulties of acquiring other languages means that languages are not social. Social phenomena can be incredibly obdurate. Nonetheless, I wanted in "Traffic" to put gender and sexuality into a social framework, and I did not want to go completely in the direction of the Lacanian symbolic and be stuck with a primary category of gender differences which might as well be inscribed in granite.

JB: So, if you would, talk about the theoretical and political circumstances that made you turn toward "Thinking Sex."

GR: "Thinking Sex" was part of a movement away from an early structuralist focus on the binary aspects of language, such as the binary oppositions you see very much in Lévi-Strauss and Lacan, toward the more discursive models of later poststructuralism or postmodernism. If you are really going to take seriously that social life is structured like language, then you need complex models for how language is structured. I think these binary models seemed to work better for gender, because our usual understandings posit gender as in some ways binary; even the continuums of gender differences often seem structured by a primary binary opposition. But as soon as you get away from the presumptions of heterosexuality, or a simple hetero-homo opposition, differences in sexual conduct are not very intelligible in terms of binary models. Even the notion of a continuum is not a good model for sexual variations; one needs one of those mathematical models they do now with strange topologies and convoluted shapes. There needs to be some kind of model that is not binary, because sexual variation is a system of many differences, not just a couple of salient ones.

We were talking earlier about the ostensible relationship of "Thinking Sex" to MacKinnon's work. Retrospectively, many people have interpreted "Thinking Sex" as a reaction to MacKinnon's work against pornography.

JB: I'm doubtless guilty of that. . . .

GR: While the early feminist anti-pornography movement was an issue, most of the work for "Thinking Sex" was done before MacKinnon became a visible figure in that movement. To many, MacKinnon has come to represent the feminist anti-porn movement, but actually she was a relative latecomer to it. She became visible as an important actor in the porn wars about 1984, after the passage of the so-called "civil rights" anti-porn ordinances, first in Minneapolis late in 1983, and subsequently in Indianapolis. Her fame tends to eclipse the early history of the feminist anti-porn movement, which is represented better by the anthology *Take Back the Night*. I mostly knew about MacKinnon from those two articles in *Signs*. The first was published in 1982, and I had seen an earlier version. I had already been working on versions of "Thinking Sex" for some time. But I could see where MacKinnon was heading, at least at the theoretical level, and I was going in a different direction. She wanted to make feminism the privileged site for analyzing sexuality and to subordinate sexual politics not only to feminism, but to a particular type of feminism. On the grand chessboard of life, I wanted to block this particular move. But it was not the impetus for the paper. At some level, I think there were some underlying social and political shifts that produced "Thinking Sex," the feminist anti-porn movement, MacKinnon's approach, and the right-wing focus on homosexuality and other forms of variant sexual conduct, among other things.

JB: You are referring to MacKinnon's "Marxism, Feminism, Method and the State."

GR: Yes. "Thinking Sex" had its roots back in 1977–78, and I started

doing lecture versions of it in 1979. I think you were at one of these, at the
Second Sex Conference at the New York Institute for the Humanities.

JB: Right. The first time I saw a copy of Michel Foucault's *The History
of Sexuality.*

GR: Was I waving it around?

JB: Yes. You introduced it to me.

GR: I was really, just totally hot for that book.

JB: Yes, you made me hot for it too . . .

(laughter)

GR: The paper actually began before I ran into Foucault, but his work
clarified issues and inspired me. In any event, the sources of this paper were
earlier, and a little different. First of all, I started to get more and more
dissatisfied with what were then the stock feminist explanations for certain
kinds of sexual behaviors. A number of different debates, incidents, and issues
forced me to start questioning the wisdom, if not the relevance, of feminism as
the privileged political movement or political theory for certain issues of
sexuality and sexual difference. One was the debate on transsexuality. Even
before that debate hit print toward the late 1970s, the discussion really flipped
me out because it was so biologically deterministic. When it finally erupted into
print over the hiring of Sandy Stone, a male to female transsexual, by Olivia
Records, there were a number of articles in the lesbian press about how women
were born and not made (House and Cowan) which I found rather . . .

GR & JB: (in unison) . . . distressing.

GR: To say the least. And then there were other issues that came up.
Around 1977–78, there was a repression, to use an old-fashioned term, going on
in Michigan, directed against gay male public sex. All of a sudden men were
being arrested in a much more aggressive way for sex in parks and tea rooms.
There were a couple of old cruising areas on the Michigan campus, one in the

Union and the other in Mason Hall. The cops came in and arrested some people. There was a truck stop on I-94 between Ann Arbor and Detroit where a number of men were arrested, and in one park sweep I think one of the officials of the Detroit public school system was nabbed and subsequently fired. And as these stories started to percolate through the feminist and lesbian communities, the most common opinion I heard was that these were just men doing horrible masculine, patriarchal things and they probably should be arrested. This was not a position I could accept. No one was going around arresting all the people having heterosexual sex in parks and automobiles. To support or rationalize the arrests of anyone for engaging in consensual homosexual sex was abhorrent to me.

There was another set of incidents that happened, again in Ann Arbor in the late 1970s, around sex work and prostitution. There was a really interesting woman named Carol Ernst. We had disagreed on many things over the years; she was very involved with ideas for which I had little patience, like matriarchy theory and the patriarchal revolt as an explanation for women's oppression, and the idea that women had political power in societies that worshipped female deities. But you know how in small communities people tend to talk to each other even if they disagree or have really different perspectives. That was the case there, and we were friends. Carol did a number of things which were very important in that community. At one point she went to work for a local massage parlor. She ended up trying to unionize the sex workers, and sometime in the early 1970s she spearheaded a labor action against the parlor management. There were hookers with picket signs on the street in front of this dirty book store in downtown Ann Arbor, and the striking sex workers even filed an unfair labor practice complaint with the Michigan Labor Relations Board. It was amazing.

Then Carol left the massage parlor and went to work for the bus company, where she was also deeply involved in labor issues and unionization. Many Ann Arbor lesbians ended up working either at the massage parlor or the bus company, which we fondly referred to as "dial-a-dyke." During the mid 1970s, the three major employers of the lesbian community in Ann Arbor were the university, the bus company, and the massage parlor. It's pretty comic but that's how it was.

Then the massage parlor where many of the dykes worked was busted. One of the arrested women was a really wonderful, good-looking, athletic butch who happened to be the star left-fielder of the lesbian softball team. The local lesbian-feminist community suddenly had to deal with the fact that many of their friends and heroes had been arrested for prostitution.

JB: Fabulous.

GR: Most of the rest of us initially had a stock response, which was that they shouldn't be doing this work and that they were upholding the patriarchy. The arrested women and their supporters formed an organization, called PEP, the Prostitution Education Project. They put the rest of us through quite an educational process. They asked how what they did was so different from what anyone else did for a living. Some said they liked the work more than other kinds of work available to them. They asked why it was more feminist to work as secretaries and for longer hours and less money. Some said they liked the working conditions; the busted parlor even had a weight room where the jocks worked out while waiting for clients. They demanded that we deal with prostitution as a work issue rather than a moralistic one. They brought in Margo St. James and had a big hookers' ball to raise funds for the legal defense.

Carol Ernst was later tragically killed in an automobile accident. But she was a visionary, and her peculiar combination of feminist and labor politics really left an imprint. She challenged me on my rhetorical use of prostitution to make debating points about the horror of women's oppression. I used to convince people to feel moral outrage by comparing the situation of women in marriage and similar sexual/economic arrangements to prostitution. Carol argued that I was using the stigma of prostitution as a technique of persuasion, and that in so doing I was maintaining and intensifying such stigma at the expense of the women who did sex work. She was right. I finally realized that the rhetorical effectiveness came from the stigma and decided that my rhetorical gain could not justify reinforcing attitudes which rationalized the persecution of sex workers. All of these incidents began to eat away at some of my preconceptions about how to think about power and sex, and the politics of sex.

I was also getting more and more alarmed at the way the logic of the woman-identified-woman picture of lesbianism had been working itself out. By defining lesbianism entirely as something about supportive relations between women rather than as something with sexual content, the woman-identified-woman approach essentially evacuated it—to use a popular term—of any sexual content. It made it difficult to tell the difference between a lesbian and a non-lesbian. These were tendencies of thought common in local lesbian communities. Adrienne Rich in a way codified a certain approach that was widespread at the time, in which people didn't want to distinguish very much between lesbians and other women in close supportive relationships. And I found this both intellectually and politically problematic. A lot of things that were not by any stretch of the imagination lesbian were being incorporated into the category of lesbian. And this approach also diminished some of what was interesting and special about lesbians. I had initially been incredibly excited about the woman-identified-woman ideas, but I was starting to get a sense of their limitations.

JB: Is it that you objected to calling "lesbian" the whole domain of female friendship?

GR: In part. I objected to a particular obfuscation of the categories, and of taking the limited world of nineteenth-century romantic friendship, bound as it was by rigid sex role segregation and enmeshed in marriage relations, as some kind of ideal standard for lesbian existence. I objected to the master narrative that was then developing in lesbian historiography, in which the shifts which undermined that world were seen as entirely negative, a fall from grace, an expulsion from Eden engineered by nasty sexologists with their knowledge of carnal desires. I did not like the way in which lesbians motivated by lust, or lesbians who were invested in butch/femme roles, were treated as inferior residents of the lesbian continuum, while some women who never had sexual desire for women were granted more elevated status. This narrative and its prejudices were expressed in the title of the Nancy Sahli article, which was called "Smashing: Women's Relationships Before the Fall." It is highly developed in Lillian Faderman's *Surpassing the Love of Men*. Caroll Smith-Rosenberg's original 1975 essay deliberately blurred some of the distinctions between categories of lesbianism as a sexual status and other types of female intimacy, but she refrained from using romantic friendship as the standard by which lesbianism should be measured. I suppose the most vulgar reduction of this "paradise lost" narrative of lesbian history can be found in Sheila Jeffreys's work.

JB: But then Rich's notion of the continuum, I take it you . . .

GR: Rich's piece shares many of the same elements and assumptions that turn up in the historical work. I was not opposed to historical research on these relationships but thought it was a mistake to privilege them in defining the category of "lesbian," either historically or in a contemporary context, and to judge other forms of lesbianism as wanting, degraded, or inferior. For example, from reading *Surpassing the Love of Men*, you might conclude that "mannish lesbians" were concocted by the sexologists as a plot to discredit romantic friendship. In addition, both Sahli's and Faderman's analyses imply that the conditions which enable the emergence of sexually aware lesbians, conscious lesbian identities, and lesbian subcultures in the late nineteenth century are regrettable, because they undermined the old innocent passions and pure friendships. Then nothing much good happened for lesbians until the emergence of lesbian feminism in the early 1970s. Unfortunately, this ostensible dark age happens to coincide with much of the early development of lesbian cultures, literatures, identities, self-awareness, and politics.

This narrative structure oversimplified the complexities of these friendships, obscured their class components, and obliterated many important distinctions. This is a much longer discussion than we can have here, but the point I want to make is just that this categorical system submerged many historical and social complexities in a romantic, politicized, and limited notion of lesbianism. It, moreover, displaced sexual preference with a form of gender solidarity. The displacement was both moral and analytical. While female intimacy and solidarity are important and overlap in certain ways with lesbian erotic passions, they are not isomorphic and they require a finer set of distinctions.

Another problem in the late 1970s was presented by gay male politics. Feminism was also used quite a bit as the political theory of gay male politics, and it didn't work very well. Very little gay male behavior actually was granted the feminist seal of approval. Most of the actual practice of gay male culture was objectionable to many feminists, who mercilessly condemned drag and cross-dressing, gay public sex, gay male promiscuity, gay male masculinity, gay leather, gay fist-fucking, gay cruising, and just about everything else gay men did. I could not accept the usual lines about why all this stuff was terrible and anti-feminist and thought they were frequently an expression of reconstituted homophobia. By the late 1970s, there was an emerging body of gay male political writing on issues of gay male sexual practice. I found this literature fascinating and thought it was not only helpful in thinking about gay male sexuality, but also that it had implications for the politics of lesbian sexual practice as well.

And then there was just the whole issue of sexual difference. I am using the terminology of "sexual difference" here to refer to what has otherwise been called perversion, sexual deviance, sexual variance, or sexual diversity. By the late 1970s, almost every sexual variation was described somewhere in feminist literature in negative terms with a feminist rationalization. Transsexuality, male homosexuality, promiscuity, public sex, transvestism, fetishism, and sadomasochism were all vilified within a feminist rhetoric, and some causal primacy in the creation and maintenance of female subordination was attributed to each of them. Somehow, these poor sexual deviations were suddenly the ultimate expressions of patriarchal domination. I found this move baffling: on the one hand, it took relatively minor, relatively powerless sexual practices and populations and targeted them as the primary enemy of women's freedom and well being. At the same time, it exonerated the more powerful institutions of male supremacy and the traditional loci for feminist agitation: the family, religion, job discrimination and economic dependency, forced reproduction, biased education, lack of legal rights, and civil status, etc.

JB: OK. Well let's go back for a minute. You spoke earlier about how you were forced to rethink the notion of prostitution, and I gather that it became for you something very different. You spoke about rethinking prostitution both as a labor question and a question of women's work. You then talked about the desexualization of the lesbian, and you also talked about how gay male politics had feminism as its theory, and yet that theory didn't really fit with the kinds of practices that gay men were engaged in.

GR: Toward the late seventies and early eighties, just before AIDS hit and changed everyone's preoccupations, there was an emergent literature of gay male political theory of sexuality. Much of this appeared in North America's two best gay/lesbian newspapers at the time, *The Body Politic* and *GCN* (*Gay Community News*). There were articles on public sex, fist-fucking, man-boy love, promiscuity, cruising, public sex, and sex ads. Gay men were articulating an indigenous political theory of their own sexual culture(s). This body of work evaluated gay male sexual behavior in its own terms, rather than appealing to feminism for either justification or condemnation.

Looking back, it seems clear to me now that many things were happening almost at once. Somehow, the political conditions of sexual practice were undergoing a shift in the late 1970s, and the emergence of creative gay male sexual political theory was part of that. The major development was the phenomenal growth of the New Right. By the late 1970s it was mobilizing explicitly and successfully around sexual issues. The New Right had a strong sexual agenda: to raise the punitive costs of sexual activity for the young, to prevent homosexuals (male and female) from obtaining social and civic equality, to coerce women to reproduce, and so forth. Then the anti-porn movement erupted into feminism in the late 1970s. WAVPM (Women Against Violence in Pornography and Media) was founded around 1976–77, and WAP (Women Against Pornography) followed in 1979. Samois, the first lesbian SM organization, was founded in 1978. There was something profound going on; some larger underlying shift in how sexuality was experienced, conceptualized, and mobilized. "Thinking Sex" was just one response to this change in the social and political weather. I think my work shifted because something different was happening and my set of operating assumptions and tools was not adequate for helping me navigate the shifts.

JB: I gather that you also objected to the available language in which so-called sexual deviants were described.

GR: I looked at sex "deviants," and frankly they didn't strike me as the apotheosis of patriarchy. On the contrary, they seemed like people with a whole set of problems of their own, generated by a dominant system of sexual politics that treated them very badly. They did not strike me as the avatars of political and social power in this society. So I asked myself, what's wrong with this picture? It seemed to me that many feminists had simply assimilated the usual stigmas and common hatreds of certain forms of non-normative sexual practice which they then rearticulated in their own framework.

I was also becoming dissatisfied with the dominance of certain kinds of psychoanalytic interpretations of variant sexualities and with the common presumption that psychoanalysis was the privileged site for interpreting differences of sexual conduct. Despite its limitations and its problems, psychoanalysis has a certain power and utility for thinking about issues of gender identity and gender difference. By contrast, much of the psychoanalytic approach to sexual variation, also known as perversion, struck me as incredibly reductionist and over-simplified. Moreover, many of these traditional approaches to "perversion" had come into feminism almost uncriticized. For me, the explanatory potency of psychoanalysis seemed much more limited with regard to sexual variation.

For example, to look at something like fetishism and say it has to do with castration and the lack, or maybe it's the knowledge of castration, or maybe it's the denial of the knowledge of castration, or maybe it is the foreclosure of the knowledge of, or the displacement of the knowledge . . . well, it says very little to me about fetishism.

When I think about fetishism I want to know about many other things. I do not see how one can talk about fetishism, or sadomasochism, without thinking about the production of rubber, the techniques and gear used for controlling and riding horses, the high polished gleam of military footwear, the history of silk stockings, the cold authoritative qualities of medical equipment, or the allure of motorcycles and the elusive liberties of leaving the city for the open road. For that matter, how can we think of fetishism without the impact of cities, of certain streets and parks, of red-light districts and "cheap amusements," or the seductions of department store counters, piled high with desirable and glamorous goods (Walkowitz, Peiss, Matlock)? To me, fetishism raises all sorts of issues concerning shifts in the manufacture of objects, the historical and social specificities of control and skin and social etiquette, or ambiguously experienced body invasions and minutely graduated hierarchies. If all of this complex social information is reduced to castration or the Oedipus complex or knowing or not knowing what one is not supposed to know, I think something important has been lost.

I want to know about the topographies and political economies of erotic signification. I think that we acquire much of our grammar of eroticism very early in life, and that psychoanalysis has very strong models for the active acquisition and personalized transformations of meanings by the very young. But I do not find the conventional preoccupations of psychoanalysis to be all that illuminating with regard to the shifting historical and social content of those meanings. So much of the input gets—to borrow some phrasing—foreclosed, denied, or displaced. There is a lot of very interesting and creative and smart psychoanalytic work. But when I wanted to think about sexual diversity, psychoanalytic approaches seemed less interesting to me. They seemed prone to impoverish the rich complexity of erotic meaning and conduct.

Moreover, it seemed that many psychoanalytically based approaches made a lot of assumptions about what certain variant erotic practices or preferences meant. These interpretations, mostly derived *a priori* from the literature, were then applied to living populations of individual practitioners, without any concern to check to see if such interpretations had any relevance or validity.

There has also been a kind of degradation of psychoanalytic approaches, when the language and concepts are applied with great enthusiasm and little discrimination. Instead of vulgar Marxism, we now have a kind of vulgar Lacanianism. Even the best ideas from truly creative minds can be overused and beaten into the ground. I remember sitting in the audience of one conference and thinking that there was now a "phallus ex machina," a kind of dramatic technique for the resolution of academic papers. I was remembering an image from a famous Japanese print, where the men have these very large cocks, and one man has a member so huge that he rolls it around in a wheelbarrow. I had this image of the phallus being brought up to the podium on a cart. I have heard a few too many papers where the phallus or the lack were brought in as if they provided profound analysis or sudden illumination. On many of these occasions, they did neither.

At some point, I went back and read some of the early sexology and realized that Freud's comments on the sexual aberrations were a brilliant, but limited, intervention into a preexisting literature that was very dense, rich, and interesting. His brilliance and fame, and the role of psychoanalytic explanation within psychiatry, have given his comments on sexual variation a kind of canonical status. Even though many of his successors ignored or reversed his insights, Freud's prestige has been used to legitimate the later psychoanalytic literature as the privileged discourse on the "perversions." This has eclipsed a vast sexological enterprise that was roughly contemporary with Freud and which was actually more directly concerned with the sexual "aberrations" than he was.

Early sexology has many problems of its own. Besides being sexist and anti-homosexual, the earliest sexology treated pretty much all sexual practice other than procreative heterosexuality as a pathology. Even oral sex was classified as a perversion. The dominant models were drawn from evolutionism, particularly a kind of Lamarckian social evolutionism that was deeply embedded in ideologies of the ostensible superiority of the societies of white

Europeans. But sexology, particularly after Krafft-Ebing, actually *looked* at sexual variety, taking sexual "aberrations" or "perversions" as its primary subject. Sexologists began to collect cases and to record studies of living, breathing, speaking inverts and perverts. Their data collecting was very un-even—some were better at it than others. And many historians are pointing out the limitations of their empirical practices. For example, from her work on the Alice Mitchell trial, Lisa Duggan has discussed how sexologists unsceptically treated newspaper reports, or reports from other sexologists, as primary data. Robert Nye and Jann Matlock have analyzed assumptions and prejudices, especially about men and women, which shaped the early configurations of the categories of sexual fetishism and perversion. Nonetheless, early sexological compendia are incredible sources to mine. Even Krafft-Ebing is useful. For example, actual "inverts" and "perverts" read his early work and wrote him. They sent him their life histories, their anguished self-examinations, and their angry social critiques. Some of these were duly published in the later editions of *Psychopathia Sexualis*. So there are these amazing voices, like the early activist invert who eloquently denounces the social and legal sanctions against homosexuality. Or there is an account of what was called the "woman-haters" ball, but was actually a drag ball in turn-of-the-century Berlin. The detailed description notes that the dancing was accompanied by "a very fine orchestra" and that many beautifully bedecked "women" suddenly lit up cigars or spoke in a deep baritone.

JB: Who were the other sexologists you were thinking of?

GR: Well Havelock Ellis is one of the best of them. Magnus Hirschfeld was also very important. Ellis and Hirschfeld probably did the most, before Freud, to normalize and destigmatize homosexuality and other sexual varia-tions. An indication of Ellis's power as a polemicist can be seen in the famous letter Freud wrote to an American mother who was worried about her homo-sexual son. Freud assured her that many great individuals were homosexual, and that homosexuals should not be persecuted. He advised her, if she didn't believe him, to go "read the books of Havelock Ellis" (Abelove 381).

Ellis and Freud both acknowledge a considerable debt to Hirschfeld. Virtually everyone who writes about homosexuality at the turn of the century cites Hirschfeld's journal, the *Jahrbuch für sexuelle Zwischenstufen* [*The Jour-

nal for Intermediate Sexual Stages]. Other important sexologists included Albert Moll, Albert Eulenberg, and Iwan Bloch. In the first footnote to his famous essay on the sexual aberrations, Freud lists several of the most influential sexologists. These are the writers with whom he is in dialogue. They each have their own approach, and some are more interesting than others. Despite a limited theoretical apparatus, there is a rich social, historical, and cultural complexity reflected in this literature that gets lost in much later psychoanalytic writings.

My sense is that Freud was not all that interested in "perverts" or "inverts"; he seemed much more excited by neurosis and the psychic costs of sexual "normality." Yet his interventions into turn-of-the-century sexology have overshadowed the context in which he was writing and the memory of that substantial and fascinating literature. In any event, instead of just taking off from Freud or later psychoanalysis, I thought it would be a good idea to go back to that literature before the psychoanalytic branch became so dominant, and see what could be learned from the issues and materials that were salient to those who first looked at sexual diversity as their main object of study.

JB: And Foucault, I presume he offered you an alternative to psychoanalysis. You were reading the first volume of Foucault's *History of Sexuality* somewhere around this time as well.

GR: Yes. That was published in English in 1978. I immediately gravitated to it. As you can see from my copy here it is very marked up and dog-eared. That was a very important book. I do think that because of his undoubted stature, other work in the field of sexuality is retrospectively credited to him. There was a debate recently on one of the gay studies lists on the Internet, in which Foucault was credited as the originator of "social construction" theory. The key roles of people like Mary McIntosh, Jeffrey Weeks, Kenneth Plummer, and a host of other historians, anthropologists, and sociologists were completely erased in the context of this discussion. It astonishes me how quickly people forget even recent history, and how much they are willing to project current attitudes back as a fictive chronological sequence. I was influenced by Weeks as much as Foucault. In my opinion, Weeks is one of the great underappreciated figures in gay studies and the social theory of sexuality. He published the basic statement of social construction of homosexuality in 1977, the year before Foucault's *History of Sexuality* was translated.

Many others who were working in the field of gay or lesbian history were rapidly coming to the same kinds of conclusions. I had been researching the history of lesbianism in the early 1970s, and quickly became aware that there was some discontinuity in the type of available data and the kinds of characteristic persons called "lesbian" before and after the late nineteenth century. There were earlier records of women who had relationships with women, and records of cross-dressing or passing women. But it seemed there was little evidence of self-conscious, self-identified lesbians, or lesbian communities, or a kind of lesbian political critique, until the late 1800s.

In 1973, I took another course that changed my life. It was "The Urbanization of Europe, 1500–1900," and was given by Charles Tilly (also at the University of Michigan). Tilly described how industrialization resulted in massive transfers of population from countryside to cities, how urban life was subsequently transformed, and how the forms of voluntary association available to city dwellers differed from those in peasant villages. Another major theme of the course was how the language and repertoire of political action changed in different historical periods. We spent a lot of time on different structures of revolutionary action and political protest in France, and how these changed over time and were specific to particular historical circumstances. Another theme of the course was the way in which forms of individual consciousness changed in the course of all these developments. We discussed E. P. Thompson's work on shifts in how people experienced time, and I was already familiar with Althusser's discussions of different forms of historical individuality (*Reading* 251–53). It was a short jump from the impact of urbanization and industrialization on repertoires of political protest, the conventions of time, and forms of historical individuality, to thinking about how different forms of sexual identity and subjectivity might have resulted from the same large scale social changes. These ideas seemed to make sense of what I was finding in my explorations of lesbian history. I didn't label any of this as "social construction," but I was reaching for ways to think about such issues. But many different scholars were taking the common approaches of social history, anthropology, and sociology, and applying these in a consistent way to homosexuality. There was a widespread convergence of this kind of thinking about male and female homosexuality, and a sudden paradigm shift, in the mid-1970s.

I was unaware of the extent of Foucault's involvement in this emerging paradigm, but I had some idea that he was doing research on sexuality and homosexuality. I had met Foucault earlier, when I was studying in France in the summers of 1972 and 1973. One of my friends was a wonderful man named Larry Shields. We were both completely obsessed with "structuralism," which was what we then called most of the contemporary French thought. We had read Lévi-Strauss and what there was of Lacan, and books of Foucault's such as *The Order of Things*. But there was so little of this material around, and we wanted to go to the source. We got grants to go off to Paris to do research on structuralism. Well, Larry dutifully sat in the main reading room at the Bibliothèque Nationale reading Godelier, Lyotard, Kristeva, and Baudrillard.

But I found that my French was inadequate to this task. As a game to find my way through the labyrinthine catalogue of the Bibliothèque Nationale, I started looking for some obscure lesbian novels that I had not been able to get my hands on for the part of my senior thesis on lesbian literature. When I found that they had Liane de Pougy's *Idylle Sapphique* (her *roman à clef* about her affair with Natalie Barney), I went up to the Réserve room to read it. I found a whole deposit of books by the Natalie Barney and Renée Vivien crowd, with penciled marginalia containing incredible biographical information on the cast of characters. So I ended up spending the summer in the Réserve, clutching my dictionary and verb book, reading dirty lesbian novels.

GR/JB: (in unison) My/Your French was good enough for that!

GR: Well, one day Larry spotted Foucault in the main reading room, and we got up our nerve and asked him out for coffee. We were totally dumbfounded when he accepted. So we went out for coffee, and he asked us what we were doing. Larry enthusiastically reported on his explorations of cutting edge theorists. When Foucault asked me what I was doing, I very sheepishly admitted that I was reading lesbian novels upstairs in the Réserve. To my surprise, he seemed completely nonplussed, and just said, "Oh, I've been studying sodomy convictions." He explained that while sodomy laws were on the books for most of European history, they were only sporadically enforced. He was curious about what determined such patterns of enforcement. This was totally unexpected; I was astonished.

He was incredibly friendly and approachable and gave us his address and phone number. I thought no more about it until I saw the *History of Sexuality* in 1978. I was just starting my research on the gay male leather community in San Francisco. I was going to France for a feminist conference.

I mailed Foucault the very rough draft of my dissertation proposal and told him how much I loved his new book. I thought my work might interest him at a theoretical level, but I expected him to be put off by specific things, like the focus on gay male SM. Once again he surprised me, by inviting me to dinner. It was not until I got to the dinner that I finally realized that he was homosexual, that he seemed perfectly comfortable about SM, and that I could stop worrying about offending him.

JB: So what was it in Foucault that you found useful to your thinking about sexual practices and sexuality in general?

GR: I thought his discussion of the emergence of a new relationship between systems of alliance and sexuality, at least in certain Western industrial countries, was very insightful. You know, I said earlier that many people seem to have overinterpreted the last few pages of "Thinking Sex." I was not arguing there that kinship, gender, feminism, or psychoanalysis no longer mattered in any way. Rather, I was arguing that there were systems other than kinship which had assumed some kind of relative autonomy and could not be reduced to kinship, at least in the Lévi-Straussian sense. When I wrote about that, I very much had in mind the section from the *History of Sexuality* where Foucault says, "Particularly from the eighteenth century onwards, Western societies created and deployed a new apparatus which was superimposed on the previous one" (106). He never says it *replaces*, he says "superimposed."

JB: Right, right.

GR: "And which, without completely supplanting the latter helped reduce its importance." That is the actual phrase. It does not supplant, it simply reduces its importance. "I am speaking of the deployment of sexuality: like the deployment of alliances it connects up with the circuit of sexual partners, but in a different way. The systems can be contrasted term by term." And then he says, "For the first"—that is, alliance—"what is pertinent is the link between partners and definite statutes. The second is concerned with the sensations of the body, the quality of the pleasures, and the nature of impressions, however tenuous or imperceptible these may be." Then on the next page he goes on to explain that "it is not exact to say that the deployment of sexuality supplanted the deployment of alliance" (107). He writes, "One can imagine that one day it will have replaced it, but as things stand at present, while it does tend to cover up the deployment of alliance, *it has neither obliterated the latter, nor rendered it useless. Moreover, historically it was around, and on the basis of the deployment of alliance that the deployment of sexuality was constructed*" (emphasis added). And then he goes on to write, "Since then it has not ceased to operate in conjunction with a system of alliance on which it had depended for support" (108). He even says the family is the "interchange" of sexuality and alliance. "It conveys the law in the juridical dimension in the deployment of sexuality, and it conveys the economy of pleasure, and the intensity of sensations in the regime of alliance." He even calls the family "the most active site of sexuality" (109). Echoing this discussion, it never occurred to me that anyone would think I was arguing that kinship or the family, and their respective dynamics, have *ceased* to have any relevance. What he was saying helped me to think about the outlines of another system that had different dynamics, a different cartography, and different lines of force. In this whole section by Foucault, you can hear the echoes of his conversations with Lévi-Strauss and Lacan. I felt that his assessment of those relationships was novel, insightful, and accurate.

There were so many things I loved about this book—the brilliance and descriptive richness of his writing, his rearrangement of the dominant concepts of sexuality, his interpretations of Freud, Lacan, Reich, and Lévi-Strauss, the dazzling insights, his models for social power, his ideas about resistance and revolution, the depth of his commitment to social and historical causality.

He generated many wonderful phrases—such as the proliferation of perversions. It gave me new ideas, provided some really clear and vivid language, and confirmed that my own preoccupations at the time were not completely absurd. I had given a couple talks on the emergence of modern lesbianism and homosexuality, and many people who heard them probably thought, politely, that I was out of my mind. Finding out that both Weeks in *Coming Out* and Foucault in *The History of Sexuality* had come to similar conclusions, and had a similar understanding of a set of historical and theoretical issues, was immensely reassuring and helped shape my subsequent work.

JB: I realize that you don't want to discount the force of kinship altogether, but isn't there another issue here, namely, developing a vocabulary to articulate contemporary configurations of kinship. I guess another question for me is whether various supportive networks within the lesbian and gay community can't also be understood as contemporary forms of kinship.

GR: You can understand them that way, but then you are using kinship in a really different way. When people talk about gay kinship, for example, they are using a different model of kinship. Instead of Lévi-Strauss, it is based more on the work of David Schneider, who wrote about kinship in America. You have to be specific about how the term is used. In a Lévi-Straussian sense, kinship is a way of generating a social and political structure from manipulations of marriage and descent. In a more vernacular sense, particularly in complex societies like this one, kinship can mean simply the social relations of support, intimacy, and enduring connection. This use of kinship is very different from the Lévi-Straussian notion of kinship.

JB: Well of course it is. But doesn't that mark the conservatism of the Lévi-Straussian notion?

GR: Yes, but I'm saying that the terms are not quite commensurate. In feminist theory, a lot rides on that Lévi-Straussian notion of kinship, which can't just be switched into a more fluid notion of modern or gay-type kinship systems. So one has to be careful about what one is then saying about kinship in this different sense. A system of voluntary association is very different from a system in which obligatory marriages create dynastic systems or other forms of political organization.

Lévi-Strauss is talking about societies in which those relations of marriage and descent *are* the social structure. They either organize almost all of the social life, or they are the most important and visible institutional apparatus. In modern systems, kinship is already a structure that is much reduced in institutional importance. It is not radical to say, in anthropology, that kinship doesn't do in modern urban societies what it used to do in pre-modern cultures. Furthermore, gay kinship closely resembles what anthropologists would call "fictive" or "informal kinship." Such systems of informal or fictive kinship are even less institutionalized and structurally stable than those relationships which are reinforced by state authority.

JB: Right. Well, I would certainly say that kinship can't possibly be the predominant way in which we try to take account of the complexity of contemporary social or sexual life. I mean, that seems clear. On the other hand, it seems to me that the Foucauldian historiography that you have just noted takes for granted the Lévi-Straussian account of kinship and presumes that this form of kinship is itself something in the past.

GR: No. I don't mean to suggest that. Again, one issue is how we are defining kinship.

JB: OK. Because if we understand kinship as obligatory relations, or we think about societies that are governed by obligatory kinship relations, then certainly we would be able to say that is not commensurate with social life as we live it. On the other hand, it seems to me that kinship itself may have lost some of that obligatory status, or is in the process of losing it. And I am wondering if there is some value in holding on to the term "kinship" precisely in order to document that shift in the way in which the social life of sexuality is reconfigured and sustained.

I guess this becomes important when people want to say that feminism, especially in its psychoanalytic or structuralist mode, could talk about kinship. But that particular discourse can't possibly describe the complexity of more modern arrangements or regulatory powers that are governing sexuality. And I think that the problem has been that some people have taken this distinction to be the basis of the distinction between what feminism ought to do, namely look at kinship and gender and psychoanalysis, and what sexuality studies ought to do. And then some people, I think, have taken that a step further and have said that sexuality is the proper "object," as it were, of gay and lesbian studies, and have based the whole methodological distinction between feminism and gay and lesbian studies on the apparent autonomy of those two domains. So maybe it would be better if I just asked you to address that question now.

GR: You have several different issues here. To take one pertinent at the time I wrote "Traffic," there was a still a kind of naive tendency to make general statements about the human condition that most people, including me, would now try to avoid. When you read Lévi-Strauss or Lacan, they make pretty grandiose generalizations. Plus they never hesitate to call something *the* theory of this and *the* theory of that. I often wonder if that usage reflects a grandiosity that is no longer possible, or if it is only an artifact of the translation. In French everything has an article in front of it. So "*la* théorie" in French can mean something quite different from *the* theory in English. In "Traffic," I simply absorbed the idioms and innocent universalism of the time. By the time I wrote "Thinking Sex," I wanted to make more modest claims. That was part of why, in "Thinking Sex," I noted that the Lévi-Straussian/Lacanian formulations might or might not be accurate for other societies, even as I was certain that they had limited applicability to our own. I had acquired some skepticism about the universality of those models.

As for this great methodological divide you are talking about, between feminism and gay/lesbian studies, I do not think I would accept that distribution of interests, activities, objects, and methods. I see no reason why feminism has to be limited to kinship and psychoanalysis, and I never said it should not work on sexuality. I only said it should not be seen as the privileged site for work on sexuality. I cannot imagine a gay and lesbian studies that is not interested in gender as well as sexuality and, as you note in your paper, there are many other sexualities to explore besides male homosexuality and lesbianism. But I am not persuaded that there is widespread acceptance of this division of intellectual labor between feminism, on the one hand, and gay and lesbian studies on the other. And it was certainly never my intention to establish a mutually exclusive disciplinary barrier between feminism and gay and lesbian studies. That was not an issue I was dealing with. I was trying to make some space for work on sexuality (and even gender) that did not presume feminism as the obligatory and sufficient approach. But I was not trying to found a field. For one thing, at that time the institutionalization of gay and lesbian studies was a fond dream that seemed far removed from the realm of immediate possibility. And yet, on the other hand, gay and lesbian studies as an enterprise was well underway. "Thinking Sex" was part of that ongoing process.

Some of the context for "Thinking Sex" was the developing project of gay and lesbian studies, especially gay and lesbian history and anthropology. There now seems to be a certain amnesia about the early work of lesbian and gay studies, as if the field only just started in the early or mid 1980s. This just isn't true. There are whole strata of work in lesbian and gay scholarship which date from the early 1970s and which came out of the gay liberation movement. These in turn built on even earlier research based in the homophile movement. Gay scholarly work was not institutionalized in academia and many of the people who did that work in the 1970s have paid a high price in terms of their academic careers. Lesbian and gay studies certainly didn't start with me, or at such a late date.

For example, the San Francisco Lesbian and Gay History Project started in 1978. A lot of work was begun in the excitement of that time: Allan Bérubé's work on gays in the military, Liz Kennedy and Madeline Davis's work on the Buffalo lesbian community, and my research on gay male leather were all undertaken then. By that time, there were many other scholars involved, and most of us were in communication and dialogue with one another and with one another's work.

Jonathan Ned Katz's *Gay American History*, John D'Emilio's *Sexual Politics, Sexual Communities*, Jim Steakley's *The Homosexual Emancipation Movement in Germany*, and Jeffrey Weeks's *Coming Out: Homosexual Politics in Britain* were from an even earlier period. There was another book on the German gay rights movement by John Lauritsen and David Thorstad published in 1974. By the very early 1970s, lesbian scholars were starting to build on the earlier, pathbreaking bibliographic studies by Jeannette Foster and Barbara Grier. I bring this work up to note that gay and lesbian studies preceded "Thinking Sex" and that it was a thriving scholarly enterprise long before it began to be institutionalized.

JB: Well, tell us what you had in mind then when you wanted to designate the provisionally autonomous status of sexuality as a field.

GR: I wanted to have better scholarship on sexuality, and a richer set of ideas about it than were readily available. I wanted to be able to articulate a sexual politics that did not assume that feminism was the last word and holy writ on the subject. Just as I had a decade earlier wanted a way to think about gender oppression as distinct from class oppression (though not necessarily unrelated or in opposition), I later wanted to be able to think about oppression based on sexual conduct or illicit desire that was distinct from gender oppression (although, again, not necessarily unrelated or in opposition to it). I felt that we had to be able to articulate the structures of sexual stratification and make them visible in order to contest them. I thought that if we did not, progressive constituencies would unwittingly play into a very reactionary sexual agenda, which has, alas, too often been the case. I was afraid that if there were no independent analysis of sexual stratification and erotic persecution, well-intentioned feminists and other progressives would support abusive, oppressive, and undeserved witch hunts.

I think by then a certain kind of feminist orthodoxy had become an edifice with some of the same problems that had earlier plagued Marxism. Instead of class, gender was often supposed to be the primary contradiction from which all social problems flowed. There was an attitude that feminism now had the answers to all the problems for which Marxism was found wanting. I remember that one Marxist scholar made a wonderful comment about a certain approach to Marxism, which I thought was beginning to be applicable to a certain kind of feminism as well. I cannot recall who made the comment, although I think it was Martin Nicolaus. But the comment criticized those Marxists who treated *Capital* as if it were a lemon, as if by squeezing it hard enough all the categories of social life would come dripping out. By the early 1980s, there were many people who approached feminism in the same way. For some, feminism had become the successor to Marxism and was supposed to be the next grand theory of all human misery. I am skeptical of any attempt to privilege one set of analytical tools over all others and of all such claims of theoretical and political omnipotence.

I approach systems of thought as tools people make to get leverage and control over certain problems. I am skeptical of all universal tools. A tool may do one job brilliantly and be less helpful for another. I did not see feminism as the best tool for the job of getting leverage over issues of sexual variation.

I certainly never intended "Thinking Sex" as an attack on feminism, any more than I intended "Traffic" as an attack on Marxism. "Traffic" was largely addressed to an audience drenched in Marxism and can be easily be misunderstood in an era whose preoccupations are so different. I find the current neglect of Marx a tragedy, and I hope to see a revival of interest in his work. Marx was a brilliant social thinker, and the failure to engage important and vital issues of Marxist thought has weakened social and political analysis.

"Thinking Sex" similarly assumed a largely feminist readership. It was delivered at a feminist conference, aimed at a feminist audience, and written within the context of feminist discussion. I do not consider it an attack on a body of work to say that it cannot do everything equally well.

Finally, I wanted to add sexual practice to the grand list of social stratifications, and to establish sexuality as a vector of persecution and oppression. In the 1960s, the important stratifications were pretty much understood to be caste, class, and race. One of the great contributions of feminism was to add gender to that list. By the early 1980s, it had become clear to me that adding gender did not take care of the issues of sexual persecution, and that sexuality needed to be included as well.

JB: Your own work has become descriptively very rich, especially the ethnographic work, and earlier, with respect to the sexologists, you applaud their efforts for being full of valuable descriptive data. You mention as well that they "looked at" cases and practices. Is "looking at" in this sense a theoretical activity? In other words, don't we look with or through certain kinds of theoretical suppositions? And are certain kinds of practices "seeable" or "unseeable" depending on which theoretical presuppositions are used? Perhaps you would like to take this opportunity to speak a bit more about the relationship between descriptive and theoretical work?

GR: Yes, of course; whenever we look at anything we are already making decisions at some level about what constitutes the "seeable," and those decisions affect how we interpret what it is that we "see." The paradigms that informed early sexology produced a certain set of interpretations and explanations which I would reject, particularly the presumption that sexual diversity equals sexual pathology. The assumptions of sexology structured many of the categories and presuppositions that we are still dealing with today, for example, the idea that women are less capable of, less prone to, and less adept at sexual perversions than men. At the same time, their approach enabled sexologists to bring sexual diversity, however misperceived, into their field of view. It is, as it were, at the center of their lens, at the focal point of their enterprise. While Freud had, in general, a lens with better optics and higher resolution, sexual diversity was more at the edge of his field of view. In a way, it remains there in much subsequent work, including large parts of feminism.

But your question raises another issue for me, and that is the way in which empirical research and descriptive work are often treated as some kind of low-status, even stigmatized, activity that is inferior to "theory." There needs to be a discussion of what exactly is meant, these days, by "theory," and what counts as "theory." I would like to see a less dismissive attitude toward empirical work. There is a disturbing trend to treat with condescension or contempt any work that bothers to wrestle with data. This comes, in part, from the quite justified critiques of positivism and crude empiricism. But such critiques should sharpen the techniques for gathering and evaluating information rather than becoming a rationalization for failing to gather information at all.

One friend of mine likes to say, "All data are dirty." Take this to mean that data are not just things out there waiting to be harvested, with intrinsic meanings that are readily or inevitably apparent. Data, too, are socially constructed, and there are always perspectives that determine what constitutes data or affect evaluations of what can be learned from data. Nonetheless, it is a big mistake to decide that since data are imperfect, it is better to avoid the challenges of dealing with data altogether. I am appalled at a developing attitude that seems to think that having no data is better than having any data, or that dealing with data is an inferior and discrediting activity. A lack of solid, well-researched, careful descriptive work will eventually impoverish feminism, and gay and lesbian studies, as much as a lack of rigorous conceptual scrutiny will. I find this galloping idealism as disturbing as mindless positivism.

I also find preposterous the idea that empirical work is always easy, simple, or unanalytical. Unfortunately, virtuoso empirical work often goes unrecognized. Good empirical research involves as much thought and is as intellectually challenging as good conceptual analysis. In many ways, it is more challenging. I know this is a completely heretical opinion, but it is often more difficult to assemble, assimilate, understand, organize, and present original data than it is to work over a group of canonical texts which have been, by now, cultivated for so long by so many that they are already largely digested. There is plenty of "theory" in the best empirical studies, even if such studies often fail to cite the latest list of twenty-five essential authorizing or legitimizing "theorists."

Moreover, many people who deal with data are trained to be sophisticated about how to evaluate empirical material. Some who proclaim the supremacy of theory and who are contemptuous of empirical research can be quite naive about the material used in their own "theoretical" work. Often, data come in, as it were, by the back door. In the absence of empirical research or training, some ostensibly theoretical texts end up relying on assumptions, stereotypes, anecdotes, fragments of data that are out of context, inaccurate details, other people's research, or material that is recycled from other so-called "theoretical texts." So some extremely dirty data get enshrined as "theory." The opposition between "theoretical" and "empirical" work is a false, or at least, distorted one; the imbalance between conceptual analysis and data analysis needs some redress. In short, I would like to see more "interrogation" of the contemporary category of "theory" and of the relationships between such "theory" and empirical or descriptive research.

There is another specific problem I see with regard to sexuality. There is a common assumption that certain kinds of conceptual analysis or literary and film criticism provide descriptions or explanations about living individuals or populations, without establishing the relevance or applicability of such analyses to those individuals or groups. I have no objection to people performing dazzling analytic moves upon a body of assumptions or texts in order to say interesting things about those assumptions or texts. I have nothing against philosophy, literary analysis, or film criticism per se. But I have a problem with the indiscriminate use of such analyses to generate descriptions of living populations or explanations of their behaviors.

For example, there is a trend to analyze sexual variance by mixing a few privileged "theoretical" texts with literary or film criticism to produce statements about either the thing (e.g. "masochism") or the population (e.g. "masochists"). The currently fashionable "theory" of sadomasochism is Deleuze's long 1971 essay on "masochism." Despite the fact that Deleuze based much of his analysis on fiction, primarily Sacher-Masoch's novel *Venus in Furs* and some texts of de Sade, he is taken to be an authority on sadism and masochism in general. Since he is known as a theorist, his comments on sadism and masochism are surrounded with the penumbra of "Theory."

Deleuze treats differences in the literary techniques of de Sade and Sacher-Masoch as evidence for ostensible differences between "sadism" and "masochism." But what are the "sadism" and "masochism" of which he speaks? Are they literary genres? Practices of living sadists and masochists? Floating formations of desire? He makes sweeping generalizations about "sadism" and "masochism," such as "sadism negates the mother and inflates the father; masochism disavows the mother and abolishes the father. . . . There is an aestheticism in masochism, while sadism is hostile to the aesthetic attitude . . ." (115). I find statements like these fairly meaningless, intelligible only because of a psychoanalytic tradition that has equated particular constellations of sexual desire with alleged universals of childhood development. What troubles me is that such generalizations are and will be taken as descriptive statements about those persons and populations who might be considered "masochistic" or "sadistic."

Deleuze is very smart, and it also seems clear from his text that he had some acquaintance with practicing perverts. But his empirical knowledge enters primarily as anecdote. He seems familiar with female dominance, particularly by professional Mistresses. He seems to generalize from some literature and some kind of personal knowledge to make statements about "masochism" and "sadism" in a broader context. This essay is fascinating, yet hardly definitive. It is nonetheless becoming an authoritative text for writing about masochism and sadism.

There are now discussions which draw on Deleuze to analyze the "masochistic aesthetic," "the masochistic text," "masochism's psychodynamics," or "masochistic narrativity." Such usage implies that masochism is an "it," a unitary phenomenon whose singular psychodynamic, text, aesthetic, or narrativity are not only knowable but known. Leaving aside the issue of what terms like this mean, I see a danger that statements about what "masochism" in this sense "is" or "does" or "means" will be taken as descriptions or interpretations of what actual masochists are, do, or mean. Yet, the authority of these statements is not derived from any systematic knowledge of masochism as it is practiced by masochists. It is derived from an analytic apparatus balanced precariously upon Deleuze's commentary, de Sade's fiction and philosophical writings, Sacher-Masoch's novels, psychoanalytic writings on the etiology of masochism, various other texts and films, and personal anecdote.

I have this quaint, social science attitude that statements about living populations should be based on some knowledge of such populations, not on speculative analysis, literary texts, cinematic representations, or preconceived assumptions. And I can hear the objection to what I'm saying already: "but Deleuze," someone is bound to say, "is Theory."

JB: So tell us more about the kind of work you are currently doing, and how it negotiates this tension between conceptual and descriptive domains. You just completed your study on the gay male leather community in San Francisco. What is it that you sought to find there?

GR: Well, when I started this project I was interested in the whole question of sexual ethnogenesis. I wanted to understand better how sexual communities form. This question came out of work I had done in lesbian history, and initially I was trying to figure out where lesbian communities came from, or how they come to exist. I became curious about gay male as well as lesbian communities. Then I realized that many sexualities were organized as urban populations, some quite territorial. I started to wonder about what stork brought all of these sexual populations, and how it happened. This was all part of reorienting my thinking about such categories as lesbianism, homosexuality, sadism, masochism, or fetishism. Instead of seeing these as clinical entities or categories of individual psychology, I wanted to approach them as social groups with histories, territories, institutional structures, modes of communication, etc.

As an anthropologist, I wanted to study something contemporary. There were a number of reasons why I picked this community, but one was that it had crystallized since World War II. There were still individuals around who were involved then, from the late 1940s on. I had access to them, and could study this fascinating process whereby some sexual practice or desire that was once completely stigmatized, hidden, and despised could actually be institutionalized in a subculture in which it was considered normal and desirable. The building of subcultural systems designed to facilitate non-normative sexualities is an interesting process.

And in many ways, the gay male leather community is a textbook case of sexual social formation, although the sexualities within it are more complex than I initially thought. For one thing, "leather" does not always mean "SM." Leather is a broader category that includes gay men who do SM, gay men who are into fisting, gay men who are fetishists, and gay men who are masculine and prefer masculine partners. Leather is a multivalent symbol that has different meanings to different individuals and groups within such communities. Among gay men, leather and its idioms of masculinity have been the main framework for gay male SM since the late 1940s. Other groups organize similar desires in different social and symbolic constellations. For example, heterosexual SM for most of the same period was not organized around the symbol of leather, idioms of masculinity, or urban territories. "Leather" is a historically and culturally specific construct in which certain forms of desire among gay men have been organized and structured socially.

I also did not know when I began this research that at least one sexual activity, fist-fucking, seems to have been a truly original invention. As others have pointed out, fisting is perhaps the only sexual practice invented in this century. It may have been practiced in the early 1960s. But it really became popular in the late 1960s and early 1970s, and then spawned its own unique subcultural elaboration and institutionalization.

Within the gay male leather community, you get this particular unity of the kinky and the masculine in a way that you don't see among heterosexuals or lesbians where those things are mapped out differently. It is a very unique and interesting way of putting certain sexual practices together.

JB: What is the significance of the combination of masculinity and kinkiness?

GR: That is a huge subject and requires a much longer discussion than we can have here. Among gay men, the adoption of masculinity is complicated, and has a lot to do with rejecting the traditional equations of male homosexual desire with effeminacy. Since the mid-nineteenth century, there has been a slowly evolving distinction between homosexual object choice and cross-gender or trans-gender behavior. A masculine homosexual (like a feminine lesbian) was once considered an oxymoron; such persons existed but were "unthinkable" in terms of the hegemonic models of sexuality and gender. The development of the leather community is part of a long historical process in which masculinity has been claimed, asserted, or reappropriated by male homosexuals.

Gay male leather, including gay male SM, codes both desiring/desired subjects and desired/desiring objects as masculine. In this system, a man can be overpowered, restrained, tormented, and penetrated, yet retain his masculinity, desirability, and subjectivity. There are also symbolics of effeminate homosexual SM, but these have been a relatively minor theme in the fifty years of gay male leather. Other communities don't combine these things in the same way. During most of the same time period, heterosexual SM was organized more through sex ads, professional dominance, and some private social clubs. For heterosexual SM, leather was a fetish, but not the core symbol which anchored institutionalization. Straight SM was not territorial, and if anything, the dominant stylistic idioms were feminine.

The imagery of heterosexual SM and fetishism draws on a lot of feminine symbolism. SM erotica aimed at male heterosexuals often has mostly female characters, and the few male characters are often effeminized. There are many reasons for this, including the idiosyncrasies of the history of legal regulation of SM erotica. But evidently many heterosexual men have fantasies of being lovely young ladies. Most of the better equipped houses of dominance have a special room for cross-dressing male clients who pay handsomely for the privilege. These "fantasy" rooms are distinguished from "dungeons" or "medical" rooms. They are often decorated in pink frills and ruffles. One typical heterosexual SM scenario may involve a woman dressed in feminine attire, dominating a man who may be overtly or covertly "effeminized." I do not mean to imply that there are no "masculine" heterosexual male masochists or sadists. Moreover, this feminine imagery is not as hegemonic for heterosexual SM as is masculine imagery for gay male SM. But a visible and common style of heterosexual SM involves a feminine woman and an effeminized man, a sort of fantasy "lesbian" couple. Meanwhile, among actual lesbian sadomasochists, there seems to be a pretty even distribution of masculine and feminine styles, genders, and symbolism.

JB: I'd like to bring us back to gender.

GR: You would! I will only say that I never claimed that sexuality and gender were always unconnected, only that they are not identical. Moreover, their relationships are situational, not universal, and must be determined in particular situations. I think I will leave any further comments on gender to you, in your capacity as the reigning "Queen" of Gender!

August 1994.

Works Cited

Abelove, Henry. "Freud, Male Homosexuality, and the Americans." *The Lesbian and Gay Studies Reader*. Ed. Henry Abelove, Michèle Barale, and David Halperin. New York: Routledge, 1993. 381–93.

Althusser, Louis. "Freud and Lacan." *New Left Review* 55 (1969): 48–66.

——. *Reading Capital*. London: New Left, 1970.

Apter, Emily, and William Pietz. *Fetishism as Cultural Discourse*. Ithaca: Cornell UP, 1993.

Bérubé Allan. *Coming Out Under Fire: The History of Gay Men and Women in World War II.* New York: Free P, 1990.

D'Emilio, John. *Sexual Politics, Sexual Communities: The Making of a Homosexual Minority in the United States, 1940–1970.* Chicago: U of Chicago P, 1983.

Deleuze, Gilles. *Masochism: An Interpretation of Coldness and Cruelty.* New York: Braziller, 1971.

Duggan, Lisa. "The Trials of Alice Mitchell: Sensationalism, Sexology and the Lesbian Subject in Turn-of-the-Century America." *Signs* 18.4 (1993): 791–814.

Engels, Friedrich. *The Origin of the Family, Private Property and the State.* Intro. Eleanor Burke Leacock. New York: International, 1972.

Faderman, Lillian. *Surpassing the Love of Men: Romantic Friendship and Love Between Women from the Renaissance to the Present.* New York: Morrow, 1981.

Foster, Jeannette D. *Sex Variant Women in Literature.* New York: Vantage, 1956.

Foucault, Michel. *The Archaeology of Knowledge and The Discourse on Language.* Trans. A. M. Sheridan Smith. New York: Pantheon, 1972.

———. *The History of Sexuality, An Introduction.* Vol. 1. Trans. Robert Hurley. New York: Pantheon, 1978.

———. *Madness and Civilization: A History of Insanity in the Age of Reason.* Trans. Richard Howard. New York: Pantheon, 1965.

———. *The Order of Things: An Archaeology of the Human Sciences.* New York: Pantheon, 1970.

Freud, Sigmund. "The Sexual Aberrations." *Three Essays on the Theory of Sexuality.* 1905. *The Standard Edition of the Complete Psychological Works of Sigmund Freud.* Trans. and ed. James Strachey. Vol. 7. London: Hogarth, 1960. 135–72. 24 vols. 1953–74.

Grier, Barbara [Gene Damon]. *The Lesbian in Literature.* 1967. 3rd ed. Tallahassee, Florida: Naiad, 1981.

Hartman, Heidi. "The Unhappy Marriage of Marxism and Feminism." *Women and Revolution.* Ed. Lydia Sargent. Boston: South End, 1981. 1–41.

House, Penny, and Liza Cowan. "Can Men Be Women? Some Lesbians Think So! Trans-sexuals in the Women's Movement." *Dyke, A Quarterly* 5 (1977): 29–35.

Jeffreys, Sheila. *The Spinster and Her Enemies: Feminism and Sexuality.* Boston: Pandora, 1985.

Katz, Jonathan. *Gay American History: Lesbians and Gay Men in the U.S.A.* New York: Crowell, 1976.

Kennedy, Elizabeth Lapovsky, and Madeline Davis. *Boots of Leather, Slippers of Gold: The History of a Lesbian Community.* New York: Routledge, 1993.

Krafft-Ebing, Richard von. *Psychopathia Sexualis, with Special Reference to the Contrary Sexual Instinct: A Medico-Legal Study.* Philadelphia: Davis, 1899.

Lacan, Jacques. *The Language of the Self: The Function of Language in Psychoanalysis.* Trans. Anthony Wilden. Baltimore: Johns Hopkins, 1968.

Lauritsen, John, and David Thorstad. *The Early Homosexual Rights Movement.* New York: Times Change, 1974.

Lederer, Laura. *Take Back the Night: Women on Pornography.* New York: Morrow, 1980.

Lévi-Strauss, Claude. *The Elementary Structures of Kinship.* Trans. James Harle Bell, John Richard von Strurmer, and Rodney Needham. Boston: Beacon, 1969.

MacKinnon, Catherine. "Marxism, Feminism, Method and the State: An Agenda for Theory." *Signs* 7.3 (1982): 515–44.

———. "Marxism, Feminism, Method and the State: Toward Feminist Jurisprudence." *Signs* 8.4 (1983): 635–58.

Mannoni, Maud. *The Child, His "Illness" and the Others.* New York: Pantheon, 1970.

Matlock, Jann. "Masquerading Women, Pathologized Men: Cross-Dressing, Fetishism, and the Theory of Perversion, 1882–1935." Apter and Pietz 31–61.

Nye, Robert A. "The Medical Origins of Sexual Fetishism." Apter and Pietz 13–30.

Peiss, Kathy. *Cheap Amusements: Working Women and Leisure in Turn of the Century New York.* Philadelphia: Temple UP, 1986.

Pougy, Liane de. *Idylle Saphique.* Paris: La Plume, 1901.

Reiter, Rayna R., ed. *Toward an Anthropology of Women.* New York: Monthly Review, 1975.

Rich, Adrienne. "Compulsory Heterosexuality and Lesbian Existence." *Signs* 5.4 (1980): 631–60.

Rubin, Gayle. "A Contribution to the Critique of the Political Economy of Sex and Gender." *Dissemination* 1.1 (1974): 6–13; 1.2 (1974): 23–32.

——. "The Leather Menace." *Coming to Power.* Ed. Samois. Boston: Alyson, 1982. 192–227.

——. "Misguided, Dangerous, and Wrong: An Analysis of Anti-Pornography Politics." *Bad Girls and Dirty Pictures: The Challenge to Reclaim Feminism.* Ed. Allison Assiter and Avedon Carol. London: Pluto, 1993. 18–40.

——. "Thinking Sex: Notes for a Radical Theory of the Politics of Sexuality." Vance, *Pleasure* 267–319.

——. "The Traffic in Women: Notes on the 'Political Economy' of Sex." Reiter 157–210.

Sacher-Masoch, Leopold von. *Venus in Furs.* Deleuze 117–248.

Sahli, Nancy. "Smashing: Women's Relationships Before the Fall." *Chrysalis* 8 (1979): 17–27.

Schneider, David M. *American Kinship: A Cultural Account.* Englewood Cliffs: Prentice-Hall, 1968.

——. *A Critique of the Study of Kinship.* Ann Arbor: U of Michigan P, 1984.

Smith-Rosenberg, Caroll. "The Female World of Love and Ritual: Relations Between Women in Nineteenth-Century America." *Signs* 1.1 (1975): 1–29.

Steakley, James D. *The Homosexual Emancipation Movement in Germany.* Salem, N.H.: Ayer, 1975.

Thompson, E. P. "Time, Work-Discipline, and Industrial Capitalism." *Customs in Common: Studies in Traditional Popular Culture.* New York: New, 1993. 352–403.

Vance, Carole S., ed. *Pleasure and Danger: Exploring Female Sexuality.* Boston: Routledge, 1984.

———. "Social Construction Theory: Problems in the History of Sexuality." *Homosexuality, Which Homosexuality?* Ed. Dennis Altman, et al. London: Gay Men's, 1989.

Walkowitz, Judith. *City of Dreadful Delight: Narratives of Sexual Danger in Late-Victorian London.* Chicago: U of Chicago P, 1992.

Weeks, Jeffrey. *Coming Out: Homosexual Politics in Britain from the Nineteenth Century to the Present.* New York: Quartet, 1977.

Wilden, Anthony. "Lacan and the Discourse of the Other." Lacan 157–311.

Extraordinary Homosexuals and the Fear of Being Ordinary

*T*he separation of sexuality from gender, suggested by Gayle Rubin in "Thinking Sex," had the potential to challenge the binary frames within which sexual practices, sexual object choices, sexual desires are collapsed with gender identities and anatomical sex. Prying open the causal and continuous relationship assumed in heterosexist, misogynist frames between gender and sexuality should help us see the surprising and diverse combinations of a range of aspects of social and psychic life; it should help both terms, gender and sexuality, move. However, some of our recent efforts to introduce desire into the definition of lesbianism and distance it from imperatives to identify with and as women have cast (feminine) gender as mere masquerade or as a constraint to be escaped, overridden, or left aside as the more radical work of queering the world proceeds. Such conceptions reproduce stereotypes of femininity and emotional bonds between women as quasi-natural, undifferentiated enmeshments that can only be shorn by way of identifications with (homosexual) men or with sexuality. Given the culture in which we live, it is no surprise that queer theorists, too, would repeat the age-old gesture of figuring lesbian desire in phallic terms in order to distinguish it from what then appears to be the fixed ground or maternal swamp of woman-identification. But making "lesbian" signify desire and difference between women too often leaves femininity's traditional association with attachment, enmeshment, and home intact, fails to reconceptualize homosocial relations among women, and damages feminist and queer projects.

What troubles me is the defensive refusal on the part of queer theorists who have defined sexuality against gender to make the figure-ground relationship between sexuality and (feminine) gender mobile, fluid, or reversible so that new or different configurations of identification and desire, homosociality and homosexuality, reproductivity and productivity can emerge, so that lesbian *desire* might make a bigger difference to the symbolic and social arrangements into which it is now more insistently inserted. Casting sexuality as that which exceeds, transgresses, or supercedes gender aborts the very promise that the separation of gender and sexuality, feminist studies and lesbian/gay studies seemed to hold. It also indulges in the kind of liberationism that inevitably plagues projects that center sex and separate it out from other dimensions of social and psychic life.

When I complain about the tendency to relegate not only femininity, but also feminism to the asexual realm of reproduction, as I do in my readings of Eve Sedgwick's anti-homophobic axioms,[1] I am not suggesting that every critic pay equal attention to every issue, nor do I mean that we should try to get everything out of the morass of the Real into the grasp of language and culture. That would assume that the Real, or everything that exceeds our grasp, could be symbolized, socialized, or rationalized. It would also falsely assume, as Luce Irigaray reminds us, that there is space for feminine difference to be something other than masculine or its negative image when it appears in the Symbolic. I *am* suggesting that we stop defining queerness as mobile and fluid in relation to what then gets construed as stagnant and ensnaring, and as associated with a maternal, anachronistic, and putatively puritanical feminism. Just as it is true that too many queer theorists have constructed feminism as a homogeneous field in need of the intervention of desire and conflict, it also true that too many feminists see queer theory and activism as disruptive of the potential solidarities and shared interests among women. Understanding the complexities of gender and sexuality and opening spaces for their reconfiguration requires that we introduce desire and conflict into the assumption of female proximity and immediacy, and that we acknowledge the vulnerabilities, identifications, and unmanageable bodies at the heart of queer sexualities.

Queer uses of Foucault are responsible, in part, for an overly sociological and negative view of gender, identity, even interiority as traps and prisons.[2] Having accepted the claim that interiorities and core gender identities are effects of normalizing, disciplinary mechanisms, many queer theorists seem to think that gender identities are therefore only constraining, and can be overridden by the greater mobility of queer desires. Predictably enough, gender of the constraining sort gets coded implicitly, when not explicitly, as female while sexuality takes on the universality of man. Our subjection to dichotomizing gender norms is then considered to be at the heart of a disciplining, regulatory psyche. But we should remember that the internalization of gender and sexual norms, the shaping of bodily surfaces and boundaries as effects of social injunctions are not coterminous with the psyche or its tasks as a whole.

Gender identity does often seem to organize or define the very processes through which it itself takes shape, thus, to constitute a ground. After all, the culture tends to arrange virtually every dimension of social and psychic life around sexual difference, as if our sex were the core and cause. To contest that construction of our sex as core and cause does not or should not negate the integration or coherence that a particular configuration of sexual difference, in its articulation with other aspects of social and psychic life, achieves and sustains in individuals over the course of time. Interactions between organisms and environments produce articulations of which our relation to sexual difference is a crucial piece, but not exclusive cause.

Neither gender nor psychic life as a whole are states; they are open processes that gestalt in ways that remain consistent over time without becoming closed or completely insular. Gender operates then at many finely differentiated levels and ought not to be conceived as one solid kernel. In addition to the performative dimension of what comes to seem essential, or relatively stable and lasting, namely, the enfoldings of an outside that become embodied as they become psyche, there are also unconscious gender-performative aspects of our defenses and resistances as well as of our pleasures. There is the most literal kind of performative expression of gender, a volitional dramatization in the service, say, of seduction. And there is the Real of sexual difference that has no fixed content, but which operates as a drag on the wish to have or be everything, as well as on illusions of mastery, knowledge, and control. It exerts its own pressures, always in some relation to what the organism-psyche is in the process of integrating and abjecting. Unmasking gender performativity, on however deep a level, does not do away with gender or even gender identity. It has the potential, however, of making "gender" less controlling, but only if we abandon the simplistic assumption that it has a completely imperial grasp on the psyche in the first place. Queer deconstructions of gender, in other words, cannot do all the earth-shattering work they seem to promise, because gender identity is not the whole of psychic life. Still, that is not to say those deconstructions are therefore insignificant.

What we come to experience as our relation to sexual difference, our most deeply felt sense of gender is, in part, the consequence of reducing a complex set of articulations to a false unity under the sign of sex. This, it seems to me, was one of Foucault's more important points. The goal, then, should not be to do away with gender, as if that were possible, or to leave it intact as though it were a state, or to override or contradict it with our more mobile desires. We might rather value it as an aspect of the uniqueness of personalities without letting it bind and control qualities, experiences, behaviors that the culture divides up rigidly between two supposedly different sexes.[3] Queer or perverse desires do not seem very transformative if the claims made in their name rely on conceptions of gender and psychic life as either so fluid as to be irrelevant or so fixed and punitive that they have to be escaped.

At the most fundamental level, where the organism's central dilemma of attachment to self and other begins, sexual difference plays a belated or secondary role, and its definition as ground may, as Elisabeth Bronfen and Carol Maxwell Miller suggest, operate as a defense against basic terrors of abandonment and suffocation. In *Over Her Dead Body*, Bronfen suggests that reducing femininity to masculinity's other, on the one hand, and/or to a pre- and unarticulable outside, on the other, may be one of the primary ways that we all defend against those primal struggles to survive. I am interested in how lesbianism comes to operate as such a defense, in work deemed to represent it positively and in explicitly homophobic work as well. I will return to this discussion of gender, sexual difference, and psychic life, but first, I want to use two texts from turn-of-the-century Germany to demonstrate that our current bind has a long history and to make the case for more finely differentiated notions of how gender and sexuality operate.

"What Interest Does the Women's Movement Have in the Homosexual Question?" Openly homosexual Anna Rueling delivered a speech on this question at the annual conference of the Scientific Humanitarian Committee on October 8, 1904, at a time when a relationship between the two movements was yet to be articulated.[4] In that speech, Rueling characterizes the women's movement as a product of civilization that has finally allowed women to take back "the ancient human right that was taken from her by raw force" (93). That characterization displays popular nineteenth-century views of the progress of civilization from the use of brutal force to more mediated forms of governance. Rueling views the homosexual question, on the other hand, as a question of the natural rights that accrue to an innate condition, not in terms of the historical achievement of a requisite level of human civilization; for her, as for the founder of the Scientific Humanitarian Committee, Magnus Hirschfeld, homosexuality was a fact of nature, but also a bridge, "the natural and obvious link beween men and women" (83). In this sense, homosexuality was both an effect of civilization and its future realization or demise, and a throwback to an earlier period, since a lack of differentiation between the sexes was considered characteristic of more primitive societies. I would suggest that the notion of a "third sex," distinct from either the first or second, and individualized into a form with its own laws, saved this form of homosexuality from appearing to fall back or regress. Advocates for the third sex emphasized the "civilized" qualities of its members.

Rueling points immediately to the invisibility of female homosexuals, which she attributes to women's absence or exclusion from the criminal code that makes male homosexuality a punishable offense. She sets out to make female homosexuality articulate within the terms of social life, claiming along the way that homosexual women are crucial to the entire social structure, despite their invisibility. And she tips her hat to the group to which she is speaking, asserting that the only homosexual group that acknowledges women's importance and puts them on an equal footing with homosexual men is Magnus Hirschfeld's Scientific Humanitarian Committee. She was right, of course, to distinguish Hirschfeld's organization from other groups, such as Benedict Friedländer's "Community of the Special," a group of men that propagated the superior value of manliness and denigrated women. Still, there would be problems for "femininity" within the third sex. In the efforts to bridge the gap between the women's movement and the homosexual question, homosexual women will be defined as more masculine and valued, even as they are stigmatized, for manly qualities. Still, it was virtually impossible in 1904 to make female homosexuality articulate as sexual without the supplement of masculinity as the means of refusing the association of women with the constraints of the private, familial sphere.

Rueling links the feminist struggle for women's independence and equality to homosexual women's need for education and jobs, making homosexual women the privileged figure of women's independence. The common fight against moralism and its studied ignorance of scientific reason is what unites the movements. For Rueling, as for many others, homosexuality and feminism constituted two crucial sites for the battle over the limits of state control, the reach of criminal law, and the rights to privacy. But the desperate association of homosexuality with science and enlightenment over against moral sentiment and irrational needs represents a paradoxical wish. The move from obscurity out into the light of scientific scrutiny and scientific fact also risks dissolving the very distinctness of homosexuality and its function as the secret key to sexual enlightenment. The dangers of science and education emerge, indeed, when Rueling contributes to the rhetoric of discipline and the good of the nation and its health, an hygienic discourse that helps her decide what institutions homosexuals are actually fit to enter.

In response to anyone who might worry about unmarried homosexual women adding to the number of spinsters, Rueling assures her audience that homosexual women display "none of the ridiculed characteristics attributed to the average single heterosexual woman." "This proves," she continues, "that sensible and moderate satisfaction of the sex drive also keeps women full of life, fresh and active, while absolute sexual abstinence easily causes those unpleasant qualities we find in the spinster, such as meanness, hysteria, irritability, etc." (88). I suppose at one level we could read this passage as refreshingly pro-sex, given the period in which it was written. Even here, however, we see the regulatory rhetorics of health and deviance at work, in the effort to circumscribe what sensible and moderate satisfactions of the sexual drive might be. The meanness and irritability of the spinster may actually be more suggestive of desire than the sensible and moderate satisfactions of homosexual women. At any rate, given the mean-spiritedness of the passage, we would have to wonder whether sex really cures the propensity to meanness in homosexual women.

Rueling enjoins leaders of the Women's Movement to educate the public about the existence of homosexuality and help fight the contempt and open scorn to which homosexuals are subject. She berates feminists for failing to acknowledge the homosexuality of its members and its leaders. "Considering the contributions made to the women's movement by homosexual women for decades, it is amazing that the large and influential organizations of the movement have never lifted a finger to improve the civil rights and social standing of their numerous Uranian members" (91).[5] She threatens a kind of outing when she suggests that many, if not most of the leaders of the women's movement are homosexual women. She could name them, if she were so inclined, but she also teases her readers by pointing out that she should not have to, because only the blindest could fail to recognize them for what they are.

Rueling distinguishes between a merely psychological and an absolute homosexuality. Psychological homosexuals have masculine characteristics but that masculinity does not generate sexual desire for women. Absolute homosexuality includes a masculine psyche and homosexual desire. Masculinity of the psyche, accompanied or not by sexual desire, makes homosexual women different from normal women, who are more prone to hysteria and whose emotionality clouds their thinking and reasoning abilities. Homosexual (read: masculine) women are "like the average man, more objective, energetic, and goal oriented than the feminine woman." Rueling hastens to add that "the homosexual woman does not imitate man, she is inherently similar to him" (85).

Rueling's mapping of sex and sexuality hints at the influence of the notoriously misogynist, homophobic, and anti-Semitic Otto Weininger, whose theories of innate bisexuality helped him make a case for the superiority of a specifically Christian masculinity and, hence, manly Aryan men. Weininger's wacky, eventually popular claims challenged the highly touted division of the sexes as mere ideals that obscured the fluidity of sex characteristics within and across bodies. But Weininger put the brakes on that fluidity in time to distinguish men from women. Anatomical males and females might have varying degrees of masculinity and femininity within them, but men were still superior to women, regardless of the relative proportions. In the chapter of *Sex and Character* devoted to women's emancipation, Weininger suggests that the masculinity in women desires independence, while feminism's most formidable enemies are the women within women. Weininger acknowledges the achievements of great women through history, citing the most famous by name and calling them homosexual. Still, he hastens to add that the most feminine man is superior to the most masculine woman, and he reserves particular contempt for effeminate men, normal women, and Jews, who were equivalent to women in his scheme.

Rueling follows Weininger in his high valuation of homosexual women's greater masculinity, their objectivity, capacity to reason, dedication to work, and transcendence of normal women's emotionality. She cites Weininger directly in order to disagree with his claim that all the most accomplished women in history have been homosexuals. She even engages in debates over the putative homosexuality of specific women named by Weininger. Despite her own propensity to overvalue masculinity in women, Rueling claims to believe that "women in general are equal to men." In the sentence that follows, however, Rueling makes homosexual women more equal. "I am convinced," she writes, "that the homosexual woman is particularly capable of playing a leading role in the international women's rights movement for equality" (91). In the end, it seems that education for Rueling functions primarily to separate the girls from the homosexuals.

The more equal status of homosexual women emerges again when she tries to alleviate the worry among men that women's emancipation means competition with men for jobs. "The combination of masculine and feminine characteristics varies so much from one person to another," she writes, "that all children, whether masculine or feminine, should be educated for independence in the name of simple justice" (89). Though all women should be educated and prepared for meaningful work, most women, according to Rueling, will continue to choose motherhood as their vocation. Normal women will inevitably choose what comes naturally to them. Manly men will still be better suited for certain forms of physical labor, women for more traditionally women's work, and both men and women will be capable of performing those tasks that require neither manly men nor feminine women. Even in the university, where men display the deepest fears of competition with women, male academics exaggerate the problem. "Homosexual women are well suited for sciences and scholarship," she says, "because they have those qualities lacking in feminine women: greater objectivity, energy, and perseverence" (90), and heterosexual women may also become doctors and scientists, but most normal women will prefer marriage and family. And, apparently, Rueling sees little chance that the number of homosexual women will pose a serious threat to male positions.

Rueling ends by linking homosexuality and prostitution, which was one of the privileged sites of regulatory concern and feminist reform efforts in Germany. "In a certain sense," she argues, "the struggle of the homosexual woman for social acceptance is also a struggle against prostitution" (93). Rueling backs up her claim by estimating that as many as twenty percent of all prostitutes are homosexual women whose heterosexual prostitution represents nothing more than income and whose private lives are organized around their homosexuality. If women in general, and homosexual women in particular, had more options, prostitution could be diminished, according to Rueling. The diminishing of prostitution leads Rueling to her concluding remarks, filled with metaphors of light, hope for the future, and the ends of false morality and darkness. But prostitution remains a drag on this way out of the darkness. Just before concluding her speech, Rueling admits that reforms might diminish prostitution, but could never eliminate it, implying unwittingly that the project of enlightenment itself requires an obscurity in relation to which it can do its scutinizing, gazing, and disciplining work.

Let me highlight what I take to be some of the strategic but ultimately problematic gestures in Rueling's speech, with particular attention to the problems that seem to anticipate current debates. First, a particular sexual identity, female homosexuality, is linked to autonomy and distinguished from the dependencies and enmeshments of the average woman. It is the phallic supplement to their "womanness" that makes female homosexuals more equal than other women and more free of particularity. Or, to put it more accurately, to make them distinct from the particularities, insularities, and quasi-natural wishes of average women Rueling represents them in phallic terms. Second, active sexual desire, independence, and uniqueness are associated with greater intelligence, increased self-awareness, and greater freedom from the constraints of a feminized psyche. Masculinity is the ingredient that makes the difference and blinds Rueling to her own unconscious complicity with the disciplining effects of enlightened sociality. Third, mobility becomes possible and visible in the form of an escape from reproduction, families, households, and private lives, with the consequence that sexual, economic, and political autonomy get defined in non-relational terms. Fourth, the category of normal women who will always want to marry and stay at home remains as crucial to homosexual women and their sense of mobility as it does to men. Those undifferentiated, privatized, maternal keepers of hearth and home remain a drag on what might otherwise mean complete rootlessness, rationalization, and societalization, not to mention the dissolution of sexual difference in a public world of abstract individualism and economic competition. Fifth, work is distinguished from what most normal women do in a way that becomes the defining feature and, perhaps, the primary defense of homosexual women. In Rueling, as in other feminist works of the period, this capacity and desire to work is associated with a freedom from particular attachments and family that ultimately serves the nation and its health. Finally, all these assumptions about the relationships among sexuality, intelligence, and modernity participate, even if unwittingly, in a colonial discourse that equates civilization with reason, autonomy, manliness, and clear differentiations between the sexes over against less individualized, less intelligent women, children, and lower races.

Aimée Duc's 1901 novel, *Are They Women?* (*Sind es Frauen?*), reproduces many of these gestures in a more entertaining form.[6] The novel introduces us to a group of women who identify themselves in the newly available terms of the third sex, terms they attribute to Richard von Krafft-Ebing and his *Psychopathia Sexualis*. Though narrated in the third person, the novel is written about and from the perspective of a main character, Minotschka Fernandoff, a student of literature and philosophy who is described as half Russian and half French. We are introduced to Minotschka and to her circle of friends at the point at which they are studying in Genf, Switzerland. From about 1870, Zurich, in particular, but Switzerland, more generally, was associated for many women (and many anti-feminists) with women's wish for education and autonomy. The experience of student life in Switzerland, where women had access to university study before they did elsewhere, is often represented as only a temporary phase in the biographies of women who lived and studied there. In her study of lesbianism in Austria at the turn of the century, Hanna Hacker exposes the extent to which "the student years" then became a code that referred to the biographical experience of social life and learning with like-minded women.

The group to which we are introduced in Duc's novel is emphatically cosmopolitan, or, in other words, European since the novel's few allusions to the exoticism and foreignness of the Orient and Australia make it completely evident what the limits of that specifically European modern cosmopolitanism were. The group includes Minotschka's lover, Marta, a Polish countess, who is independently wealthy and studies music for the fun of it, and a Russian physician, Dr. Tatjana Kassberg, who is described as a cynical, somewhat false, and unpopular woman and is assumed by the entire group to be a nihilist. Her mysterious connections with Russians who have been deported from Switzerland anticipate her own necessary flight out of Genf to avoid arrest for running a secret press in the service of Russian nihilist groups. Frau Annie is a married woman who remains married for the sake of children and who often feels uncomfortable in the group's discussions of marriage and men. Pierette is described as a second-rate Swiss actress; Zeline Ardy is a Viennese medical student; and her partner, Berta Cohn, is a Jew from Prague who is only seventeen or eighteen years old, but said to be taller, stronger, and apparently smarter than the rest of them. Two uninteresting Germans and a French woman who speaks no German round out the group.

Other than their national heritage, we learn nothing about the family backgrounds of these women; indeed, they are cast as happily orphaned and at home in any major city with a significant number of women like themselves. The novel seems to be structured by a shift from this initial celebration of cosmopolitan rootlessness and alternative affiliations to what becomes an ultimately melancholic longing for attachments that recapitulate identifications with home, family, and nation. I am going to suggest, however, that that apparent shift opens up the possiblity of rethinking the relations between the more public world of knowledge and commerce and the supposedly private and constraining world of home, family, and love.

Minotschka Fernandoff is described in terms that echo those characteristics that Krafft-Ebing and a range of other sexologists highlight as typical of contrary female sexual types.[7] The novel opens with Minotschka's exit from a lecture hall at the university. In terms that immediately set her apart from her fellow students, she leaves the university building before the great mass of students, hurries down the steps and onto the streets of Genf where she attracts the attention of passers-by, to whose looks Minotschka seems oblivious. That form of oblivion to the gaze of others protects Minotschka and displays her refusal to shy away from the stigma she knows is attached to her.

In the two paragraphs that describe Minotschka's external appearance, we get a range of Krafft-Ebing's favored symptoms of contrary sexual types: Minotschka combines a mannish gait with an underlying feminine coquettishness and her boyish, youthful, energetic movements give her unconsciously feminine coquettishness a unique quality. She is wearing a simple black dress, a tie, and a straw hat; she carries a walking stick, which Krafft-Ebing lists along with umbrellas and other self-evidently phallic objects typically carried by women who constitute the third sex. It is the walking stick that attracts the attention of the people in the streets who, we are told, fail to notice the limp that makes the stick necessary, and instead impute dark, ugly motives to Minotschka's insistence on carrying such an object. Minotschka requires the walking stick in order to climb the steep streets of Genf because she suffers from a nervous weakness in her left ankle. This attribution to her of nervous weakness coheres with various nineteenth-century constructions of homosexuality but is less interesting than the attribution to her of a psychic wound for which the phallic stick compensates and which only the complement of a feminine woman can ultimately heal or cover up. And this novel makes room for the most feminine of women in the category of the third sex, even as it seems to valorize manliness and to turn the feminine woman into Minotschka's walking stick. In the process, however, it may also expose manliness in men and in women as a defense, rather than a state of interiority.

At one level, the plot of this "Trivialroman" is simple and true to cheap romances. Girl falls in love with girl, girl loses girl, girl finds girl again and they live happily ever after. If I were to put it in more modern terms, the plot would sound a little more complicated and a lot campier: manly young woman, henceforth, butch, falls in love with feminine homosexual woman, or femme; that "falling" is masked by the butch's dedication to work, politics, and the deflection of emotion. Butch loses femme to a man; butch falls apart and gives up her work to return to mother(land); butch and femme meet again by chance over the dead body of the femme's husband in a Paris cemetery; butch uses her wounds but also her pride to force the femme to explain, defend, and justify herself, then plead for the reconciliation that the butch knows will heal her own pain. Or, we could read it another way. Feminine woman falls in love with *Mannweib*, masks that falling with various forms of caretaking that expose the only apparently stronger butch's wound. Femme abandons butch for wounded father figure, then emerges again over the husband's dead body. Femme lets the butch think that the butch has the power to decide to reconcile, instead of exposing the femme-mommie, butch-baby dynamic that is really at work. Butch is granted the role of tyrant by a supposedly contrite, obedient femme who leads the butch by the hand into the sunset.

Now, let me offer a slightly more detailed version of the plot, such as it is. We learn from a number of broad hints and explicit assertions early on that Minotschka and the Countess Marta are a couple. Marta is called away from Genf to tend to her sick father. While she is gone Mintoschka is tempted by another feminine woman, the actress Pierette, who begs Minotschka to take her along to Munich, where Minotschka has plans to pursue her studies. Minotschka has a hostile encounter during this period with a certain Dr. Laum who comes to Genf to propose marriage to her for the second time, only to find himself barraged by feminist diatribes about his disgraceful views of women. When the countess returns from her father's sickbed, the two women spend an idyllic vacation together that ultimately makes them restless about neglecting their work. Work, we are told, staves off the hysterias and romantic longings that plague normal women. When Marta's father dies suddenly, the countess leaves Genf again without knowing when she will be able to return. In the meantime, Minotschka moves with her Russian friend Boris and Pierette to

Munich. The move to Munich occurs sooner than planned because the university has been interrupted by the explosion of a set of scandals. One of the members of the third-sex group, Dr. Kassberg, has been forced to flee Switzerland for illegal political activities in support of nihilists in Russia.

In Munich, Minotschka works, attends the gatherings of the third-sex group, joins a group of avowed third-sex bikers (bicyclers), and works some more. After a period of only sporadic and lackluster correspondence from Marta, Minotschka receives the letter that brings her world crashing down around her. The Countess writes that she has married an officer she met while on a rest cure on the North Sea. In response to this news, Minotschka suffers a prolonged, severe breakdown. For four weeks she locks herself in her apartment and refuses all visitors. Her landlady excuses her distance from her friends by telling them she is working on a book and cannot be disturbed. When she finally emerges, she attends one of the third sex gatherings in order to make Marta's exclusion from the group official.

For the next two years, she ceases to participate in any social life, watches as the circle of homosexual women disperses to all parts of the Eurocentric globe, returning "home" out of necessity or choice. Minotschka prepares for the job she has been offered as head of an Australian school, but her despair remains too great to allow her to pursue her professional goals. She buries herself in fantasies or memories of "Heimat," the homeland which she associates with the mother, her mother country, mother tongue, France. Eventually, she refuses her position in Sydney and travels to Paris where she hopes to fight off what she now considers to have been the arrogance of her student years and to begin a new life. Apparently, she hopes to make her student years a mere stage to be outgrown. Minotschka resists her memories of the countess by immersing herself in the past, in home, in familiar bread, familiar food, familiar wine. But her longings return and interrupt her good intentions. On a walk through a Paris cemetery, where she seeks peace and quiet, Minotschka just happens to come upon a woman in mourning clothes whose sexiness and appeal remind her of Marta. Lo and behold, it turns out to be Marta, who is visiting the grave of her dead husband and who recognizes and embraces Minotschka. After pleading for forgiveness, Marta convinces Minotschka to make a life with her, half a year every year in Warsaw and the other half in Paris, their respective parental homes. They go off into the sunlight arm and arm and we presume they live happily ever after.

It is easy to see why this novel has been hailed as one of the first "positive" representations of lesbian love. That is how it was advertised by the Amazon Press when it was reissued in 1976 and by scholars of turn-of-the-century homosexual literature.[8] After all, not a single one of the women dies or commits suicide and the homosexual couple ends up together in the end. Readers have celebrated not only this happy romance plot, but also the book's feminist politics. The love story I have just recounted takes up remarkably little space in this short novel which is more fully devoted to the representation of political discussions among the women, as well as to their political debates with unwitting men. (We neither meet nor hear from a single "normal woman.") At one level, it is a deeply conservative novel, one that appears to renege on its early dedication to an educated, politically aware elite community of women. But I prefer to read it as a reminder to Minotschka and then to us of how braided the only apparently distinct worlds of average women and extraordinary homosexuals are.

For now, I want to dwell on a series of those political discussions and diatribes that offer what for me has always been an amusing view of what the feminist politics of these homosexual women were, and I will in turn relate those politics to other definitions of female homosexuality. Two discussions dominate the first gathering described in the novel. Shortly after the women arrive at Minotschka's apartment, they are engaged by their host in a heated discussion of a former member of the group who is now married to a man.[9] In response to their host's pedantic diatribe, other women work to reestablish the boundaries around what they wish were the non-contradictory category of the "third sex" by supposing that this particular woman had never really been one of them, that her claims to have been part of the third sex were fraudulent, and that she was actually a woman all along. The difficulty sustaining the neat division between real and unreal members of the third sex, between the inside and outside of the category, emerges when one of the women reminds Minotschka, the most vociferous critic of this woman's fraudulence, that she herself had once been married to a man. In response to this reminder, Minotschka can manage only the ultimately weak assertion that her earlier marriage "was different." Duc's novel is filled with conversations in which Minotschka and her circle of friends expend considerable effort keeping the category of women, that is, the second sex distinct from themselves. Those boundary concerns are characteristic of other writings on female homosexuality at the time. Duc's novel takes a slightly different tack than Rueling's speech, making feminine women homosexual, but representing them as lacking, as waiting for "the human being" in them to be saved.

Minotschka and friends spend the second half of the evening lamenting the systematic suppression of evidence of the existence of a third sex, and Minotschka attacks her friends who study medicine for failing to focus their research and writing on its existence. Dr. Kassberg, the only woman who ever seems to contest Minotschka's pedantry in any serious way, challenges her host to offer evidence for the existence of a third sex with its own laws. She wonders instead whether such women as themselves are merely exceptions, anomalies whose "extraordinary intelligence has lulled their sexuality to sleep or even killed it off" (17). Minotschka rejects the doctor's view without making explicit their at least slight disagreement over the relationship between sexuality and intelligence. The intensity of Minotschka's impassioned speechifying suggests, when her relationship with Marta may not, that sexuality might have been sublimated, even repressed, but not killed off.

Minotschka then claims that if medical scientists were to inform the public about what they know, the woman question would not only take a different turn, it would no longer be a woman's question at all, but a question of the third sex. In the first of many such gestures, Minotschka takes the lead in separating the category of normal women from the category of women who belong to the third sex and want, therefore, to be emancipated. Such views are consistent with other contemporary efforts, anti-feminist as well as feminist, to confine the desire for emancipation to members of the third sex, to homosexual women. In her speech Rueling more radically phallicizes the desire for emancipation and female homosexuality, but does not obscure the emancipatory concerns of heterosexual women as thoroughly as does Minotschka's equation of feminism with female homosexuality.

Minotschka's girlfriend, Marta, the Polish countess, sustains the evening discussion at her lover's home by lamenting how little they do to make the existence of a third sex public, with the consequence that women commit themselves to marriages that make them and their husbands miserable. Distinguishing third-sex women from real women, the countess speaks of her frustration over the requirements of feminine masquerade, the injunction to act or perform like normal women which is a painful struggle for them. Other than the attention Minotschka attracts in the streets, the women never cause any suspicion (of deviance) among the people they encounter in the world of bars, concerts, and universities. Their difference makes its appearance in their own insistent verbal attempts to define their uniqueness.

In an affect-laden bit of sarcasm, Minotschka points to the sorry state of heterosexual marriage, those "unhealthy relationships on which the foundation of the state is supposed to rest" (22). And Dr. Kassberg concurs, adding that hysteria is caused by "the false sexual life imposed on unsensual normal women and on members of the third sex in marriage" (23). She speaks more than once of the brutalities of the marital bedroom and makes a plea, along with her colleagues, for women's education and preparation for work. All the women emphasize how offensive it is to be forced into marriages that offend their sense of aesthetics, but their eugenicist interests in the health of marriage and the nation do not emerge as explicitly as they do in Rueling's speech with its disciplinary and hygienic gestures.

The conversation among Minotschka and friends shifts to love, to the incredibly irrational, self-destructive things women do for love. Minotschka argues that love is always more or less about sex and leads to irrationalities for that reason. Because well-developed minds and intelligence stand in inverse proportion to more vulgar or brutal sexual instincts, she suggests that "the more intelligent person will necessarily always love more happily." "A person who puts a lot of energy and intensity into intellectual life has no time to think so much about the satisfactions of love," she waxes with great confidence (24). Minotschka's conclusions can be paraphrased in the following terms. Love is a preoccupation of women with lesser intelligence who lack the most important ingredients of happiness, namely, work and the development of their minds. People of greater intelligence and with purposeful lives love more happily, because they are less given to the deleterious effects of excessive fantasy and imagination. Minotschka's own susceptibility to love's unhappinesses becomes painfully obvious only after we have been treated to a number of these protests distancing her from the unhappinesses and hysterias of the average woman.

This lengthy discussion takes up twenty-seven pages of a ninety-five-page novel. And, then, we are treated to another lengthy example of Minotschka's pedantic, if articulate, outbursts during the visit of a certain Dr. Laum, a male acquaintance who has announced his intention to propose to her for a second time. Unable to avoid seeing him, Minotschka invites her friends Frau Annie and Boris to join her for the encounter. Boris is a medical student who wisely keeps the true nature of his affections for Minotschka concealed. The minute Dr. Laum has made himself at home, Minotschka offers him sherry and proposes the following toast: "So, Dr. Laum, let's toast on the occasion of this first reunion, to my future—that it should bring me happiness! And to my remaining happy in my independent life, just as I am now" (31–32). The good doctor displays some embarrassment at this all too obvious refusal of his unarticulated marriage proposal and responds by saying he will toast to her happiness, but not in its current form, rather to her happiness "at the side of a beloved man." As the narrator assures us, Dr. Laum could not have made a bigger mistake. "Nothing infuriated Minotschka, that strong independent nature more than the eternal reference to men as Happiness-Attributes" (32).

Just when the conversation seems to be taking a less problematic turn, Dr. Laum makes the mistake of reporting that his sister has studied music only as a way of passing time until she is married, and though she is already twenty-five years old, he hopes that something will soon work out. This inspires another set of angry speeches from Minotschka about the disgrace involved in thinking of women's education as mere preparation for marriage, for the manhunt, as she calls it. Dr. Laum, who is completely out of his league, suggests that all women should marry and want to marry. Frau Annie decides to respond to this indignity, explaining to Dr. Laum that not all women want to marry and some most definitely should not. "We are all human beings, and only then sexual beings. All sexual beings are certainly humans, but not all human beings are sexual beings," she says (34). Dr. Laum finds this argument confusing and asks whether they understand the burden placed on families and the state by women who remain spinsters forever. This opens the way for another moment of pedantry from Minotschka about the importance of women's work and women's education. Suddenly Dr. Laum goes on the offensive and argues that only emancipated women oppose marriage and want education. "We shouldn't give in to them," he allows, "because in its truest form women's emancipation is the negation of marriage. Unfeminine women are a monstrosity for every-one" (35–36). In one of her more subtle rejoinders, Minotschka concedes Dr. Laum's point, only to give his definition of femininity a new twist. "What is the concept 'femininity,'" she asks with her usual rhetorical flourish, "but a wish dictated and enforced by men who want to shape the woman according to their own tastes." She holds forth again, that the women who are made in the image of man are actually the "unfeminine" ones. "The truly 'feminine' ones," she claims, "would be those who hold their own individuality completely for themselves, and who constitute a particular species, psychically and physically" (36). In a rare allusion to motherhood, Minotschka allows that woman as mother is feminine by definition and apparently constitutes a category separate from truly feminine women and unfeminine ones as well.

How, asks the doggedly confused Dr. Laum, does one discover femininity then? To this Minotschka offers one of her few potentially off-color responses when she suggests that she "has [her] ways." But she goes on to explain the importance again of education for all women, so that they can make informed choices about what they want to do with their lives. As always, Minotschka and Frau Annie assure Dr. Laum that most women will still prefer marriage and family over career, but Dr. Laum cannot be comforted about the problem of competition between men and women, about the reduction of the relations between the sexes to that. Minotschka's hard edge allows her to be positively joyful about the survival of the fittest, a survival and triumph that have nothing to do with physical strength, according to our lovable pedant, but everything to do with intelligence. "Sex makes no difference," she claims, "and in the end hard work and competence will be decisive" (38). In a final desperate attempt to win a point, Dr. Laum warns against the dissolution of households and the end of domesticity. "The word 'Hausfrau' will eventually be completely devalued" (40), he argues. Frau Annie applauds the very trend that Dr. Laum fears. She suggests that social life has already moved out of the home and into public places, and she offers a wonderful description of how much better it is for women to have holiday dinners at restaurants or inns rather than at home, where they are also served rather than being exhausted from waiting on men and children. This move out away from home, then, is inevitable and positive. Dr. Laum worries that "the domestic hearth will become more and more monotonous, boring, and empty." Yes it will, responds Minotscka, "because even now it cannot compete with what is available outside the home" (41).

The autonomy of these women haunts the heterosexual male characters in the novel who fear that the rationalization of the domestic will destabilize not only gender relations, but the social contract and the nation as a whole. Their relation to the women who identify as members of the third sex could be characterized as fetishistic; they actively seek discussion and debate with these women only to disavow the difference, in particular the specifically sexual difference, that these women represent. But, of course, Minotschka's relation to femininity, vulnerability, and attachments other than intellectual ones is also characterized by disavowal. Despite her often brilliant exposés of men's tendency to eroticize women's obscurity, she replicates that very dynamic as she projects onto normal women those psychological weaknesses from which she imagines herself to be free. In the end, love and unconscious identifications prove to be as powerful in determining Minotschka's fate as are her professional ambitions or her identification with the category of the third sex.

The novel, written about Minotschka Fernandoff, also seems to have enough distance from her perspectives on herself to allow for an ironic reversal in the end. The characters around her operate as a kind of chorus for her diatribes about the status of women, the deplorable state of marriage, and scientists' shameful disavowals of what they know, namely the existence in nature of a third sex. The minor characters have little life of their own and the arrangement of these figures around the lead has a number of effects. First, their lack of individuality seems to support Minotschka's claims to independence and self-sufficiency, which, in turn, depend for their intelligibility on a dependent, feminine chorus. Second, in the process through which Minotschka is distinguished not only from so-called normal women, but also from the women in her group, the more mannish woman that she is becomes the ideal or at least most prominent type of third sexer, making cross-gender identification and homosexual object choice cohere, and autonomy a decidedly, or at least, apparently, masculine preserve. The consequence of her prominence as ideal type is that the more feminine women ultimately become marginal, even suspect, by virtue of their apparent ability to pass more easily into a heterosexual role, this in spite of those very women's disclaimers. The feminine women become visible primarily as objects of Minotschka's desire, introducing conventional gender differences into a category that has often been characterized only in the terms of cross-gender identifications.

This recognition and representation of differences between and among homosexual women distinguishes the novel from the prejudices of the sexologists for whom feminine homosexual women could not be real homosexuals. In *Are They Women?* the category of feminine homosexual women causes trouble but is not uniformly dismissed as inauthentic. Still, in her relationships with the actress Pierette, for example, Minotschka demonstrates how the assumption of the masculine position is linked to an intolerance of what feminine women, even feminine homosexuals, supposedly lack. When Pierette begs Minotschka to take her along to Munich, she begins with a series of apologies and hestitations that provoke Minotschka to command her to get on with it and forget all the introductions. The narrator informs us, as if we didn't know by now, that Minotschka could be brutal in response to indecisive, hesitant women. "She hated everything that lacked energy or force" (46). The dashes that punctuate the rest of Pierette's efforts to convince Minotschka to take her with her to Germany make the feminine homosexual woman's timidity even more evident. Minotschka's sense of superiority is displayed not only in her position as caretaker, perhaps as maternal caretaker, but also in her tone. When Pierette breaks into tears, Minotschka refers to her as a "little goose" in a tone described as deeper and darker than usual. She comforts Pierette with the words "you nutty, dumb little thing" and, along the way, agrees to take Pierette with her to Munich, but not without educating the actress in the value of independence, making her promise that she will learn German in the meantime. "I just want to save and sustain the human being in you," Minotschka says, "that is our obligation" (48). But Minotschka's sense of obligation to the human being in Pierette becomes Pierette's experience of passion, in passages that associate Minotschka with autonomy, work, and political commitment and Pierette with timidity, irrational frivolity, dependence, and love. Pierette will become independent, but not masculine, and Minotschka will fall apart without becoming a femme.

Minotschka's mannish independence (or defense) suffers an enormous blow when her lover leaves her for a man, exposing not only the vulnerability at the heart of Minotschka's defenses, but also the fragility of the boundaries around the category of the third sex and the always ambiguous status of the feminine homosexual woman. The loss of the loved object creates a crisis in Minotschka that exposes her genuine desire for the countess, but also her vulnerability to love's unhappinesses. Her response takes the form of a melancholic longing for home, specifically for the mother's home, for France, the mother tongue, and for what she describes as the smells, the sounds, the sights, and associations of childhood. This return to Paris does not represent a return to actual family or friends, but to a fantasmatic identification with what has been lost or disavowed in the effort to define female homosexuality against female afflictions.

Suddenly, it is as if Minotschka's political and intellectual ideals had only temporarily defended against a wound or loss that structures not only her relation to gender and sexuality, but also to nation and home. And what is lost is not only the loved object, but faith in the stability of the boundaries between the second and third sexes, between homosexuality and heterosexuality, faith also in the possibility of sustaining alternative forms of attachment and affiliation in opposition to those deemed more primary.

Whereas the movement between cities, countries, and languages was once the condition of her freedom, but also apparently of her identity, it is now experienced as symptomatic of confusion, detachment, and loss. A positive, mobile, denaturalization of gender and national identity becomes a negative, melancholic homelessness. The structures of melancholy that differentiate the two women from one another—Minotschka's loss of the mother, Marta's of the father—also motivate their erotic relation to one another and their plan to live half a year on Marta's father's estate in Poland and the other half in Minotschka's mother's country of origin, France. On the face of it, this fantasy relationship conceived in a cemetery prevents the women's return home from being reduced to heterosexual normalcy, even if their agreement to be tyrant and obedient wife to each other recapitulates primary attachments to lost parental objects and is a profoundly melancholic reproduction.

But there are other sources of loss and melancholy, the loss, for instance, of the community of homosexual women that supported Minotschka's political, emotional, and intellectual certainties. The novel indeed demonstrates the absence of social, institutional, and discursive supports for female homosociality or non-sexual heterosociality for women. In this story, Minotschka loses faith in the community before she actually loses that community, faith in the stability of distinctions, boundaries, and differences. Her loss of her walking stick, Marta, shatters her faith in the power of science to make a discrete third sex with its own laws, and to control gender and sexuality in a way that would protect her from wayward women, but also from the qualities in herself that fail to fit the rigid forms of disidentification and cross-identification that she champions.

The loss also shatters what come to seem like bourgeois pretenses. When Minotschka first reads Marta's fateful letter, she has her friend Boris accompany her through the streets of Munich, streets she is suddenly unable to negotiate. She walks in circles, aimlessly, unable to find her way, and eventually ends up on the bad side of town, as though her bourgeois certainties, her knowledge, and goals had constituted only a thin veil over inner and outer chaos, a chaos represented by the uncivilized sexualities of the lower classes. Minotschka rediscovers, finds Marta again not on the streets of Paris, in the midst of the sensations of smell, taste, and sight she associates with home, but in what she describes as the stillness of the cemetery, and, even more specifically, the peacefulness of the graves of the poor, whose plots are covered with the natural beauty of colorful flowers, eschewing all pomp and pretense. What supports the attachment now is each woman's relation to abandonment and death.

How do we read Mintoschka's identifications with science, objectivity, and work, once those identifications and their supporting disidentifications seem to shatter? We could read her "butchness" as phallic imposture that cracks to expose the real woman underneath. Or, we could read her butch performances as strategic masquerades that allow her entry into the male-defined realms of scholarship and exchange. Both interpretations are based on superficial accounts of how gender and sexual difference operate. Underneath Minotschka's butch defenses is not "a woman" but a butch who has defended against a range of things, including the qualities of vulnerability, dependence, and attachment too often associated with femininity and women. Minotschka is clearly constrained by social constructions of manliness and citizenship, defined as objective, abstract, disembodied, and independent. She is also constrained by the association of vulnerability, emotionality, hysteria, and particularity exclusively with women. When she is forced to encounter her own overwhelming emotionality and vulnerability, those qualities may feel like cross-gender behaviors or feelings, and they may change her relation to her butchness, but they do not change her relation to gender.

Minotschka appears to go through a period of regression to the point of a certain fantasized confluence or loss of self in the (m)other, but she emerges out of the dead to discover her own desire and her capacity to attach from a position that remains butch, even though it can now be characterized as tyrannical only with a great deal of irony. Dissolving the defense against qualities that have been made to seem cross-gendered does not change the configuration of sexual differences consolidated over time as gender identity, but such dissolution could change the affective and behavioral dimensions that she allows as part of her felt sense of gender. Minotschka does not become a femme, nor does she become androgynous; she becomes less defended, but her butchness remains important to her, as well as to the countess. When the hysterical Pierette agrees to try to do what would mitigate her helplessness, hysteria, and dependence, those new behaviors might seem cross-gendered to her, but her new-found strength, independence, ability to earn her own living does not turn her into a butch or an androgyne. They change her relation to her own femeness. Dissolving defenses and resistances reveals what the women share, the terrors of attachment and its potential failures that our tenacious insistence on sexual division may help us conceal. The redistribution of qualities and experiences and behaviors across only apparently definitive divisions by sex does not undo the tight psychic braid that comes to be defined as or in relation to our gender. Of course, our only access to those regions is through the tight braid of sexual difference with the various dimensions and levels of psychic life. But to suggest that we can never dispense with the lenses of gender is not the same as imagining that gender actually organizes social and psychic life in an absolutely imperial way.

What of the countess, the feminine homosexual woman? How do we avoid the trap of casting Minotschka's phallic performances as veils or defenses and Marta's femininity as somehow self-evident or psychologically undifferentiated? Marta's return home to her dying father, her assuming of his estate, her connection then to a family history, to land, and to country isolate her from the alternative public that was possible in Genf or in Munich, and, according to her, make her vulnerable to the seductions of heterosexual marriage. Her marriage was a mistake caused by the confusions of grief and loneliness. If Minotschka has defenses against the possibility of abandonment and loss of control, Marta had defences throughout against attachment to self and to others. Her apparent function as walking stick/phallus for her partners masks what may well be a resistance to losing herself, a resistance that takes the form of an appearance of pure devotion. In that sense, Minotschka and Marta are both confronted with fundamental psychic dilemmas against which Marta has as many defenses as Minotschka. In any case, the relationship between them is generated by similarities, proximities, and shared interests, but also by erotic differences that demonstrate the profound effects of kinship on these women so intent on disavowing family life.

I dwell on this point in order to challenge the false alternatives to which we are so often treated—rigid gender differences or androgynous indifference. Over against both of those possiblities, some queer theory, as I argue above, has embraced the notion that gender is infinitely changeable and/or irrelevant to the far greater mobility of our desires. Such notions are often tied, however loosely and problematically, to the Foucauldian argument that power in the modern world operates primarily by way of the normalization, discipline, and regulation of sexuality, by way of norms that are internalized and then begin to appear to be the truth of our selves or subjectivities. Foucault's model of bio-politics, its disciplinary mechanisms, and its strong critique of enlightenment as itself an unstable and defensive policing has proved crucial to reading late-nineteenth-century or turn-of-the-century texts. However, I see two problems with becoming too enamored of a stripped-down version of this conceptual model. First, it seems to lead some theorists to abandon the discourse of rights completely in favor of the "real" workings of power that are masked by democratic rhetoric and legal rights. Despite the disapproving stares of Swiss citizens and Minotschka's own policing of her self, normativity may not have been these homosexual women's biggest problem. What they needed were rights to education, jobs, housing, and resources that would have allowed them new concerns and new configurations of private and public spaces and concerns.

Second, the focus on normalization has led some to represent psychic life as nothing more or less than the interiorization of a punitive outside and to suppose, somewhat paradoxically, that the psyche is therefore easily manipulable or a mere ruse that discursive change, awareness and/or desire will help us overcome. In this view, gender, considered by some to organize psychic life, becomes voluntary and fictional in the strongest sense as well. Such a view adopts the simplistic assumption that the line of force operates in only one direction, from outside in, which then seems to imply either the dystopian or utopian possibility of total social control. Even more sophistocated versions of constructionism fall into the trap of making femininity or the female body a fixed ground against which an implicitly male, masculine, or abstracted social has the power to move, to change, and to influence. But neither the psyche nor the body are direct or simple effects of internalized norms. They are also irreducible to their conceptualization as inevitable failures to replicate those norms. They are, at any given moment, rich, densely overdetermined, and open sites that exert their own pressures, not primarily through conscious will, but by virtue of the agency of a never static givenness, and its convergences and interactions with what it encounters, internally, and in the world thought to be outside itself.

The assumption that a thoroughly gendered psychic life constitutes only a burden seems to have led to a radical anti-normativity and a romantic celebration of queerness or homo-ness as the very demise of current forms of societalization. In some queer work, the very fact of attachment has been cast as only punitive and constraining because already socially constructed, so that indifference to objects, or the assumption of a position beyond objects—the position, for instance, of death—becomes the putative achievement or goal of queer theory. To be radical is to locate oneself outside or in a transgressive relation to kinship or community because those relationships have already been so thoroughly societalized, normalized, and then internalized as self-control and discipline. Radical anti-normativity throws out a lot of babies with a lot of bathwater, family along with its normalizing and constraining functions and forms; concerns about children, along with the disidentification of sexuality from reproduction; psychological health, along with its history of discipline and punishment, responsibility to what is given, in the effort to destabilize what has incorrectly and destructively been considered unchangeable essence. Implicit in these constructions of queerness, I fear, is the lure of an existence without limit, without bodies or psyches, and certainly without mothers, as well as a refusal to acknowledge the agency exerted by the givenness of bodies and psyches in history, or by the circumstances in which we find ourselves with others. An enormous fear of ordinariness or normalcy results in superficial accounts of the complex imbrication of sexuality with other aspects of social and psychic life, and in far too little attention to the dilemmas of the average people that we also are.

Notes

1   I develop my critiques of Sedgwick's construction of gender and feminism in a recent essay entitled "Sexualities without Genders and Other Queer Utopias."

2   Here I am thinking of Judith Butler's analysis of gender performativity in *Gender Trouble*, which seems at times to subject Foucault's *History of Sexuality* to too strict a reading of *Discipline and Punish* in order to avoid the kinds of voluntarist and idealist readings of her work that have marked queer theory nonetheless.

3   I am indebted to the work of Dr. Carol Maxwell Miller and to my discussions with her for these ideas and their formulation.

4   The Scientific Humanitarian Committee was founded by Dr. Magnus Hirschfeld in 1897 to study sexuality and homosexuality, in particular, and to advocate for the rights of "the third sex."

5   The term Uranian came into use as a term for homosexual in the work of Karl Heinrich Ulrichs (1825–1895), a lawyer who wrote and lobbied for the legal rights of homosexuals. Ulrichs took the term from Greek mythology and it was used interchangeably with homosexual by a range of thinkers, including Rueling.

6   "Aimée Duc" was a pseudonym. The author was born in 1869 in Straßburg and grew up in France. She was married to a Swiss man and eventually landed in Berlin where she was the chief editor of a women's magazine and publisher of the Berlin *Modekorrespondenz.* She published several other short novels in addition to her journalistic writing. Sections of the novel are translated in Fadermann and Eriksson, *Lesbians in Germany: 1890s–1920s.* The translations in this essay are my own.

7   For a more detailed account of how Krafft-Ebing's constructions of female homosexuality entered into lesbian literature and self-representations, see Hanna Hacker's study of lesbianism in Austria.

8   For a thorough study of homosexual literature or literature on the third sex at the turn of the century, see Jones.

9   This account of the women's efforts to define the third sex appears in a slightly different version in my "Sexual Practice and Changing Lesbian Identities."

Works Cited

Bronfen, Elisabeth. *Over Her Dead Body: Death, Femininity, and the Aesthetic.* New York: Routledge, 1992.

Butler, Judith. *Gender Trouble: Feminism and the Subversion of Identity.* New York: Routledge, 1990.

Duc, Aimée. *Sind es Frauen? Roman über das dritte Geschlecht.* 1901. Berlin: Amazonen Frauenverlag, 1976.

——. Excerpts from *Sind es Frauen? [Are These Women?]*. Fadermann and Eriksson 1–23.

Fadermann, Lillian, and Brigitte Eriksson, eds. and introd. *Lesbians in Germany: 1890s–1920s*. New York: Vintage, 1980.

Foucault, Michel. *Discipline and Punish: The Birth of the Prison*. Trans. Alan Sheridan. New York: Vintage, 1979.

——. *The History of Sexuality: An Introduction*. Vol. I. Trans. Robert Hurley. New York: Vintage, 1980.

Hacker, Hanna. *Frauen und Freundinnen: Studien zur weiblichen Homosexualität am Beispiel Österreich 1870–1938*. Weinheim: Beltz, 1987.

Jones, James. *"We of the Third Sex": Literary Representations of Homosexuality in Wilhelmine Germany*. New York: Lang, 1990.

Krafft-Ebing, Richard von. *Psychopathia Sexualis*. Ed. and trans. Franklin S. Klaf. Trans. of the 12th German edition. New York: Stein and Day, 1905.

Martin, Biddy. "Sexual Practice and Changing Lesbian Identities." *Destabilizing Theory: Contemporary Feminist Debates*. Ed. Michèle Barrett and Anne Phillips. Cambridge: Polity, 1992. 93–119.

——. "Sexualities without Genders and Other Queer Utopias." *Diacritics* 24.2/3 (1994): 104–21.

Rubin, Gayle. "Thinking Sex: Notes for a Radical Theory of the Politics of Sexuality." *Pleasure and Danger: Exploring Female Sexuality*. Ed. Carole S. Vance. Boston: Routledge, 1984. 267–319.

Rueling, Anna. "What Interest Does the Women's Movement Have in the Homosexual Question?" Fadermann and Eriksson 83–94.

Sedgwick, Eve Kosofsky. *Epistemology of the Closet*. Berkeley: U of California P, 1990.

Weininger, Otto. *Sex and Character*. 1903. London: Heinemann, 1906.

EVELYNN HAMMONDS

Black (W)holes and the Geometry
of Black Female Sexuality

The female body in the West is not a unitary sign. Rather, like a coin, it has an obverse and a reverse: on the one side, it is white; on the other, not-white or, prototypically, black. The two bodies cannot be separated, nor can one body be understood in isolation from the other in the West's metaphoric construction of "woman." White is what woman is; not-white (and the stereotypes not-white gathers in) is what she had better not be. Even in an allegedly postmodern era, the not-white woman as well as the not-white man are symbolically and even theoretically excluded from sexual difference. Their function continues to be to cast the difference of white men and white women into sharper relief.
(O'Grady 14)

When asked to write for the second special issue of *differences* on queer theory I must admit I was at first hesitant even to entertain the idea. Though much of what is now called queer theory I find engaging and intellectually stimulating, I still found the idea of writing about it disturbing. When I am asked if I am queer I usually answer yes even though the ways in which *I* am queer have never been articulated in the *body* of work that is now called queer theory. Where should I begin, I asked myself? Do I have to start by adding another adjective to my already long list of self-chosen identities? I used to be a black lesbian, feminist, writer, scientist, historian of science, and activist. Now would I be a black, queer, feminist, writer, scientist, historian of science, and activist? Given the rapidity with which new appellations are created I wondered if my new list would still be up to date by the time the article came out. More importantly, does this change or any change I might make to my list convey to anyone the ways in which I am queer?

Even a cursory reading of the first issue of *differences* on queer theory or a close reading of *The Lesbian and Gay Studies Reader* (Abelove, Barale, and Halperin)—by now biblical in status—would lead me to answer no. So what would be the point of my writing for a second issue on queer theory? Well, I could perform that by now familiar act taken by black feminists and offer a critique of every white feminist for her failure to articulate a conception of a racialized sexuality. I could argue that while it has been acknowledged that race is not simply additive to, or derivative of sexual difference, few white feminists have attempted to move beyond simply stating this point to describe the powerful effect that race has on the construction and representation of gender and sexuality. I could go further and note that even when race is mentioned it is a limited notion devoid of complexities. Sometimes it is reduced to biology and other times referred to as a social construction. Rarely is it *used* as a "global sign," a "metalanguage," as the "ultimate trope of difference, arbitrarily contrived to produce and maintain relations of power and subordination" (Higginbotham 255).

If I were to make this argument, I wonder under what subheading such an article would appear in *The Lesbian and Gay Studies Reader*? Assuming, of course, that they would want to include it in the second edition. How about "Politics and Sex"? Well, it would certainly be political but what would anybody learn about sex from it? As I look at my choices I see that I would want my article to appear in the section, "Subjectivity, Discipline, Resistance." But where would I situate myself in the group of essays that discuss "lesbian experience," "lesbian identity," "gender insubordination," and "Butch-Femme Aesthetic"? Perhaps they wouldn't want a reprint after all and I'd be off the hook. Maybe I've just hit one of those "constructed silences" that Teresa de Lauretis wrote about as one of the problems in lesbian and gay studies ("Queer" viii).

When *The Lesbian and Gay Studies Reader* was published, I followed my usual practice and searched for the articles on black women's sexuality. This reading practice has become such a commonplace in my life I have forgotten how and when I began it. I never open a book about lesbians or gays with the expectation that I will find some essay that will address the concerns of my life. Given that on the average most collections don't include writers of color, just the appearance of essays by African-Americans, Latinos, and Native Americans in this volume was welcome. The work of Barbara Smith, Stuart Hall, Phillip Brian Harper, Gloria Hull, Deborah McDowell, and, of course,

Audre Lorde has deeply influenced my intellectual and political work for many years as has the work of many of the other writers in this volume.

Yet, despite the presence of these writers, this text displays the consistently exclusionary practices of lesbian and gay studies in general. In my reading, the canonical terms and categories of the field: "lesbian," "gay," "butch," "femme," "sexuality," and "subjectivity" are stripped of context in the works of those theorizing about these very categories, identities, and subject positions. Each of these terms is defined with white as the normative state of existence. This is an obvious criticism which many have expressed since the appearance of this volume. More interesting is the question of whether the essays engaging with the canonical terms have been in any way informed by the work of the writers of color that do appear in the volume. The essays by Hull and McDowell both address the point I am trying to make. Hull describes the life of Angelina Weld Grimké, a poet of the Harlem Renaissance whose poetry expressed desire for women. This desire is circumscribed, underwritten, and unspoken in her poetry. McDowell's critical reading of Nella Larsen's *Passing* also points to the submersion of sexuality and same-sex desire among black women. In addition, Harper's essay on the death of Max Robinson, one of the most visible African-Americans of his generation, foregrounds the silence in black communities on the issue of sexuality and AIDS. "Silence" is emphasized as well in the essay by Ana Maria Alonso and Maria Teresa Koreck on the AIDS crisis in "Hispanic" communities. But the issue of silence about so-called deviant sexuality in public discourse and its submersion in private spaces for people of color is never addressed in theorizing about the canonical categories of lesbian and gay studies in the reader. More important, public discourse on the sexuality of particular racial and ethnic groups is shaped by processes that pathologize those groups, which in turn produce the submersion of sexuality and the attendant silence(s). Lesbian and gay theory fails to acknowledge that these very processes are connected to the construction of the sexualities of whites, historically and contemporaneously.

Queer Words and Queer Practices

I am not by nature an optimist, although I do believe that change is possible and necessary. Does a shift from lesbian to queer relieve my sense of anxiety over whether the exclusionary practices of lesbian and gay studies can be resolved? If queer theory is, as de Lauretis notes in her introduction to the first special issue of *differences*, the place where "we [would] be willing to examine, make explicit, compare, or confront the respective histories, assumptions, and conceptual frameworks that have characterized the self-representations of North American lesbians and gay men, of color and white," and if it is "from there, [that] we could then go on to recast or reinvent the terms of our sexualities, to construct another discursive horizon, another way of thinking the sexual," then *maybe* I had found a place to explore the ways in which queer, black, and female subjectivities are produced (iv–v). Of course, I first had to gather more evidence about this shift before I jumped into the fray.

In her genealogy of queer theory, de Lauretis argues that the term was arrived at in the effort to avoid all the distinctions in the discursive protocols that emerged from the standard usage of the terms *lesbian* and *gay*. The kind of distinctions she notes include the need to add qualifiers of race or national affiliation to the labels, "lesbian" and "gay." De Lauretis goes on to address my central concern. She writes:

> *The fact of the matter is, most of us, lesbians and gay men, do not know much about one another's sexual history, experiences, fantasies, desire, or modes of theorizing. And we do not know enough about ourselves, as well, when it comes to differences between and within lesbians, and between and within gay men, in relation to race and its attendant differences of class or ethnic culture, generational, geographical, and socio-political location.* We do not know enough to theorize those differences. *(viii; emphasis added)*

She continues:

> *Thus an equally troubling question in the burgeoning field of "gay and lesbian studies" concerns the discursive constructions and constructed silences around the relations of race to identity and subjectivity in the practices of homosexualities and the representations of same sex desire. (viii)*

In my reading of her essay, de Lauretis then goes on to attribute the problem of the lack of knowledge of the experiences of gays and lesbians of color to gays and lesbians of color. While noting the problems of their restricted access to publishing venues or academic positions, she concludes that "perhaps, to a gay writer and critic of color, defining himself gay is not of the utmost importance;

he may have other more pressing priorities in his work and life" (ix). This is a woefully inadequate characterization of the problem of the visibility of gays and lesbians of color. Certainly institutional racism, homophobia, and the general structural inequalities in American society have a great deal more to do with this invisibility than personal choices. I have reported de Lauretis's words at length because her work is symptomatic of the disjuncture I see between the stated goals of the volume she edited and what it actually enacts.

Despite the presence of writers of color, the authors of the essays in the *differences* volume avoid interrogating their own practices with respect to the issue of difference. That is to say to differences of race, ethnicity, and representation in analyzing subjectivity, desire, and the use of the psychoanalytic in gay and lesbian theory. Only Ekua Omosupe explicitly addresses the issue of black female subjectivity, and her essay foregrounds the very issue that queer theory ostensibly is committed to addressing. Omosupe still sees the need to announce her skepticism at the use of the term *lesbian* without the qualifier, "black," and addresses the lack of attention to race in gay and lesbian studies in her analysis of Adrienne Rich's work (108). For her, the term "lesbian" without the racial qualifier is simply to be read as "white" lesbian. Despite her criticism, however, she too avoids confronting difference within the category of black lesbian, speaking of "the" black lesbian without attention to or acknowledgment of a multiplicity of identities or subject positions for black women. She notes that the title of Audre Lorde's collected essays is *Sister Outsider*, which she argues is "an apt metaphor for the Black lesbian's position in relation to the white dominant political cultures and to her own Black community as well" (106). But metaphors reveal as much as they conceal and Omosupe cannot tell us what kind of outsider Lorde is, that is to say what sexual practices, discourses, and subject positions within her black community she was rebelling against. As with the Hull and McDowell essays, Omosupe's article acknowledges silence, erasure, and invisibility as crucial issues in the dominant discourses about black female sexuality, while the essay and the volume as a whole continue to enact this silence.

Thus, queer theory as reflected in this volume has so far failed to theorize the very questions de Lauretis announces that the term "queer" will address. I disagree with her assertion that we do not know enough about one another's differences to theorize differences between and within gays and lesbians in relation to race. This kind of theorizing of difference, after all, isn't simply a matter of empirical examples. And we do know enough to delineate what queer theorists *should* want to know. For me it is a question of knowing specifically about the production of black female queer sexualities: if the sexualities of black women have been shaped by silence, erasure, and invisibility in dominant discourses, then are black lesbian sexualities doubly silenced? What methodologies are available to read and understand this perceived void and gauge its direct and indirect effects on that which is visible? Conversely, how does the structure of what is visible, namely white female sexualities, shape those not-absent-though-not-present black female sexualities which, as O'Grady argues, cannot be separated or understood in isolation from one another? And, finally, how do these racialized sexualities shaped by silence, erasure, and invisibility coexist with other sexualities, the closeted sexualities of white queers, for example? It seems to me that there are two projects here that need to be worked out. White feminists must refigure (white) female sexualities so that they are not theoretically dependent upon an absent yet ever-present pathologized black female sexuality. I am not arguing that this figuration of (white) female sexuality must try to encompass completely the experiences of black women, but that it must include a conception of the power relations between white and black women as expressed in the representations of sexuality (Higginbotham 252).[1] This model of power, as Judith Butler has argued, must avoid setting up "racism and homophobia and misogyny as parallel or analogical relations," while recognizing that "what has to be thought through, is the ways in which these vectors of power require and deploy each other for the purpose of their own articulation" (18). Black feminist theorists must reclaim sexuality through the creation of a counternarrative that can reconstitute a present black female subjectivity and that includes an analysis of power relations between white and black women and among different groups of black women. In both cases I am arguing for the development of a complex, relational but not necessarily analogous, conception of racialized sexualities (JanMohamed 94). In order to describe more fully what I see as the project for black feminist theorists, I want to turn now to a review of some of the current discussions of black women's sexuality.

The Problematic of Silence

*To name ourselves rather than be
named we must first see ourselves. For*

some of us this will not be easy. So
long unmirrored, we may have
forgotten how we look. Nevertheless,
we can't theorize in a void; we must
have evidence. (O'Grady 14)

Black feminist theorists have almost universally described black women's sexuality, when viewed from the vantage of the dominant discourses, as an absence. In one of the earliest and most compelling discussions of black women's sexuality, the literary critic Hortense Spillers wrote: "black women are the beached whales of the sexual universe, unvoiced, misseen, not doing, awaiting *their* verb" ("Interstices" 74). For writer Toni Morrison, black women's sexuality is one of the "unspeakable things unspoken," of the African-American experience. Black women's sexuality is often described in metaphors of speech-lessness, space, or vision, as a "void" or empty space that is simultaneously ever visible (exposed) and invisible and where black women's bodies are always already colonized. In addition, this always already colonized black female body has so much sexual potential that it has none at all ("Interstices" 85). Histori-cally, black women have reacted to this repressive force of the hegemonic discourses on race and sex with silence, secrecy, and a partially self-chosen invisibility.

Black feminist theorists, historians, literary critics, sociologists, law-yers, and cultural critics have drawn upon a specific historical narrative which purportedly describes the factors that have produced and maintained percep-tions of black women's sexuality (including their own). Three themes emerge in this history: first, the construction of the black female as the embodiment of sex and the attendant invisibility of black women as the unvoiced, unseen everything that is not white; second, the resistance of black women both to negative stereotypes of their sexuality and to the material effects of those stereotypes on their lives; and, finally, the evolution of a "culture of dis-semblance" and a "politics of silence" by black women on the issue of their sexuality. The historical narrative begins with the production of the image of a pathologized black female "other" in the eighteenth century by European colonial elites and the new biological scientists. By the nineteenth century, with the increasing exploitation and abuse of black women during and after slavery, U.S. black women reformers began to develop strategies to counter negative stereotypes of their sexuality and their use as a justification for the rape, lynching, and other abuses of black women by whites. Although some of the

strategies used by black women reformers might have initially been characterized as resistance to dominant and increasingly hegemonic constructions of
their sexuality, by the early twentieth century black women reformers pro-
moted a public silence about sexuality which, it could be argued, continues to
the present.[2] This "politics of silence," as described by historian Evelyn Brooks
Higginbotham, emerged as a political strategy by black women reformers who
hoped by their silence and by the promotion of proper Victorian morality to
demonstrate the lie of the image of the sexually immoral black woman (262).
Historian Darlene Clark Hine argues that the "culture of dissemblance" that
this politics engendered was seen as a way for black women to "protect the
sanctity of inner aspects of their lives" (915). She defines this culture as "the
behavior and attitudes of Black women that created the appearance of open-
ness and disclosure but actually shielded the truth of their inner lives and
selves from their oppressors" (915). "Only with secrecy," Hine argues, "thus
achieving a self-imposed invisibility, could ordinary Black women accrue the
psychic space and harness the resources needed to hold their own" (915). And
by the projection of the image of a "super-moral" black woman, they hoped to
garner greater respect, justice, and opportunity for all black Americans (915).
Of course, as Higginbotham notes, there were problems with this strategy.
First, it did not achieve its goal of ending the negative stereotyping of black
women. And second, some middle-class black women engaged in policing the
behavior of poor and working-class women and any who deviated from a
Victorian norm in the name of protecting the "race."[3] My interpretation of the
conservatizing and policing aspect of the "politics of silence" is that black
women reformers were responding to the ways in which any black woman
could find herself "exposed" and characterized in racist sexual terms no matter
what the truth of her individual life, and that they saw this so-called deviant
individual behavior as a threat to the race as a whole. Finally, one of the most
enduring and problematic aspects of the "politics of silence" is that in choosing
silence black women also lost the ability to articulate any conception of their
sexuality.

    Without more detailed historical studies we will not know the extent of
this "culture of dissemblance," and many questions will remain to be an-
swered.[4] Was it expressed differently in rural and in urban areas; in the north,
west, or south? How was it maintained? Where and how was it resisted? How
was it shaped by class? And, furthermore, how did it change over time? How did

something that was initially adopted as a political strategy in a specific historical period become so ingrained in black life as to be recognizable as a culture?
Or did it? What emerges from the very incomplete history we have is a situation
in which black women's sexuality is ideologically located in a nexus between
race and gender, where the black female subject is not seen and has no voice.
Methodologically, black feminists have found it difficult even to fully characterize this juncture, this point of erasure where African-American women are
located. As legal scholar Kimberlé Crenshaw puts it, "Existing within the
overlapping margins of race and gender discourse and the empty spaces
between, it is a location whose very nature resists telling" (403). And this
silence about sexuality is enacted individually and collectively by black women
and by black feminist theorists writing about black women.

It should not surprise us that black women are silent about sexuality.
The imposed production of silence and the removal of any alternatives to the
production of silence reflect the deployment of power against racialized subjects, "wherein those who could speak did not want to and those who did want
to speak were prevented from doing so" (JanMohamed 105). It is this deployment of power at the level of the social and the individual which has to be
historicized. It seems clear that we need a methodology that allows us to
contest rather than reproduce the ideological system that has up to now defined
the terrain of black women's sexuality. Spillers made this point over a decade
ago when she wrote: "Because black American women do not participate, as a
category of social and cultural agents, in the legacies of symbolic power, they
maintain no allegiances to a strategic formation of texts, or ways of talking
about sexual experience, that even remotely resemble the paradigm of symbolic domination, except that such a paradigm has been their concrete disas-
ter" ("Interstices" 80). To date, through the work of black feminist literary
critics, we know more about the elision of sexuality by black women than we do
about the possible varieties of expression of sexual desire.[5] Thus what we have
is a very narrow view of black women's sexuality. Certainly it is true, as
Crenshaw notes, that "in feminist contexts, sexuality represents a central site
of the oppression of women; rape and the rape trial are its dominant narrative
trope. In antiracist discourse, sexuality is also a central site upon which the
repression of blacks has been premised; the lynching narrative is embodied as
its trope" (405). Sexuality is also, as Carol Vance defines it, "simultaneously a
domain of restriction, repression, and danger as well as a domain of explora-

tion, pleasure, and agency" (1). The restrictive, repressive, and dangerous aspects of black female sexuality have been emphasized by black feminist writers while pleasure, exploration, and agency have gone under-analyzed.

I want to suggest that black feminist theorists have not taken up this project in part because of their own status in the academy. Reclaiming the body as well as subjectivity is a process that black feminist theorists in the academy must go through themselves while they are doing the work of producing theory. Black feminist theorists are themselves engaged in a process of fighting to reclaim the body—the maimed immoral black female body—which can be and still is used by others to discredit them as producers of knowledge and as speaking subjects. Legal scholar Patricia Williams illuminates my point: "no matter what degree of professional I am, people will greet and dismiss my black femaleness as unreliable, untrustworthy, hostile, angry, powerless, irrational, and probably destitute . . . " (95). When reading student evaluations, she finds comments about her teaching and her body: "I marvel, in a moment of genuine bitterness, that anonymous student evaluations speculating on dimensions of my anatomy are nevertheless counted into the statistical measurement of my teaching proficiency" (95). The hypervisibility of black women academics and the contemporary fascination with what bell hooks calls the "commodification of Otherness" (21) means that black women today find themselves precariously perched in the academy. Ann duCille notes:

> Mass culture, as hooks argues, produces, promotes, and perpetuates the commodification of Otherness through the exploitation of the black female body. In the 1990s, however, the principal sites of exploitation are not simply the cabaret, the speakeasy, the music video, the glamour magazine; they are also the academy, the publishing industry, the intellectual community. (592)

In tandem with the notion of silence, black women writers have repeatedly drawn on the notion of the "invisible" to describe aspects of black women's lives in general and sexuality in particular. Lorde writes that "within this country where racial difference creates a constant, if unspoken distortion of vision, Black women have on the one hand always been highly visible, and on the other hand, have been rendered invisible through the depersonalization of racism" (91). The hypervisibility of black women academics means that visibility too can be used to control the intellectual issues that black women can and cannot speak about. Already threatened with being sexualized and rendered inauthentic as knowledge producers in the academy by students and colleagues alike, this avoidance of theorizing about sexuality can be read as one contemporary manifestation of their structured silence. I want to stress here that the silence about sexuality on the part of black women academics is no more a "choice" than was the silence practiced by early twentieth-century black women. This production of *silence* instead of *speech* is an effect of the institutions such as the academy which are engaged in the commodification of Otherness. While hypervisibility can be used to silence black women academics it can also serve them. Lorde has argued that the "visibility which makes us most vulnerable," that of being black, "is that which is the source of our greatest strength." Patricia Hill Collins's interpretation of Lorde's comment is that "paradoxically, being treated as an invisible Other gives black women a peculiar angle of vision, the outsider-within stance that has served so many African-American women intellectuals as a source of tremendous strength" (94).

Yet, while invisibility may be somewhat useful for academicians, the practice of a politics of silence belies the power of such a stance for social change. Most important, the outsider-within stance does not allow space for addressing the question of other outsiders, namely black lesbians. Black feminist theorizing about black female sexuality, with a few exceptions— Cheryl Clarke, Jewelle Gomez, Barbara Smith, and Audre Lorde—has been relentlessly focused on heterosexuality. The historical narrative that dominates discussion of black female sexuality does not address even the possibility of a black lesbian sexuality, or of a lesbian or queer subject. Spillers confirms this point when she notes that "the sexual realities of black American women across the spectrum of sexual preference and widened sexual styles tend to be a missing dialectical feature of the entire discussion" ("Interstices" 91).

At this juncture, then, I cannot cast blame for a lack of attention to black lesbian sexuality solely on white feminist theorists. De Lauretis argues that female homosexualities may be conceptualized as social and cultural forms in their own right, which are undercoded or discursively dependent upon more established forms. They (and male homosexualities) therefore act as "an agency of social process whose mode of functioning is both interactive and yet resistant, both participatory and yet distinct, claiming at once equality and difference, and demanding political and historical representation while insisting on its material and historical specificity" ("Queer" iii). If this is true, then theorizing about black lesbian sexuality is crucially dependent upon the existence of a conception of black women's sexuality in general. I am not arguing that black lesbian sexualities are derivative of black female hetero-sexualities, but only that we cannot understand the latter without understanding it in relation to the former. In particular, since discussions of black female sexuality often turn to the issue of the devastating effects of rape, incest, and sexual abuse, I want to argue that black queer female sexualities should be seen as one of the sites where black female desire is expressed.

Discussions of black lesbian sexuality have most often focused on differences from or equivalencies with white lesbian sexualities, with "black" added to delimit the fact that black lesbians share a history with other black women. However, this addition tends to obfuscate rather than illuminate the subject position of black lesbians. One obvious example of distortion is that black lesbians do not experience homophobia in the same way as do white lesbians. Here, as with other oppressions, the homophobia experienced by black women is always shaped by racism. What has to be explored and historicized is the specificity of black lesbian experience. I want to understand in what way black lesbians are "outsiders" within black communities. This, I think, would force us to examine the construction of the "closet" by black lesbians. Although this is the topic for another essay, I want to argue here that if we accept the existence of the "politics of silence" as an historical legacy shared by all black women, then certain expressions of black female sexuality will be rendered as dangerous, for individuals and for the collectivity. From this it follows then that the culture of dissemblance makes it acceptable for some heterosexual black women to cast black lesbians as proverbial traitors to the race.[6] And this in turn explains why black lesbians who would announce or act out desire for women—whose deviant sexuality exists within an already pre-existing deviant sexuality—have been wary of embracing the status of "traitor" and the attendant loss of community such an embrace engenders.[7] Of course, while some black lesbians have hidden the truth of their lives, there have been many forms of resistance to the conception of lesbian as traitor within black communities. Audre Lorde is one obvious example. Lorde's claiming of her black and lesbian difference "forced both her white and Black lesbian friends to contend with her historical agency in the face of [this] larger racial/sexual history that would reinvent her as dead" (Karla Scott, qtd. in de Lauretis, *Practice* 36). I would also argue that Lorde's writing, with its focus on the erotic, on passion and desire, suggests that black lesbian sexualities can be read as one expression of the reclamation of the despised black female body. Therefore, the works of Lorde and other black lesbian writers, because they foreground the very aspects of black female sexuality which are submerged—that is, female desire and agency—are critical to our theorizing of black female sexualities. Since silence about sexuality is being produced by black women and black feminist theorists, that silence itself suggests that black women do have some degree of agency. A focus on black lesbian sexualities, I suggest, implies that another discourse—other than silence—can be produced.

I also suggest that the project of theorizing black female sexualities must confront psychoanalysis. Given that the Freudian paradigm is the dominant discourse which defines how sexuality is understood in this postmodern time, black feminist theorists have to answer the question posed by Michele Wallace: "is the Freudian drama transformed by race in a way that would render it altered but usable?" (*Invisibility* 231) While some black feminists have called the psychoanalytic approach racist, others such as Spillers, Mae Henderson, and Valerie Smith have shown its usefulness in analyzing the texts of black women writers. As I am not a student of psychoanalytic theory, my suggested responses to Wallace's question can only be tentative at best. Though I do not accept all aspects of the Freudian paradigm, I do see the need for exploring its strengths and limitations in developing a theory of black female sexualities.

It can readily be acknowledged that the collective history of black women has in some ways put them in a different relationship to the canonical categories of the Freudian paradigm, that is, to the father, the maternal body, to the female-sexed body (Spillers, "Mama's"). On the level of the symbolic, however, black women have created whole worlds of sexual signs and signifiers, some of which align with those of whites and some of which do not. Nonetheless, they are worlds which always have to contend with the power that the white world has to invade, pathologize, and disrupt those worlds. In many ways the Freudian paradigm implicitly depends on the presence of the black female other. One of its more problematic aspects is that in doing so it relegates black women's sexuality to the irreducibly abnormal category in which there are no distinctions between homosexual and heterosexual women. By virtue of this lack of distinction, there is a need for black women, both lesbian and heterosexual, to, as de Lauretis describes it, "reconstitute a female-sexed body as a body for the subject and for her desire" (*Practice* 200). This is a need that is perhaps expressed differently by black women than by white women, whose sexualities have not been subjected to the *same* forces of repression and domination. And this seems to me to be a critical place where the work of articulating black female sexualities must begin. Disavowing the designation of black female sexualities as inherently abnormal, while acknowledging the material and symbolic effects of the appellation, we could begin the project of understanding how differently located black women engage in reclaiming the body and expressing desire.

What I want to propose requires me to don one of my other hats, that of a student of physics. As I struggled with the ideas I cover in this essay, over and over again I found myself wrestling with the juxtaposed images of "white" (read normal) and "black" (read not white and abnormal) sexuality. In her essay, "Variations on Negation," Michele Wallace invokes the idea of the black hole as a trope that can be used to describe the invisibility of black creativity in general and black female creativity specifically (*Invisibility* 218). As a former physics student, I was immediately drawn to this image. Yet it also troubled me.[8] As Wallace rightfully notes, the observer outside of the hole sees it as a void, an empty place in space. However, it is not empty; it is a dense and full place in space. There seemed to me to be two problems: one, the astrophysics of black holes, i.e. how do you deduce the presence of a black hole? And second, what is it like inside of a black hole? I don't want to stretch this analogy too far so here are my responses. To the first question, I suggest that we can detect the presence of a black hole by its effects on the region of space where it is located. One way that physicists do this is by observing binary star systems. A binary star system is one that contains two bodies which orbit around each other under mutual gravitational attraction. Typically, in these systems one finds a visible apparently "normal" star in close orbit with another body such as a black hole, which is not seen optically. The existence of the black hole is inferred from the fact that the visible star is in orbit and its shape is distorted in some way or it is detected by the energy emanating from the region in space around the visible star that could not be produced by the visible star alone.[9] Therefore, the identification of a black hole requires the use of sensitive detectors of energy and distortion. In the case of black female sexualities, this implies that we need to develop reading strategies that allow us to make visible the distorting and productive effects these sexualities produce in relation to more visible sex-ualities. To the second question—what is it like inside of a black hole?—the answer is that we must think in terms of a different geometry. Rather than assuming that black female sexualities are structured along an axis of normal and perverse paralleling that of white women, we might find that for black women a different geometry operates. For example, acknowledging this difference I could read the relationship between Shug and Celie in Alice Walker's *The Color Purple* as one which depicts desire between women and desire between women and men simultaneously, in dynamic relationship rather than in opposition. This mapping of the geometry of black female sexualities will perhaps require black feminist theorists to engage the Freudian paradigm more rigorously, or it may cause us to disrupt it.

Can I Get Home from Here?

I see my lesbian poetics as a way of entering into a dialogue—from the margins—with Black feminist critics, theorists and writers. My work has been to imagine an historical Black woman-to-woman eroticism and living —overt, discrete, coded, or latent as it might be. To imagine Black women's sexuality as a polymorphous erotic that does not exclude desire for men but also does not privilege it. To imagine, without apology, voluptuous Black women's sexualities. (Clarke 224)

So where has my search taken me? And why does the journey matter? I want to give a partial answer to the question I posed at the beginning of this essay. At this juncture queer theory has allowed me to break open the category of gay and lesbian and begin to question how sexualities and sexual subjects are produced by dominant discourses and then to interrograte the reactions and resistances to those discourses. However, interrogating sites of resistance and reaction did not take me beyond what is generally done in gay and lesbian studies. The turn to queer should allow me to explore, in Clarke's words, the "overt, discrete, coded, or latent" and "polymorphous" eroticism of differently located black women. It is still not clear to me, however, that other queer theorists will resist the urge to engage in a re-ranking, erasure, or appropriation of sexual subjects who are at the margins of dominant discourses.

Why does my search for black women's sexuality matter? Wallace once wrote that she feared being called elitist when she acted as though cultural criticism was as crucial to the condition of black women as health, the law, politics, economics, and the family. "But," she continued, "I am convinced that the major battle for the 'other' of the 'other' [Black women] will be to find voice, transforming the construction of dominant discourse in the process" (*Invisibility* 236). It is my belief that what is desperately needed is more rigorous cultural criticism detailing how power is deployed through issues like sexuality and the alternative forms that even an oppressed subject's power can take. Since 1987, a major part of my intellectual work as an historian of U.S. science and medicine has addressed the AIDS crisis in African-American communities. The AIDS epidemic is being used, as Simon Watney has said, to "inflect, condense and rearticulate the ideological meanings of race, sexuality, gender, childhood, privacy, morality and nationalism" (ix). The position of black women in this epidemic was dire from the beginning and worsens with each passing day. Silence, erasure, and the use of images of immoral sexuality abound in narratives about the experiences of black women with AIDS. Their voices are not heard in discussions of AIDS, while intimate details of their lives are exposed to justify their victimization. In the "war of representation" that is being waged through this epidemic, black women are victims that are once again the "other" of the "other," the deviants of the deviants, regardless of their sexual identities or practices. While white gay male activists are using the ideological space framed by this epidemic to contest the notion that homosexuality is "abnormal" and to preserve the right to live out their homosexual desires, black women are rendered silent. The gains made by queer activists will do nothing for black women if the stigma continues to be attached to their sexuality. The work of black feminist critics is to find ways to contest the historical construction of black female sexualities by illuminating how the dominant view was established and maintained and how it can be disrupted. This work might very well save some black women's lives. I want this epidemic to be used to foment the sexual revolution that black Americans never had (Giddings 462). I want it to be used to make visible black women's self-defined sexualities.

Visibility in and of itself, however, is not my only goal. Several writers, including bell hooks, have argued that one answer to the silence now being produced on the issue of black female sexuality is for black women to see themselves, to mirror themselves (61). The appeal to the visual and the visible is deployed as an answer to the legacy of silence and repression. As theorists, we have to ask what we assume such reflections would show. Would the mirror black women hold up to themselves and to each other provide access to the alternative sexual universe within the metaphorical black hole? Mirroring as a way of negating a legacy of silence needs to be explored in much greater depth than it has been to date by black feminist theorists. An appeal to the visual is not uncomplicated or innocent. As theorists we have to ask how vision is structured, and, following that, we have to explore how difference is established, how it operates, how and in what ways it constitutes subjects who *see* and *speak* in the world (Haraway, "Promises" 313). This we must apply to the ways in which black women are seen and not seen by the dominant society and to how they see themselves in a different landscape. But in overturning the "politics of silence" the goal cannot be merely to be seen: visibility in and of itself does not erase a history of silence nor does it challenge the structure of power and domination, symbolic and material, that determines what can and cannot be seen. The goal should be to develop a "politics of articulation." This politics would build on the interrogation of what makes it possible for black women to speak and act.

Finally, my search for black women's sexuality through queer theory has taught me that I need not simply add the label queer to my list as another naturalized identity. As I have argued, there is no need to reproduce black women's sexualities as a silent void. Nor are black queer female sexualities simply identities. Rather, they represent discursive and material terrains where there exists the possibility for the active production of speech, desire, and agency.

My thanks to Joan Scott, Mary Poovey, Donna Penn, and Geeta Patel for their support and for their thoughtful and incisive critiques of the ideas in this essay.

Notes

1 Here I am referring to the work of Stuart Hall and especially Hazel Carby: "We need to recognize that we live in a society in which dominance and subordination are structured

through processes of racialization that continuously interact with other forces of socialization. . . . But processes of racialization, when they are mentioned at all in multicultural debates are discussed as if they were the sole concern of those particular groups perceived to be racialized subjects. Because the politics of difference work with concepts of individual identity, rather than structures of inequality and exploitation, processes of racialization are marginalized and given symbolic meaning only when subjects are black" ("Multicultural" 193).

2 See Higginbotham, Hine, Giddings, Carby (*Reconstructing*), and Brown ("What").

3 See Carby, "Policing." Elsa Barkley Brown argues that the desexualization of black women was not just a middle-class phenomenon imposed on working-class women. Though many working-class women resisted Victorian notions of womanhood and developed their own notions of sexuality and respectability, some also, from their own experiences, embraced a desexualized image ("Negotiating" 144).

4 The historical narrative discussed here is very incomplete. To date there are no detailed historical studies of black women's sexuality.

5 See analyses of novels by Nella Larsen and Jessie Fauset in Carby (*Reconstructing*), McDowell, and others.

6 I participated in a group discussion of two novels written by black women, Jill Nelson's *Volunteer Slavery* and Audre Lorde's *Zami,* where one black woman remarked that while she thought Lorde's book was better written than Nelson's, she was disturbed that Lorde spoke so much about sex and "aired all of her dirty linen in public." She held to this even after it was pointed out to her that Nelson's book also included descriptions of her sexual encounters.

7 I am reminded of my mother's response when I "came out" to her. She asked me why, given that I was already black and that I had a non-traditional profession for a woman, I would want to take on one more thing that would make my life difficult. My mother's point, which is echoed by many black women, is that in announcing my homosexuality I was choosing to alienate myself from the black community.

8 I was disturbed by the fact that the use of the image of a black hole could also evoke a negative image of black female sexuality reduced to the lowest possible denominator, i.e. just a "hole."

9 The existence of the second body in a binary system is inferred from the periodic Doppler shift of the spectral lines of the visible star, which shows that it is in orbit, and by the production of X-ray radiation. My points are taken from the discussion of the astrophysics of black holes in Wald, chapters 8 and 9.

Works Cited

Abelove, Henry, Michèle Barale, and David Halperin, eds. *The Lesbian and Gay Studies Reader*. New York: Routledge, 1993.

Alonso, Ana Maria, and Maria Teresa Koreck. "Silences, 'Hispanics,' AIDS, and Sexual Practices." Abelove, Barale, and Halperin 110–126.

Brown, Elsa Barkley. "Negotiating and Transforming the Public Sphere: African American Political Life in the Transition From Slavery to Freedom." *Public Culture* 7.1 (1994): 107–46.

——. "'What Has Happened Here': The Politics of Difference in Women's History and Feminist Politics." *Feminist Studies* 18.2 (1992): 295–312.

Busia, Abena, and Stanlie James. *Theorizing Black Feminisms: The Visionary Pragmatism of Black Women*. New York: Routledge, 1993.

Butler, Judith. *Bodies That Matter: On the Discursive Limits of "Sex."* New York: Routledge, 1993.

Carby, Hazel. "The Multicultural Wars." Wallace and Dent 187–99.

——. "Policing the Black Woman's Body in the Urban Context." *Critical Inquiry* 18 (1992): 738–55.

——. *Reconstructing Womanhood: The Emergence of the Afro-American Woman Novelist*. New York: Oxford, 1987.

Clarke, Cheryl. "Living the Texts Out: Lesbians and the Uses of Black Women's Traditions." Busia and James 214–27.

Collins, Patricia Hill. *Black Feminist Thought, Knowledge, Consciousness, and the Politics of Empowerment*. Cambridge: Unwin Hyman, 1990.

Crenshaw, Kimberlé. "Whose Story Is It Anyway? Feminist and Antiracist Appropriations of Anita Hill." Morrison 402–40.

de Lauretis, Teresa. *The Practice of Love: Lesbian Sexuality and Perverse Desire*. Bloomington: Indiana UP, 1994.

——. "Queer Theory: Lesbian and Gay Sexualities: An Introduction." *differences: A Journal of Feminist Cultural Studies* 3.2 (1991): iii–xviii.

duCille, Ann. "The Occult of True Black Womanhood: Critical Demeanor and Black Feminist Studies." *Signs* 19.3 (1994): 591–629.

Giddings, Paula. "The Last Taboo." Morrison 441–65.

Gomez, Jewelle. "A Cultural Legacy Denied and Discovered: Black Lesbians in Fiction by Women." Smith 110–123.

Haraway, Donna. "The Promises of Monsters: A Regenerative Politics for Inappropriate/d Others." *Cultural Studies*. Ed. Laurence Grossberg, Cary Nelson, and Paula Treichler. New York: Routledge, 1992. 295–337.

———. "Situated Knowledges: The Science Question in Feminism and the Privilege of Partial Perspective." *Simians, Cyborgs, and Women: The Reinvention of Nature*. New York: Routledge, 1991.

Henderson, Mae Gwendolyn. "Speaking in Tongues: Dialogics, Dialectics, and the Black Woman Writer's Literary Tradition." Wall 16–37.

Higginbotham, Evelyn Brooks. "African-American Women's History and the Metalanguage of Race." *Signs* 17.2 (1992): 251–74.

Hine, Darlene Clark. "Rape and the Inner Lives of Black Women in the Middle West: Preliminary Thoughts on the Culture of Dissemblance." *Signs* 14.4 (1989): 915–20.

hooks, bell. "Selling Hot Pussy: Representations of Black Female Sexuality in the Cultural Marketplace." *Black Looks: Race and Representation*. Boston: South End, 1992. 61–76.

Hull, Gloria T. "'Lines She Did Not Dare': Angela Weld Grimké, Harlem Renaissance Poet." Abelove, Barale, and Halperin 453–66.

JanMohamed, Abdul. "Sexuality On/Of the Racial Border: Foucault, Wright, and the Articulation of 'Racialized Sexuality.'" *Discourses of Sexuality: From Aristotle to AIDS*. Ed. Domna Stanton. Ann Arbor: U of Michigan P, 1992. 94–116.

Lorde, Audre. *Sister Outsider, Essays and Speeches*. Trumansburg, NY: Crossing, 1984.

———. *Zami: A New Spelling of My Name*. Trumansburg, NY: Crossing, 1982.

McDowell, Deborah E. "'It's Not Safe. Not Safe at All': Sexuality in Nella Larsen's *Passing*." Abelove, Barale, and Halperin 616–625.

Morrison, Toni, ed. *Race-ing Justice, En-gendering Power: Essays on Anita Hill, Clarence Thomas and the Construction of Social Reality.* New York: Pantheon, 1992.

Nelson, Jill. *Volunteer Slavery: My Authentic Negro Experience.* Chicago: Noble, 1993.

O'Grady, Lorraine. "Olympia's Maid: Reclaiming Black Female Subjectivity." *Afterimage* (1992): 14–23.

Omosupe, Ekua. "Black/Lesbian/Bulldagger." *differences: A Journal of Feminist Cultural Studies* 3.2 (1991): 101–11.

Smith, Barbara. "Towards a Black Feminist Criticism." *Conditions* 2 (1977): 25–44.

——, ed. *Home Girls: A Black Feminist Anthology.* New York: Kitchen Table, 1983.

Smith, Valerie. "Black Feminist Theory and the Representation of the 'Other.'" Wall 38–57.

Spillers, Hortense. "Interstices: A Small Drama of Words." Vance 73–100.

——. "Mama's Baby, Papa's Maybe: An American Grammar Book." *Diacritics* Summer 17.2 (1987): 65–81.

Vance, Carole, ed. *Pleasure and Danger: Exploring Female Sexuality.* London: Pandora, 1989.

——. "Pleasure and Danger: Toward a Politics of Sexuality." Vance 1–24.

Wald, Robert. *Space, Time, and Gravity: The Theory of the Big Bang and Black Holes.* 2nd edition. Chicago: U of Chicago P, 1992.

Walker, Alice. *The Color Purple.* New York: Harcourt, 1982.

Wall, Cheryl, ed. *Changing Our Own Words: Essays on Criticism, Theory, and Writing by Black Women.* New Brunswick: Rutgers UP, 1989.

Wallace, Michele. *Invisibility Blues: From Pop to Theory.* New York: Verso, 1990.

Wallace, Michele and Gina Dent, eds. *Black Popular Culture.* Seattle: Bay, 1992.

Watney, Simon. *Policing Desire: Pornography, AIDS and the Media.* Minneapolis: U of Minnesota P, 1989.

Williams, Patricia J. *The Alchemy of Race and Rights: Diary of a Law Professor.* Cambridge: Harvard UP, 1991.

KIM MICHASIW

Camp, Masculinity, Masquerade

> One might even say that the masculine
> ideal and the feminine ideal are repre-
> sented in the psyche by something other
> than this activity/passivity opposition. . . .
> Strictly speaking, they spring from a
> term that I have not introduced, but of
> which one female psycho-analyst has
> pin-pointed the feminine sexual
> attitude—the term masquerade.
> (Lacan, *Four* 193)

Parody in the Masculine

> Parody is an erotic turn-off, and all gay
> men know this. Much campy talk is
> parodistic, and while that may be fun at
> a dinner party, if you are out to make
> someone you turn off the camp. Male
> gay camp is, however, largely a parody
> of women, which, obviously, raises
> some other questions. (Bersani 208)

I begin with two photographs. Each is found on the back cover of a paperback edition of a relatively recent work by a North American male academic. Both works and both writers occupy portions of the boundary territory between literary criticism, cultural theory, and overt political intervention. Both works and both writers have had considerable influence. And the packaging of the paperbacks is notable in both cases for featuring a photograph of the author, a practice that is not unknown but is occasional enough among academics to solicit notice.

The first is of D. A. Miller on the back cover of his *The Novel and the Police*.[1] Against a background of beach-chair striped wallpaper we have Miller's torso, from the line of about the base of the rib cage up, clad in a monochrome tank-top, his bare, gym-worked arms clasped in such a way as to frame the chest (while squeezing the chest together to make it appear to sport highly developed pectorals). Above the square of arms, torso, and shoulder, Miller's head tilts to one side, toward a strong light that smoothes and tightens the line of his jaw. The mouth is open slightly as if caught in the moment of speech, and is also asymmetrical, the side toward the light more open. Above this: a standard-issue police mustache; eyes almost closed, mirroring the lines of the eyebrows above; a high square forehead; hair a shade short of too tidy.

There are several ways of understanding this image. One is that this is a caricature of a gay man of a certain age; another is that this is a professor masquerading as a surfer-cop; a third is that the first two are indissoluble as both are interdependent modalities of the masculine. Beyond these, for a certain order of academic reader, there is the suggestion of a far more particular and directed mode of perhaps parodic masquerade. Which brings me to the second of the photographs: the famous photo of Frank Lentricchia on the back cover of *Criticism and Social Change*. Of this image Kenneth Burke writes in his postscript to the volume: "The picture . . . is enough to make an author relieved on learning that Lentricchia is largely on his side" (165). Lentricchia's pose is almost identical to Miller's, save that both arms are visible and the hands do not extend so far—the sense that Miller is containing or hugging himself is not present. A wedding ring is visible, even highlighted by the positioning of the left hand. Lentricchia wears a striped short-sleeved K-Mart issue sport shirt and looks straight at the camera. His mouth is closed and his mustache turns slightly down at the corners of his mouth. There is a faint light from the same side as the intense light on Miller. This light has, however, the effect of vaguely shadowing the right side of Lentricchia's face, of showing up a doubling chin, creases descending from the nose, and dark circles under the eyes. These eyes are open and the hair looks in need of a cut and a comb. Lentricchia stands against a concrete wall adorned with somewhat faded and apparently crayoned rather than spray-painted graffiti. The shapes of these graffiti are picked up by the strong shadows on Miller's body even as the stripes of Lentricchia's shirt are echoed by Miller's wallpaper. Writing on concrete becomes writing on the body; the apparently comfortable, pay-as-you-play golf course, horizontal

Figure I
Courtesy of Frank
Lentricchia

stripes of Lentricchia's shirt are turned ninety degrees and projected onto the walls to become the bars of the prison-house. Lentricchia, as Burke observes, presents himself as an enforcer;[2] Miller, in some ways at least, as the enforced.

How are we to go about comprehending the relation between these two images? That Miller's photograph appropriates the conventional signs of aggressively straight masculinity and transforms them is clear enough. Is it sufficient, though, to label this appropriative transformation parody? If so, on what terms does the parody operate? Does the Miller photograph assert the homosexual/homosocial continuum heterosexist males have worked so long to occlude or erase? Is its implicit argument a variation on Lacan's charge that "in the human being, virile display itself appears as feminine" (*Feminine* 85)? That is, does the Miller photo reinscribe in Lentricchia's the anxiety about effeminacy—and its cognate exhibitionistic desire to be seen as male—underwriting assertive masculinity? Or is the point to highlight separation, to illumine the distance between the iconically gay and the conventionally straight? If so the illumination shows the gap to be narrow, if deep, especially given the trim, fashionable athleticism of Miller's image. The straight male of a certain age has run to flesh and dresses badly; the gay male of the same age far more closely approximates the ideal of youthful masculinity. The Miller photo suggests a distanced adoption of and continuing adherence to a set of attributes straight masculinity would associate with itself but from which straight males fall away with age. Which is to claim that Miller's photo operates almost precisely on the logic—suggested by Mary Ann Doane in her fine-tuning of Joan Riviere—of masquerade. Doane is concerned only with women and femininity-as-mask but her observations may, I think, be trans-sexed.

> Masquerade . . . attributes to the woman the distance, alienation, and divisiveness of self [denied her by psychoanalytic theory]. The theorization of femininity as masquerade is a way of appropriating this necessary distance or gap in the operation of semiotic systems, of deploying it for women, or reading femininity differently. (37)

Gay male masquerade, then, would be a mode of appropriating and articulating the gap between masculinity understood in heterosexist terms—as being bounded by heterosexual object-choice—and masculinity understood differently.

In this, gay masquerade would appear to pair itself with drag, or more broadly with camp in the sense that camp is understood by Leo Bersani, as a mode that "desublimates and desexualizes a type of femininity glamorized by movie stars." Bersani opposes camp to "gay-macho style [which] . . . is intended to excite others sexually" (208). This "gay-macho" parallels, trans-sexedly, the articulation of femininity-as-mask accounted by Doane. There may, however, be a telling difference in what Bersani characterizes as the "dead seriousness" of this male masking, a masking that makes no attempt to "pass." This seriousness opposes itself to the "playful" logic of camp. That masquerade is performed as a distanced mode of identification in the service of desire argues for a degree of investment in the performance different from that in evidence in the distanced, ironized identifications of camp. It suggests also the need to query further the oblique, elusive placement of desire in camp. Might one conjugate a Freudian binary and suggest that masquerade offers identification in the service of desire while camp displays desire in the service of identification? A too tidy formulation perhaps, but one serving at least for the moment to suppress the interimplication and resistance to hierarchy of its paired terms. Whether or not this suppression can be maintained, I wish to consider the terms masquerade and camp as cognate and opposed, each designating a mode of distanced adoption of a gender position against and through which the individual subject perpetuates itself. This consideration may permit a coming to terms with several patterns of identification determining at least some strands in male identity politics at a time when the multiple forces of the old Gang of Four title, "I Love a Man in a Uniform," vibrate behind American political debate.[3]

Camp-Recognition

The term is Eve Kosofsky Sedgwick's and she employs it to designate a specific function of the gay male (or gay male-identified) gaze. In proposing the term Sedgwick shifts our attention from the understanding of camp as a mode of performance and turns it to comprehending camp as a modality of perception. But here we need to consider what is at stake in distinguishing camp-as-performance from camp-recognition. The camp defined by Daniel Harris as "something that can be donned like formal wear for occasions of state and similarly doffed when the situation demands" (78) is clearly a performative. Moreover it is a performative that depends on a relatively stable ironic context—the formal wear depends very much on a prior agreement as to form. I am and am not invested here and you my ideal viewer will know roughly the degrees of each and will appreciate your separation from those who read the performance straight. I am an object that establishes a certain community from within *and* from without, fixing the pales. What is constructed by the camp-performative is a set of sets of limits, the several skins of the shallot, fixing the viewers in ranges of ironic contract: those who do not know at all; those who think they know but do not; those who know, but only from without and are afraid really to know; those who *do* know but are appalled,[4] or are laughing, or are laughing at the wrong pitch; and you. All of these limits depend, of course, on recognition on the part of the viewer but these recognitions are structured by the individual viewer's relative ignorance or knowledge of a stable set of codes and on the attitude characteristically struck by the viewer to that ignorance or knowledge. The camp-performative, as it is understood by Harris (and by Kaja Silverman and D. A. Miller, of whom more below) is highly codified and can be recognized readily enough by hordes of straight teenagers watching Erasure's Andy Bell croon Tammy Wynette's "Stand By Your Man" in a sparkling sky-blue cowboy jump-suit with the buttocks cut out.[5] Camp-performativity is a lure for the gaze and is ensured as such by a collective agreement from one segment of the voyeuristic classes and by a collective projection onto another.[6]

This is not, I think, what Sedgwick means to mean by camp-recognition, an act requiring something rather different from the viewer. For her, camp-recognition is not the registration of established codes; rather it is a sudden fracture and expansion of those codes, an opening onto something outside the pales of the *parole* each subject has framed within the *langue* of the socio-symbolic order. Or rather it appears to offer an opening until we read Sedgwick's description with more attention than she affords it. For this reason I quote at length:

> *Unlike kitsch-attribution, then, camp-recognition doesn't ask, "What kind of debased creature could possibly be the right audience for this spectacle?" Instead it says* what if: *What if the right audience for this were exactly* me? *What if, for instance, the resistant, oblique, tangential investments of attention and attraction that I am able to bring to this spectacle are actually uncannily responsive to the resistant, oblique, tangential investments of the person, or some of the people who created it? And what if, furthermore, others whom I don't know or recognize can see it from the same "perverse" angle? (156)*

Camp-recognition comes as a democratizing surprise. Coming upon an object at which straight taste jeers I feel a sudden pull, am arrested in mid-derision, and see in the object myself invested. In this formation we can see what Sedgwick calls "a gayer and more spacious angle of view" (156); we can see also perhaps what Susan Sontag diagnosed as "the democratic *esprit* of Camp" ("Camp" 291).

There are, however, two elements in this movement at odds with such politically hopeful stylings. These are elements contributing to the normalizing of camp, the limiting of its potential for psychic subversion, especially for those male subjects who once found in camp an oppositional alternative to the prevailing modes of masculinity. The first, to which I will return at greater length below, is the effacement, or erasure, of the object itself. As Sedgwick herself allows, camp-recognition deals "in reader relations and in projective fantasy." The object becomes a screen, or an oblique mirror through which the viewer glimpses both the object's creator and other like-minded viewers. The recognized object offers no resistance to being engulfed in projective fantasy and turned into a relay point linking a network of looks. The second is the epiphanic quality of the moment. Recognizing the object becomes the epiphanic denouement of some mass-produced late modernist short story. And with this modernist moment comes a revenant modernist subject, suddenly unary, individuated, the split healed at last. The structure of the process is almost identical to that of the Kantian sublime. The subject takes a momentary loss that is immediately recuperated and recuperated twice, first at the level of identity ("the resistant, oblique, tangential investments of attention and attraction that *I* am able to bring . . . ") and then at the level of community ("others whom I don't know or recognize . . . "). The progress moves from the surprising blow to the narcissistic ego, to the healing of that ego, and to the promise of integration of that ego into a wider community. Thus the subject moves, through a recognition of the falseness of an initial identity and an admission of what has been hidden by that false self, to self-recognition and toward a quest for another who is essentially identical. Anything of otherness or difference in the object is gentrified in the precise sense of being completely enframed by the engulfing subject. Like the front-yard shrines sometimes preserved by white painters buying into formerly working-class neighborhoods, the recognized object appears to retain itself but has in fact been wholly redescribed by its transformed context. Moreover the otherness of other viewers is split between those who see and those who do not.[7]

Camp-recognition may be understood as an epiphanic dawning of irony. This is an obvious enough suggestion and underlies the title of Philip Core's *Camp: The Lie That Tells the Truth*. The structure of irony requires there to be those in on the code and those outside. Irony necessarily establishes an oppositional structure; it can be the weapon equally of hegemonic groups and of the oppressed. Yet ironic structures also divide within, establish elites, organize networks of mentors and ephebes. This renders somewhat more problematic the epiphany of recognition. If recognition is simply a matter of discovering a fragment of an established code that overturns the apparent intent of the object—the small "subversive" detail in the apparently bourgeois-directed creation, the one that says "they don't know what they're *really* getting here"—then the epiphany merely confirms the observant subject's existing being. That is, however novel and surprising its object, camp-recognition is no more than picking up on an hitherto hidden instance of camp-performance.

This subsumption of apparent difference in the projection of identity—the tacky object vanishing except as a contact point between two like beings—assumes a greater political force when the issue shifts to what I take to be Sedgwick's primal scene of camp-recognition. "The kid in Ohio who recognizes in 'Somewhere Over the Rainbow' the national anthem of a native country, his own, whose name he's never heard spoken is constructing a new family romance on new terms" (144). Sedgwick wishes to bring together the song's thematics of escape and domestic nostalgia with the iconic force of Judy Garland as failed, doomed femininity, and to style the moment of recognition as somehow preexisting knowledge of the symbolic order in which "Somewhere" functions. That is, the kid from Ohio recognizes the song as a quilting point, a *point de capiton*, for the North American sentimental economy that determines the available modalities of gay male being. As such, the signifier is not arbitrary; it has a "natural" referential and relational value. Thus the kid from Ohio, though constructed as a subject in dialogue with an homophobic hegemony, finds himself without need for a guide.

But this opens the question of transition: if sentimental investment in "Somewhere Over the Rainbow" is an instance of recognition, why is this investment ironized in the move from the song as transitional object (enabling the kid from Ohio to find himself) to the song as diagnostic instrument (enabling the kid to find others like himself)? The simplest answer, and one in accord with Sedgwick's logic, is that the moment of recognition's first phase—that of radical individuation and separation from the false self—is temporally divided, in Ohio, from the second phase's recognition of community. When the second phase "kicks in" and the Ohioan comes to know the commonness of his experience, the sense of radical difference of the one is replaced by a dual sense of difference from many in common with some. The experience then founds a communal irony—we know, they do not. This foundational irony also weans the subject from individual over-investment in the object, in any object. Effacing uniqueness—aside from assuaging alienation—screens off the radical alterity of desire. And *screens* is important: camping the over-invested object filters sentiment in a way wholly fitting a North American male and allows also

for a fixed bond of nostalgia—I remember when I thought I was the only one—
that allows a certain degree of free emotional energy to be bound. Moreover,
and this may be the crucial distinction, the camp icon serves as the discursive
equivalent of the screen memory, adapting the individual's structure of desire
to the prevailing discourse, while defending against the particularity of desire,
against the object recognized and the psychic function on which its force
depends.

Recognition Proper

*[P]ower resides in the capacity to
advance into emptiness. All of that
gives us the figures of the apparatus of
a domain in which the recognition of
another reveals itself [s'avère] as an
adventure. The meaning of the word
recognition tends toward that which it
assumes in every exploration, with all
the accents of militancy and nostalgia
we can invest in it.* (Lacan, *Seminar
VII* 196–97)

Sedgwick's formulations of epiphanic recognition, of transforming
encounters with difference, collapse back into consoling and consolidating
affirmation of identity. Might there be another way to frame the notion of
recognition that serves to evade, or at least to defer, this collapse? The Lacan
citation above appears to point both to the inevitability of recognition's return
to the sovereign subject and to another end. In the linkage of recognition and
exploration, of militancy and nostalgia, there is perhaps a demystifying difference to which we might attend. What is being described here is the mode of
false discovery, the route to that sequence of *méconnaissances* serving to affirm
the ego's delusive domination of the subject. This falseness is perhaps best
understood by analogy with the apparently self-defeating but actually self-
affirming paradox which John Frow has identified at the heart of that debased
form of exploration called tourism, the longing for the untouched, the unde-
filed other scene that is, of course, sullied by the tourist's presence there (146–
47). The yearning for the time before one set foot in the undiscovered country,
a yearning that does not stop the foot from placing itself on the beach, a
yearning indistinguishable from that bringing the foot to the beach in the first

place, and one all the more piquant for the taint that recognition holds within it. Yet this undiscovered country can only be known as such if it conforms to contours preestablished by the tourist: no tawdry beach cabanas, no indigenous people in baseball caps, no industrial flotsam littering the verge of the sea. Save, of course, that such impediments are signs of fallen-ness and bring on a nostalgic awareness of how only the tourist preserves the place in its original purity. The litter and trash bring on also, perhaps, a dedication, a commitment to restoration, a dedication to return the place to what only the tourist still knows it once was.

As with the eco-tourist so with the psychic investigator. To recognize is to see what is already known and to acknowledge the subject's implication in the scene. I have seen this before and have seen myself seeing this before, and in my admission that I know what I am seeing I confess myself. The subject divides along time lines—and thence comes the nostalgia—the time of knowing, the time of knowing again, and the time intervening. Each of these defines its own subject; yet that subject strives to link, to narrativize, to frame the affective response as a homesickness. Either: I have re-found myself here and lament the sad waste time in self-exile, or: I have now lost forever what I just was, in this place I am no longer. Or both, the divisions fudged by an ontological sentimentality founded on a Wordsworth as reread by Kodak and the discourse of self-help.

Which is not all Lacan means, especially in passing lightly over the militancy. The relation Lacan sketches between exploration, recognition, nostalgia, and militancy appears to founder on its last term. Any exploration of objects is an attempt to re-find; the quest is always for the lost which may be recognized. That nostalgia should accent this process is unsurprising but whence militancy, unless the term is the unconscious product of the Boy's Own Annual chain of signifiers strung through this passage.[8] Lacan's power of recognition is a self-authentication through a fiction of going boldly into a void—supposedly of the Other but entirely prescripted by the subject—where no one has gone before. On this heroic journey militancy and nostalgia are affective boon companions.

If we change focus for a moment and take another word as the passage's *point de capiton*, these lines of connection clarify further. "Accents," especially in their shifting, are prime markers of displacement. As Freud writes in the *Introductory Lectures*, displacement is in evidence when "the psychical accent is shifted from an important element to another which is unimportant" (174). In this instance displacement is a vicissitude of affective investment: "By the process of displacement one idea may surrender to another its whole quota of cathexis" ("Unconscious" 186). Hence, the *accents* falling upon nostalgia and militancy are displaced from that which the subject mourns and/or pursues but does not seek to find. Nostalgia and militancy, like Douglas Crimp's mourning and militancy, are apparently opposed but actually cognate affective vicissitudes: nostalgia a gentrified keeping buried of loss, militancy an ordered regime of misdirection understood as a cause or a code. Militancy is a skewed fixing of the subject's affective position, an assertive, even manic manliness. Pinned and sentimentalized by the nostalgia at its root, the militancy of the subject who would recognize walls of contingency, flux, play. Militancy allows the subject to go on about its business of appearing to search while averting its gaze from anything that might give the lie to its aboriginality. Militancy marks the subject's commitment to maintaining itself as it is, whatever it might discover, while nostalgia marks a limitation of the subject's past. Together the two armor the subject against anything that might dissolve its cocooning carapace. The latter assures the subject that what is lost will stay that way while the former ensures that the subject will make its way without stumbling across what it marches in search of.

Lacanian recognition is a study in avoidance, a misrecognition that keeps empty the emptied place against which subjectivation lies. Moreover, with its affective adjuncts it sops up any affective spillage—unbound energy that might frame itself as anxiety or worse—in stylized lament and purpose. Recognition by its very "failure" marks the limit of the human subject's possible acknowledgment of the Thing, *das Ding*. Lacan's *Ding* is "the central place . . . the intimate exteriority or 'extimacy'" (139) against which the formation of any subject both strives and props itself. It is not quite what Julia Kristeva makes of it, the abject, for the abject comes reeking of sour milk and Melanie Klein and is the primal object defined maternally and viewed in its malignancy and decay (8–13). This location of the maternal body as site of nauseous enjoyment is another face of the phallus, another face of the object cause of desire that is the *objet a*, and another face of that "leftover of enjoyment beyond meaning, resisting symbolization," called the *sinthome*. But all of these, as readers of *Seminar XX* will know, fan out from a central abyss, a vacuole of which all are thetic grasps at symbolizing (83). The problem, then, with *das*

Ding, is not that it is unsymbolizable but that it is too easily, if always incommensurably, symbolized. It leaves avatars littering the psyche, proliferating on all registers. The point for us, as Lacan insists in *Seminar VII*, is that viewing any object aesthetically marks a symptomatic swerve away from recognizing a given object's derivation from *das Ding*. If to recognize camp, then, is in some measure an aesthetic judgment, it is in the same measure the mark of a defense against the object's allure. If the camp object lies entirely outside the canonical aesthetic fields of sublime and beautiful, it marks — like its categorical ancestor the picturesque — an attempt to expand the regions of the judging subject's mastery. This attempt is the more daring, and more psychically risky, as camp at least on the surface transgresses the founding principle of Kant's aesthetics and of the tradition of Western thought his work codifies: the negation or foreclosure of enjoyment in or of the object.

For Kant and his tradition any taste involving appetite, hence embodied pleasure, has not yet emerged from barbarism (65). Hence any implication of desire in the act of looking, an implication that would show itself in the form of embodied pleasure, removes the act from the aesthetic field. To employ the distinction Kaja Silverman has teased out of Lacan's *Seminar XI*: the aesthetic is concerned with the gaze (*le regard*), while any scopic act touched by desire must be called the look (*l'oeil*) (129–31, 145–46).[9] As Silverman suggests, "the relationship between eye [or look] and gaze is . . . analogous in certain ways to that which links penis and phallus; the former can stand in for the latter, but can never approximate it" (130). The gaze then is the enabling condition for the individual eye especially as it misrecognizes itself as masterfully judging. But the gaze, like the phallus, is a fantasy and a fantasy leading to paranoia, as it is always in the possession of the Other. The fantasy underwriting aesthetics is that of the subject succeeding to the position and possession of the gaze, of becoming not the subject presumed to see but the subject who sees. In practice, though, there is a guilty knowledge that the gaze comes from somewhere over our shoulders and pauses, momentarily, to shame us on its way to its object. Here lies the lure of the community of judgment: if we see the object as others do we must be approximating the gaze. And to align our look with the presumed community of looks we have mistaken for the gaze that look must be purged of quirks, of odd bits, of all intractable particularities of desire and enjoyment. As Silverman concludes, only because we bring symptomatic criteria which we call, defensively, Kantian to judging the relation between look and gaze, does power fall all on one side: "if the gaze always exceeds the look, the look might also be said to exceed the gaze—to carry a libidinal supplement which relegates it, in turn, to a scopic subordination. The gaze, in other words, remains outside desire, the look stubbornly within" (130).

The question posed here concerns the whence of the symptomatic swerve from particularity and it is here that the inextricable link between enjoyment (*jouissance*) and *das Ding* is essential. That Silverman retains the term desire is a sign of her enmeshment in the very process she describes, as desire is that organization of the drive allowing it to function in the symbolic order. Required here is Slavoj Žižek's stubborn insistence on prizing apart desire and *jouissance* (or, in his tendentious translation of the supposedly untranslatable, enjoyment). For Žižek desire performs essential services in the subject's self-maintenance. To desire an object is to place it within a pre-existing organization of the drives, a structuring through fantasy defending the subject against the potentially annihilating enjoyment the desire purports to facilitate (*Sublime* 118–19). But, and this is crucial to the dangers posed by recognition, somewhere in the object may inhere a trace of that against which both the subject and the subject's desire have been structured. Both subject and desire are propped against the embodied enjoyment that is *das Ding*.

It is for this reason that attempts to find in consummated desire a line of flight from compulsory subjectivity have foundered. Exemplary of this process is the contradiction marring the utopian close of Bersani's "Is the Rectum a Grave?": "If sexuality is socially dysfunctional in that it brings people together only to plunge them into a self-shattering and solipsistic *jouissance* that drives them apart, it could also be thought of as our primary hygienic practice of nonviolence" (222). As Tim Dean has pointed out, Bersani's argument here employs the experience of self-annihilation as a spiritual exercise directed toward "a redemption of *subjectivity*—if not of self-hood—as such" (114). In this, even Bersani's strenuous efforts to theorize a sexualized, achieved desire as destructive of the egoic structures on which the Western social order depends end in a discipline of hygiene for another sort of self. We are left, then, with desire as a defense, and with canonical aesthetics, in its purging of appetite and embodied pleasure, as a refinement of that defense.

Camp too is a defense but one that does not (or need not) precisely follow the beaten track of aesthetics. If the aesthetic turn defends against the defense that is desire, it moves the subject still further from the disturbance prompting defense. Camp, on the other hand, may reverse the swerve, may return the subject to a place perilously near *das Ding*. That is, if one attaches desire to an object and a form in order to defend against the destabilizing force of desire in itself, and if camp is an aestheticizing, ironic defense against such formatted desire, might camp not bring the subject back to a point close to the desubjectifying chaos that the domestication of desire forecloses? I would suggest that the question is worth asking, however speculative the answers provided might be, and that those answers can bring us back to the opposition posed at the beginning of the essay between camp and masquerade. Consider, for instance, the relative stability of camp icons, a stability that ought not to be in place if Sedgwick's model of sudden epiphany were in fact the rule. Camp appears to require a canon, shared objects in which the subject is simultaneously invested and disinvested, which maintain their value as signifying links but are intrinsically emptied. The invested object that cannot be shared with even one other cannot be camped. It may be disavowed as an instance of bathos, or subsumed into a larger, enveloping category of "things like that" but the nagging site-specificity of the object cannot be allowed.

One can frame any number of "what if" questions here. What if the song in which Sedgwick's Ohioan had heard the national anthem of a native country had been another song, one less canonical—The Smiths' "How Soon Is Now," for instance—or one completely idiosyncratic—a certain yearning ache in Eddie Vedder's voice on "Crazy Mary"? What if the community-forming second phase is neither instantaneous nor inevitable?[10] What if the native country is as tenantless as Crusoe's beach before the wreck? What if the moment of self-recognition radically separates the subject not only from the former self but from any possibility of community with other subjects, however minoritarian their subjectivity may be? What if there is a terrifying gap between the moment of recognition and the saving transition from object to mirror, from trap for the look to reflector of the gaze?

The Obscene Object of Camp

Might one suggest, then, that there is such a gap and that it inheres in the camp-performance while being foreclosed by the canon-forming act of camp-recognition. The logic of camp-recognition, in devoting itself entirely to affairs of consciousness, elides any issue of unconscious investment. Performance, on the other hand, in confronting identification, allows a moment in which the unconscious may "speak" audibly. To account for this moment we must return to *das Ding*. The Thing which is, according to the Lacanian formula, "in you more than you," is an wholly foundational concept. It is that which recalls to the subject a time before it was and suggests some possible return of a vital enjoyment that will annihilate the subject, not only in its current configuration but in any configuration at all. It is the primordial, impossible object of which other key Lacanian objects—the phallus and the *objet a* in particular—are defensive, symptomatic derivatives. The *objet a*, as object cause of desire, is that instrument by which "the subject separates himself off, ceases to be linked to the vacillation of being" (*Fundamental* 258). This is the essence of alienation but it is also that which makes the subject possible. We desire through the *objet a* in order not to be drawn back to the Thing, to that reliquary of impossible *jouissance* for which we may say we long but do not.

No object can be *das Ding*, the formlessness of which is essential. Certain objects, particularly the miserable, the maligned, the exiled, the obscene, may bring intimations. Žižek wishes to align such intimations with the apperceptive structure of the sublime in which the miserable material clod is "elevated to the status of the impossible Thing" (*Sublime* 71). And certainly, as I have noted above, the camp object is subjected by Sedgwick and others to sublimation in at least two senses. At the same time, if we follow Thomas Weiskel's reading of the sublime and understand the sublime object as standing for the (inaccessible) phallus, for mastery and authority, hence as being wholly integrable either with Oedipus or with the Lacanian hysteric's compulsive address to the subject presumed to know, we can see the sublime as a secondary function, an affair of the symbolic order (91–94). The camp object may well be treated by the psyche as if it were sublime but it is, I think, something other. Žižek emphasizes "the terrifying impact of the Thing" and our "attempt to domesticate the Thing by reducing it to its symbolic status, by providing it with a meaning" (71). This employment of terror—a determinate affect—is part of Žižek's project of wedging intimations of *das Ding* into the canonical aesthetics of the sublime, a project structurally parallel to Sedgwick's "subliming" of camp-recognition noted above. If we step back, however, and suggest the possibility that a disturbing affect of indeterminate designation may assail the subject only to be framed as terror and diffused into knowledge, something very like the process of moving from camp-performance to camp-recognition reveals itself.

Defensive transitions from affect to knowledge are common enough. It is, however, precisely the primary perception of affective disturbance against which the various modes of defense enumerated above are engaged. The question, then, is of the source of the disturbance. The first resort on such questions is to the forbidden desire, the wish to have that has been interdicted. In this case, however, the interdiction falls not on the register of desire but that of identification. And it is because identification is at issue that the psychic shift to recognition plays so large a role. Recognition inevitably operates within the range of epistemology; identification, even in the debased, defensive form of parodic mimicry, breathes of the ontic. This opposition is central to the logic of camp-performance and to Sedgwick's displacement of emphasis from the psychodynamics of the one performing to those of the one recognizing. Sedgwick's formulation, which is seconded by Harris's formal dress model, shifts the accent to camp as identificatory marker. Camp-performance becomes an element in a sign system and one performs as a means to an end. This reading accords also with Bersani's assurance that "if you're out to make someone you turn off the camp" (208). For Bersani, campiness is a lure, one exterior, if perhaps adjunct, to desire. Moreover Bersani's camp is entirely parodic, a self-conscious approximation of what one is not (female, feminine, tasteless, trailer-trash, whatever).

In differing but parallel ways Sedgwick and Bersani quietly elide the possibility of identification *in* rather than through or by means of the camp-performance.[11] But if the possibility of identification is the repressed of the current models of camp performance, and if a sudden breaking of boundaries between the habitual subject and the not-I always haunts—as impossible jouissance—acts of identification (which we might argue are always less thoroughly and repressively policed by the self-perpetuating subject than are the actings out of desire), then in the relation between the camp-performer and the object performed lies some possibility of the dissolution brought on by encounters with *das Ding.*

Why, after all, is the camp object characteristically feminine?[12] And why feminine in the egregious, caricatural fashion of a Liz Taylor, a Maria Montez? Femininity is masquerade, but this masquerade, whether mapped by

Riviere, Doane, or Tania Modleski, is such in the precise sense of a turning away from the female, insofar as the female is understood to inhere in the maternal body, from which each subject is torn in order to be subjectified. As argued above, the maternal body is not *das Ding*; it is rather that portion of primordial indistinction that is available to symbolization, that portion analysts can metonymize as "the breast" (good or bad). The primal indistinction, when divided into subject and maternal object, leaves a residuum resistant to symbolization. This residuum cannot be wholly accounted by the thetic *objet a* (not an object in itself but a parasitic lamella appearing to inhere in objects), cannot be covered entirely by the paternal interdiction, or the imagined trace of maternal desire that yields the phallus. As Elisabeth Bronfen observes, "mastering the maternal body . . . means mastering the forbidden and the impossible, for the maternal body serves as a figure doubly inscribed by the death drive—as trope for the unity lost with the beginning of life and also as trope for loss and division always already written into life, pleasure and imaging" (35). The maternal body exists under a dual prohibition; hence the sheer, brutal rigor of the inscriptions of the maternal in the heterosexist imaginary. Femininity, as coded by Hollywood cinema, for instance, tropes the maternal even as the maternal "itself" tropes the cloven-off portion of primal unity. Thus acting out the feminine ought to dramatize the subject's enmeshment in the symbolic order: I am, as camp-performer, taking on the most extreme signs of the imposed artifice that is the feminine, while knowing (or so I think) that I am not castrated. Thus I am only underscoring the security of my place as male. I am not identifying with the female but rather with the constellation of male-made signs that construct the feminine, with the law of the father that puts mother in her place.

But the extremity of the signs through which the camp-performer identifies himself—from high drag through bitchy repartee—suggests something rather more than Bersani's desublimation and desexualization is going on (208). This is not quite to argue, with Doane, that "the assumption of a mask conveys more of the 'truth' of sexuality . . . than any recourse to 'being' or 'essence'" (37). Neither truth nor essence has much to do with it unless we mean by the terms the truth or essence of fantasy, whereby the subject both tames and enables desire. The elements of the masculine construction of the feminine with which the camp-performer identifies are exactly those where masculine desire shades over into terror, where an increasing panicked defense against what the female might signify produces monsters of semiosis. Hence the camp-performer identifies with exactly that weak point in the male heterosexist symbolic order, that point at which the groping to symbolize, thus to contain, has encountered intimations that can be kept at bay only through hyperbole, and only then if the hyperbole is understood as parodically abject-able. In the camp-performance, where the clothing has rooted itself to the performer's skin, the attitude cannot be shelved the moment someone "to make" enters the room; the feminine signs, as masks, dissolve revealing the apotropaic as mere tropes. Here looms the possibility of identity with an obscene object, not the desiring mother—a being entirely adaptable to Oedi-pus—but the enjoying being to which the maternal label can be affixed only with a phallic spike. This looming does not lure those engaged in camp-recognition, fenced round as they are by epistemophilic mirror-games, but it may draw the performer. The identification with hyperbolic signs of the feminine is tied by its desperate artifice to that which is of that being belatedly titled mother but escapes the maternal, that against which the scenarism of maternality is erected. In identifying through those feminine signs inscribed by masculinist terror at its most hysterical, the camp-performer aligns himself beside that gap in the symbolic order and fairly partners the symbol-less object that is, in the most literal sense, obscene.

Can we suggest, then, that the camp-appropriation of the feminine-as-object—especially as this object displays the primary sign of an origin in the Thing, its permeation with obscene enjoyment[13]—offers another, more supple, mode of negotiating the necessary domestication of *das Ding* than is offered by canonical forms of becoming masculine? Through absorption into the order of the camp-performative, the obscene object becomes available for a mediated identification. That is, if, as the late Lacan insists, the final movement of a non-normalizing cure is that of identifying with the symptom ("Joyce" 34–35), then perhaps camp-performativity is part-way there.

Which may offer an opening to explaining both the drive to understand camp as identificatory plumage and the insistence of Bersani and Daniel Harris on camp as ever-doffable formal dress. In both cases the subject exercises complete mastery over the possible lure of the camp object. For both Bersani and Harris camp is fixedly outside the subject and is in no way transformative. Viewed this way camp-performance becomes an identity-affirming version of the *fort-da* game. The camp-performer takes on the signs of the obscenely feminine and then casts them off, proving again and again his freedom from the Thing. The moment at which, in Bersani's phrase, "you turn off the camp," that moment at which you actively begin to practice your chosen practice of desire, you are putting away, yet again, the most dangerously childish of childish things. Hitting the off switch reaffirms the subject's self-mastery and that the identificatory lure of the camp object has been disavowed once more is only a bravura demonstration that this masterful subject is immune to change.

Yet there is an unease around camp that will not quite be stilled by either Sedgwick's or Bersani's domestications. The attempts of Pride Day Committees to ban drag are motivated by more than fear of photos in the mainstream press. And this unease coalesces around another form of gender masquerade, that of masculinity. This masquerade manifests itself in relation to camp in several discreet and symptomatic ways, most notably in its production of objects of detestation and fear and it is to this form of gendered cultural production that I now turn.

Militancy and Phobia

The obscene object is not the phobic object. They are, however, related and related in ways bound up with the fractured antinomy of identification and desire. The phobic object, as Kristeva suggests, reframing D. W. Winnicott, is a transitional object marking the transit route from one identity to another (32–33). More precisely, the phobic object is a defensive metonym, a displacement enabling the subject to identify itself in its separation from objects. In the case of Freud's Little Hans, for instance, the phobic horses permit Hans to identify himself in relation to a father who can, through the intervention of phobia, become an object proper. The phobic object displaces the subject's investment in *das Ding* and in so doing allows both the subject's assumption of a relatively stable position and the coming into being of relatively stable objects.

It is here that Freud's assertion that identifications are incorporated triumphs over object-choices comes into play. The object of phobia marks a residuum in this process—that which is unassimilable to the psychic act of incorporation is cloven off, is left without, and is figured as filth, danger, defilement. It is reviled in order that the subject's stabilizing identifications take place and that its objects of choice fix—I am this; I desire that; I loathe and fear and repudiate constantly that other (which was once attached, lamprey-like, to me and my objects).

This may be going roundabout, but only through a consideration of the phobic object can we locate precisely the opposed stakes of camp and masculine masquerade. Especially when the phobic object of gay discourse around camp and identity has assumed what seems, initially at least, so odd a form— that of Susan Sontag. It is unsurprising that Sontag's name should arise in discussions of camp; her 1963 article on the topic stands as an almost inevitable point of reference if not of departure. Nor is it surprising that those coming after should be at pains to document the failings, the blindnesses of "Notes on Camp." What is surprising is the virulence, or to employ a Sontag word to which D. A. Miller takes particular exception, the "vehemence" of these critiques and their studied refusal of even the most pro forma of acknowledgments. It may be that some of the violence of this response is an effect of my reading but I am unconvinced that the effect is merely my own projection.

Consider the remarks of Miller and of Michael Moon. In "Sontag's Urbanity," Miller commences by remarking on Sontag's "intellectually fatuous, politically repellent desire to scale AIDS down to the import of what one might cook for dinner" (91–92). He continues to accuse her recent work on AIDS and metaphor of "the same irrationally phobic relation to AIDS that she alleges an interest in demystifying" and her earlier work as featuring a "phobic de-homosexualization of Camp" (93). She is further guilty not only of the "homophobia 'of omission,'" but of more active forms that are indistinguishable from those practiced by "Jerry Falwell, Pat Robertson, Norman Podhoretz, and their like 'specialists in ugly feelings'" (94–95). Sontag not only practices an "unrelenting intellectualization of AIDS" (as those orthodox Foucauldians who take AIDS to be an epidemic of signification apparently do not) but also a "no less insistent colonization of AIDS for high culture" (99).

Moon's criticisms of Sontag are analogous, if less sweeping.[14] In reconsidering Jack Smith's *Flaming Creatures*, Moon turns to Sontag's 1963 essay on the film to observe how

> *from the vantage point of twenty-five years . . . one may well be struck rereading her essays by the extreme degree to which they depoliticize the sexual and artistic practices that are their subjects. For example, Sontag praises* Flaming Creatures *for its "joy and innocence" . . . and while I can see speaking of it as a* joyous *film, the other half of the formulation makes one want to paraphrase Mae West; "innocence had nothing to do with it." (35)[15]*

Sontag has also imposed upon Smith "extreme and extremely reductive hypostatizations."

> [C]ategories and categorical dyads such as Jewish moral seriousness versus gay "playfulness" fall explanatorily flat, especially in view of the subsequent history of these two groups in the quarter-century since Sontag's essay, during which time many of her New York Jewish liberal intellectual confrères . . . have turned neoconservative and gays have been engaged in a series of political struggles that have for the most part been anything but "playful." (36n17)

What, aside from having had the misfortune to have written twenty-five years ago, has Sontag done that was so wrong? And what are readers to make of the ways in which Miller and Moon respond? Is there something symptomatic in their procedures? Sontag, it appears, de-homosexualizes, de-politicizes, demetaphorizes, and, in a turn that moves Miller to his impassioned denunciative conclusion, demilitarizes. Moon finds Sontag infantilizing in her emphasis on playfulness and innocence; his Sontag cuts gay men off from the real scene of action and denies them adulthood. Miller's charges are more scatter-shot but his Sontag commits similar outrages. His Sontag strives to strip gay men of the cultural proprietorship of camp. To suggest that camp was an inevitable styling of sensibility is a phobic attack on gay origins and gay cultural agency.

Worse still, Miller's Sontag "tribalizes" gay culture, an ethnographic avatar of infantilizing. The process of this accusation is worth observing closely as it leads toward answering the question of symptomaticity. Miller takes particular exception to what he calls Sontag's "ethnographic perspective" on gay culture.

> If one form of the homophobia in Sontag's text takes the high ground of opposition to racism, by urging us to consider, instead of the gay men implied to be monopolizing all our unstintingly expended concern and resources, those who are sick or infected with AIDS in West Africa ("were AIDS only an African disease . . . few people outside of Africa would be concerned with it" [83], "people are being told that heterosexual transmission is extremely rare, and unlikely—as if Africa did not exist" [26]), another form is by no means above relying on that very racism, however unintentionally, by inscribing gay men in

the most abusive stereotypes of our popular mythology of the African
"tribe" (e.g., "in the 1970s . . . many male homosexuals reconstituted
themselves as something like an ethnic group, one whose distinctive
folkloric custom was sexual voracity" [76]). ("Urbanity" 95)[16]

This passage, aside from suggesting that Miller has failed to anticipate Douglas Crimp's "How to Have Promiscuity in an Epidemic," features displacements across associative chains that speak symptomatic volumes. The very intensity of the sentence's nestings of brackets inside the extended frame of the "if . . . then" construction suggests much about the need to bound, to contain, to police Sontag. The accusation of ethnography shifts to Sontag's presumed accusation of racism, which leads to a zero-sum equation opposing American gay men to African heterosexuals.[17] Setting out the opposition in this way argues that the act of recalling, even mentioning, Africans "sick or infected with" (not dead or dying of) AIDS is one form of homophobia. The other form of Sontag's homophobia depends on another, Millerian, use of Africa. Sontag's phrase "something like an ethnic group" is understood by Miller, not as a relatively neutral, if disputable, statement about gay group identity, but rather as "inscribing gay men in the most abusive stereotypes of our popular anthropology of the African 'tribe.'" The shift from ethnic group to tribe is not motivated by anything in Sontag's texts; rather it stems directly from the phobic avoidance of things African in the sentence's "if" clause. The provenance and referent of "our" are mysterious and telling—with whomever else, Miller partakes wholly in this "popular" anthropology. The root problem in both ends of the sentence is that gay American men are being accused, by Sontag, of being like Africans.[18] That this "accusation" is actual in the first clause (Sontag insists that gay white men and black Africans are dying of the same disease) and exists only in Miller's phobic fantasies in the second is, I think, a significant clue as to how Sontag's place in the scene of American gay male identity is to be understood.

Sontag is figured by Miller and by Moon as one who denies identity, as one who travels the terrain of gay male culture armed with the prefix "de-" and does dreadful damage. As noted above, in Sontag's work gay men and gay culture are de-homosexualized, depoliticized, demilitarized, demetaphorized. Most reductively Sontag is understood as castratory, and worse, as constructing a "phobic" portait of gay masculinity which accepts tamely its cutting off from the phallus and its metaphors. She infantilizes, tribalizes, feminizes, and she does so as the servant of traditional male elite culture, as intellectual, as mandarin ("Urbanity" 99). Sontag's unapologetic adherence to traditional culture, her insistence on camp's oblique implication in this culture and the masculinity that props it, her doubts that those gay stylings that have succeeded camp are so oppositional as their predecessor, her daring to employ food metaphors, her having had cancer: all provoke. All suggest a pleasurable ease in the presence of the paternal metaphor that can only derive from an obscene proximity to varieties of foreclosed enjoyment and to *das Ding*'s immersive deliquescence of gendering. Sontag, in short, becomes a figure for the unspeakable enjoyment of the mother.[19]

And what is the response? Perhaps the best term would be Lacan's underemployed suggestion: *jalouissance*, an interpellatingly phobic outburst in the face of allo-enjoyment (*Séminaire XX* 91). This assumes form in an insistent reimaging of the gay male as warrior, as militant, as a conventionally aggressive masculine icon. In response to Sontag's playful and innocent Jack Smith, Moon presents a Smith "highly serious, perhaps in some ways painfully overserious" (38). But seriousness is not enough, Moon must offer us Jack Smith, heroic munitions expert, who "knew how to make a cultural product 'guaranteed' to explode closets, [who] knew where and how to detonate it, and [who] was aware that setting people's closets on fire is not simply a liberatory act: inevitably some people would get burned, including, quite possibly, the incendiaries themselves" (36). Nothing playful here, nothing innocent. Moon's metaphors place Smith firmly in the boot camps of urban guerrillas, perhaps the only form of military identification possible pre-Stonewall.[20]

Miller makes the same move more programmatically at the close of his attack. Objecting to Sontag's call to retire the military metaphors guiding our comprehension of epidemics, he writes that Sontag "overlooks how vital another such metaphor—the one conveyed in the word *militancy* (from the Latin *miles* [soldier])—is proving to people with AIDS and to the AIDS activism of which they stand at the center. 'Fight back, fight AIDS,' is a chant of this activism, one of whose many organizations calls itself Mobilization Against AIDS" (101). Lost in this response is Sontag's suggestion that one might query why military metaphors are so comforting, why it is that AIDS activism has turned to a radical overidentification with an obsessively masculinist military culture. Like a good member of the NRA or staffer at the Pentagon, Miller wants to stick to his guns, maintaining and exalting his polemic, his militancy, his fighting.

Yet this militant masculinism comes from one whom we found initially striving to *parody* Lentricchia's enforcer stance. And it is here that the need to distinguish camp from masquerade becomes most apparent. Both camp and masquerade are structured around a conscious parody overlying an unconscious identification. The objects of unconscious identification, however, differ radically. Camp's identification, as we have seen, is with the signs of the symbolic father at his most hystericized; masquerade's identification is with that father's ego-ideal. In this context the appearance of parody might well be seen as masking a case of what Bersani has identified as "the dead seriousness of the gay commitment to machismo . . . [and] the potential for a loving identification of the gay man's enemies . . . a fantasy-luxury that is at once inevitable and no longer permissible" (208). That is, if I follow Bersani correctly, the relation between the Miller photograph and that of Lentricchia follows the logic of identification negated by parody and masks an ontological yearning that finds anodyne but not release in desire. Similarly the embrace of masculine militancy in the face of Sontag employs the mask of different object-choice to obscure the ontological yearning for the reabsorption of gay male identity into the canons of American masculinity.

A less full version of this paper was presented at the Canadian Association for American Studies conference at Mount St. Vincent University, Halifax, in October 1993. Subsequent revisions have benefited greatly from the perceptive questions and objections of Stephen Bruhm, Peter Schwenger, Robert K. Martin, Sandra Tomc, and particularly Nicola Nixon. Thanks are due also to my advisors on all essential matters of style: Sheila Barry, Kevin Rowe, Shane St. George, and Ken Mattheson.

Thanks to Frank Lentricchia for permission to reprint his photograph. That this permission was granted should in no way suggest that he endorses my interpretation, or grants the accuracy of my description, of this image.

Notes

1   Permission to reproduce the cover photo from *The Novel and the Police* was denied by D. A. Miller. See *differences* 6.2+3 (147) for a reproduction of the photo.

2   A citation from Maureen Corrigan below the picture insists on the connection by labeling Lentricchia "the Dirty Harry of contemporary critical theory."

3   It is remarkable, if not surprising, how unconcerned the debate over "gays in the military" has been about lesbians. The crisis of morals and morale has centered entirely on the relations between gay and straight male soldiers and the relations of both to the ideal of American masculinity perhaps best summarized by the recruiting ads proclaiming the Marines wish to find a "few good men." An abler critic than I could do much with the impeccably set out square-jawed Marine with his sword featured in that ad and the relations of this image to various registers in the masculine erotic imaginary.

4   I'm thinking of the Toronto Pride Day Committee which tried, with limited success, to ban drag from the 1992 parade.

5   Tammy Wynette's ambiguous iconicity and its appropriation in various places in pop culture might prove an ideal occasion for a finer-grained study of readerly investment and projective fantasy. One might commence with a comparison of Erasure's use of Wynette references in their stage show with the actual employment of Wynette's voice and video presence by The KLF in their 1992 remake/remix of "Justified and Ancient." On both vocal track and video Wynette camps herself to a startling degree. Dressed as a female impersonator she wails, with all the ache of Ozark soul, such lines as "Ooooo, bound for Mu Mu Land" and leaves this viewer's semio-symbolic processing systems reeling.

6   This may point to a political problem implicit in camp's oppositionality. As suggested here and as discussed in more detail below, the camp-performative requires an uncomprehending mass *and* an outraged sector. As such Pat Buchananism is a godsend, as it were, to camp-performatives everywhere. The dependence on opposition, however, suggests an equal dependence on a largely homophobic and/or philistine dominant culture. Is camp possible in a nonhomophobic environment? If so what forms would it assume? How would the ins and outs on which its structure depends be transformed?

7   Which, one assumes, is why D. A. Miller needs Sontag's "phobic de-homosexualization of camp" (93) to prop his own view and why Sedgwick requires "the jello-phobic J. M. Cameron" (149) as straw figure for hers. Of interest here are the opponents chosen. I have grave doubts that either Sontag or Cameron is a suitable representative from homophobia in its more rampant forms. This may suggest one answer to the question posed in the note above. If one can recruit opponents from the ranks of those who are not oppositional in legal or political ways, from those whose homophobia is aestheticized, then there is no need for potential bashers in the audience.

8   Dennis Porter's translation works to limit this sense especially in its rendering of Lacan's *s'avère* as "reveals itself," a translation glossing over the French's sense of proving or authenticating, of earning one's badge (*Séminaire VII* 231).

9 In making this distinction Silverman joins the ranks of those attempting to redress Laura Mulvey's vastly influential misrecognition of the heterosexist male look, a misrecognition curiously similar to the heroine's attribution of power to the specious villain of a Gothic novel. It is to be hoped, though, that Silverman's subtle and brilliantly suggestive rethinking of look and gaze will wholly displace the Mulveyan view in cultural studies of the specular.

10 Which, it should be noted, it *is not* for the kid from Ohio but *is* in the paradigmatic description. The Ohioan's sudden intimations of community may remain no more than intimations for years. In turning exemplary anecdote into paradigm Sedgwick's argument quietly suppresses the process's segmentarity and duration.

11 Bersani's elision is polemically necessary as part of his purpose is to contrast the consciously controlled, and relatively benign, affectation of the feminine in camp with the largely unconscious and dangerous identification of gay men with the very masculinity that produces homophobia. I will return to this issue below.

12 I am concentrating on gender transgression as the essential element of camp-performance, despite the awareness that class transgression plays also a key role. I would suggest, though, that the tacky objects that are campily prized are valorized through a variant on the adoption of a feminized position, specifically that maternalized position of doting on the hideous, as in the homely phrase "a face only a mother could love." For reasons argued below I would suggest that this "maternal" love of the tawdry is more easily absorbed into a masculinist discourse than are more caricaturally "feminine" dismissals of trash, or prizing of such trash on aesthetic rather than affective grounds.

13 Including, dare one say, the enjoyment of the degradation, decay, and death of so many canonical camp figures. Sedgwick's sentimentalization of the sentimental does much to erase the viewer's pleasure in defilement and death. Would "Somewhere Over the Rainbow" enjoy its status were it not for the pleasurable juxtaposition of the youthful unsullied singer in *The Wizard of Oz* and the incoherent, shambling wreck we know she became? Some of this pleasure might be explained as fretful, self-endangering identification, but does this do anything effectual to separate our enjoyment from its implication in the death drive?

14 Moon's criticisms of Sontag are distinctly more concrete and witness conflicting interpretations. Hence to synonymize the attacks is somewhat unfair. At the same time, the *fact* of Miller's litany of charges appears a precondition for more site-specific critiques. In more recent works a footnoted reference to "Sontag's Urbanity" permits the author to proceed as if Sontag's homophobia had been proved beyond doubt. For examples, see Joughin 148 and Dickinson 235–36; 243n11.

15 I will discuss the dispute about innocence below but I would observe here how the "period" flavor of Sontag's anti-moralism and her conviction of the importance of vindicating bodily innocence as a cultural intervention is balanced by Moon's very contemporary assumptions that moralism is a political necessity and that innocence is inherently anti-political.

16 One should note that the quotation marks around "tribe" are scare-quotes rather than indicators of a citation from Sontag's text. The way Miller sets out the sentence suggests that the tribalizing is Sontag's not his, but this is not the case.

17 This is not to suggest that Sontag's First World gay/African straight dichotomy is un-problematic. As Cindy Patton has argued, much North American discourse concerning "African" AIDS appears to assume the non-existence of gay male sexual activity in Africa. At the same time, Patton herself encounters the difficulties presented by AIDS in Africa to AIDS activism in the First World. In critiquing Western discourse about "African" AIDS, Patton finds herself obliged to deny any possibility of an African origin (the disease must have been spread by the "huge quantities of unscreened blood" exported to the developing world by the West), to suggest that there are no sexual practices anywhere in Africa that are different from those common in the West, and (practically) to characterize as racist suggestions that standards of health care in many African nations are appalling (and this last despite her own assertion that "The fall from 'previous health' is not a feasible diagnostic distinction in countries . . . where people have received little health care or where infectious diseases make it difficult to distinguish between clinical AIDS and malaria, anemia, tuberculosis, etc."). Patton is caught between her recognition of the fantasies infesting western discourse about Africa and her need to de-heterosexualize AIDS transmission (223).

18 In exactly the manner of the Bush White House's assurances that the Gulf War produced practically no casualties, Miller's condemnation of Sontag depends on the assumption that no number of dead foreigners of color can count as real death, and that if people over there are dying of some disease it certainly can't be the same disease that my white friends are dying of. Miller's sentimental appeal depends on the suburbanite assumption that the early deaths of middle-class male Americans are violations of the natural order in a way that the deaths of probably impoverished Africans are not.

19 A point emphasized by Annie Liebovitz's photo of Sontag on the dust-jacket of *The Volcano Lover*. The reclining figure of the author, the self-containment and self-delight of her facial expression, the near-impossibility of locating her figure in space: all suggest access to a pleasure impossible for the viewer even to imagine.

20 Moon also strives to rescue Smith from his own unfortunate adoption of a style "alter-

nately glacially ironic and self-distancing but also aggressively 'deviant' and exhibitionistic." Some might mistake this alternation—whatever precisely the poles obscured by Moon's syntax are—for playfulness. Moon, however, thinks it "undeniable that [Smith's] career represents a highly serious, perhaps in some ways painfully overserious, attempt to work out an exemplary role for himself and others on the sexual and artistic fringes" (37–38). The guerrilla warrior becomes, simultaneously, Matthew Arnold, or someone like him.

Works Cited

Bersani, Leo. "Is the Rectum a Grave?" *October* 43 (1987): 197–222.

Bronfen, Elisabeth. *Over Her Dead Body: Death, Femininity and the Aesthetic.* New York: Routledge, 1992.

Core, Philip. *Camp: The Lie That Tells the Truth.* New York: Delilah, 1984.

Crimp, Douglas. "Mourning and Militancy." *October* 51 (1989): 3–18.

Dean, Tim. "The Psychoanalysis of AIDS." *October* 63 (1993): 83–116.

Dickinson, Peter. "'Go-Go Dancing on the Brink of the Apocalypse': Representing AIDS, An Essay in Seven Epigraphs." *English Studies in Canada* 20.2 (1994): 227–47.

Doane, Mary Ann. *Femmes Fatales: Feminism, Film Theory, Psychoanalysis.* New York: Routledge, 1991.

Freud, Sigmund. *Introductory Lectures on Psychoanalysis.* 1916–17. *The Standard Edition of the Complete Psychological Works of Sigmund Freud.* Trans. and ed. James Strachey. Vols. 15–16. London: Hogarth, 1963. 24 vols. 1953–74.

——. "The Unconscious." 1915. *The Standard Edition.* Vol. 14. 159–215.

Frow, John. "Tourism and the Semiotics of Nostalgia." *October* 57 (1991): 123–51.

Harris, Daniel R. "Effeminacy." *Michigan Quarterly Review* 30.1 (1991): 72–81.

Joughin, John J. "Whose Crisis? AIDS/Plague and the Subject of History." *Uses of History: Marxism, Postmodernism, and the Renaissance.* Ed. Francis Barker, Peter Hulme, and Margaret Iverson. New York: Manchester UP, 1991. 140–52.

Kant, Immanuel. *The Critique of Judgement*. Trans. James Creed Meredith. Oxford: Oxford UP, 1952.

KLF, The, with Tammy Wynette. "Justified and Ancient." Arista, CD5-2403, 1992.

Kristeva, Julia. *Feminine Sexuality: Jacques Lacan and the école freudienne*. Ed. Juliet Mitchell and Jacqueline Rose. Trans. Jacqueline Rose. New York: Norton, 1982.

——. *Powers of Horror: An Essay on Abjection*. Trans. Leon S. Roudiez. New York: Columbia UP, 1982.

Lacan, Jacques. *The Four Fundamental Concepts of Psycho-Analysis*. Trans. Alan Sheridan. New York: Norton, 1977.

——. "Joyce le symptôme I & II." *Joyce avec Lacan*. Ed. Jacques Aubert. Paris: Navarin, 1987. 21–36; 37–67.

——. *Le Séminaire de Jacques Lacan: livre XX: Encore, 1972–73*. Paris: Seuil, 1975.

——. *The Seminar of Jacques Lacan: Book VII: The Ethics of Psychoanalysis, 1959–1960*. Trans. Dennis Porter. New York: Norton, 1992. Trans. of *Le Séminaire de Jacques Lacan: livre VII: L'ethique de la psychoanalyse, 1959–60*. Paris: Seuil, 1986.

Lentricchia, Frank. *Criticism and Social Change*. Chicago and London: U of Chicago P, 1983.

Miller, D. A. *The Novel and the Police*. Berkeley: U of California P, 1988.

——. "Sontag's Urbanity." *October* 49 (1989): 91–101.

Moon, Michael. "Flaming Closets." *October* 51 (1989): 19–54.

Mulvey, Laura. "Visual Pleasure and Narrative Cinema." *Screen* 16.3 (1975): 8–18.

Patton, Cindy. "From Nation to Family: Containing 'African AIDS.'" *Nationalisms & Sexualities*. Ed. Andrew Parker, Mary Russo, Doris Sommer, and Patricia Yeager. New York: Routledge, 1992. 218–34.

Ross, Andrew. "The Uses of Camp." *No Respect: Intellectuals and Popular Culture*. New York: Routledge, 1989. 135–70.

Sedgwick, Eve Kosofsky. *Epistemology of the Closet*. Berkeley: U of California P, 1990.

Silverman, Kaja. *Male Subjectivity at the Margins*. New York: Routledge, 1992.

Sontag, Susan. "Notes on Camp." *Against Interpretation and Other Essays*. New York: Dell, 1969.

——. *The Volcano Lover: A Romance*. New York: Farrar, 1992.

Straub, Kristina. *Sexual Suspects: Eighteenth-Century Players and Sexual Ideology*. Princeton: Princeton UP, 1992.

Weiskel, Thomas. *The Romantic Sublime: Studies in the Structure and Psychology of Transcendence*. Baltimore: Johns Hopkins UP, 1976.

Žižek, Slavoj. *Looking Awry: An Introduction to Jacques Lacan through Popular Culture*. Cambridge: MIT, 1991.

——. *The Sublime Object of Ideology*. London: Verso, 1989.

TREVOR HOPE

Melancholic Modernity: The Hom(m)osexual Symptom and the Homosocial Corpse

For Michael J. Current

*T*he work of Luce Irigaray has provided an enormously powerful analysis of the operations of sexual difference in the structures of the social symbolic. Extending and critiquing the readings offered by Jacques Lacan and Claude Lévi-Strauss, she has emphasized the manner in which an apparent hetero-sexual economy of desire operative within the laws of kinship and language in fact reproduces itself through a profound sexual *in*difference. The patriarchal symbolic reproduces itself at the site of a destituted femininity. Behind the charade of an apparently dialectical hetero-sexuality, the "specularization" of the feminine sustains the sublation of the phallus and permits the male imaginary to enjoy itself according to a phallomorphic photo-logic and narcissistic cinematography.[1] Structures of kinship in fact suppress the possibility of symbolic relations between women in favor of the maintenance of the imaginary male bonds that underlay the regulatory operations of exogamy.[2] In practice, hetero-sexuality maintains an economy of Semblance that displaces and replicates itself along the male genealogy through the extraction of (representationally as well as sexually) reproductive labor from femininity— from women.[3] Irigarayan theory, in particular in its critical engagement with Lacan and Hegel on the question of the operation of desire and the imaginary in the articulation of a social field, provides a profoundly productive critique of normative heterosexuality. It fails, however, I would contend, to be sufficiently critical of the regulatory operations of homophobia within the social symbolic, and within psychoanalytic theory, when it hermeneutically recovers male homosexuality as the fundamental libidinal force of the patriarchal male imaginary that underpins the economics of exogamous exchange:

> *The law that orders our society is the exclusive valorization of men's needs/desires, of exchanges between men. What the anthropologist calls the passage from nature to culture amounts to the reign of the empire of hom(m)o-sexuality. Not in an "immediate" practice, but in its "social" mediation. . . . In this new matrix of History, in which man begets man as his own likeness, wives, daughters, and sisters have value only in that they serve as the possibility of, and potential benefit in, relations among men. . . . Reigning everywhere, although forbidden in practice, hom(m)o-sexuality is played out through the bodies of women, matter, or sign, and heterosexuality has been up to now just an alibi for the smooth workings of man's relations to himself, of relations among men.* (This Sex 171–72)

The notion of an archaic and foundational male homosexuality at the base—or even literally at the origin—of civilization is profoundly Freudian, but it is not my intention here to provide an in-depth critique of the manner in which Irigaray perpetuates the logic whereby male homosexuality is analytically "archaicized" and "retrojected," but rather to offer a critique of how the concept of a male homosexual imaginary has been taken up in post-Irigarayan feminist theories of modernity, in which it figures as a sign of a societal regression and possibly even as an atavistic phenomenon: a symptom of the perverse and pathological operation of the male imaginary in the liberal democratic socius.[4]

Melancholic Modernity

One of the most striking recurrent themes in psychoanalytic political theorization of modernity is that of loss. Rosi Braidotti, in *Patterns of Dissonance*, is concerned not only to identify the sense of loss that afflicts us as contemporary subjects, but also to provide a political account of the gendered nature of the nostalgia and morbidity with which contemporary discourses of "crisis" are imbued:

> *We are all epistemological orphans, and the ontological insecurity we suffer is our unavoidable historical condition. Afflicted by the melan-*

*choly which henceforth marks the end of this millennium, haunted by
a feeling of loss, philosophy is no longer the queen of knowledge, nor
is it the master-discipline any more. (2)*

*François Châtelet proposes the "practice of disrespect" as the distinc-
tive trait of contemporary philosophy: the philosophers of today
"invite us scrupulously and learnedly to follow—in mourning clothes
but in a spirit of intense jubilation—the funeral cortege of the Family,
the Word and Being." The crisis of philosophy is thus translated into a
climate of loss, of a break in filiation, or, as Jean-François Lyotard
observes, into a loss of legitimacy which obliges the sons to celebrate
with all due traditional ceremony the death of the philosophical
father. The decline of the paternal metaphor is the subtext of the
philosophical discourse of modernity. . . . What sort of thought can a
fatherless society have? (16)*

Braidotti points out that the alterations in structures of power in a
society in which the disappearance of the paternal metaphor has placed
modern epistemological projects in a crisis of legitimation are of particular
concern for women. In fact, she suggests, the eclipse of patriarchal legitimacy,
while it produces a proliferation of figurations of the feminine, is a cause of
great concern for the future of sexual difference: for the future of women, that
is, as political subjects. Indeed, the metaphorization of the feminine in its
contemporarily hyperbolic intensity may mediate to us the extent of the threat
to the social bond and the emergence of the deathly forces it has served to keep
at bay. The feminine, it appears, sutures the social, keeping a primal death
instinct at bay. Picking up on a passage by Robert Castel, she urges:

*Notice, once again, the crossing of ways which, acting as real axes of
research, structure the landscape of modernity: the climate of loss and
crisis, "where the symbolic structures are gradually crumbling away";
deterioration of the social bond, because of the progressive decay of
the paternal metaphor as the bearer of Law. What is at stake in this
radical change is the status of difference in a society resistant to seeing
difference as a positive value. In this perspective the paternal metaphor's loss of authority implies the risk of dissolution of the social
bond: the consequences of this would be disastrous: a frenzied individualism would replace the notion of contract and the brothers'*

rivalry that Freud presents in Totem and Taboo *as the basis for the model of the social contract would triumph over all other modes of relation. An important implication of Freud's mythological anthropology is the association of masculinity with war and, on the other hand, the positioning of women as objects of exchange in a symbolic discourse dominated by men. The feminine is the symbolic glue that sticks the contract together. (34–35)*

Like Michel Foucault and Gilles Deleuze, Braidotti is concerned with hearing the rumblings of war deep within the symbolic structures of modernity. Her psychoanalytic account operates, then, as a symptomatic account of a certain return of the repressed, or of a regressive return *to* an atavistic state of development. Mikkel Borch-Jacobsen has traced this logic of symptomaticity in Sigmund Freud and Gustave Le Bon:

Like Freud, Le Bon uses "pathological" states as the key to decoding "normalcy." The two share a common conviction (along with the vast majority of late-nineteenth century psychologists) that the pathological return to a previous state bears witness to the existence of a state of ontogenetic and phylogenetic development that has been surpassed (that is, integrated and by the same token recovered). "Pathological," in this sense, does not mean abnormal; on the contrary, it is archi-normality itself, primary normality. And the origin (the essence) can thus be read in the symptom. (135)

I think the extent of Braidotti's participation in this perhaps insistently late-nineteenth-century epistemology is apparent in her final account of contemporary philosophy, and, by association, modernity as a whole, as existing in a state of degeneration:

Whatever the dangers, the advantages and disadvantages, I have been arguing so far that the philosophy of the crisis and the decline of classical philosophical notions of the subject have put on the agenda the question of "women and philosophy," in terms of the feminine of thought. It arises all the more urgently because the wounded, diseased subject of modern knowledge seems unable to cure and take care of himself. Modern philosophy is in mourning, and in the climate of diffuse angst *new forms of reflection on women attempt to fill in the*

form of a void which is synonymous with both nothingness and
excess. (132)

While Braidotti's analysis of an evacuated and excessive femininity as conform-
ing to a masculinist imaginary is clearly both justified and useful, her unques-
tioned perpetuation of the logics of symptomaticity worries me. It is odd, I feel,
that an account that is intensely engaged with Foucauldian analysis is not more
self-conscious of the manner in which it reproduces the disciplinary hermeneutics of clinical discourse. This discourse tends to reinscribe a regulatory
and normative authority formerly legitimated by the divine within a depth
hermeneutics installed at the site of the body. In an earlier article, "The Ethics
of Sexual Difference: The Case of Foucault and Irigaray," Braidotti demonstrates in hyperbolic form the logic of her participation in a disciplinary
discourse of symptomaticity:

> *Over a century ago, Nietzsche stated that all decadent, diseased and*
> *corrupted cultures acquired a taste for "the feminine"—if not for the*
> *effeminate. The "feminine" thus described is nothing more than a very*
> *elaborate metaphor, or a symptom, of the profound discontent that lies*
> *at the heart of the phallo-logocentric culture. It is a male disease. (1)*

The danger, of course, is that an account of modernity as a decline of
the patriarchal law—a decline that threatens disorder, de-differentiation, and
an intensification of the forces of death—produces a nostalgia that is wholly in
the services of the patriarchal law. Indeed, if the decline of the paternal
metaphor is definitive of modernity, as Braidotti's work, along with that of other
theorists, suggests, is it not possible that it is precisely through the production
of accounts of its eclipse and decline that the patriarchal law holds its subjects
enthralled? Is the paternal law perhaps not always, already, dead or *in extremis*,
insinuating itself into subjects, interpellating subjects, through its melancholic
incorporation?

But this melancholics, if it is, as I am suggesting, a ruse of the
patriarchal symbolic, seems insistently also to refer to that archaic substratum
of sociality that manifests itself in the logic of symptomaticity, as an always
already overcome prior state of development: male homosexuality. This too, I
would argue, is an important implication of the Freudian "mythological anthropology" on which Braidotti draws. It is disturbing that the reinscription of

femininity within the masculine subject in the modality of "disease" coincides with a Nietzschean pathologization of decadence, disease, and corruption as a sign of male effeminacy. The danger of Braidotti's psychoanalytic "symptomatology" is made clear by the more contemporary site of pathology that she identifies in *Patterns of Dissonance*:

> *Once again, women's discourses and practices, and their specific*
> *relation to the symbolic run the risk of being occulted, before they*
> *have been even completely expressed. This risk is all the more striking*
> *in an age of advanced post-industrialism where the social manifesta-*
> *tions of difference between the sexes are displaced by new forms of*
> *androgyny or unisex. . . . This can be exemplified clearly through the*
> *"gender-bender" syndrome, illustrated by popular culture figures such*
> *as Boy George, Annie Lennox and many others. J. Baudrillard, an*
> *acute observer of contemporary ideas, has pointed out in a provoca-*
> *tive paper called "We are all trans-sexuals" that the phenomenon of*
> *gender-bending is symptomatic of our era. (122–23)*

In view of this fairly overt pathologization of a queer symptomaticity at the heart of (post)modern sexual indifference, it is interesting to look at Braidotti's critique of the Foucauldian privileging of male homosexuality as a historical discourse and social resource. Noting the centrality of a "relational ethics" in Foucault's explication of the role of the other "as director of conscience, philosopher, friend, lover and so on," Braidotti detects an elevation of pre-Christian male homosexuality to paradigmatic status in the elaboration of a new ethical genealogy:

> *[I]n order to legitimate this relational ethics [Foucault] uses the*
> *example of classical male homosexuality in the pre-Christian era. The*
> *male homosexual bond thus acquires for him not only the status of a*
> *paradigm, but also functions as a lost horizon that got displaced in*
> *the coming of the new technologies of the self in Christianity. (91)*

> *By enthroning male homosexuality as the lost paradigm, Foucault is*
> *diametrically opposed to the feminist analysis that situates the social*
> *contract in a male homosocial bond of sublimated homosexuality*
> *requiring the circulation of women as objects of exchange between*
> *men. Feminist scholars as different from each other as Rubin and*

*Irigaray have stressed this point, also signaling that female homo-
sexuality is one of the dark continents of patriarchy. It seems to me
that on this point the dialogue between Foucault and feminism simply
breaks down. (96)*

Braidotti's point about the plight of lesbianism in any theory of sexuality that
fails to take seriously the profound asymmetry of sexual difference is well
taken. Obviously this does not, in itself, however, imply that male homosexuality should operate as a communicational impasse between Foucault and
feminism. And if male homosexuality, for Braidotti, necessarily represents the
end of any possible dialogue with Foucault, I want to suggest that the two
supposedly opposed accounts of male homosexuality offered here are, in fact,
surprisingly similar. For, whilst they diverge on the point of the ethical and
political value to be attributed to male homosexuality, Foucault and Braidotti
do at least entirely agree here on the question of its status as a repressed
historical horizon to be hermeneutically, symptomatically recovered: an interpretive bedrock to be struck in the political analysis of sexuality. My aim here
is not to remark the difference between Foucault and feminism with a counter-
valorization of the emancipatory potential for a gay male hermeneutics that
would seek to recover the lost, barely perceptible traces of an archaic and
displaced male homosexuality beneath the historical functionings of a heterosexual symbolic. On the contrary, I might hope to reinitiate a dialogue that
acknowledges that both feminist and gay male critical enterprises might have
a stake in questioning the disciplinary operations of discourses of symptomaticity
as they melancholically constitute both the social field and the sexed body.

Modernity, the Dead Father and the *Corpus Socians*

If, for Braidotti, the paternal metaphor is in crisis, for Juliet Flower
MacCannell, in *The Regime of the Brother*, the rule of the father has definitively
been eclipsed, in the state of modernity, by the ascension of the brother.
Fraternity has become the legitimating discourse of sociality since the Enlightenment, and pervades the myths of the liberal democratic *polis*. The overt
gendering of premodern patriarchal power has given way to a far more
insidious set of power structures that operate through the erasure of sexual
difference, and of all other differences for which this (according to Mac-
Cannell's argument) is a paradigm. What is most powerful about MacCannell's

account of a postpatriarchal political structure is the manner in which it enables liberal assumptions about Enlightenment to be questioned, revealing the disciplinary operations of emancipatory discourses of individualism and equality in the context of the rise of the State and the decline in the political functions of the family. Rooted in a post-Irigarayan psychoanalytic feminist methodology, MacCannell's account is able to perform a questioning of grand narratives of power that seek to explain it as unproblematically the possession of an identifiable subject (individual or collective): a questioning that parallels the Foucauldian project as outlined in the introductory volume of *The History of Sexuality*. For MacCannell, as for Foucault, power does not precede or determine a given set of power relations, but rather is their differential effect. Power exceeds and produces the subjects that it interpellates (indeed, subjectivates) within a matrix of relations behind which it succeeds in cloaking itself.[5] For MacCannell, the analysis of the relationship between power and subjectivation begins with an account of a historically specific manifestation of the superego or ego ideal. The first issue to be "couched," as she puts it, "is a question of the ego."

> *To answer it has implications for the structure of what is the "ego ideal" in modern culture, its "superego." It is no longer an unquestioned "Father": for, when I say the familial root has been attacked, I am speaking not just of the maternal relation, but also of the paternal one—the ego stands alone, or so it imagines, after the patriarchy. (1)*

> *It takes some effort even to recognize that there is a superego, operating without check, in a modernity whose cardinal feature is "la mort de Dieu" (at least from the eighteenth century on). The Enlightenment decided upon the construct of an ego rather than an obvious superego as the synthesizer (not creator) of all social and political forms. As Georg Simmel put it, "[The ego] stands so much on itself alone that even its world,* the world can stand on it." (2)

It seems to me that MacCannell's analysis brilliantly surpasses many of the limitations both of psychoanalytic social theory and of traditional liberal political thought. First of all, far from producing an account of sociality that merely analogizes it to individual psychology (which is Freud's procedure, for example, in "Group Psychology and the Analysis of the Ego"), she performs a critique of the ego that locates it as a foundational myth of Enlightenment.

Unlike liberal (including liberal feminist) political theory with its hypostat-
ization of individuals who are said to possess liberty as an inalienable right,
MacCannell's account produces a genealogical analysis of the disciplinary
effects of discourses of individualism, analyzing the manner in which they
systematically disavow the operations of power in its modern specificity. Unlike
Foucault, however, she is able to account for the fact that the impersonal matrix
of power relations operating in the field of sociality does, nevertheless, reproduce sexual difference as a stable hierarchical distribution of power inherent
within the founding legitimating narrative of liberal democracy:

> *I argue for the necessity of employing a combination of psychoanalytic
> and rhetorical methods to criticize the central concepts (liberty/
> equality/fraternity) produced at the birth of the Enlightenment version
> of modernity—in order to reach a structural and formal understand-
> ing of the failure of modernity. (1)*

> *We can no longer beg the question the modern ego refuses to be asked:
> its familial status. "Whose ego" is being privileged in modernity—
> privileged by modeling a superego whose existence it denies? My
> answer is—the Brother's. (2)*

In the same way that the operations of power—conceived as superego—are
eclipsed by the political subject this matrix of power interpellates in "its"
image—the Brother's—so too is authority within the modern social field misunderstood insofar as we persist in trying to trace its genealogy back to a mythical
Father:

> *The time has come to subject the hidden superego to a radical critique:
> the society formed by it and which it forms is not one of fathers, not
> one ruled by elders, but by sons. Unfortunately they have managed to
> act as sovereigns (like the* père *jouissant of* Totem and Taboo, *or
> Rousseau's* Second Discourse*) rather than "well-meaning" Oedipal
> patriarchs. Their privilege is the freer in modernity, where we claim
> an absolute right brought about by the death of the tyrannical
> "father" to self-governance and an absolute equality for everyone. (2)*

> *In this book, then, I confront the cardinal implications both of elimi-
> nating the woman (or more exactly, sexual difference) under the*

Regime of the Brother, and of erroneously equating the modern order
with a patriarchy. (5)

Where MacCannell's analysis puts Irigarayan psychoanalytic methods most effectively into play is in her account of the production of a seeming neutrality in the operations of the modern social field, the manner in which the neuter and the neutral erases (or, more precisely, imaginarily "specularizes") the feminine, which becomes the screen and support for a cinematographic economy authored in the name of the phallus:

> *Freud's last texts deal with a crucial displacement: the unconscious,*
> *the id takes over from the father-superego as the model for the*
> *collective. In these late works the id becomes the equal and rival of the*
> *superego for defining the form of the human collective: the "It." Ever*
> *since the Enlightenment, "It" has seemed to be the embodiment of a*
> *principle of impartiality. Neutral, the impersonal third term is*
> *necessary, as Benveniste reminded us, to found every discourse, to set*
> *up every relation of "I" and "you," and to speak every general will.*
> *The very figure also of judgment, the neuter is neutral: supervisory,*
> *the umpire chaperons between players who cannot speak to each*
> *other in its absence. (9)*

We should note here the importance of the disembodied "umpire" who seems to dominate (with a gaze—He/It is a "supervisory" power) the social field from a removed position. This disembodied entity that apparently exhausts and sutures the democratic socius in the scope of its gaze is in itself, I would argue, an idealization and a political fiction. It is an ideological production in the sense that, functioning as the apparent source of democratic legitimacy, it is, in itself, an encoding of its disciplinary effects, and hence closely related to the death drive. The rigid *im*personality of the disembodied gaze, in other words, anchors the *Gestalt* of the *corpus socians* to the onto-logic (and morbid *patho*-logic) of the deceased father: of the paternal corpse. The social body is held—sustained and gripped—within a morbid structure of cognition which requires the perpetual sublation of paternity within the always-already defunct metaphor of paternal legitimacy. As the empty, fantasmatic "author" or fictional subject of the discourse of liberal democracy, the empty site of this metaphoricity is most famously sustained and re-marked by the function of the State. There is a powerful line of thought in psychoanalytic political theory (including Irigarayan thought) which reads the systems of exchange that traverse and bind the social—the exchange of women in one register, of commodities, money, labor, in another—as a fetishistic symbolic surface that sustains and disavows the deathly economy that results from the sublation of the paternal phallus. In these accounts the State, in its unicity, serves both as a reassuring representation of the positivity of the foundational ontology of sociality—enjoying the absolute value of the gold standard—and as the infinitely unstable and transparent fiction of a unicity not constituted on the asubjectal void of sociality, of a collective jouissance not already oriented towards the crypt. As Eugène Enriquez puts it in *De la horde à l'état*:

> *"Civil society," privileging the economic realm above all else, risks engendering the "war of all against all" in the form of conflict between the new domains of the sacred, money and work. Men [sic] too have been led to create a new transcendent principle: the State, which tends to construct a social body along new lines in order to subjugate civil society and to mobilize, in the real, the phantasm of the One.*
>
> *The functioning of the State, and of the sundry institutions and organizations which constitute it and assure its regulation, mobilizes mechanisms of power grounded just as much on the discourse of love as on the production, in global society and in the individual psyche, of those perverse and paranoiac desires which permit the death drive a locus of application and justification. (28; my translation)*[6]

For the time being I want to focus on the issues of loss and erasure evoked in this image of an idealized state that functions as a kind of melancholic legitimating resource for the democratic field of power, the "dead" author or transcendent principle—the Other—of the libidinal and political discursive matrix of modernity, sustained as the fantasmatic source of power through a collective paranoid projection.

If the law of the Brother is in a certain sense prohibitive ("[A] new 'No!' rises to the lips of the leader in imitation of the father: the brother utters a prohibition, or rather acts it out silently" [13]), MacCannell's account nevertheless moves beyond the repressive hypothesis to discern, in a manner suggestive of the psychoanalytic political theory of Slavoj Žižek, the positive legislation of enjoyment at the heart of the collective:[7]

> *It is less a matter, that is, of a "feminine id" opposing a "masculine ego" and superego than of a previously unknown form: an unconscious that, though liberated and* jouissant *like the pre-Oedipal mother and child, is also a ruler, a sovereign.* It *demands;* It *commands us to "pursue happiness." That* It *is telling us to "Enjoy!" has obscured its imperative nature. We have thought ourselves to be "self-governed" and no longer, with our rights of "man" intact, fulfilling the desire of the Other, the commands of a king (the evident gender of this formula is now fully exposed). Our "collective" logic—our naive belief—is that we no longer have a superego, that* It *wants nothing. (11)*

I want to suggest that the categorical imperative to "Enjoy!" at the heart of the Enlightenment is more intimately connected to the death drive than Mac-Cannell's account suggests. Once again, as with Braidotti's account of the demise of the paternal metaphor, I suggest that we need to take a closer look at the libidinal investment of modernity in the preservation of a death—an *empty* paternal metaphor—at its melancholic heart. It is this continuing investment—one might say this *fixation* with the *corpse* of the father—that is overlooked when MacCannell states that "Technically, the Enlightenment dispensed with the patriarchy: it gave up the cult of the ancestor in the particular way it defines its turn toward modernity."

MacCannell does, indeed, indicate the centrality of the death drive to the libidinal operations of the regime of the brother:

> *Thus, far from being a paternal moral lawgiver or a self-governed liberated self, the modernized fraternal superego is both ego and* It, *changing roles whenever it suits him. The* It *becomes—narcissistically modeled—a mute, destructive sovereign; the ego the fixed center (as opposed from the "shifter" I of linguistics and of the kinship system) of a kinship network from which it is pleased to cut itself free. . . . And we know that the life-instincts, the self-conserving forces are never ultimately served by the narcissistic Eros: Narcissus wants to mix love and death. In dedicating ourselves to the ego as the principle of the collective, then, we have unconsciously pooled our desires and created*

> *in* It *a collective death-wish.* It *seems to want to die in the service of its own pleasure principle, the plenitude of its romance with its own image. (17)*

What I want to suggest, however, is that the installation of the death drive within the fraternal symbolic is not merely a side effect of a regime that has effectively "given up" or turned away from the cult of the ancestor. Rather, it is through its melancholic enjoyment of the paternal corpse that the fraternal regime operates its mimetic cinematographics of representational authority. For it is precisely insofar as the "Oedipal cut" that installs and sublates the phallus (as Irigaray has demonstrated) is taken up and repeated within the mimetic operations of the fraternal modern imaginary that the phallic *Gestalt* of the "patriarch" continues to be produced as a specter which may not enter the symbolic operations of sociality in its living positivity, but which nonetheless commands its melancholic enjoyment.[8] The fraternal imaginary and the operations of Oedipal authority (however fantasmatic it may be) are more closely related than MacCannell's habitual opposition of Narcissus and Oedipus might suggest:

> *Here the crucial contradiction of the modern, artificial collective, founded on the ego, appears in the starkest light. Oedipus was intended to overcome primary narcissism through a castration that is the price of full citizenship in group life. Instead, it has not prevented the triumphal return of Narcissus, the same, who imagines himself to be another. And, in contrast to the classic Oedipal patriarch, this fellow lacks for nothing: he does not desire, but fully enjoys—himself. His longing is always being satisfied. (20)*

If Narcissus stands securely at the beginning and end of this political-historical mythography, it is surely worth questioning whether this "return" is not, in fact, part of the mythical narrative whereby Oedipality installs and perpetuates its own heroic reproduction. Is the pathos of Oedipal decline—that is, the eternal threat of narcissistic degeneration—not intricately bound up with the triumphant narrative of modernity itself? Once again, I want to stress that there is an intensely paradoxical relationship between melancholy—the installation of lack precisely in relation to the dead Father *at the heart* of the imaginary self-reflection of Narcissus—and enjoyment.

The continued operation of the father's fantasmatically sustained corpse within the social body is intrinsically part of the operations whereby power, in modernity, pervades the social and yet conceals its own operations. Indeed, there never was a father, except insofar as he was constituted as the corpse around which a melancholic fraternal sociality coheres. As Enriquez puts it:

> And this is Freud's stroke of genius: . . . it is his assassination that constitutes the leader of the horde as father. There is, then, no father except insofar as the object thus cathected not only possesses the women, but, also and above all is the object of a death-wish. The father as such only exists once he has been killed, actually or symbolically. (34)
>
> There has never been a real father. The father is always a dead father: the dead father a mythical father. (35; my translation)[9]

Insofar as the father's corpse—the sign of a universal guilt—is nonetheless an essential function within the operations of the fraternal symbolic of modernity, we must beware of the temptation to read the father's demise as an actual historicizable event. The father's passing, as it is rehearsed and repeated through the Oedipal structure does, in fact, ground the very historicity of modernity, but, once again, we must be aware of the paradoxical relationship between this melancholic "origin"—this originary spacing as an incitement to history—and the disciplinary operations of enjoyment that MacCannell describes. For Žižek also, the liberal democratic polity coheres, in its enjoyment, around a melancholic mantra of loss, lack, foreclosure:

> The Lacanian answer [to the question: Who is the "subject" of democracy] is unequivocal: the subject of democracy is not a human person, "man" in all the richness of his needs, interests and beliefs. The subject of democracy, like the subject of psychoanalysis, is none other than the Cartesian subject in all its abstraction, the empty punctuality we reach after subtracting all its particular contents. In other words, there is a structural homology between the Cartesian procedure of radical doubt that produces the cogito, an empty point or reflective self-reference as a remainder, and the preamble of every democratic

proclamation "all people without regard *to (race, sex, religion, wealth, social status)." (*Looking *163)*

Once we problematize the dichotomization of the paternal injunction and the festivities of fraternal totemism, recognizing the installation of the dead father at the heart of the modern regime of male homosociality, the intrication of loss within enjoyment, it is surely the link between the paternal corpse, the (narrative of) the demise of traditional authority and the melancholic and guilt-ridden injunction to "Enjoy!" that explains Freud's somewhat elliptical statement in *Totem and Taboo* that "an explanation of taboo might throw a light upon the obscure origin of our own categorical imperative" (76).

It is once again in MacCannell's failure to question the historical literalness of the turn away from the father, the uncritical opposition that she maintains between a traditional Oedipal structure and the modern Narcissus, *as if Oedipus were not precisely dependent upon the generalization of the paternal murder as the founding narrative for the incorporation of the same and its "historical"/intergenerational replication and displacement*, that she ends up representing pre-modern sociality nostalgically, implying, I would maintain, that she has been misled by the very corpse that maintains, from its spectral sublation/interment, the disciplinary hold of the modern *polis*, the *rigor* of the *corpus socians*. For we should surely be far more critical of the communitarian privileging of "traditional" societies for their organicism, their inherent vitality and respect for difference, than MacCannell's text allows:

> *Since the Enlightenment "traditional" society has been supplanted by what Freud calls an "artificial group" (*die Masse*) making its patriarchal ideals at best a charming fraud, at worst an ideological cover for another kind of exercise of power, the command to conformity in mass society. (11–12)*

> *Although Freud placed the problematic of the modern symbolic under the sign of Oedipus, we must conclude, especially after reading* The Ego and the Id, *that he found it dysfunctional under conditions of modernity. For in modernity group life—both "mass society" and a remodeled family—is self-consciously artificial. Like the good old "God," the good "father" is only a name, one that is clearly no more than a figure. While it seems therefore freer, it licenses many abuses,*

*especially sins against "natural" groups (families) and communal
forms (tribe, clan, ethnicity) it was supposed to symbolize, enable, and
endorse. (28)*

Con/Founding Male Homosexuality

Again, what is disturbing about MacCannell's final return to a chronological account of the move from patriarchal to fraternal authority is the
manner in which it, once again, is underpinned by the specter of an archaic
male homosexuality. If, on the one hand, the past is associated with the
relatively reassuring operations of the Oedipal order, on the other hand, the
modern Narcissus is, of course, once again, insistently read as the symptom of
an insidiously lurking perversion that subtends the functionings of the modern
imaginary:

> *Collectively, modern society is a fraternity—the "universal" brother-
> hood of man. Its desire, we have been told, is* hommosexuel*: homo,
> homeo-, and man-sexed (which makes it, technically, anal-sadistic).
> According to Lacan, "social feeling" is rooted in the period of "infan-
> tile homosexuality" when "fraternal objects" are eroticized: this is the
> period when "the social instincts form." (Lacan bases this on Freud's
> analysis of the fraternal love-object in infantile homosexuality.) But it
> is a modern social instinct insofar as its desire is neither for the
> mother nor the father, but the brother. In this way, the heated opposi-
> tion in the positions of Lacan and Irigaray can be partially recon-
> ciled, seen now as two sides of the same critique of what is less a
> psychocultural constant than of the same historical situation, re-
> marked by both from two sexual vantage points. (18)*

This specter of a reconciliation over the pre-historic installation of
male homosexuality should surely be a matter of concern. Once again, it seems
that male homosexuality has become the interpretive bedrock for an epistemology of sexual difference in both Irigarayan and Lacanian forms. This
interpretive move ultimately fails to question the narrative function of the
symptom—of male homosexuality as a privileged symptom—within the disciplinary cognitive regime of Enlightenment. I want to suggest that it is the
inherence of a certain obscurity within the symptom that enables it to function

as the eroticized foundation for a sociality that coheres around a retrojectively disavowed libidinality. Once again, what this means is that we must move from the vicious hermeneutic circle that insists on discovering male homosexuality symptomatically as the literal pre-historic origin of sociality, to an analysis of the manner in which this perception is always necessarily belated in relation to the origin that it thus temporally disavows. Such a hermeneutics might best be described as fetishistic. It grounds itself in a disavowed cognition, but more precisely it installs disavowal as the basis of cognition. I am arguing that, indeed, the disciplinarity of the ideology of Enlightenment that governs modernity bears a particular relationship to the manner in which male homosexuality is the "object" of a structural disavowal. Enlightenment is thus, evidently, to be understood as itself a structural injunction and categorical imperative: "Enjoy (knowledge)!" "Know!" But this would be an epistemophilic regime founded upon a fetishistic economy. The injunction to "Know!" would repeatedly install male homosexuality as that which is most insistently to be epistemologically re-covered: both gestured towards and yet, in this very gesture of referentiality performatively distanced and veiled.[10] It is the operations of power in this paradoxical logic of referentiality that are overlooked by the repeated gesture that unites Irigaray, Lacan, and MacCannell within the shared disciplinary enjoyment of psychoanalytic revelation.[11] In MacCannell's words:

> *Denial of difference is the basis of our homoerotic order (desire marked with a male sign) in so far as, in Lacan's thesis, "heterosexuality" is a metaphor/symptom which marks by substitution a lack of distinction. For Lacan, as for Freud, homophobic declaratives, homosexual conjugations and hysterical defenses of fixed, natural or permanent gender distinctions (women are like this, men are like that: they're "just naturally different") are all transformations of the root declarative sentence—that cannot be uttered—"I, a man, love him [a man]." (194n20)*

The fetishistic operations of the epistemology of the closet—an epistemology which maintains this sentence at the heart of all social relations—make all gestures of referentiality, even those that would propose a "symptomatic" critique of homophobia, ultimately ambivalent. This is true of the recent debates in lesbian, bisexual, and gay politics about the strategy of "outing" public figures who have, either actively or through indifference, persecuted lesbians, bisexuals, and gay men and courted heterosexual privilege and homophobic approval. The problem with such a strategy is that it implies, once again, that ultimately the responsibility for the closet—indeed the pathological core of homophobia, its symptomaticity—is to be detected within the psyches of lesbians, bisexuals, and gay men themselves, rather than in the structure of power relations that insistently maintain homosexuality within the structure of the "open secret."

We might begin to unpack the dense relationship among male homosexuality, homophobia, the death drive, and the melancholic constitution of modernity in relation to the celebrated, incorporated paternal corpse by looking at one point where MacCannell's text attempts to hermeneutically uncover the insidious desire of the modernity which strives to conceal its aim. Her interpretive gesture insistently sutures the melancholic nature of this desire around the figure of male homosexuality:

> [W]hile it is easier to picture the collective body as iconically a him or her, the thought is deeply repugnant to modern social forms. We find gender designations strangely inappropriate to the modern democratic collective. Mother countries and fatherlands are associated with radical political variants, and the great emblem of democracy, the United States, has settled on the "primitive" solution, the figure of the mother's brother, Uncle Sam, who can fill in for a parent without needing to be one.
>
> It is even more impolite to ask what It wants, to suggest that It desires. (10)

In accordance with the etiquette of modern desire, then, MacCannell here politely confines her moment of hermeneutic recovery to a footnote:

> In wartime, of course, Uncle Sam wants soldier males: his concrete response appears in First World War recruiting posters where his finger points directly at the viewer and the legend reads, "Uncle Sam wants You!" (184n3)

This, then, should we be impolite enough to ask, is the bedrock of the injunction to "Enjoy!" We might, of course, see the very gesture of ostentation in this

narrative as simultaneously a categorical imperative and a moment of interpellation, a subjectivation through desire. Thus, running beneath the neutrality of the collective and binding *It* that grounds sociality lies the suspicion (for
we are dealing, here, with a hermeneutics of suspicion, a footnote hermeneutics, an obscure and agonistic epistemological recovery whose relationship to the referential melancholics of Cartesian doubt we would do well to
bear in mind) of a lingering pathology, a perversion: male homosexuality.
Beneath the polite veneer of the fraternal regime, if one is indelicate enough to
pursue the point, there lies an obscene homosexual desire. The *corpus socians*
finally coheres, in wartime, in extremis (and the generalization of war, of
death, is, of course, the very heart of liberal democracy's pursuit of life, liberty,
and happiness) around the exquisite, because exquisitely mortal, tragically
youthful corporeality of the soldier male. The American citizen is thus interpellated not only according to a gendered circuit of desire, but according to the
deathly erotics of male homosexuality. "You!" (regardless of sex or, rather,
through the active denial of sexual difference) are bound to the sociality of
nationhood through the entrapping desire of a kinky Uncle. Furthermore, his
accusatory finger and beady gaze ensure that You! are not unaware of the
compulsory nature of Uncle Sam's wants: his desire holds You! and penetrates
You! You! are petrified in that supervisory stare. Indeed, that petrification is
your substance, your ontology, the self-consciousness of guilt your only consciousness. If You! enjoy citizenship and its attendant rights of life, liberty and
the pursuit of happiness, it is precisely only insofar as You! in your petrification—your symptomaticity—have embodied, incorporated, encrypted, that fraternal Gestalt caught in the *jouissance* of deathly combat. It is, indeed, at the
price of this morbid substitutability, this constant proximity to, embodiment of,
death, that your life is purchased.

  The enjoyment of the soldier male's exquisite body is the enjoyment at
the heart of the modern socius, but in its very onto-logic it is an enjoyment in
the grip of—or at the end of the finger of—death: melancholic, masochistic,
paranoid, constructed and de-structed in the shadow of the phantasm of
annihilation, apprehending itself tragically, cathecting itself hypochondria-
cally, "de-sisting" at the point of the melancholic loss that is its kernel, enjoying
and purchasing its "presence" only in (the anticipation of) its archaic grounding in loss: pre-siding only in the certainty that it has always already fallen,
enjoying its liberty only in the knowledge of the judgment of guilt that hovers

over it, desiring, at the end of finger, only where a policing gaze has already entrapped it.

Yet You! are also not interpellated "merely" as single, bodied, subject, but as a political subject in relation to a social field. Your melancholic jouissance binds you into the fraternal social body that coheres around the morbid fascination of and seductive power of the soldier's anticipated, deferred, promised, encrypted corpse. The gaze that singles You! out does so precisely by binding you into a deathly metonymic chain of substitution, a referential chain of signification anchored at either end in an inadmissible referentiality, a foreclosed object-relation: You! (a man) Love! Him! (a man).

But finally, maybe, in the substitutability of the liberal subject, there is no Him and no You. No body, no murderer, no judge. Maybe there is no kinky Uncle at all, except insofar as You! wished to displace, to retroject, to memorialize your desire, installing it in a discretely bodied gaze and finger, the Other, the seducer, the police. What if there is no He, just a series of You!s, the others, and He is just a phantasm that You! enjoy remembering? Perhaps He, It, the gaze, the finger, the law, is just a device, a referent and a deferent, an encryptment and an ostentation of what is nothing more than the obscene underside of all that unites You! Perhaps You! are at the center of the desirous, seductive, disciplinary, punitive, petrifying, constitutive, devastating, murderous, initiatory gaze in more than one sense? If You! enjoy yourself through transubstantiation with the social corpse, at the price of a fraternal sacrifice, is it perhaps your guilt, your knowledge of your guilt, that pierces you, pins you, con-stitutes and de-stitutes you with its phallomorphic, deathlike rigor? Can you hide your guilt? Encrypt it, maybe? Bury it deeper? What, ultimately, binds you in this chain of guilt? Is it a primitive and perverse desire? Is it the law? Is it mere paranoia? Perhaps we should break the analytical gaze and look politely away. But there again, what if we are already held by that gaze? Should we proceed in penetrating the secret or has it, perhaps, always already penetrated us, perpetrated us as crime, as a certain, unutterable murderous offense?

I think, ultimately, that MacCannell's account of the post-Oedipal "Pseudo-symbolic," her conception of the liberal democratic collectivity is rather too seamless in its operations. What I have tried to do in relation to her account of this imaginary is to emphasize the manner in which its cinematographics of reflection and narcissistic competition is always founded upon a traumatic referential loss *within the operations of fraternal homosociality itself.*

This founding loss relates in complex ways (which, given considerations of space, will have to be more carefully elaborated elsewhere) to the reproduction of the father's death and also to the production of the space of the closet—a site strictly speaking not occupied by any subject but which yet functions as a crucial *point de capiton*—a quilting point around which the symbolic coheres neither as the imaginary and belated translation of a founding male homoerotic desire, nor as its erasure and site of repression, but rather as a cognitive field— a homosexual/homophobic discursive matrix. Within this cognitive field the closet operates as an ever-suspended signification, with all the promissory and threatening qualities of the secret in its paradoxical relation to the overseeing gaze of Enlightenment that founds the social collectivity.

The point, then, of this homosexual/homophobic matrix that abyssally grounds the symbolic and the phallomorphic imaginary is that it has no author except insofar as that author is precisely dis/embodied, simultaneously en-crypted and sublated. The "legitimation crisis" of modernity stems from the *essentially* an-originary nature of the "patriarchal" symbolic. In fact, the father does not exist, and if the Law is scripted in his name, it is precisely, as Lacan and Irigaray have noted, insofar as it refuses itself to circulation within the symbolic. If commentators on the modern democratic state pathologize it as a narcissistic play with mirrors, what is occluded in this account is the fact that this specular play interpolates a certain distance between the (definitively masculine) citizen-subject and his autoerotically perceived image. It is the very logic of this spacing that exceeds the imaginary suturing of the social and that constitutes the fraternal citizenry as individuals subjectivated and yet also socially bound in their guilt. The brothers become subject to the regime of modernity and are subjectivated *as* liberal democratic citizens only insofar as they submit to such an originary spacing. Guilt and death inhere in that spacing precisely insofar as it is a melancholically constituted site of primal loss, one which is phenomenologically apprehended through a masochistic delight in the rigors of a law that has no ontology beyond its loss, its nostalgically sustained eclipse. The author(ity) behind that law is the effect of a constitutive ostentation, a performatively installed and constatively evacuated referen-tiality. The sublation of the name of the father, the idealization of the phallus as that which must eternally remain veiled within the operations of the symbolic, represents precisely the possibility of the establishment of the modern *demos* as a field of substitutability, a chain of simulacra whose origin exists only in its *différance.* The question that must be raised is the complex relationship between the "disappearance" of the paternal name, the suspension of its return as a promissory parousic lure—the possibility of an end to the alienating operations of the symbolic, of History—and the regulatory regime that constructs male homosexuality as a significatory vanishing point capable of entering the symbolic only as a traumatic absence.

The Irigarayan account is, perhaps, correct in analyzing heterosexuality as a form of alibi, but it is one which operates also as a complex hermeneutic lure: a disciplinary red herring. It invites (and initiates) the interpretive and policing gaze that mourns the father even as it forecloses the possibility of his apprehension as simple other. Indeed, a careful reading of *Totem and Taboo* would suggest that the father gets installed as Other—as the Law, precisely in its a-subjectivity, that saturates the *corpus socians* with a paranoid economy of the policing gaze (what Lacan calls the *"voyure"*)—at the very moment that male homosexuality is installed (or "retro-jected") as irretrievably lost through a founding disavowal. That sociality is penetrated (and "spaced") by this disavowal and deferral of the (unrealizable) "hom(m)osexual declarative" "I (a man) love him (a man)" implies that we need to be cautious about assertions of the foundational nature of male homosexual desire in modernity. What we need to move towards is an analytics sensitive to the manner in which it is a social symbolic both patriarchal and homophobic that launches the phallacious dialectic of hetero-sexuality.[12] The brothers, the fraternal citizen-subjects, remain loyal to the paternal corpse in according to it a "deferred obedience," encrypting the relation to the masculine other in the homophobic and misogynist ritual of the "totemic meal," the fraternal feast which permits them to *eat* (to *be* according to a melancholic logic of de-sistence, to in-corporate) that father precisely through the evasion of *having* him (or some fraternal substitute).

The social contract is a pact of fraternal concord. It fundamentally destitutes the feminine, as Braidotti and MacCannell, following Irigaray, so effectively argue. It is also profoundly melancholic in its evasions and deferrals. The homosocial pact is signed according to a logic I am tempted to call "necrographic." We must beware of the lure of historicity with which it seduces us when we fall for its ruse of pathos, for the fraternal regime succeeds in duping us with its initiatory melancholics when we literalize its sense of loss. Oedipus has always already *fallen* for Narcissus, and patriarchy has always already constituted merely a representational *père-version* in the brotherly regime of modernity. According to this reading, male homosexuality is not a logic that subtends and founds, but an abyssal ground that confounds the masculine subject and launches it into its phobic ex-sistence. The analytic gaze that insists on discovering it at the origin is complexly complicit in the symbolic that archaicizes it, maintains it under erasure and forbids it (as Irigaray would say) "in practice."

The attempt to historicize the operations of sexual in/difference in modernity is a valuable and productive one, but I hope that this reading has suggested the need, as we turn to psychoanalytic mythological anthropology, to produce a critical analysis of the political production of historicity (as the melancholic loss, archaic repudiation, degeneration, *fall* that informs symptomatology) in its relation to sexuality. I am certainly not suggesting that we abandon the line of feminist thought that would question the erotic nature of the bonds that bind the modern fraternal collectivity. I believe that those bonds are essential to the production and reproduction of the modern social symbolic. I would insist, however, that feminist and gay male theorists should acknowledge the ambivalent significance of hermeneutically recovering a triumphant male homosexuality shrouded in the guise of the quotidian commerce — business as usual — of phallocentric heterosexuality. For male homosexuality is tangled in incredibly dense ways within the operations — prohibitive and proscriptive, juridical and productive — of the symbolic as it pervades the social field and continuously writes the social contract. Ultimately, I believe that further consideration will reveal that it is unlikely that male homosexuality inhabits the modern symbolic either as its insidious underlying logic or as a force of unequivocal opposition. Yet insofar as it seems, within a wide range of political discourses to be anchored fairly resolutely to the question of "crisis" — however suspicious we should be of the ends to which discourses of "crisis" may be mobilized — I would urge that we explore the potential of male homosexuality as a potentially *pro*ductive and *pro*spective site of intervention within genealogies of legitimation and filiation, resisting what seems to be the melancholic draw of a retrospective symptomatology.

Notes

1   For one account of the "cinematography" of the male imaginary see "Plato's *Hystera*" (*Speculum* 241–364). Crucially, it is in her elaboration of cinematography as a spatial and temporal representational regime marked by a profoundly asymmetric economy of sexual

difference that Irigaray most certainly evades the charges of a naive biologism or essentialism of gender difference sometimes leveled at her. The emphasis on the techniques of scenography within a morphological and representational economy of Semblance counters the possibility of a sociologically reductive reading of Irigaray's work that would understand sexual difference as merely the field of power and conflict between discreetly positioned and embodied social agents or classes. The notion of a cinematographic regime will be useful in the argument I am making here precisely because it underscores the social and psychological production of Semblance—and of the erotics of narcissism, so often bound, in psychoanalytic thought, to the question of homosexuality—rather than taking sameness, mimesis, even unicity, as pre-given, natural or foundational phenomena.

2   On exogamy and the symbolic exchange of women see "Women on the Market" and "Commodities Among Themselves" (*This Sex* 170–91, 192–97).

3   For an Irigarayan critique of the sham dialectic of heterosexuality see "Une Chance de vivre" (*Sexes* 197–222).

4   For a particularly bizarre Freudian myth of originary male homosexuality see the footnote on page 90 of *Civilization and Its Discontents*. The locus classicus is, of course, *Totem and Taboo*. For a critique of this logic in Freud and an account of how it is reproduced in Irigaray's work see my essay "Sexual Indifference and the Male Homosexual Imaginary."

5   To trace the vicissitudes of the concept of "power" and its relation to terms such as "the Law," "disciplinarity," and "authority" in Foucauldian and psychoanalytic thought would be a large-scale enterprise in its own right. Whilst Foucault (along with others such as Gilles Deleuze and Félix Guattari) has done much to criticize psychoanalysis for a lop-sidedly juridical account of power as the prohibitive (Oedipal and paternal-symbolic) Law inappropriate to the disciplinary operations of modernity, there is a current in psychoanalysis which would align it with the Foucauldian, and more broadly poststructuralist, analyses of power as relational and matricial: constitutive of and constituted within the contours of agency, identity and subjecthood. MacCannell very effectively mobilizes the critical resources of both traditions against the liberal-democratic and sociologistic conception of power as a differential current that ebbs and flows between preexisting and securely ontologically anchored subjects, agents and classes. The Law, in this hybrid reading, is no longer a rigidly totalizing narrative of the social, but rather a fantasmatic effect of and resource for the hegemonic self-representations of sociality, read as a matrix of power. At the same time, however, psychoanalysis continues to insist—more effectively, I believe, than Foucault, and in a manner which is surely indispensable to feminism—on the aspect of "structurality" which enables the reproduction of certain predictable power- and subject-effects within representational, political, and even bio-genealogical regimes.

6 "La 'société civile' donnant la primauté au monde des affaires risque d'engendrer la 'lutte de tous contre tous' par le truchement du combat entre les nouvelles sphères du sacré, l'argent et le travail. Aussi les hommes ont-ils été conduits à créer un nouveau principe transcendant: l'Etat, qui tend à construire un corps social suivant différentes perspectives pour s'asservir la société civile et mettre en œuvre, dans le réel, le phantasme de l'Un.

Le fonctionnement de l'État comme des institutions et des organisations diverses qui le constituent et en assurent sa régulation, met en œuvre des mécanismes de pouvoir fondés aussi bien sur le discours d'amour que sur le développement dans la société globale, comme dans la psyché individuelle, de désirs paranoïaques et pervers permettant à la pulsion de mort de se trouver un champ d'application et de justification" (28).

7 See, in particular, Žižek's "How Did Marx Invent the Symptom" (*Sublime* 11–53) and "On the One" (*For They* 7–60) for an analysis of the relation of enjoyment and the symptom to the ideological "quilting" of sociality.

8 Again, I refer to a *cinematographics* of phallic mimesis in order to emphasize the extent to which, as Irigaray clearly demonstrates, mimesis, far from being a self-evident process, is installed within the workings of a dense political and scopic economy of Semblance. There is a problem with accounts (I am thinking here of Borch-Jacobsen and René Girard) that I think place so much emphasis on primary identification and its ambivalences as that which projects the subject into the conflicts of sociality, as if identification and mimesis were not somehow already caught within the disciplinary workings of specularization and Semblance.

9 "Et voici le coup de génie de Freud: . . . c'est son assassinat qui constitue le chef de la horde en *père*. Il n'y a donc de père que si celui qui peut être ainsi investi non seulement possède les femmes, mais encore et surtout est l'objet *d'un désir de mort*. Le père en tant que tel n'existe qu'une fois tué réellement ou symboliquement" (34).

"Il n'y a jamais de père réel. Le père est toujours un père mort, le père mort un père mythique" (35).

10 The manner in which homosexuality—according to an "epistemology of the closet"— confounds the avowed categorical imperative of Enlightenment has, of course, been most poignantly elaborated in the work of Eve Kosofsky Sedgwick, and, in particular, in *Epistemology of the Closet*: "If ignorance is not—as it evidently is not—a single, Manichean, aboriginal maw of darkness from which the heroics of cognition can occasionally wrestle facts, insights, freedoms, progress, perhaps there exists instead a plethora of *ignorances*, and we may begin to ask questions about the labor, erotics and economics of their production and distribution. . . . [T]hese ignorances, far from being pieces of the originary

dark, are produced by and correspond to particular knowledges and circulate as part of particular realms of truth" (8).

11   Again, I refer here to the "operations of power" to emphasize the insight that authority constitutes itself across the social field (in its an-originary dissemination, one might say) at the same time as part of the disciplinary force of these operations depends on their ability to sustain (fantasmatically, or under a peculiarly morbid erasure) the image of an originary and eclipsed paternal Law.

12   And, while I have here focused on the homophobic ban placed on *male* homosexuality, lesbianism is also, of course, one of those symbolic practices of the *entre-femmes* which, as Irigaray has pointed out, the male imaginary keeps under erasure in order that women can be specularized according to the requirements of the phallomorphic imaginary.

Works Cited

Borch-Jacobsen, Mikkel. *The Freudian Subject*. Trans. Catherine Porter. Stanford: Stanford UP, 1988.

Braidotti, Rosi. "The Ethics of Sexual Difference: The Case of Foucault and Irigaray." *Australian Feminist Studies* 3 (1986): 1–13.

——. *Patterns of Dissonance*. Cambridge: Polity, 1991.

Enriquez, Eugène. *De la horde à l'état: essai de psychanalyse du lien social*. Paris: Gallimard, 1983.

Foucault, Michel. *The History of Sexuality: An Introduction*. Trans. Robert Hurley. New York: Pantheon, 1978. Vol. 1 of *The History of Sexuality*. 3 vols. 1978–86.

Freud, Sigmund. *Civilization and Its Discontents*. 1930. *The Standard Edition of the Complete Psychological Works of Sigmud Freud*. Trans. and Ed. James Strachey. Vol. 21. London: Hogarth, 1961. 57–145. 24 vols. 1953–74.

——. *Group Psychology and the Analysis of the Ego*. 1921. *The Standard Edition*. Vol. 18. 65–143.

——. *Totem and Taboo*. 1913. *The Standard Edition*. Vol. 13. ix–161.

Hope, Trevor. "Sexual Indifference and the Male Homosexual Imaginary." *Diacritics* 24.2–3 (1994).

Irigaray, Luce. *Sexes et parentés*. Paris: Minuit, 1987.

———. *Speculum of the Other Woman*. Trans. Gillian C. Gill. Ithaca: Cornell UP, 1985.

———. *This Sex Which Is Not One*. Trans. Catherine Porter. Ithaca: Cornell UP, 1985.

MacCannell, Juliet Flower. *The Regime of the Brother: After the Patriarchy*. London: Routledge, 1991.

Sedgwick, Eve Kosofsky. *Epistemology of the Closet*. Berkeley: U of California P, 1990.

Žižek, Slavoj. *For They Know Not What They Do: Enjoyment as a Political Factor*. London: Verso, 1991.

———. *Looking Awry: An Introduction to Jacques Lacan through Popular Culture*. Cambridge, Mass: MIT P, 1991.

———. *The Sublime Object of Ideology*. London: Verso, 1989.

Revisiting Male Thanatica. *Response*

I enjoyed Trevor Hope's incisive and brilliantly formulated essay on feminist theory. The author shows an impressive level of understanding of and commitment to issues that are central to feminism, and I consider it a privilege to engage in a discussion with him. I shall start my comment on Trevor Hope's extremely interesting essay from footnote 12, in which the author draws an analogy between male homosexuality and lesbianism, claiming that they are both subjected to the requirements of the phallomorphic imaginary. Mr. Hope then goes on to apologize for not having dealt more extensively with the lesbian issue. This analogy comes from what I consider a very uncomfortable place, which I will question. Throughout, the essay pursues what Irigaray, among others, chastises as the illusion of symmetry in the position the two sexes occupy vis-a-vis the phallic symbolic. In what strikes me as a variation on this theme, Mr. Hope pursues an argument that tacitly assumes a symmetry between male homosexuality and lesbianism. It is this approach I would like to challenge.

What's in a Myth?

Clearly, Freud's metapsychology provides a set of foundationalist narratives, or political myths, that allow us to come to terms with—in the sense of politically accounting for—the present. I would approach the narrative of the archaic male homo-sexual/social bond as a cartography, in Foucault's sense of the term. A cartography is a politically informed reading of the present; it offers more than hermeneutical grids of analysis: it also allows for the identification of points of resistance to dominant formations in the social field as well as in terms of sexual identity.

What is so interesting about the cartographic gesture, as Deleuze brilliantly points out in his study on Foucault, is that each cartographic rendition is always external, or relational, and retrospective. It is external because it situates the subject not in the hallowed space of his/her interiority, but rather in a web of relations to others. It is retrospective in that it can be drawn *a posteriori*: we can only grasp what we have been and consequently have ceased to be. In other words, each political myth is a map of places, positions, and situations in which we no longer are.

This emphasizes the eternal delay of theory over experience, but it also points to a structural aporia in theoretical discourse about the present moment (*l'actuel*). Politically informed maps or cartographies cannot fully account for the *hic et nunc*, the here and now of the gesture that binds self-reflective consciousness to political accountability; they merely draw a diagram of the power conditions that frame this gesture and, by framing it, act as its genealogical pre-conditions.

Donna Haraway, in her commentary on Foucault, puts it very succinctly: Foucault's diagrams of bio-power describe a system at the moment of its implosion, i.e. when it has already ceased to be. We no longer live in a regime of bio-power, but rather in the informatics of domination, under the tyranny of psycho-babble. I would even suggest that the social imaginary that underpins Foucault's analysis of power—and certainly his reading of the history of the bio-sciences and the medicalization of sexuality—rests on a nineteeth-century imaginary, which I would want to reassess critically. It is quite clear that Freud's own metapsychological account of the "origin" of the social contract is fully immersed in a world view and in a perception of socio-sexual relations which no longer describe *who* we are, but rather allow us to retrace the steps of what we have been or where we are coming from. It is an archeology of modernity.

My point is firstly methodological: I want to suggest that Mr. Hope's argument does not fully account for the complexity of the temporal scale of myth. He even suggests that the myth of the archaic male homo-sexual/social bond is posited as a moment *prior* in time to the constitution of adult, conscious citizenship. I would argue that such a political myth cannot be considered as being "prior" in any sense of chronological priority, quite to the contrary, it functions on the mode of the continuous present—that is to say of something that needs to be enforced and reasserted at each step of the socialization process. His account collapses mythical time with historical time, thereby blurring the crucial boundary between history and genealogy. I suggest that the myth of the archaic male homo-sexual/social bond is a genealogical tale, full of sound and fury, signifying nothing other than the emergence of male dominance as a factor in a world-wide system of domination which is always already here and now.

Respecting the specific temporality of political myths has another important implication for the role of the intellectual. I think a cartography provides us with politically informed, workable descriptions of the present and, as such, enables critical thinkers to engage actively in the process of resistance. Following Foucault, I see resistance as a way of politically activating counter-memories, that is to say sites of non-identification with or non-belonging to the phallogocentric regime. Feminist consciousness is one of the best examples of this sort of resistance and Foucault was honest enough to acknowledge his debt to the women's movement on this score. Thus, the political function of the intellectual is closely linked to her/his capacity to bypass or deconstruct the linearity of time, in a set of counter-genealogical moves. The cartographies or political narratives that sustain and express this process become objects of discursive exchange among such intellectuals; they function like transitional objects. I think we should approach the myth of the archaic male homo-social/sexual bond in this mode.

Although I agree whole-heartedly with Mr. Hope's call for a new dialogue between gay men and feminists and lesbians, so as to question the disciplinary operation of discourses of symptomaticity, I do think that for this dialogue to be beneficial to both sides we need to stop awhile and discuss more rigorously the terms of the debate. Similarly, if we are to take sexuality as a historical horizon that needs to be hermeneutically recovered as an interpretative bedrock, we need to do so in a manner that respects sexual difference in the sense of a fundamental dissymmetry between the sexes, all the way to their respective relationships to homosexuality.

I have no problem with the idea of taking male homosexuality not as foundational, but as the abyss that confounds the masculine subject and confronts him with his eclipse. But we need to do so in a manner that accounts for the transhistorical phenomenon of male dominance and does not attempt to cover it up under the illusion of a renewed symmetry between homosexual of the male and the female kind. Power differentials need to be taken into account.

Pathology and the Discourse of the Crisis

Mr. Hope argues that feminist readings of the patriarchal social symbolic are overdependent on the political myth of an atavistic male homosexual/social order, along the lines of the exogamous marriage proposed by Lévi-Strauss, Lacan, and other "fathers" of structuralism. Commenting on the fetishistic nature of this myth, which is both foundational and disavowed, he also points out that disavowal thus gets installed at the basis of cognition: male homosexuality is evoked only to be immediately bracketed off. He also notes the phobic effects of this political positioning of an archaic male homosexuality. In other words, the anteriority of male homosexuality does not confer any "priority" upon it, quite to the contrary: it ends up pathologizing this archaic, retrojected, homo-sexual/social economy that becomes specularly opposed to normal adult citizenship. The male homosexual "other" thus becomes phobically inscribed as the negative of normal masculine subjectivity. My question is, over again: what is the place of sexual difference in this account ? What about the symbolic position of lesbianism?

Feminist analyses of the last forty years agree on one fundamental assumption: that the masculine symbolic rests on a false universalization of the subject position, which is colonized by white, heterosexual men and the forceful creation of a set of "others" among whom the "second sex" — women — is the most prominent. This peculiar division of socio-symbolic labor constructs a fundamental asymmetry between the sexes. The price the masculine pays for the prerogative of subjectivity is a flight into abstract virility, which feminists read also as a form of disembodiment. The price women pay, on the other hand, is the confinement to immanence through being over-identified with their embodied condition and especially with sexuality. The relationship between the two poles is postulated in terms of compulsory heterosexuality.

As a consequence, if we want to alter this division of labor and institute a different socio-symbolic contract, the issue men need to confront is their disembodiment, the issue women need to confront is their over-embodiment. This is a set of very different and, I would argue, dissymmetrical problems which, in order to get adequately solved, must not be mixed up and lumped together under the banners of an allegedly "common" revolution within the symbolic order. Mr. Hope argues that these feminist readings reproduce a normative hermeneutics at the site of the sexed body and also make it constitutive of the social field. He takes my suspicion of male gender-benders and female impersonators as extremely revealing in this respect.

My answer to this is by now familiar: the feminist position consists in anchoring the deconstruction of identities based on the phallus, and especially of the feminine in its many figurations, to the lived experience of real-life women as bio-cultural agents of a massive political movement. The crucial issue for feminists is precisely that knot of identification, loss, and pain, that binds women to a feminine that is not one, but a web of multiple sites. My problem with male impersonators is that I see them playing with what Irigaray rightly calls "the other of the same"—mirroring the masks of the hyper-feminine which the patriarchal imagination adores, since it has created it in its image. My concern as a feminist is, however, how to bring into representation "the other of the other"—a feminine redefined by women in their collective effort to repossess a broken and destituted genealogy of their own. This is quite another issue, which would give to female homosexuality a different role in both society and the structures of identity.

The point of discussion between us here is that I do not think the positions of the lesbian and of the gay man are reversible or in any way symmetrical, though they both may be equally involved in and committed to the task of redesigning sexuality. The invisibility of the lesbian as other of the other is of a different conceptual and qualitative order. For one thing, within patriarchy, we do not dispose of any political myth or foundational narrative that assigns to female homosexuality an archaic, threatening, or structuring function. Whereas the gay man needs to resurrect the shreds of an identity from under the detritus of a triumphant masculine heterosexuality, the lesbian is coming in from the cold. Whereas the gay man needs to deconstruct a representation of the homosexual as the phobic other, the lesbian must move, symbolically, from *unrepresentability* into some sort of representation. The problems may appear analogous, but they are quite different.

Where they differ the most is in their assessment of the crisis of modernity. The same conditions that men encounter as a difficulty and a loss, are for women the opening out of brand new possibilities. The decline of the paternal metaphor simply does not resonate the same way in the "sons" as in the "daughters."

Modernity and the Sickness unto Death

Mr. Hope goes on to argue that the feminists' vision of archaic male homosexuality colors the poststructuralist reading of the crisis of modernity, which gets described as marked by degeneration, loss, nostalgia, pathology, and morbidity. It is a pathologized imaginary of disease and clinical remedies, haunted by the death of the father. Following the specular logic which marks the Western mind set, however, this pathology is the key to understanding normality and it thus ends up being archinormality.

What I most challenge in Mr. Hope's account is the allegation that we feminists fail to see through the discourse of the crisis. He suggests that we do not even contemplate the possibility that such a discourse may be a ruse of patriarchal discourse. He argues that we should ask instead what is the libidinal investment of modernity in the preservation of the notion of the loss or the death of the father. In response to this, I would like to draw attention to the wide spectrum of feminist positions, poststructuralist and not, that raise serious questions as to the credibility, feasibility and outcome of the alleged crisis of the paternal metaphor in the age of modernity. As a matter of fact, I think the majority of feminists have applied a healthy dose of suspicion to the melancholy discourse of the loss of legitimation of the master-narratives.

In answer to the question, "Is the paternal law not always already insinuating itself into subjects through its melancholy incorporation?" my reply is unequivocally yes, but the ways in which the internalization of that loss occurs and more specifically the pivotal role played by the mother as the conveyor of both the inevitability of the law and the necessity of the loss differs considerably in the two sexes. All are equal under the phallic symbolic, but when it comes to the inscription of the embodied subject into the signifying chain, some are definitely more equal than others. Melancholia, of all states, is deeply affected by sexual difference and for the "dutiful" daughters the mourning period is never really over; patriarchy would have them forever lingering in the twilight zone at the margin of the phallic empire.

Not only are most feminists mistrustful of the apocalyptic tones of the discourse of the crisis, but also we have devised a range of extremely valuable discursive and political strategies to come to terms with it. The need to reassert sexual difference implies that some attention be paid to these strategies. In my work, following Irigaray, I stress the importance of mimetic repetition as a way of moving out of the contradictions of the present. Repetitions are ways of revisiting sites and positions in order to disengage ourselves from the hold they may still have upon us. It is a process of working through, for which the psychoanalytic process of remembrance is one adequate model (though by no means the only one). Working through is a way of walking backwards through what we have been; this process of retracing the steps of an itinerary is the applied side of the counter-genealogies which I mentioned earlier.

With respect to the crisis of the paternal metaphor and the sense of loss and dejection that seems to accompany it, I wish to dwell upon that loss and not rush headlong into an allegedly radiant post-phallus future, because I believe we need to take the time to consume the process. I think the time of consciousness requires intervals and repetitions that contrast with the more linear logic of historical time. If the culture is to work its way out of the crisis of modernity, we critical thinkers of the feminist or other kind, need to take the time not only to think about loss and dejection, but also to devise adequate burial ceremonies for the dead. I am struck how, at each political revolution, as in eastern Europe since 1989, the winning party rushes on to destroy the documents and the monuments of the previous regime. The melting of Lenin's preserved corpse is the macabre detail that crystallizes this tendency. I do wonder what documents and monuments of the phallus we would have to destroy in order to accomplish the symbolic revolution of our dreams? Where do changes like that originate from? And how would we go about finding new, alternative representations of the new forms of desire and subjectivity that we already partly embody and experience?

This is the process I have in mind when I say that we need to take the time for the burial of the dead, to mark the transition, the difference. The death of the paternal metaphor is less important than the burial ceremony that follows it. Think of how perfectly adequate and fair is the Freudian notion of the totemic meal in this regard. It is the assimilation of the old that will allow us to move on to the new. I maintain that we have not yet buried our dead and that it should be the task of those of us who elect to be "dutiful" sons and daughters to fulfill it.

The only kind of intellectuals I know who are taking time off for the burial ceremony are the cyberpunk artists and science fiction writers. It seems to me that they are lingering on the process of death and dissolution of identities and are putting it back on the agenda, without nostalgia or false sentiments. I wish academics could do the same: think the death and the burial of classical understanding of subjectivity, dissolving the received ideas about the sexed body, as a matter of ceremonial fact.

The Riot Girls

Mr. Hope is perfectly right in pointing out that feminists such as myself over-emphasize the roars of war within the patriarchal bosom, an explosive violence contained within the divided heart of the patriarchal social symbolic. Where I would question Mr. Hope is in his assumption that such violence is intimidating to us. The point I wish to make here is that not all feminists are "dutiful" daughters, mourning the death of the father, lost in the melancholia. And even some of the "dutiful" ones have their limitations and in no way fit the traditional bill of the eternally black-clad mourning female. Most are actually not. The feminist reactions to the crisis and the sense of loss are many and manifold. I actually feel close to the mixture of anger and ego-defeating irony that marks so much of contemporary popular culture, like that of the riot girls, which I could paraphrase—somewhat provocatively—as follows: there is a war going on out there and women did not start it. We are not naturally pacifists, we are neither Cassandras nor Antigones. We are the guerrilla girls, we are the riot girls, we want to resist but we also want to have fun. We women want our imaginary, we want our own projected selves, we want to design the world in our own glorious image. It is time for the unholy alliance with Dionysian forces, time for the female death force to express itself, but in expressing itself also work towards workable networks of translation into socially livable modes of behavior. It is time for history and the female unconscious to strike up a new deal. We want to revisit male Thanatica—the discourse of death and the death trappings that lie at the empty heart of the phallic empire.

Besides, the realities and the figurations of war are all around us. Rock 'n' roll—which used to be the sound of life-giving rebellion—died when it started being used by the U.S. Army as a combat weapon in Vietnam and more recently against Noriega in Panama. It has since been replaced by rap and its masculinist warmongering tendency. Fortunately, female rappers like the band "Salt 'n' Pepa" have started a female counter-rebellion. Women want their own dreams and fantasies. We want the opportunity to work our way out of the old, decayed, seduced, abducted and abandoned corpse/corpus of phallogocentric patriarchy. We are sick of the death squads of the phallus with its essential accessories: abstract masculinity, iconic femininity, racism, and violence. In our lively, burning eyes, the male-dominated death apparatus—also known as Thanatica—is doomed.

Works Cited

Deleuze, Gilles. *Foucault*. Minneapolis: U of Minnesota P, 1988.

Foucault, Michel. "Le jeu de Michel Foucault." *Ornicar* 10 (1978): 62–93.

Haraway, Donna. "A Cyborg Manifesto: Science, Technology, and Socialist Feminism in the Late Twentieth Century." *Simians, Cyborgs, and Women: The Reinvention of Nature*. New York: Routledge, 1991.

The "Returns" of Cartography:
Mapping Identity-In(-)Difference. *Response*

I would like to thank Rosi Braidotti for her thoughtful and thought-provoking response to my essay. The engagement in productive "discussion" always implies a certain generosity. Where such discourse takes place across the differential political space of identities at the same time as it takes the cartography of identities as its object, that generosity involves a certain staking of ontology, a questioning of integrity, a willingness to risk, relinquish, divert certain cathexes in favor of new connections, new communicational currents, and, I am certain, new communicational stumbling blocks and impasses which both promise and withhold the possibility of a "return" on one's epistemological and ontological investment. It is a privilege for me to be engaged in dialogue with a scholar whose work has already so enriched my own thought. These connections and blockages—the promises and delays of cognition: synaptic relays, if you will—across the spacings of the social field, mark not just points of proximity and contiguity, but also points of articulation. I think we should not congratulate ourselves when they run too smoothly, but should listen carefully to the moments where they jar and send a shudder through a social body which too often presents itself as unarticulated, as fabulously, brilliantly singular in its organicity and self-semblance. For this reason I value Professor Braidotti's sense that we should "wait awhile," exercising extreme caution about appeals to symmetry, commonality, and perhaps even contiguity. I think we share, from our different emplacements and embodiments, a belief in a political engagement which respects the fundamental fractures of the social as sites to visit and revisit, places to linger, in the project of forging an ethics of difference.

Footnoting Lesbianism

It is for these very reasons that it makes me sad that Professor Braidotti has identified a moment in my text where my writing might be understood as having sutured itself rather too quickly across precisely such a space of difference. The dismissive, homologizing reference to lesbianism within work which takes male paradigms of homosexuality as its organizing principle has played such a massive and pernicious role in the mapping of asymmetric discourses of gender and sexuality that it seems there should, by now, be a universal moratorium on any footnoted reference to lesbianism in such texts. Professor Braidotti's insistence that we revisit the location of this (my) fault of scotomization and articulate it anew as a prospective point of visibilization is entirely welcome, and I do not wish to withdraw in a defensive reterritorialization. When I resituate the footnote within a broader context of my avowed intentions in the more encompassing (more differentiated? more fractured? more articulated? not, I hope, simply more integrative, more acquisitively wide-ranging) project of which this essay is truly a small fragment, I hope I can reread the significance of this moment in a manner which is also more positive. That dreadful homologizing of the footnote—"lesbianism is also . . . "—stems from a fear I had about a certain danger inherent in my assertion, within the body of my text, that "it is a social symbolic *both patriarchal and homophobic* that launches the phallacious dialectic of hetero-sexuality" (emphasis added). The danger of that sentence—a danger, as Professor Braidotti points out, that is perhaps exacerbated rather than alleviated by the apologia of the footnote—is that lesbianism gets occluded precisely where the operations of a social field which is, indeed, in a certain sense, both homophobic and patriarchal are too swiftly dichotomized into two discrete axes of identity and power: a set of discursive practices aimed at homosexuality and an array of disciplinary techniques directed at femininity.

The truth, of course, is that the political and representational regimes of asymmetric in/difference are never simply mapped onto one another in such a manner that subjects are mere palimpsestic accretions of diverse codifications and encryptments of jurisdiction. The embodied subject is the point at which a non-quantifiable heterogeneity of legislation converges, fractures, consolidates, contradicts, articulates, and disarticulates itself in such a manner as to produce an infinitude of subjectivities, positionalities, embodiments interimplicated in a fragmented and spaced social symbolic: a symbolic which, nonetheless, in its deployment of the mirror-tricks of scotomization, specularization, and objectification manages to cohere in the emplacement of a fatally solipsistic occular political regime. Moreover, the interimplication of "diverse" political subjects places them not at discrete points on a single cartography of social positioning, but rather enmeshes and knots them within a weblike textuality that produces appallingly repetitive and predictable effects of semblance and discrimination around the hegemonic faultlines, territorializations, and articulations of race, gender, class, and sexuality.

And again, Luce Irigaray's work would also insistently bring into question the notion that power actually ever flows between discretely embodied individuals occupying geometrically singular positions on a level social field: positions closer to or further from a "central" resource of capital, power, prestige. Her work reminds us that the regimes of semblance legislate the disembodiment of certain subjectivities—their "transcendence" into political agency and symbolic articulacy at the price of the threat of disciplinary abjection and overembodiment of others who serve the reproductive needs of the corpus socians.

In this respect I think that Professor Braidotti's deployment of the Irigarayan notion of the "Other of the Other" (which also figures in my own work on the relation of lesbianism to female homosociality beyond the faulty footnote) surpasses the limitations of the insertion of lesbianism within a "both/and" analytics of the regimes of gender and sexuality. A vast amount of productive thought has emerged in feminist and lesbian theories over the past twenty-five years—and, in another (though still limited) sense, during at least the last century—around the question of the relationship of the category of gender to that of sexuality. What I take the concept of the "Other of the Other" to offer is an understanding which renders gender and sexuality neither as identical nor as dichotomous matrices of subject-formation and political inquiry, and which consequently renders lesbians neither homologous to, nor different from, the categories of "women" and "homosexuals" unitarily conceived. Moreover, the "Other of the Other" is neither the point where critical projects of gender and sexuality abut nor where they banally overlap. It is certainly not the ground (for, indeed, it is never a place of geometric unicity but rather one of articulate spacing) for the jubilant unification of feminist and queer agendas. It is a site and a fracture in which that "and" is foregrounded for the territorial fault that it marks, and held under erasure for the faulty territorialization that it suggests.

It is tempting to stop here, at this statement of an articulate divide, and yet I think another, less confident "revisitation" of that mediatory impasse is necessary. There is still a structural fault that traverses the "dialogue" as I have conceived it here and, I believe, as it gets institutionalized within the academy. The faulting of the lesbian footnote within this dialogue is useful because it associates lesbianism with a certain privileged perspective on the articulation of queer "and" feminist politics, and indeed I am committed, in a certain sense, to the maintenance of that privilege. On the other hand, lesbianism is only rehomologized with discourses of sameness as long as it figures as a carefully mapped space of negativity for the self-consciousness of projects that mobilize the identities "women" and "queers": so long, that is, as it becomes, once again (as I fear the eagerness of the above paragraph to deploy it to deconstructive ends might imply), a specularized point of negativity that simply returns the current—the cathectic circuits of interest and dialogue—of feminist and queer theories reflexively back to "themselves."

The "privileging" of the Other of the Other also means that it must not function as an objectified focal point, nor as a specularized negative image, but rather must "return" feminism and queer theory in all their articulations to a differentially emplaced terrain in which homophobia "and" sexism are recognized as tediously insistent and appallingly trenchant within women's and lesbian, bisexual, and gay studies. As a gay male critic emplaced and embodied in, articulated and empowered through, subjected to and subjectivated by the densely palimpsestic cartographics of power that map and traverse the social body, I cannot not refer to lesbianism and sexual difference, least of all should I refuse simply to make reference to them. The ethical project of gay male criticism must surely be to refer to and even to privilege lesbianism and sexual difference in a manner that does not simply reap the returns of a momentarily diverted investment of attention: that does not specularize, objectify, or scotomize. The lesbian footnote will not do.

Passing: Narcissism, Identity, and Difference

*O*urs is the era of the passing of *passing* as a politically viable response to oppression. It seems fitting that passing is a verb with no noun-subject form since it is an activity whose agent is obscured, immersed in the mainstream rather than swimming against the tide, invisible to the predatory eye in search of its mark. Passing has become the sign of the victim, the practice of one already complicit with the order of things, prey to its oppressive hierarchies—if it can be seen at all. For the mark of passing successfully is the lack of a mark of passing, of a signifier of some difference from what one seems to be. In fact, passing can only name the very failure of passing, an indication of a certain impossibility at its heart, of the contradictions which constitute it: life/death, being/non-being, visibility/invisibility, speech/silence, difference/sameness, knowledge/ignorance, coming out/mimicry. Passing is the *e*ffect of a certain *a*ffect, an uncanny feeling of uncertainty about a difference which is not quite invisible, not quite unknown, not quite non-existent—a sort of life in death, in which otherness appears on the verge of extinction, dying into the self-sameness it still lacks even as it lacks difference.

Passing is commonly supposed to be the effect of "closetedness," whose paradoxical qualities Eve Sedgwick articulates in her description of it as "a performance initiated as such by the speech act of a silence—not a particular silence, but a silence that accrues particularity by fits and starts, in relation to the discourse that surrounds and differentially constitutes it" (3). Passing speaks of a secret behind a closed door, which it opens as a space of difference in the heart of the same, disrupting identity. Something we cannot quite make out begins to take on shape and color, growing visible in our midst, passing through us, unsettling us, troubling the homogeneity of our group and our identifications with one another which, as Freud and others have noted, are the support of group identity.[1] Sometimes that something is one's self, as the focus of an almost nameless anxiety narrows to one's own image, in what Sedgwick calls "circuits of intimate denegation" (61), and one finds oneself—and not the other—in the closet. But to find oneself there is already to come out, to name one's doubts and fears and repudiate them together with the old identity as a disguise which deceived no one. Passing is always passing through, from coming out to mimicry, since coming out reconstitutes one's past as mimicry, but also from mimicry to coming out, because the former becomes the cause of the latter, the ambiguity—or ambivalence—about an identity that calls it into question, rendering it unnatural, exposing it as a fake.

Coming out and mimicry are critical practices which currently interest many activists and scholars. They are at the center of debates about identity politics and postmodernism, essentialism and antiessentialist social constructionism, which structure the discussion of resistance in the wake of passing in many fields today, including lesbian and gay, queer, feminist, postcolonial, and African-American studies. Participants in these debates voice the desire to be subjects rather than objects of difference, to speak, write, and desire differently without reproducing the phallogocentric subject's fetishistic ambivalence about difference, even to be absolutely and essentially different from the hegemonic subject. They would *fix* resistance (in both senses of the word) by fixing difference—which in the end can only fetishize it as a play of masking and unmasking. The difference from and within coming out and mimicry, passing passes between and through them like the ghost of a phenomenon, the spectre of identities past and future. As the uncanny experience of the *lack* of an identity, passing is not quite not resistance, which we want to be a thing of substance with a name and an identity. Coming out and mimicry would unmask the face of resistance disguised by passing. They insist on the other's right to be other—to be seen, heard, known, and named as different—affirming that difference, the one directly, the other indirectly, through negation and irony. Each is the other's limit, but a limit passed by passing, which splits and doubles them as the effect of a symbolic lack which haunts them: the *passing* of the castration complex, not quite not there, the skeleton of the phallus in the closet, not fixed, neutered, or neutralized.

Coming Out

Coming out, one affirms an identity, declaring and displaying it as a positive difference from a presumptive norm which has also served as the measure of superiority. One names oneself, refusing one's assigned or hegemonic name in what Kimberly Bentson describes as a simultaneous unnaming, "affirming at once autonomy and identification in the relation to the past" (153). Bentson describes this topos in African-American culture:

> *[The former slave's] social and economic freedom—a truly new self— was incomplete if not authenticated by self-designation. The* unnaming *of the immediate past ("Hatcher's John," etc.) was reinforced by the insertion of a mysterious initial, a symbol of the unacknowledged, nascent selfhood that had survived and transcended slavery. On the other hand, the association with tropes of American heroism ("Lincoln," "Sherman," etc.) was also an act of naming, a staging of self in relation to a specific context of revolutionary affirmation. . . . (153)*

After transsexual surgery Richard Raskind is reborn as Renee Richards; after Stonewall the homosexual is gay. Sometimes such renaming involves reclaiming the old name and inflecting it differently, something that has happened with "queer." The hierarchies may even be inverted and the devalorized, revalorized: black is beautiful; women on top. Asserting the right to name oneself this way is asserting the right to be oneself, which is why the fundamental realization of "coming out" is in the use of the phrase itself. As Sedgwick explains, the text on a T-shirt that ACT UP New York sells—"I am out, therefore I am"—functions performatively rather than constatively (4); it is in effect a continuing renewal of being through the repetition of the gesture that explicitly affirms one identity and implicitly repudiates another.

In a performance piece which seems to work in a similar way, Adrian Piper has passed out "calling cards" to those who "pass over her racial difference." The cards read:

> *Dear Friend:*
>
> > *I am black.*
> >
> > *I am sure that you did not realize this when you made/ laughed at/agreed with that racist remark. In the past I have attempted to alert white people to my racial identity in advance. Unfortunately, this invariably causes them to react to me as pushy, manipulative, or socially inappropriate. Therefore, my policy is to assume that white people do not make these remarks, even when they believe there are no black people present, and to distribute this card when they do.*

> *I regret any discomfort my presence is causing you, just as*
> *I am sure you regret the discomfort your racism is causing me.*
> Sincerely Yours,
> Adrian Margaret Smith Piper
> (qtd. in Phelan 97–98)

Piper's difference goes unremarked because she is camouflaged—but by the others around her, against her will, "disappeared" into the presumptive universal, the unmarked "same." Piper is the object, not the subject, of a desire for white mimicry since she has not consented to practice it. She seems to be the victim of a crime, the theft of her identity, in which her desire or will is deeply invested. We feel we have an inalienable right to our desire and identity, but unfortunately, our narcissistic investment in them binds us deeply to others who have the power to alienate us from ourselves by calling into question the character(s) we are in the fantasies which structure our reality, for as a staging of desire, fantasy cannot do without performers, spectators, and props. Piper's cards, the ACT UP T-shirt, and other assertions of a "proper" name suggest that it is never enough to name oneself by oneself in a private fantasy. Identity is always dependent upon others of whom a demand for recognition is made—paradoxically, in terms one calls one's own. As a relation to others, fantasy is necessarily public, and the public, therefore, has a fantasmatic dimension.

"Natural" Signs

The wish for one's own terms and one's proper identity, perhaps the most deeply private property of all, is an impossible desire since both are held in common with others in the community as an effect of the symbolic. We can never be sure what is "coming out" of us for the other, or from the other. Nevertheless, there persists a paradoxical desire to be self-present to others, to come out as our proper self to ourselves through the other's recognition of our proper name and image. As signifiers of our selves with which we are deeply identified, we wish our name and image to transparently reflect our being, like an iconic sign, and to be existentially or naturally bound to it, like an index.[2] Such signs are supposed to be "motivated" rather than "arbitrary" or conventional and artificial, and therefore less susceptible to the disarticulations of signifier and signified, sign and referent, which make communication confusing. The absence of the real in them is disavowed, just as in fetishism the

mother's difference, which the subject sees and scotomizes, knows and ig-
nores, is disavowed.

The classic examples of such realist fetishism are photography and
film. At once iconic and indexical, their truthful representation of the referent
seems to have a double "guarantee." Because both are recorded, rather than
live, they are marked by what Roland Barthes calls "the photo effect."[5] According to Barthes, the photograph functions as a witness of "what has been,"
certifying the presence of the past by mortifying the living it would immortalize
(85, 87–88, 13–14). Its proper tense is the future perfect: this *will have been*. As
the agent of that action, the camera-mortician "will have been" in the same
space at the same time as what it embalms, preserving the referent's reality
through the light rays which have touched the living and the filmic bodies,
creating an existential bond between them. The photograph, Barthes writes,
"carries its referent with itself. . . . [T]hey are glued together, limb by limb, like
the condemned man and the corpse" (5–6). For film critic and theorist André
Bazin, this indexical relation is the basis for a more persuasive argument for
cinematic realism than an appeal to its supposed iconicity (9–16).

However, neither indexical nor iconic signs preserve the real of the
referent, whose relation to both is arbitrary, a matter of conventions. As
Umberto Eco observes, indexical relations are based on inferences which
come to be socially sanctioned and systematically coded through a discourse,
whether of science or "common sense," and it is this cultural coding which
transforms them into "semiosic acts" (17). He emphasizes the importance of
convention in reading the photograph as "real" by undermining the latter as
the natural consequence of "analogue" (as opposed to "digital" or purely
arbitrary) form: "[A] photograph is perhaps 'motivated' (the traces on the paper
are produced by the disposition of the matter in the supposed referent) but it is
digitally analyzable, as happens when it is printed through a raster . . . " (190).
Classic Hollywood cinema's realism is no less realistic when a movie is
projected from a laser disk, rather than film stock, or when an entirely fictional
scene manufactured by the computer wizards of special-effects departments is
edited together with more conventionally filmed footage. Our inference that
the camera was in the space of the mise-en-scène, which therefore "must have
been," is simply false in the case of special-effects sequences, and in fact in
realist film we are never allowed to see in the diegetic world the camera or
anything else that might suggest the staging of the real.

Eco most persuasively demonstrates the arbitrary relation of the iconic sign to its referent through a discussion of the double, which effectively deconstructs the logic of iconicity. It would seem the referent must appear without mediation in its double, which would exactly resemble it, being identical to it. Yet according to Eco, doubles are impossible, "for it is difficult to reconstruct all the properties of a given object right down to its most microscopic characteristics" (180). Furthermore, even if doubles could be fabricated they would cease to be doubles, since they would become instead signs of some more real Ideal which they could never quite double or duplicate.

> Given a wooden cube of a given size, matter, color, weight, surface structure and so on, if I produce another cube possessing all the same properties (that is, if I shape the same continuum according to the same form) I have produced not a sign of the first cube, but simply another cube, which may at most represent the first inasmuch as every object may stand for the class of which it is a member, thus being chosen as an example. (180)

Any particular instance of a category necessarily lacks some of the properties of the category as a whole, if only because by definition a category is general rather than particular and at least potentially includes more than just one instance. The instance which functions as its own category splits itself into an absence and a spectral presence, a ghost of an ideal which it re-presents but whose vital property it must miss, that ineffable "difference" between the member and the class. Something of the real must be absent in a sign for it to function as a sign or representation rather than the referent itself. Paradoxically, the double negates itself and its original, constituting both as signs of something else which is ineluctably absent, which passes through its signifers without a trace except what the conventions themselves make perceptible as "the realistic."

According to Lacan, the real is quite literally a matter of mirages and doubles when we refer to the subject. Our representations appear to belong to us as sovereign subjects although they come to us from the Other (*Four* 81). This is so especially for "our" representations, the signifiers which represent us, with which we are deeply identified, and which in fact constitute us in the first place: the mirror image, the proper name, and the first person pronoun. The other founds the subject by alienating him or her from a part of the self, those very signifiers which provide the fiction of a "self." The subject can never reconcile the split between itself and its mirror imago, the eye which sees and the eye which is seen, the I who speaks and the I who is spoken, the subject of desire and the subject of demand, who must pass through the defiles of the Other's signifiers. It is this alienation, this gap between being and meaning, subject and signifier, self and other, which the classical realist system of representation would suture. The subject does not exist except through the Other by whom s/he is "photo-graphed" (*Four* 106), initially in the mirror, the illusion which founds the self as if it were always already there before the mirror which would simply reflect it. The imaginary "ideal ego" is "the total form of the body by which the subject anticipates in a mirage the maturation of his power . . . [and] symbolizes the mental permanence of the *I*, at the same time as it prefigures its alienating destination . . . the statue in which man projects himself" through the libido which is invested in it (*Ecrits* 2).

The imago is at once an iconic and indexical sign: it "resembles" the subject only because it assembles him, fixing him to the *gestalt* image of himself as whole through the libidinal flow which binds him to it as his "self," like the picture which mortifies the subject it would immortalize, preserving him in a statue. The mirror other as primordial subject is the foundation for the later identifications with ego-ideals which build up the ego itself. It is an uncertain foundation, however, based on a fundamental confusion of identification with identity, spectator with model, the condemned man with his corpse. In fact, it is the mirage which "appropriates" the human being as it attracts and engulfs much of the "hommelette," or infant libido, making it a subject by enclosing it in a fragile shell. The subject is therefore an effect of impersonation or "mimicry," which results from and expresses an alienating identification with something outside it (*Ecrits* 23). The mirror sign imprints itself on the real, constituting the real as a copy or double and thereby alienating it. The mirror imago constructs, rather than reconstructs, the properties of what it would reflect. The subject is only retroactively the cause of what brings it into being, an imitation of a reflection or copy of which it "will have been" the original (so that there can be a copy at all).

As Eco explains, people mistake for an icon the condition for iconicity, cultural coding itself: "Thus a schematic representation reproduces some of the properties of another schematic representation" (213, 208). If the iconic sign is finally arbitrary and conventional, the conventions of the symbolic are themselves a principle of iconicity, forming subjects and objects through the splitting and doubling of signs as the realistic and the real and binding the one to the other through the fiction of their indexical relation. There can be neither subject nor intersubjectivity without the narcissistic perception of a similarity where there is only difference, including self-difference. And there can be no similarity without difference: a thing cannot be itself and its double, yet there is no thing without its double, which brings it into being as "itself," an instance of a larger class of similar things. Beyond and before the self is the founding other, cathected by an object libido which is always already ego libido, in the name of an illusory mastery which serves a pleasure principle that is also a reality principle. Beyond and before narcissism is the self-critical aggression of the death drive, which is always already at work when the subject so radically confounds itself with the other that it *is* the other and attacks "itself" as an other with which it can never be reconciled. Who has assimilated whom in such a mimicry? The death drive must take the self as its object if the other is to survive, yet it must be directed outward, against the other, if the self is to survive. There is no possibility of a just "balance" when self and other, subject and object, narcissism and aggression, eros and thanatos are so profoundly con/fused through the splitting and doubling which found them. Sexuality always already diverges both from self-preservation or the reality principle and from the pleasure principle. Narcissism must be—and is— critiqued and preserved by subjects through the fetishistic disavowal of the other's difference, including that other which is the "self."

There is always an aggressive and narcissistic or sado-masochistic dimension to the critique of narcissism, which concerns the preservation of self or other, subject or object. Piper's calling cards exemplify this. As Peggy Phelan explains, Piper very cannily attacks the narcissism of the white self by calling into question that subject's mastery of the visual field—empiricism itself. Piper "establishes . . . the failure of racial difference to appear within the narrow range of the visible and registers her refusal to let the visual field *fail* to secure it. The card itself ruptures the given to be seen and exposes the normative force of everyday blindness: if no one looks black, everyone is white" (98). However, Piper repeats in uncanny fashion that which she would critique. She assumes she can see—or hear—who is white, interpellating people as white by giving them her card. She divides the world into black and white, passing over people of color unless they are (black) like her and share her sense of what racism is.

Hers is the inverse of white narcissism: if no one looks (or acts) white, everyone is black. Piper's policy is not so much to assume that white people do not make racist remarks, as her cards claim (otherwise she would not carry them), but to assume that people of color do not make racist remarks and are all alike in their understanding of racism. She imagines them as her mirror counterparts, what Seyla Benhabib calls the "generalized other," part of a homogeneous collectivity which the expression "people of color" itself creates as the term which designates all those who are not white (the "absence" of color, the unmarked universal). Piper abstracts a new universal from concrete differences, coming out by "passing" others into whiteness or blackness, whatever they "really" are, as she herself was "passed," making them into mimic men and women. She disavows their differences in order to "fix" her own.

Name-Calling

Is it possible to recover our genuine differences from the other's narcissistic representations without being narcissistic ourselves? Is a self-reflexive "mimicry" a less narcissistic response to the problems of (self-) representation than coming out is, given the name can no more represent the self's real difference than the image? Both naming and imaging involve violence, the violence of the "cut" when signs cleave the continuum of "real" differences into culturally significant identities. Names represent nothing of people's uniqueness; they categorize and therefore reduce specificities, alienating something of the "real." As Jacques Derrida has observed in his landmark work on the topic, writing ineluctably effaces the proper name as what is intimately one's own, as the index which would point to one person only, bound to him or her in space and time in a moment of primal baptism:

> *The death of absolutely proper naming, recognizing in a language the*
> *other as pure other, invoking it as what it is, is the death of the pure*
> *idiom reserved for the unique. Anterior to the possibility of violence in*
> *the current and deriviative sense . . . there is, as the space of its*
> *possibility, the violence of the arche-writing, the violence of difference,*
> *of classification, and of the system of appellations. (110)*

Language is public rather than private property, the realm of the iterable rather than the unique. One is white or black, straight or gay, male or female, Dick or Renee, common names for identities held in common as mutual acts of recognition. There can be no "I" without a "you," and these pronouns gain their meaning from their difference rather than from any intrinsic link to the subjects whose being they designate, given that anyone can deploy them. The subject is the effect of impersonation or mimicry, the assumption of an alienating signifier ("I" or "you"), and the imitation/repetition of the practices of the apparatus in which it is produced. "I am out, therefore I am" cannot close the gap between performance and utterance, performative and constative, subject and T-shirt, the one who is "outing" and the one who is out. "I" will have been out only at the end of the "outing," which is not in its beginning, except retroactively. Being "out" is a moebius movement of deferral without end and renewal without beginning—the future perfect as past perfected. The subject of the enunciation must pass through the statement in which his "I" is uttered. All subjects therefore are *passing* through the signifers which represent them for an other, to whom a demand for recognition and a question about being is addressed: "(Do you) Hear what I'm saying!? (Do you) See what I am!?"

How and for whom is this confidence game staged? Louis Althusser implies that it is "for" the subject who "*is interpellated as a (free) subject in order that he shall . . . (freely) accept his subjection*, i.e., in order that he shall make the gestures and actions of his subjection 'all by himself'" (182). However, if we are duped by our act, if we believe our illusions, it is because "the system" requires our subjection so that it may reproduce itself. In the final analysis, self-deception is for the Other, the symbolic network: "[T]hose who should be deceived by the ideological 'illusion' are not primarily concrete individuals but, rather, the big Other" (Žižek, *Sublime* 198). The subject does not have to believe in his act so long as the show goes on—he knows better but some Other does not.

This splitting of belief between "I" and "you" is a form of disavowal most critics have failed to recognize as such, which includes the possible variations on the kernel sentence of the fetishistic fantasy: "I know very well, but all the same. . . . " We are in the grip of ideology when we continue to behave in a way consistent with it even if we disavow what we are doing or the beliefs that are supposed to motivate it. We still believe, Christian Metz writes, "but always in the aorist tense. . . . The beliefs of 'long ago' irrigate the unbelief of today, but irrigate it by denegation (one could also say *by delegation*, by attributing credulity to . . . former times)" (73). Emotions, including belief, can even be transferred to others as they are to our younger, "more naive" selves.

The Other can do our believing for us so that our fantasy is not disrupted. But the Other is also our self, having constituted us through its signifiers; on some Other level, therefore, we still believe—on the level of actions and not thoughts. No matter how self-consciously we deconstruct identities, no matter how self-reflexively we perform our selves, we are still "doing" them. What's more, we demand that the Other recognize both our identities and our "cynicism" about them—the Other is at once our credulous dupe and the "subject supposed to know" that we know better.

This disavowal structures the current version of identity politics. Poststructurally savvy, we "know" that coming out is a naively essentialist notion. Since we are always already caught up in a system of conventional differences that preclude the recovery of a "genuine" difference, we can only reverse the discourse that has produced us and embrace the identity we have assumed as if it represented what we really are. When Jeffrey Weeks opens his book on coming out by describing it as "a historic process, the gradual emergence and articulation of a homosexual identity and public presence" (i), he might well be discussing the discursive production of the homosexual as elaborated by Michel Foucault (*History* 36–49; 101) rather than any radical reconstruction of gay identity. In Foucauldian terms, coming out is still complicit with the regulation of sexuality even as it functions as a reverse discourse by making demands in the name of the devalued identity constituted by dominant sexual discourses. It involves no "real" liberation or authentic self-expression but is instead another identity fiction, neither self-generated nor adequate to the diversity and heterogeneity of the interests, desires, and identifications of the subjects who take up its signature image. Judith Butler makes this point about the limitations of "queer" as the name in which all the (prospective) members of the gay community would recognize themselves (*Bodies* 227–30). Lauren Berlant and Elizabeth Freeman express similar reservations about the interpellative power of "Queer Nation" and the imaginary community it would construct (197, 220–25). However, all observe that similar totalizations of identity seem to be a necessary political stratagem in the ongoing war of hegemony and resistance to it. Deploying identity fictions we recognize as such we wish to practice what Gayatri Spivak has called "strategic essentialism" ("Criticism" 11).[4]

Strategic essentialists operate in the realm of choice and conscious knowledge, "deliberately" differentiating themselves from naive essentialists, who are not supposed to know what they are doing—even when they seem to be doing the very same thing. The naive essentialist is necessarily someone else, even if only a "younger" version of ourselves. Who really is at risk when— "strategically" of course—we take the "risk of essentialism"? What other within the community—or the self—must be excommunicated when we attempt to secure our identity through it? Such strategems are the province of the ego and are inevitably caught up in aggressive rivalry with the other. R. Radhakrishnan quite rightly worries that when practiced on behalf of ethnic identity, they simply counter one oppression with another: "Doesn't all this sound somehow familiar: the defeat and overthrow of one sovereignty, the emergence and consolidation of an antithetical sovereignty, and the creation of a different, yet the same, repression?" (208) He argues for the critical thematization of the problem of alterity when affirming identity. Such a self-analysis might direct a portion of the death drive against the narcissistic ego. Otherwise, we may be compelled to "act out" over and over again the imaginary struggle between egos, as the death drive is directed against others. For, as Lacan observes in his seminar on the ethics of psychoanalysis, this rivalry can inform morality itself. When we do unto others as we would have them do unto us it may be because we love our neighbor as our self, whether or not this is what he wants (*Ethics* 179–204). There is something beyond a desire for the good in the mirror relationship of friendship, something we confront when our friend refuses the good we have wished for him. He is not my counterpart after all if he does not desire my desire. What does he want? More importantly, what does he want from me? What wicked pleasures will he take in me—or from me? I reveal my own evil when I respond to what I fear is his by imposing myself on him, "saving" him from himself by insisting that he enjoy what I do, for his own good—and my own, since I then become the instrument of his salvation. As Philippe Julien explains, "This is a perversion of the love-passion, or, to define it precisely: a pretense to *knowledge* (*savoir*) about the Other's *jouissance*, which serves to support my devotion to it" (86–87).

Signifying Clones

Perversions too are in the name of a law, a code of behavior which regulates intersubjectivity and promises to make it satisfying by confusing self and other in a narcissistic strategy of assimilation. Is the law any less repressive because "perverse"? Are the identities and behavior it legislates less normalized because "abnormal"? In his own community, the other may be an oppressor, the one whose word is not supposed to be just another law but a just law. Desire my desire and (be) like me as "the good" itself. Is it perverse to note that coming out is similarly oppressive, since it attempts to *fix* an ideal identity and a community which necessarily recognizes that identity (because everyone shares it) by reflecting it back? It disavows the split in the self by disavowing the split in discursive address, between self and other, as the other is made the double of the self. When the self and mirror other communicate there is supposed to be no double talk, as is implicit in Ferdinand de Saussure's work. In his outline of the "speaking circuit," signifiers are matched with the "proper" signifieds by sender and receiver in acts of perfect communication because human sign producers are entirely absent in one version of his diagram (12), and represented in the other as identical talking heads, twins without the desiring bodies which might subject them to Freudian slips of the signifier in their relation to one another (11). Saussure's speech community is populated by mirror egos, signifying clones. But such doubles necessarily signify an ideal they cannot fully embody; they divide each other from their ideal and themselves in the murderous/suicidal rivalry of self and/as other of the imaginary. This anxiety of mimicry emerges whenever signifying clones strive to come out as themselves without the mediation (and difference) of the Other, who must nevertheless recognize them as what they are if they are to be out at all.

It is just this anxiety Barthes articulates in his analysis of the photograph, which "represents that very subtle moment when, to tell the truth, I am neither subject nor object but a subject who feels he is becoming an object: I then experience a micro-version of death. . . . I am truly becoming a specter" (14). As Barthes explains it, the subject of the photograph passes on because he passes through the object as signifier of some other's desire, whose curious effect is the *passing* of identity itself as it becomes imposture:

> *In front of the lens, I am at the same time: the one I think I am, the one I want others to think I am, the one the photographer thinks I am, and the one he makes use of to exhibit his art. In other words a strange action: I do not stop imitating myself. . . I invariably suffer from a sensation of inauthenticity, sometimes of imposture. . . . (13)*

His image, his body, is no longer his own; some other is stealing the very stuff of his "self" and using it for his own purposes. What is coming out of Barthes for this other? To what has Barthes consented in posing for him? What right does he have to see Barthes as Barthes cannot see himself, to turn Barthes into a mere facsimile of himself by shooting him with his camera and gaze? Yet how can this mortifying gaze be evaded when it must be solicited so that Barthes can be recognized as himself? There is no "I" without a "you," but no you without an eye "through which . . . I am *photo-graphed*" (Lacan, *Four* 106). The Other provides me with the signifiers of my self which imprint themselves on me (I incorporate them, identify with them), but not without a remainder, the negative that calls into question the ego as positivity, what Lacan calls the stain or *tychic* point on the picture of myself, which is where "you" look at me (*Four* 74, 77).

Lacan recounts a parable about himself to illustrate the stain's functioning, a fish story in which the big one does not get away, although it turns out to be only a sardine. As Lacan tells it, when he was in his twenties, a young, bourgeois intellectual, he liked to "get away" and do something which challenged him and the working classes against whom he would measure himself in the pursuit of their regular occupation. Out on such a fishing expedition one day with a family from Britanny, Lacan was hailed by one of the boat's crew, Petit Jean, who laughed and pointed to something sparkling on the surface of the water: "You see that can? Do you see it? Well, it doesn't see you" (*Four* 95). As Lacan recognizes, it did see him, despite Petit Jean's assertion to the contrary, and actually gave him the fish-eye, a cold hard stare which cut him down to size. "It was looking at me at the level of the point of light, the point at which everything that looks at me is situated," he writes, adding,

> The point of this little story, as it had occurred to my partner, the fact that he found it so funny and I less so, derives from the fact that, if I am told a story like that one, it is because I, at that moment—as I appeared to those fellows who were earning their livings with great difficulty, in the struggle with what for them was a pitiless nature— looked like nothing on earth. In short, I was rather out of place in the picture. (Four 96)

There was something fishy about one of the fishermen in the photo, the *poseur* in the group, whose imposture appeared as such. Thinking to reassure himself with a little game of mimicry, which is linked not only to camouflage but also to travesty and intimidation, as Lacan tells us, he discovered he did not have the biggest one after all; when he pulled in the nets they were empty—not even a sardine in them (*Four* 98). In the struggle for recognition the other does not always provide a reassuring image of the self as whole, lacking nothing. There is no perfect reciprocity, no purely satisfying sexual or social relation; there is always something missing or lacking in one. Beyond the narcissism and paranoia of the imaginary there is something real, but it cannot be caught in the signifying nets of the symbolic either since it remains resistant to meaning, driving the subject to new relations with the Other, in which he continues to encounter that traumatic real Lacan calls *tuch* (*Four* 53). The illegible detail or stain on Lacan's picture of himself, it makes his face a mask and his acts a masquerade that questions his very being. It is the mark of his desire for what he does not have and cannot be: no sardines for the would-be analyst whose desire is for an unsatisfied desire, like that of "the beautiful butcher's wife," the hysteric whose dream of not having the caviar she wanted both Freud and Lacan analyzed (*Interpretation* 180–84; *Ecrits* 256–64). As Homi Bhabha has argued, drawing on Lacan, mimicry is at once camouflage, travesty, intimidation, and assimilation, a (su)stained imitation through which we are hailed into place but also called into question. Beyond our eye is the gaze of the Other, which ensures the I is not secured by vision. I never see what I want or exhibit what is desired in the fetishistic masquerade, whose effects are ambiguous.

(Re)Signifying Difference(s)

At once worshipped and castrated, the fetish signifies both knowledge and ignorance of difference. The fetishistic effort to fix identity and community, therefore, must fail no matter how strict the panoptic (self-)surveillance. Hegemony is always in process, as subcultures engage in a style politics which denaturalizes the apparent universality of the meanings and identities of the dominant culture. Yet subcultures themselves seek to consolidate identity and community through their appeals to counter-norms and essences, to motivated, rather than purely arbitrary signs. These appeals attempt to legitimate and naturalize certain meanings or "appropriations" of forms and outlaw others as misappropriations or thefts. Kobena Mercer resorts to just such a strategy in his ground-breaking analysis of black hairstyle politics. He seeks to celebrate the diversity of black hairstyles as testimony to "an inventive, improvisational aesthetic" and as resistance to white cultural norms, a resistance which he asserts need not be founded on the recovery of a black essence or nature (53). The Afro or "natural" was no more an iconic or indexical sign of its referent, African ancestry, than the curly perm, and, as Mercer sees it, both have been effective weapons in the political struggle over the meaning of blackness through their revalorization of "the ethnic signifier" (37). Surprisingly, however, Mercer appeals to the "nature" of black hair when he asserts that only it can be matted into dreadlocks, which is belied by the spread of the style into other racial groups (as happened with cane-rows or braids as well as with African-American and Caribbean music) (40). As he has argued himself, no hairstyle is a natural or iconic signifier of blackness; in fact, the effort to "fix" such signifiers in the nineteenth century was part of a racist science of anthropometry. Nor is there a hairstyle which is indexically bonded to a racial identity, as Mercer suggests cane-rows are. He contends the Afro was readily depoliticized and incorporated into the mainstream because it—like dreads— was the product of an "imaginary Africa" and, as such, caught up in a dualistic logic of opposition to Europe; cane-rows, however, were an expression of a genuine African aesthetic, rather than an African biology (41–42).[5]

Can any counter-hegemonic strategy be radically outside the logic of hegemony it seeks to oppose? Are cane-rows in America really the same as those in Africa, given their different cultural context, even if they look the same—like doubles? Once imported, they are surely as "hybrid" or "creole" a signifier as any other African-American (and American) cultural construct, something an iconic representation of them, like an anthropometric drawing or photograph, cannot convey. Mercer's undoubtedly strategic claim risks reinvoking a notion of history as a reflection of the real composed of a priori timeless essences rather than as a cross-cultural construct which itself constructs the meaning of cross-cultural events. How can one directly access the "real" Africa through its history without "history," a genre whose protocols owe as much to Europe and its codes for story-telling (and producing indexical, cause-effect relations) as do many of the actual events themselves? History as events and characters and as the discourse about them is a creole artifact according to Stuart Hall, one which we continually reconstruct as we reimagine ourselves and our past and future: "[C]ultural identity is not a fixed essence at all, lying unchanged outside history and culture. . . . The past continues to speak to us . . . [but] [i]t is always constructed through memory, fantasy, narrative and myth" (226). Forms cannot be permanently normalized. The object of "love and theft" (Lott), African-American signifiers are themselves subject to the reappropriation from which Mercer at times seems to want to "save" them. Their resignification may be a depoliticization of a style (if such a thing is possible), but it may be simply a different politicization of it, which is not necessarily conservative. "So who, in this postmodern age of semiotic appropriation and counter-creolization, is imitating whom?" Mercer asks, recognizing the two-way traffic in signs whose inevitable doubleness can secure no identity—or identity politics—on a permanent basis (52).[6] When there are no traffic cops or natural signs there can only be reappropriations of contingent signifiers and mimicry of the identities to which they refer as their retroactive origins. The same does not repeat itself without a trace of difference that unsettles the identity of the subject hailed by a name or image (mis)-recognized as the self.

Phallic Identities

Do meaning, identity, and hegemony take place at all, or are they endlessly deferred, in process? Both Hall and Slavoj Žižek express reservations about what they describe as the poststructuralist play of the signifier, which they link to Derridean deconstruction. Perhaps recalling Derrida's analysis of writing as violence, Hall emphasizes the metaphorical "cut" or "arrest" of identity and meaning, "the contingent and arbitrary stop—the necessary and temporal 'break' in the infinite semiosis of language" (230). Whereas Hall describes this cut as "strategic," which may suggest that it is within our control, Žižek, like Lacan, believes it exceeds our consciousness of it and links it to the law by describing it as symptomatic, neurotic, or even perverse: "[T]he fundamental gesture of post-structuralism is to deconstruct every substantial identity. . . . [T]he notion of symptom is the necessary counterpoint to it, the substance of enjoyment, the real kernel around which this signifying interplay is structured" (*Sublime* 72). The cut is made by and sutured through the prohibition of the Other, leaving a scar, the mark of symbolic castration. It determines identity as impersonation, the masquerade or display of what one "has" to offer the other, which is a matter of fetishes—not what one really wants to give, not what the other really wants to get (there is no sexual relation). The phallus functions as the occluded signifier of this lack in both the subject and the Other, setting in motion the displacements and substitutions of desire and the identifications with traits which will make the subject "lovable" and therefore loving. It is the "nodal point" or *point de capiton* which seeks to totalize meaning so that overdetermined, polysemous signifiers become fixed as part of a structured network of (common) sense about the identities of subjects, objects, and acts or aims, policing identities by determining which signs are one's own and which have been stolen. The law tells us what we "really" are and what we "really" have (or can have) by naturalizing the arbitrary name assigned us and legalizing some mimicries, which then appear as the real thing.

Unlike Derrida, Žižek stresses not only the radical contingency of naming but also the fixity and apparent necessity of a name once it has been assigned. He argues that the name is a "rigid designator," in effect a principle of iconicity which ensures identity in difference, a self-sameness beyond all the alterations in content or properties time and circumstances make in a person, thing, or action: "[T]his guaranteeing the identity of an object in all counterfactual situations—through a change of all its descriptive features—is *the retroactive effect of naming itself*: it is the name itself, the signifier, which supports the identity of the object" (*Sublime* 94–95). In Lacanian theory, the rigid designator is the Name-of-the Father (*nom/non du père*), which institutes sexual difference and identity: "It's a boy!" The designation is based on the naturalization of sexual difference in which the penis functions as an analogue sign (iconic and indexical) of the phallus which, as Lacan's description suggests, is (con)fused with it.

> It can be said that this signifier is chosen because it is the most tangible element in the real of sexual copulation, and also the most symbolic . . . since it is equivalent . . . to the (logical) copula. It might also be said that, by virtue of its turgidity, it is the image of the vital flow as it is transmitted in generation. (Ecrits 287)

The god-like creative power of the phallus, which makes human subjects, is attributed to the penis, the element at once "the most tangible" and the most visible (as "the image of the vital flow") in sexual reproduction. Through a slip of the signifier, sexual copulation and the logical copula are rendered equivalent and substitutable, so that the penis and phallus become interchangeable. The tangibility of the penis is displaced onto the phallus, and the predication the latter inaugurates—the process of attribution and substitution that constitute language and subjects—is associated with the penis, which is made the progenitor of life itself as its first predicate. By implication, the woman participates in conception only passively, contributing little more than the lifeless matter (the egg) that is animated by "the vital flow" of active sperm, a rather sexist version of reproduction which was lampooned as early as 1948 by Ruth Herschberger, who narrated a very different "matriarchal" story with a large and powerful egg as heroine (75–84). As Lacan tells it, the penis-phallus is the proper representative of life and death, and so of desire itself. The real is not entirely absent from such a signifier, a "fetish," according to Lacan (*Ecrits* 290), which not only identifies but hierarchizes subjects, since some "really" seem to have what others want. If (heterosexual) men are less able than women to tolerate the lack of satisfaction in the object, which drives them on to other women (like Don Juans) as Lacan asserts, it may be because for the fetishist of the penis the feminine object is more lacking than the masculine, which can beget life—the baby as phallic substitute for the woman suffering from penis envy.

More generally, in a patriarchal culture men have the means to provide the "gifts" which serve as a symbol of the phallus at the anal level which is the "domain of oblativity": "Where one is caught short, where one cannot, as a result of the lack, give what is to be given, one can always give something else. That is why, in his morality, man is inscribed at the anal level. And this is especially true of the materialist" (*Four* 104). The fetish is that ephemeral something in the object, the "shine on the nose" in the case with which Freud opens his essay on the topic, which fascinates the subject. It is a contingent element of the object which comes to signify the "deliberate" gaze the Other seems to make himself in mimicry for the subject's eye, the stain on the picture of his imago which opens the subject to the question of desire: What do you want from me? What do I want from you? But it also fixes the subject with/as a definite answer because mimicry is fetishistic, a disavowal of symbolic castration. The fetishist of the penis allays his anxiety about his own and the Other's lack with a pretense to knowledge about the Other's desire: the M/Other enjoys the Father's gifts, especially the penis as phallus. This axiom of heterosexual "normality" makes the latter a perversion sanctioned by the law, which assimilates woman to man in the name of his "good," which he wishes her to enjoy for the good of civilization itself. If the Father did not have what the M/Other wanted, how could our symbolic, our identities, have any consistency? What would guarantee sexual difference—or any difference, for what other motive could the mother have for turning from her child to someone else for narcissistic satisfaction, enabling the child's differentiation into a separate subject?

The anxiety these questions provoke results in the sometimes hysterical

disavowal by (generally male) psychoanalytic theorists of the difference between the phallus and the penis.[7] Like the patient of Freud who "pressed her
dress to her body with one hand (as the woman) while trying to tear it off with
the other (as the man)" ("Hysterical" 151), they remind us that the penis is not
the phallus while insisting that it is especially well suited to play the part. If
perversions contain a kernel of neurosis, as Elizabeth Grosz suggests Freud
believed by the time he wrote "A Child Is Being Beaten" ("Lesbian" 53n3), then
hysterical bisexuality could be a symptom of the "civilized" fetishist's desire as
a continuing question about the name of the rigid designator. What am I? Do I
have the means to be the cause of the Other's desire or am I passing? If gender
as masquerade or parade is fetishistic transvestism, as we can conclude from a
careful reading of Lacan, perhaps it is also hysteria. Lacan and Wladimir
Granoff seem to rule this out in their discussion of fetishism, implying that
there is a radical disjunction between fetishism and neurosis. Because Freud
defines neuroses (like hysteria) as the negative of perversions (*Three* 31), we
might expect fetishism to have a neurotic analogue, yet Lacan and Granoff
assert there is no such thing (265). However, Freud himself suggests there is a
neurosis within, and not just parallel to, fetishism. He notes that the fetishist
does not simply scotomize the traumatic sight of castration like a psychotic, but
represses it, like a neurotic ("Fetishism" 215–16). He also describes the fetish,
like the neurotic symptom, as a compromise formation, contrasting the perversion with psychosis, in which "the true idea which accorded with reality would
have been *really* absent" ("Fetishism" 218). Curiously, what is repressed seems
to return in the real for at least some fetishists, albeit in disguised form; there
is an element of psychotic hallucination or "mirage" in the distinction between
women with and without shiny noses, for instance. The consistency or identity
of things has an imaginary and psychotic, as well as symbolic, dimension—in
fact, according to Lacan, human knowledge itself is paranoid in form (*Ecrits*
17). It seems Lacan must remain ignorant of the neurotic and psychotic
dimension of fetishism if his fetish, the penis, is to "work" as the phallus or
support of patriarchal identities. To accept that the penis is only a signifier for
an occluded signifier is to acknowledge that the genital organ of "normal
sexuality" is in fact the hystericized site of an inherently displaced sexuality,
which is what actually follows from Lacan's description of desire as hysterical
in structure, as the desire of the other. This hysteria is normalized through the
psychotic (mis)recognition of the penis as the phallus in a fetishism sanctioned

by the law of the rigid designator. No one has the phallus any more than a shiny nose, but in our patriarchal culture the man's "theft" of it goes unreported.

These issues of theft, psychosis, and the consistency of sexual identity were the implicit focus of a recent Jerry Springer talk show which featured Shawn, a female-to-male transsexual (originally "named" Tanya) who was not yet taking male hormones and had not made any plans for surgery. "I have always felt like a boy," Shawn insisted at the beginning of the program, a statement typical of transsexuals, who have had to affirm this in order to be eligible for surgery whether or not it is true. Jerry Springer's response was to declare that assertion meaningless since Shawn was *not* a boy. In an implicit appeal to the rigid designator, Springer explained that whatever he did and felt must be what a man did and felt because he *was* a man. As far as Springer was concerned masculine identity had no content—there were no iconic or indexical signs of it—aside from the rigid designator itself. Sex was therefore completely arbitrary and absolutely fixed, not amenable to social (and surgical) reconstruction after its initial construction. This sentiment was seconded by an apparently male audience member who sought to show the absurdity of Shawn's claim by asking, "What if I said I have always felt like a snake?" Yet another man in the audience told Shawn he was depriving men of two good women (Shawn appeared on the show with his girlfriend) and alluded to the satisfactions only a real penis could provide. In reply, Shawn resorted to the now classic line of feminists and sex-therapists that bigger is not necessarily better, a recognition that "[w]here [*sic*] one is caught short, where one cannot, as a result of the lack, give what is to be given, one can always give something else" (*Four* 104). For Shawn, the designator was not so rigid; he simply reappropriated it for his "nub," as he called it. It could substitute for the penis, which also comes up short when measured against the phallus.

The fetishist only believes in *his* fetish; what works for one fetishist will not always work for another, as is suggested by the history of the realist fetish— nothing looks more phoney to undergraduate film students today than the classic Hollywood cinema (they believe in Industrial Light and Magic instead). Shawn was not going to convert to apostasy the disciples of the patriarchal rigid designator. Such conversions are not a matter of rational persuasion in any case but of transference, which, as Žižek explains, "consists of the illusion that the meaning of a certain element (which was retroactively fixed by the intervention of the master-signifier) was present in it from the very beginning as its immanent essence" (*Sublime* 102). Shawn still believes in sexual difference; however, the phallus no longer looks like a penis to him, unless it is a penis seen through an anamorphic lens, so that it resembles a "nub." What Žižek calls the "rock of castration," the "peter" (*petrus*) upon which psychoanalysis has built its faith, is shifted ever so slightly; from a certain angle it can appear as a pebble or nub (*Sublime* 50).

Phallocentrism is "Not-All"

Žižek provides several examples of the logic of what he calls "not-all," the paradox of the non-totalized totality which governs any ideological or symbolic discourse because there is always something (real) which exceeds it, which slips through the signifying net as its "outside." Churchill's famous statement about democracy is one instance of this: "It is true that democracy is the worst of all possible systems; the problem is that no other system would be better!" (qtd. in *Looking* 28). Can the same be said of phallocentric psychoanalysis? Is phallocentrism all there is to it—or is it "not-all"? Is there something more to psychoanalysis, in excess of its apparent (hetero)sexism, which might help us overcome our own narcissism and do justice to difference? Is psychoanalysis part of the cure or is it the disease itself? To date, those in lesbian and gay or queer studies have been more skeptical of its possibilities than feminists have been, although feminists are not exactly defenders of the faith. Feminist interest in psychoanalysis grew from its systematic attention to sexual difference, which other radical critical programs like Marxism had not made central. Gender is often in danger of being ignored as a significant difference within theories and activisms which seek to construct a community of adherents who share identities and a commitment to a single "master signifier"—whether it is class, race, or sexuality—as that which can explain everything (the inverse is also true, and in recent years feminism has focused intensively on "differences within"). As long as gender still matters, phallocentrism has not been "fixed," neutered, or neutralized.

What feminists have found most useful about psychoanalysis, however, is the notion of the unconscious, which calls into question the conclusions of every empiricist, realist theory based on a faith in the self as the ego, the system of rational perception-consciousness. According to psychoanalysis, identities and demands are not "implanted" and "incorporated" (to use Foucault's terms) without a remainder of repressed desire which troubles them. As Freud notes, "[A]ll human beings are capable of making a homosexual object-choice and have in fact made one in their unconscious" (*Three* 11, 1915 note). However, the inverse is also true; for Freud, the fixity of any object choice is the effect of narcissistic ego defences since initially the subject ranges equally over female and male objects. The community of signifying clones whose identities are clear, communications transparent, and desires identical is therefore a fantasy based on the repression of differences within both the self and the community. The value of the concept of symbolic castration is its insistence on the impossibility of narcissism, especially in self-other relations. There is always something missing in the meeting with the other who is necessary to the constitution of the self, which makes for the lack of a social or sexual relation and a subversion of self-satisfied narcissism.

If psychoanalysis has stressed the difficulty of identity and desire as "love" (the narcissistic object choice which never quite seems to secure the sexual relation), it also seeks to account for their symptomatic fixity, what could be described as the difficulty of non-identity and desire without love. The "poststructuralization" of lesbian and gay or queer identities and desires, as Žižek might phrase it, expresses our wish for a paradoxical fixity of unfixity, a pure enunciation of a non-identity which would not pass through the statement(s) of it, whose objects would not narcissistically support it. This may account in part for the preference in queer studies for Foucauldian approaches. Foucault seems to imagine a subject who is fully conscious, in control of his signifers when he represents himself and others, an illusion Gayatri Spivak has criticized as that of the "transparent intellectual" ("Can" 271–80). Furthermore, while Foucault takes issue with "the repressive hypothesis" about sexuality, insisting that the latter is not repressed but produced (via its "implantation"), he nevertheless describes it at least some of the time as the effect of a restriction of "the free choice of indeterminate individuals" (viii), a theory which helps support a problematic utopic politics of liberation as a return to a golden age or stage of "development," the founding nature or pre-cultural origin of humanity before the "fall" into human history and identities. In his introduction to the memoirs of the nineteenth-century hermaphrodite Herculine Barbin, for example, Foucault argues that until the doctors and the state imposed one on him/her, Barbin never had a definite sex. Instead, s/he experienced "the happy limbo of a non-identity" that allowed for a proliferation of pleasures and a dispersal of bodily functions and meanings which are unified and hierarchized by such sexual discourses as psychoanalysis (xiii).

As Butler trenchantly observes, Foucault's analysis seems to indulge in the very essentialism he critiques, imagining that there is a sexuality before the law, which would repress it rather than produce it, so that it could be "liberated" in hermaphroditism. Butler very persuasively demonstrates that Barbin's sexuality is actually constituted and regulated by various narratives, including romantic/sentimental stories of impossible loves and Christian legends about the lives of the saints (*Gender* 98–99). Because his/her pleasures are always already generated by the law(s) they are said to defy, "[t]he temptation to romanticize Herculine's sexuality as the utopian play of pleasures prior to the imposition and restrictions of 'sex' surely ought to be refused" (*Gender* 98). Butler suggests that Barbin is really a lesbian whose sexuality recapitulates the ambivalence of its construction: the demands of a double-bind (the doubling and splitting of demand which creates desire) to love and not to love her "sisters" and "mothers" at the various convent schools in which she grows up (*Gender* 98–100). Foucault hints at this, Butler says, but ultimately makes Barbin's sexuality the effect of a non-identity, rather than feminine identities, because he wants to reject sex altogether (*Gender* 100–01). Rather than leave him at home in his uncanny error, having retraced a path to the naive essentialism and celebration of sexual liberation he thought to bypass, Butler provides Foucault with a canny intention which would save him from his own desire to *lack* a lack of sexual identity. She "outs" him, turning his reading of Herculine into a writing, in the Derridean sense, of coming out in which he affirms his and other gay identities as "non-identities" by signing himself not with his "proper" name but with the name of the hermaphrodite whose memoirs then become his own (*Gender* 101–02). Her Foucault must come out in drag because Butler believes homosexual contexts produce sexual non-identity (*Gender* 123). She represents him as simulating a hermaphroditic identity which is a non-identity, a "poststructuralist" mimicry, currently *the* sign of the refusal of identity, the antiessentialist double of coming out which, like the latter, is presumed to unmask the face of resistance disguised by passing.

This notion of mimicry received perhaps its first poststructuralist formulation by Luce Irigaray. The mimic, she writes, "must assume the feminine role deliberately. Which means already to convert a form of subordination into an affirmation, and thus to begin to thwart it" (*This Sex* 76). Irigaray's phrasing in this passage suggests not mimicry but a reverse discourse; she seems to urge women to "come out" as women, to take on the identity they have already been assigned. However, she goes on to emphasize not *taking it on* but *putting it on* so as to display it as a put-on, a fake rather than the natural or real thing. The mimic resubmits herself to masculinist ideas about the femininine, Irigaray asserts, but "so as to make 'visible,' by an effect of playful repetition, what was supposed to remain invisible: the cover-up of a possible operation of the feminine in language" (*This Sex* 76). Hers is a femininity under the sign of ironic negation; the woman is not what she appears to be, not where she appears to be. For, as Irigaray adds, mimicry points to the "elsewhere" which is the "real" location of woman even as she seems to be in her usual place (*This Sex* 76). If coming out functions as an iconic sign of difference, mimicry functions as an index of it, gesturing toward it in symptomatic fashion and maintaining a certain contiguity with it. Something of "real" difference seems to cling to the difference conventionally associated with femininity, as Irigaray's momentary confusion of coming out and mimicry implies.

In fact, it is not momentary but systematic. For Irigaray, mimicry is in effect a reappropriation of femininity to which woman is not resigned but which she re-signs, revalorizing it because it represents another way of relating to the self, to others, and to language—a real alternative to masculine subjectivity and phallocentric desire. The dilemma facing woman is not unlike the dilemma facing the postcolonial subject as outlined by Albert Memmi. The colonized can strive to become like the colonizer through assimilation, refashioning himself as a "mimic man." But such mimicry exacts a high price, the rejection of the self, and in any case proves impossible because it is disallowed by the colonial situtation, which demands a difference so as to enable exploitation (120–27). The mimic man is finally just that, "not quite not white," in Bhabha's memorable phrase ("Mimicry" 132). Alternatively, the colonized can attempt to reconquer what colonization took away, embracing those differences left to him, even delegated to him—a past, traditions, and beliefs no longer available in a pure form, if they are available at all (Memmi 127–39). In effect, he "goes native," mimicking what (the colonizer thought) he once was, not quite passing as the real thing because "not quite not white." Mimicry, like coming out, is not quite not passing, not quite not different from its uncanny double. The past which the "colonized" woman is supposed by Irigaray and others to recover is the prehistory of the (masculine) subject of the symbolic, the pre-Oedipality which is the retroactive effect of the castration and Oedipal complexes, and a mythic matriarchy as the golden age before patriarchy which had as its law the mother's enjoyment rather than the father's.[8]

What makes the difference—the visible difference for which Irigaray

calls—between mimicking and "being"—or passing as—a woman? Most theorists have relied on conscious intentions as the guarantee of ironic effects, as
Irigaray does when she speaks of a "playful" or "deliberate" repetition (*This Sex*
76). However, irony, like anxiety, is a subjective thing, an *e*ffect of *a*ffect, in the
mind of the beholder. The attempt to "fix" mimicry is an effort to heal the split
in its discursive address, disavowing the differences between women. In
mimicry the "other" woman is fetishized as a subject presumed to know about
the self-difference signified by her style, with which the white, middle-class
woman "plays" so as to display her own ironic dis-identification from femininity. For her, the other woman's femininity could only ever be a mimicry of
genuine femininity, "unnatural," a sign of a self-conscious dis-identification,
even when such a woman simply wants to pass as feminine. The white, middle-
class woman preserves her belief in her identity, naturalizing it as the real thing
by delegating disbelief to her "others," which she performs for them by
mimicking their styles. So long as she is not quite not the other woman, she is
lacking nothing—not even lack—just as Foucault is lacking nothing so long as
he is not quite not a hermaphrodite.

Like coming out, mimicry ultimately represents a desire for a natural
sign. Paradoxically, it achieves its truth-effects not through realism but modernism, which is supposed to foreground contradiction and irony through such
techniques as montage. Something of the "real" of contradiction is not lost for
the fetishist of the modernist sign, for whom realism is a successful cover-up of
it. On the one hand, the fragmentation and disjunction of the modernist object
are theorized as if the latter simply mirrored the truth of reality, like an iconic
sign. On the other, that object is said to cause and be caused by a fragmentary
and disjunctive modernity, including the modern subject himself, an indexical
(both symptomatic and constitutive) relation. Modernism's effects are discussed as unified because its objects are not, the obverse of realism, whose
effects are critiqued as unified because its objects are too. However, as Lacan
explains, the realist picture inevitably has a stain, like the anamorphic skull in
Holbein's famous painting *The Ambassadors*, which speaks of death and desire,
subverting empiricism and its imaginary subject, whose representations can
never confirm his narcissistic wholeness. The modernist picture of the self as
the good object also would have such a stain. Since self-difference and
jouissance are now valorized—at least in academia—the attributes idealized
and appropriated by the (scholarly) ego are no longer quite what they were. To

appear to have the phallus has become the mark of lack in what is an inverted economy of sexual—and other—differences, as Jane Gallop suggests when she notes that being antiphallic has become the new phallus for postmodernist male critics, who once again find women and feminism lacking (*Thinking* 100). But in an earlier essay, Gallop makes a similar argument about postmodernist feminist women. If *jouissance* is defined as "a loss of self, disruption of comfort, loss of control," then "it cannot simply be claimed as an ego-gratifying identity, but must also frighten those who 'know' it." When it "becomes a banner and a badge for French feminine writing, the accompanying fear or unworthiness is projected outward and we—militant and bold—lose the ambiguous link to fear and emotion, which are catapulted beyond the *jouissance* principle . . . " ("Beyond" 114). This is exactly the sort of "defeat and overthrow of one sovereignty" and "emergence and consolidation of an antithetical sovereignty" of which Radhakrishnan has been critical (208). In effect, the feminists Gallop describes are phallic women, misrecognizing a "hole" as whole in the obverse of the masculinist misrecognition of difference as castration. Their "nothing" to see is something to show the Other. They expose his lack in an exhibitionist gesture of intimidation, flaunting the goods he wants: the signifier of self-difference they "have" ("two lips," etc.).

However, the subject never sees nor shows what is desired. Something is always missing in the picture and, therefore, in the relationship with the Other, with whom there cannot be a self-affirming reciprocity. The Other may not recognize the self-difference which must be "right before his eyes" because we *intended* him to see it. The masquerade then does not appear as such, despite the best of intentions; the Other passes over our ironic refusal of identity, passing us against our will; we are photo-graphed for an ID. Even the (post)modernist picture we make of ourselves in mimicry cannot guarantee its effects. Any object, including a (post)modernist object like the queer ego, must have some principle of coherence if it is to be recognized as an object or whole (*gestalt*) at all, but that principle is necessarily in the eye of the beholder—like the fetish. It is just such a fetishism which leads Butler to repeat in uncanny fashion the gesture she points to in Foucault. "Herculine's anatomy does not fall outside the categories of sex," she writes, "but confuses and redistributes the constitutive elements of those categories. Indeed, the free play of attributes has the effect of *exposing* the illusory character of sex . . . " (*Gender* 101, emphasis added). If her Foucault must come out in drag, as a hermaphrodite, it is because for her as well as for Foucault hermaphrodites are obviously female imperson-ators—through a (post)modernist pastiche which is "natural" to them and legible to all. Theirs could only ever be a mimicry of genuine femininity, regardless of a desire to pass, which Barbin expresses throughout most of the memoirs (first as a woman, then as a man), or the fact of passing, as Barbin did for many years (even Sara, her lover, initially saw her as a woman). Ironically, Butler preserves gay identity by fetishistically disavowing the differences between gays and hermaphrodites. A would-be antiessentialist, she delegates disbelief to hermaphrodites, which her gay subjects—like Foucault—perform for them by mimicking their "style." This is the narcissistic fantasy behind Butler's assertion that lesbian butch-femme roles are "obviously" transgres-sive (*Gender* 123–24). It at once supports and subverts a belief in a non-phallocentric lesbian essence as a self-identical non-identity whose self-difference makes it whole and therefore phallic once again. It is our desire for an essence, and a proper name which would express and expose it, that generates this fetishistic and transvestic play with masking and unmasking at the heart of both mimicry and coming out, which throws our identities *en abîme*—or in the closet, where the phallus still rattles like a bone.

Passing Is "Not-All"

The fetishist is not quite not ignorant of differences, responding to them with the anxiety of passing. When neither the self nor the group with which one identifies is homogeneous and unified, one may find oneself and not the other in the closet, passing from one identity to another over which one has no mastery, not quite not fixing difference, not quite not resisting hegemony. The phallus as the signifier of lack and desire can account for these narcissistic effects, including the hierarchies in which they are caught up, when it "ap-pears" as the fetish. The fetish is invested in as the "real" of identity and the sexual relation, which is always a social relation involving more than just gender signs, since we are never simply men or women but men or women of a particular race, class, ethnicity, etc., marked as lacking by these signs as well. As Freud notes, perversions (such as fetishism) are difficult to cure; this is because they mimic the "norm," taking the form of an ethical injunction or law which situates the subject within but also beyond the pleasure principle.[9] For that reason some Lacanians see perversion *as* the norm, with neurosis the symptom in need of a cure.[10]

How can one tell the "real" law from its perverse double? Žižek emphasizes that we recognize the difference between them because transference and the love of the Other supposed to know has always already happened. We cannot be reasoned with about the law—it is always already persuasive. Nevertheless, there are hysteric and psychotic components to the fetishistic phallic (mis)recognitions the patriarchal law institutes which may move the "rock" of castration, in effect disseminating the phallus. That process begins with the hysterical question to the Other: "Why am I what I'm *supposed* to be, why have I this mandate?" (*Sublime* 113, emphasis added). It may conclude with a refusal to answer it "correctly" and accept the law of identity, retroactively suturing identity differently, as the subject, like a psychotic, begins seeing things that others cannot, such as the phallic woman. The phallus may well be the stain on the picture of psychoanalysis, but only because it does not always appear as the penis or just as the penis, which is the fetishistic substitute for it naturalized by patriarchal law. Its symbolic self-identity is the effect of a single trait: size. It is size which makes the "nub" so hard to see in patriarchy that it can only appear as a hole. The size fetish also fuels fantasies about the over- or under-endowment of men of certain races, ethnicities, and classes— evidence that men can suffer from penis envy. It is the fantasmatic other who is never "caught short"; his penis is always just the right size to enable real enjoyment.

There is something beyond the penis in the phallus, which drives signification. Carolyn Steedman recognizes this when she demonstrates how the working-class penis can be missing that something the M/Other desires which makes the Father's name law. Bhabha also seeks to articulate that "something" through his analyses of racial stereotypes as fetishes ("Other"). Butler therefore is right to be critical of Žižek's effort to stabilize the law of patriarchy, which like all laws is inherently unstable (*Bodies* 196–97). In patriarchy, the penis is "the answer of the real" to the psychotic question about desire, a contingent signifier which comes to function as a fetish, keeping the question open even as it also seems to answer it. Because castration is about a certain impossibility of narcissism in self-other relations, it cannot be dismissed as just a (hetero)sexist investment in Oedipality. There is always something missing in the meeting with the Other which makes for the lack of a social or sexual relation, a missed encounter or encounter with what is missing, with the real (*tuch*) of lack, the subject's ineluctable misfortune; it constitutes every relationship as a *dustuchia* (Lacan, *Four* 80, 245). This lack is behind and beyond the symbolic *automaton* and repeats in and as the subversion of each *eutuchia* or fortunate encounter to which we would be returned through signs and the substitutions governed by the pleasure and reality principles. The penis is not the phallus—what it lacks must be supplemented by other (commodity) fetishes we offer the Other in the effort to secure his/her enjoyment, such as a baby. According to Freud, both boys and girls wish to give one to—and get one from—the M/Other. They are not yet law-abiding citizens, adults "secure" in their proper identities and "gifts," their different properties—their difference itself ("Sexual" 34; "Femininity" 106). Nevertheless, they already understand the anal economy of exchange which makes signification possible, even if no substitutions have been ruled out or fixed for them.

Beyond and between and within them is their *différance*, that difference which has not yet been caught in the signifying network but which leaves its trace there as lack, a "hole" which takes on a certain shape and size, however ephemeral, through what it is not. It is a sign of the injustice of the patriarchal law. When Žižek asserts that there is no homeostasis, no natural balance to which sexual relations, social relations, or even ecological relations could be restored, he reminds us of the fundamental impossibility of justice, of an absolutely just relationship within the law (*Looking* 38). True reciprocity always appears to be lacking because of lack itself; we inevitably feel the Other has deprived us of what we want, including recognition of our identity. There are no just relationships—just relationships, which seem more or less unfulfilling. Yet the desire for justice remains strong and is expressed not only by a Don Juan–like compulsive changing of objects but also by the criminal "reappropriation" of fetishistic signifiers by subcultures (and, eventually, hegemonic culture itself). "Caught short" because short-changed, one can also resort to theft.

Such kleptomania, which psychoanalysis understands as the "feminine" analogue to fetishism, is testimony to a desire to pervert the law of identity and fashion a different symbolic coherence, one which might successfully suture the self and social relation. It is the stake in what sometimes seems the psychotic effort to make the body visibly different by patching it with stolen bits and pieces. The fantasy these fetishistic signifiers have been ripped from the body of the other, leaving a gaping hole, is imaginary, since the body's wholeness is an imaginary *gestalt*, but as it is sanctioned by the law, it is "realistic." The perverse law that counters the norm expresses the subject's feeling that first something was taken by force from him—as Frantz Fanon implies, his "full" humanity, his "right" to enjoyment, his "real" being—a theft the law does not recognize as such, having legislated it. The counter-law cannot restore that lost wholeness, which is fantasmatic. It too is unjust; lack remains—but with a new "look," as it is reconfigured by subcultural civil disobedience in the name of a "perverse" civic code. Another ideal of justice arises as a new law's *différance*, passing through the hole it leaves in the signifying network which has been knotted differently by another phallic fetish. For the castration complex has the function of a knot, Lacan says, punning on the French slang for penis (*noeud*), which sounds like "no" (*non*) (*Ecrits* 281). The penis is (k)not the phallus, even if it passes as it in a patriarchal culture, which means that the heralding of the passing of the castration complex in any community is a matter of mimicry rather than an effect of a death sentence.

We have to be careful when we act as judges in such criminal matters. What notion of justice animates our accusations of the theft of the signs of an identity, whether our own or the other's? Are we trying to protect imaginary phallic wholeness or *différance*? Do we serve the law or justice, narcissistic love or desire? What use are we sanctioned to make of what are ultimately always the Other's signs? Are Herculine Barbin's signifiers finally private or public property? What "appropriations" of them should lead to an "arrest"—or meaningful sentence? These are the kinds of questions with which ideological criticism traditionally has struggled because, like psychoanalysis, it assumes that there is something problematic about desire, unlike theories of desire as a pure productivity. For ideological criticism that problem is the split between desires and interests, as Spivak makes clear: we can desire against the best interests of others, but more importantly, we can desire against our own best interests ("Can" 275–79). Who can know what is in our best interests if there are no "transparent intellectuals"? Only the Other of transference, according to psychoanalysis, who always already is "supposed to know" what we want if we are in a transferential relationship with him or her. The ideological critic plays the role of the analyst who is—or "will have been"—this Other for the analysand, if the latter is persuaded by such a critic that the truth of his desire is not what he thought it was. Reasons are only persuasive for those who through transference are convinced in advance of the truth they support.

For psychoanalysis, on the other hand, the problem is the split between desire and love. Desire is always for what is against one's interests since it is beyond the (ultimately impossible) "just" balance of the reality and pleasure principles which is the zone of love and imaginary reciprocity. The psychoanalytic critique of interests in the name of desire may well reinscribe the law, however, incidentally affirming the narcissism and interests of those whose fetishes pass as the real thing. The Name of the Father sanctions the misrecognition of the penis as the phallus, as if it were a natural sign of the lack — or presence — of the latter. A contingent signifier, the penis as fetish is invested with a certainty that makes the patriarchal law seem necessary and inevitable. But the penis is only one answer of the real to the question of the M/Other's desire; other answers are possible which would be equally (in)effective in ending the anxiety about it. Fetishism situates the subject somewhere between the imaginary and the symbolic (Lacan and Granoff 272). However, we cannot long inhabit any other space but that borderland which, as the site of the projection of our fantasies, screens us from the twilight zone of the real. "Reality" is only an ideological fantasy which masks the truth of the real as the pure death drive. The latter can explode in the psychotic outburst of revolutionary violence against others, as described by Fanon (*Wretched* 35–106) and Julia Kristeva (199–205), or it can be turned against the self in suicide, as happened with Barbin. Unable to be a woman or a man, Barbin became, as s/he says, an "angel," "whose earthly ties to humanity have been broken" (*Herculine* 99). What was a dream of non-identity for Foucault and ultimately for Butler as well was a nightmare for Barbin; when s/he truly became a hermaphrodite, s/he discovered there was no role as a living being for such a creature.

Once our analysis is finished, we are left with a pure desire we are not supposed to renounce (Žižek, *Sublime* 124–29). Acting on this desire, we would cease to try to supplement the lack in the Other with our love because we would recognize we do not have and can never even know what the Other wants — nor does the Other (there is no Other of the Other). We would see that we have been playing a game of mimicry whose stake is life itself, since the mask is our identity. Beyond it there is the nothing from which we must screen ourselves if we are to go on living. Fantasy is that screen which preserves us from desire as the pure death drive. It is, in effect, the latter's difference from itself, the "life drive" as a synthesizing, unifying aspect of libido which, according to Jean Laplanche, was Freud's real discovery in the years leading up to the writing of

Beyond the Pleasure Principle (*New* 146). Ultimately, the imaginary narcissism of fantasy is what binds together the three orders in Lacan's Borromean knot (if any one loop is cut, the whole thing falls apart). We are that knot, an unstable coherence whose principle is the perverse law of which the norm is just a variant, at once imaginary and symbolic. Beyond it there are only bits and pieces, the traits or differences of the symbolic, and the light which seems to reflect off them in the otherwise impenetrable fog of the real as twilight zone.

The imaginary is "(k)not-all," the best and worst thing of its kind. If we are to avoid autism, we cannot do without its iconic and indexical illusions as the possibility of resemblance, coherence, and an existential link to our surroundings, including our image of ourselves and our objects or others. We cannot live (quite literally) without its narcissism, the erotic cathexis of an ideal image of the self, and the deflection outward, onto others, of a portion of the self-critical aggressivity of the death drive. In both cases, there is a disavowal of difference, as the other is assimilated by the self which is so confused with it we might well argue the self is assimilated by the other, which calls its identity into question. There can be no just balance of ego libido and object libido, eros and thanatos, narcissism and aggression, respect for the self and for the other—and, therefore, of ideological and psychoanalytic critiques. That lack of balance, the trace of an ineradicable injustice, unsettles any law and the status quo it serves, which is why for both Freud and Lacan the repetition compulsion is not about the return of (or to) the same, but the recurring encounter with a traumatic lack of identity and similarity, the enigma of desire which is the result of our difference from others and even our self. We cannot master resistance, but it happens nonetheless. Yet we cannot cease to try to master it, since that narcissism is the life force which binds us to the world around us, including others and our "self," which ineluctably remains an other.

Should we condemn as narcissistic and imaginary Butler's theft of Barbin's difference, which she appropriates for a gay identity? Undoubtedly, it is both; nevertheless, that is "not all" there is to it. Barbin represents for Butler—and Foucault—an "other" identity beyond those the law legislates, one which does not yet really exist. Neither male nor female, straight nor gay, their Barbin is a fantasy self patched together from bits and pieces of different bodies, aims, and pleasures which already exist. S/he is an "other" identity, a different "self," like the butterfly with which Choang-tsu, the popularizer of philosophical Taoism, identifies in his well-known dream discussed by Lacan

(*Four* 75–76). Has Choang-tsu netted the butterfly or has it flown off with him? According to Lacan, as long as Choang-tsu can reflect on whether he is a man dreaming he is a butterfly or a butterfly dreaming he is a man, he is not mad (*Four* 76). Neither the one nor the other, he knows he is only *passing* through the signifier—on his way to something else that remains an open possibility.

I would like to thank Diana Fuss, Parama Roy, and Kathleen McHugh for their invaluable comments on an earlier draft of this essay.

Notes

1   See Ch. VII on "Identification" in *Group Psychology and the Analysis of the Ego*, in which Freud explains the mechanisms of group dynamics he believes to be correctly described but not accounted for in the work of his predecessors, primarily Le Bon's *The Crowd: A Study of the Popular Mind* and McDougall's *The Group Mind* (which he discusses in earlier chapters).

2   The icon and the index are, for Charles Sanders Peirce, the two types of signs which are motivated, rather than purely arbitrary, in their relation to the referent (Saussure had only one class of such signs, the symbol). An iconic sign is supposed to resemble its referent, like a picture, diagram, or onomatopoeia. An indexical sign is supposed to be existentially bound to its referent, with which it is physically contiguous (as when a part substitutes for the whole) or causally connected (as with symptoms, outcomes, or antecedents).

3   John Ellis argues that this is true of both photography and film (58). Barthes himself makes a distinction between the phenomenology of photography and of cinema, which combines the actor's "this has been" with the role's and denies the pose (and the confusion of life and death) through animation (78–79). However, he does say, "I can never see or see again in a film certain actors whom I know to be dead without a kind of melancholy; the melancholy of Photography itself (I experience this same emotion listening to the recorded voices of dead singers)" (79).

4   Spivak is more critical of "strategic essentialism" in a later interview; see "In a Word."

5   For Mercer, this might partially explain the reappropriation of dreads by other subcultures, although if it is an iconic sign of blackness the style should not be subject to such theft.

6   For a discussion of just how complex creolization is in the global context of the multi-

directional "flow" of people, finance capital, ideas, and mass media images and sounds, see Appadurai.

7   See, for example, Boothby. He asserts that what is at stake is a symbolic function, like a differential feature in linguistics, but then argues that the penis is particularly "well-suited" for the job because "even in the male alone . . . [it] embodies a principle of difference in its alternance of flaccidness and erection" and *"aside from the mother's breasts* . . . is the only bodily appendage unsupported by bone and the only appendage incapable of voluntary movement" (153, emphasis added). Because he never explains this "aside," we are left to draw our own conclusions about why breasts cannot function as the *rigid* designator in our culture.

8   I have expanded on this argument in a chapter in the forthcoming book from which this essay is drawn, "Female Impersonation." For a published discussion of the politics of Irigarayan mimicry, see my essay, "The Feminine Look," which also references some of the growing body of material on this topic. One passage in which Irigaray is quite clear about the myth-making in which she is engaged is *Sexes* 118–22.

9   Kaja Silverman has demonstrated this of masochism; see chapters 5 and 6 of *Male Subjectivity at the Margins.*

10   See, for example, Samuels. He maps psychosis, neurosis, and perversion onto the Lacanian real, imaginary, and symbolic. These correspond to being-in-itself or primary narcissism (autism), being-for-itself or narcissism, and being-for-others or anaclisis, in which the subject has no relationship with the other, relates to the other as an alter ego, or desires a relation with the Other of language and the law (55). I have argued in this essay that the norm is not only perverse but also neurotic.

Works Cited

Althusser, Louis. *Lenin and Philosophy and Other Essays.* Trans. Ben Brewster. New York: Monthly Review, 1971.

Appadurai, Arjun. "Disjuncture and Difference in the Global Cultural Economy." *Colonial Discourse and Post-colonial Theory: A Reader.* Ed. Patrick Williams and Laura Chrisman. New York: Columbia UP, 1994. 324–39.

Barbin, Herculine. *Herculine Barbin: Being the Recently Discovered Memoirs of a Nineteenth-Century French Hermaphrodite.* 1978. Trans. Richard McDougall. Introd. Michel Foucault. New York: Pantheon, 1980.

Barthes, Roland. *Camera Lucida: Reflections on Photography.* Trans. Richard Howard. New York: Hill and Wang, 1981.

Bazin, André. *What Is Cinema?* 1959, 1960. Ed. and trans. Hugh Gray. Berkeley: U of California P, 1967.

Benhabib, Seyla. "The Generalized and the Concrete Other: The Kohlberg-Gilligan Controversy and Feminist Theory." *Feminism as Critique.* Ed. Seyla Benhabib and Drucilla Cornell. Minneapolis: U of Minnesota P, 1987. 77–95.

Benston, Kimberly. "I Yam What I Am: The Topos of (Un)naming in Afro-American Literature." *Black Literature and Literary Theory.* Ed. Henry Louis Gates, Jr. New York: Methuen, 1984. 151–72.

Berlant, Lauren, and Elizabeth Freeman. "Queer Nationality." *Fear of a Queer Planet: Queer Politics and Social Theory.* Ed. Michael Warner. Minneapolis: U of Minnesota P, 1993. 193–229.

Bhabha, Homi. "Of Mimicry and Man: The Ambivalence of Colonial Discourse." *October* 28 (1984): 125–133.

——. "The Other Question: Difference, Discrimination and the Discourse of Colonialism." *Literature, Politics, and Theory: Papers from the Essex Conference, 1976–1984.* Ed. Francis Barker, Peter Hulme, Margaret Iversen, Diana Loxley. New York: Methuen, 1985. 148–72.

Boothby, Richard. *Death and Desire: Psychoanalytic Theory in Lacan's Return to Freud.* New York: Routledge, 1991.

Butler, Judith. *Bodies That Matter: On the Discursive Limits of "Sex."* New York: Routledge, 1993.

——. *Gender Trouble: Feminism and the Subversion of Identity.* New York: Routledge, 1990.

Derrida, Jacques. *Of Grammatology.* 1967. Trans. Gayatri Spivak. Baltimore: Johns Hopkins UP, 1976.

Eco, Umberto. *A Theory of Semiotics.* Bloomington: Indiana UP, 1979.

Ellis, John. *Visible Fictions: Cinema, Television, Video.* 1982. New York: Routledge, 1992.

Fanon, Frantz. *Black Skin, White Masks.* 1952. Trans. Charles Markmann. New York: Grove, 1967.

——. *Wretched of the Earth*. 1961. Trans. Constance Farrington. New York: Grove, 1963.

Foucault, Michel. *The History of Sexuality: An Introduction*. Trans. Robert Hurley. New York: Pantheon, 1978. Vol. 1 of *The History of Sexuality*. 3 vols. 1978–86.

——. Introduction. Barbin vii–xvii.

Freud, Sigmund. *Civilization and Its Discontents*. 1930. Ed. and trans. James Strachey. New York: Norton, 1961.

——. "Femininity." *New Introductory Lectures on Psychoanalysis*. 1933. Ed. and trans. James Strachey. New York: Norton, 1965. 99–119.

——. "Fetishism." 1927. Trans. Joan Riviere. *Sexuality and the Psychology of Love*. Ed. Philip Rieff. New York: Collier, 1963. 214–219.

——. *Group Psychology and the Analysis of the Ego*. 1921. Ed. and trans. James Strachey. New York: Norton, 1959.

——. "Hysterical Phantasies and Their Relation to Bisexuality." 1908. Trans. Douglas Bryan. *Dora: An Analysis of a Case of Hysteria*. Ed. Philip Rieff. New York: Collier, 1963. 145–152.

——. *The Interpretation of Dreams*. Trans. James Strachey. New York: Avon Books, 1965.

——. "On the Sexual Theories of Children." 1908. Trans. Douglas Bryan. *The Sexual Enlightenment of Children*. Ed. Philip Rieff. New York: Collier, 1963. 25–40.

——. *Three Essays on the Theory of Sexuality*. 1905. Ed. and trans. James Strachey. New York: Basic, 1965.

Gallop, Jane. "Beyond the Jouissance Principle." *Representations* 7 (1984): 110–115.

——. *Thinking Through the Body*. New York: Columbia UP, 1985.

Grosz, Elizabeth. "Lesbian Fetishism?" *differences: A Journal of Feminist Cultural Studies* 3.5 (1991): 39–54.

Hall, Stuart. "Cultural Identity and Diaspora." *Identity: Community, Culture, Difference*. Ed. Jonathan Rutherford. London: Lawrence, 1990. 222–37.

Herschberger, Ruth. *Adam's Rib*. New York: Pellegrini, 1948.

Irigaray, Luce. *Sexes and Genealogies.* 1987. Trans. Gillian Gill. New York: Columbia UP, 1993.

——. *This Sex Which Is Not One.* 1977. Trans. Catherine Porter. Ithaca: Cornell UP, 1985.

Julien, Philippe. *Jacques Lacan's Return to Freud: The Real, The Symbolic, The Imaginary.* Trans. Devra Beck Simiu. New York: New York UP, 1994.

Kristeva, Julia. "Women's Time." Trans. Alice Jardine and Harry Blake. *Signs* 7.1 (1981): 13–35. Rpt. in *The Kristeva Reader.* Ed. Toril Moi. New York: Columbia UP, 1986. 188–213.

Lacan, Jacques. *Ecrits: A Selection.* 1966. Trans. Alan Sheridan. New York: Norton, 1977.

——. *The Ethics of Psychoanalysis, 1959–1960.* Book VII of *The Seminar of Jacques Lacan.* 1986. Trans. Dennis Porter. Ed. Jacques-Alain Miller. New York: Norton, 1992.

——. *The Four Fundamental Concepts of Psycho-Analysis.* 1973. Trans. Alan Sheridan. New York: Norton, 1978.

Lacan, Jacques, and Wladimir Granoff. "Fetishism: The Symbolic, the Imaginary and the Real." *Perversions.* Ed. Sandor Lorand. New York: Gramercy, 1956. 265–76.

Laplanche, Jean. *New Foundations for Pyschoanalysis.* Trans. David Macey. Oxford: Blackwell, 1989.

Lott, Eric. "Love and Theft: The Racial Unconscious of Blackface Minstrelsy." *Representations* 39 (1992): 23–50.

Memmi, Albert. *The Colonizer and the Colonized.* 1957. Trans. Howard Greenfeld. Boston: Beacon, 1967.

Mercer, Kobena. "Black Hair, Style Politics." *New Formations* 3 (1987): 33–54.

Metz, Christian. *The Imaginary Signifier: Psychoanalysis and the Cinema.* Trans. Celia Britton, Annwyl Williams, Ben Brewster, Alfred Guzzetti. Bloomington: Indiana UP, 1982.

Peirce, Charles Sanders. *The Essential Writings.* Ed. E. C. Moore. New York: Harper, 1972.

Phelan, Peggy. *Unmarked: The Politics of Performance.* New York: Routledge, 1993.

Radhakrishnan, R. "Ethnic Identity and Poststructuralist Differance." *Cultural Critique* 6 (1987): 199–220.

Samuels, Robert. *Between Philosophy and Psychoanalysis: Lacan's Reconstruction of Freud.* New York: Routledge, 1993.

Saussure, Ferdinand de. *Course in General Linguistics.* Ed. Charles Bally, Albert Sechehaye, with Albert Riedlinger. 1915. Trans. Wade Baskin. 1959. New York: MacGraw–Hill, 1966.

Sedgwick, Eve Kosofsky. *Epistemology of the Closet.* Berkeley: U California P, 1990.

Silverman, Kaja. *Male Subjectivity at the Margins.* New York: Routledge, 1992.

Spivak, Gayatri. "Can the Subaltern Speak?" *Marxism and the Interpretation of Culture.* Ed. Cary Nelson and Lawrence Grossberg. Urbana: U of Illinois P, 1988. 271–313.

——. "Criticism, Feminism, and the Institution." Interview with Elizabeth Grosz. *The Post-Colonial Critic: Interviews, Strategies, Dialogues.* New York: Routledge, 1990. 1–16.

——. "In a Word." Interview with Ellen Rooney. *differences: A Journal of Feminist Cultural Studies* 1.2 (1989): 124–56.

The Jerry Springer Show. Metromedia. KCAL, Los Angeles. 13 September 1994.

Steedman, Carolyn. *Landscape for a Good Woman: A Story of Two Lives.* New Brunswick: Rutgers UP, 1987.

Tyler, Carole-Anne. "The Feminine Look." *Theory Between the Disciplines: Authority/ Vision/ Politics.* Ed. Martin Kreiswirth and Mark A. Cheetham. Ann Arbor: U of Michigan P, 1990. 191–212.

Weeks, Jeffrey. *Coming Out: Homosexual Politics in Britain, from the Nineteenth Century to the Present.* New York: Quartet, 1977.

Žižek, Slavoj. *Looking Awry: An Introduction to Jacques Lacan through Popular Culture.* Cambridge: MIT P, 1991.

——. *The Sublime Object of Ideology.* New York: Verso, 1989.

The More Things Change

Displacing Gender

*E*ve Sedgwick's move to separate sexuality from gender in *Epistemology of the Closet* is no more or less surprising than Gayle Rubin's by now familiar moves to separate gender from sex ("Traffic") and, more recently, feminist theory from theories of sexuality ("Thinking"). Like Rubin, Sedgwick is concerned with opening up a fresh critical discourse. Like Rubin, she pries her term away from another that blocks its force, producing not some neat differentiation but an unexpected critical space from which to read differently. And just as Rubin's early disengaging of gender and sex generated countless readings for feminism, so has Sedgwick's already made its mark on "queer"— or to use Sedgwick's language, "antihomophobic" or "gay affirmative"—work.[1]

Such critical spaces are not achieved without cost, however, and it is tempting for feminists to suspect that what we are seeing is somehow the chiasmic revenge of sex: sex, having been once displaced by gender, now returns the favor. Things are more complicated, of course. Sedgwick's "sexuality" is not—or is not only—Rubin's "sex." The latter refers to the relatively restricted notion of sexed reproduction whereas sexuality is that Foucauldian phenomenon produced by the densely entangled discourses of religion, science, and the sciences of man, with its historically privileged relationship to identity, truth, and knowledge. Intervening in these entangled discourses, Sedgwick wants to keep the slippery terms of sex, gender, and sexuality from always sliding into one another, so that sex is not always already chromosomal difference and reproduction, so that acts and sensations of "sex" are not always caught in a gendered genital economy, and so that sexuality can be inflected outside the homo-hetero axis.

It is, then, not quite right to say that Sedgwick seeks to disengage sexuality from gender. More accurately, the analytic space she opens up looks to drive a wedge not simply between sexuality and gender, but between sex-sexuality and sex-gender:

> [E]ven usages involving the "sex/gender system" within feminist theory are able to use "sex/gender" only to delineate a problematical space *rather than a crisp distinction. My own loose usage in this book will be to denominate that problematized space of the sex/gender system, the whole package of physical and cultural distinctions between women and men, more simply under the rubric "gender." I do this in order to reduce the likelihood of confusion between "sex" in the sense of "the space of differences between male and female" (what I'll be grouping under "gender") and "sex" in the sense of sexuality.* (Epistemology 29)

If, as she says, the sex/gender distinction is far from clear, the line between sex and sexuality is no better defined; indeed "*something* legitimately called sex or sexuality is all over the experiential and conceptual map." All the more reason, argues Sedgwick, to produce the necessary critical space: if sex and sexuality do not easily yield determinate meanings, "[i]f all this is true of the definitional nexus between sex and sexuality, how much less simple, even, must be that between sexuality and gender" (29). For Sedgwick, the recognition of this difficult nexus between gender and sexuality leads to two critical positions. The first is an affirmation of the very possibility of forcing the terms apart:

> It will be an assumption of this study that there is always at least the potential for an analytic distance between gender and sexuality, even if particular manifestations or features of particular sexualities are among the things that plunge women and men most ineluctably into the discursive, institutional, and bodily enmeshments of gender definition, gender relation, and gender inequality. (29–30)

The second is the impossibility of knowing what such a forced separation will bring forth. Although, as she says, the study of sexuality is not the same thing as the study of gender, nor antihomophobic inquiry the same thing as feminist inquiry, "we can't know in advance how they will be different" (27). We can't know their difference in advance; were we to know there would be no need to pry sexuality loose from gender. What differences we discover will be in the critical readings themselves, the critical work that reads *for* sexuality *apart* from gender.

My interest here is not with the powerful differences Sedgwick's readings have clearly made in the study of sexuality. Nor is my concern with some of the larger questions of sexuality's analytic relationship to gender. I am interested, rather, in the effects that a reading for sexuality apart from gender has on a particular reading of *sexual difference*.

For at least a decade, the dominant feminist criticism in the United States has taken "gender" rather than "sexual difference" as its privileged critical category. It is as if the enormous productivity of the constructedness of gender has eclipsed the other term with its more troublesome connections to the sexed body, the sexed subject.[2] In this context, Sedgwick's displacement of gender can be seen to be the double distancing of sexual difference, and in that its final death knell. Yet, at the same time, her very move to separate sex-sexuality from sex-gender—and the theoretical care with which she makes that move—renders visible in a unique way the complex connections among the terms and the stakes involved in their displacement.

By way of exploring what the stakes are for sexual difference, I want to look at a critical category which has been crucial to analyses of gender and which has proven to be indispensable to sexuality studies: the thematic. It is in looking at the particular relationship of the thematic to readings of sexuality that I hope to shed light on the banishment of sexual difference.

The Queer Turn to Thematics

The blurb on the back cover of a 1993 collection of essays, *The Return of Thematic Criticism*, begins with the following:

> *In the glory days of high modernist formalism, it was anathema to speak about the content of the work of art. Those days are gone, and critical practice is largely thematic practice. A focus on the themes of literature informs feminist, new historicist, ethnic, and even second-generation deconstructionist approaches. However, such practice is not always recognized. The specter of theoretically impoverished positivism still haunts thematic analysis, making it the approach to literature that dare not speak its name.*

Almost two decades earlier, in an essay originally published in 1976 which looks at the commonality of a different group of critical practices (thematics, structural semantics, and poststructuralism), Naomi Schor begins her "For a Restricted Thematics: Writing, Speech, and Difference in *Madame Bovary*" with this declaration: "It is time to say out loud what has been whispered for some time: thematic criticism, which was given a first-class funeral a few years ago, is not dead. Like a repressed desire that insists on returning to consciousness, like a guilty pleasure that resists all threat of castration, thematic criticism is coming out of the shadows" (3).

Whether as a practice shamed by the specter of a theoretical impoverishment, or one driven by a guilty but irresistible pleasure, contemporary thematics seems to be thematized by a certain persistent coming out. What thematics comes out *as* when it comes out for queer criticism is the question.

For neither Werner Sollors, the editor of the collection on thematics, nor for Schor seventeen years earlier, is the return of thematics a simple repeat performance; it is not, as Schor says, a "retro" criticism, "a regression to the styles of reading of the 1950s" (3). For Sollors it is a pervasive practice which has recently taken on a new life in the work of "Women's Studies, Black Studies, Ethnic Studies, Cultural Studies, Ideological Criticism, and New Historicism" (xiv). And yet for all of its importance, the thematic nature of the work is rarely if ever acknowledged, Sollors observes: "the antithematic affect seems so deeply ingrained that one might think of it as an episteme of contemporary criticism," one which ultimately keeps the thematic approach to literature from speaking its name (xiii–xiv).

In contrast, the notion of thematics Schor brings out for her reading of *Madame Bovary* is something more precise. Thematics for her are "all textual practices that suffer from what might be called . . . an Ariadne complex, all readings that cling to the Ariadne's thread (*'fil conductuer'*), whether it be the 'synonymous chains' of Barthes, the 'chain of supplements' of Derrida, or the 'series' of Deleuze" (3). These are practices that in holding on to the Ariadne's thread are inscribed metonymically under the sign of the feminine, that Freudian "plaiting and weaving" which represents women's contribution to civilization. It is the femininity of thematism, says Schor, that would explain both its culpabilization and its masculine recuperation (5).[5]

It is revealing to look at Sedgwick's thematics in contrast to those of both Sollors and Schor. In her work the thematic is also not retro, but that is where the similarity ends. For in Sedgwick the thematic is not read as feminine, it is not culpable as a reading practice, nor does it in any way disavow its work. On the contrary, it is seen as cognate with masculinity and, in its generalization to a vast array of texts and social configurations, crucial to the critical work of the book. Moreover, Sedgwick's extended, "masculine" thematics is of a very particular kind, situated squarely within a Foucauldian framework. The broad object of her inquiry is indeed the discursive mobilization of meanings: "Repeatedly to ask how certain categorizations work, what enactments they are performing and what relations they are creating, rather than what they essentially *mean*, has been my principal strategy" (27). With such a project, the thematic is not something for which one apologizes.

A consideration of this unapologetic thematics requires, if only in a very general way, a brief look at the Foucauldian thematic itself. In a short essay in *The Return of Thematic Criticism*, Nancy Armstrong offers a suggestive understanding of Foucault's special relationship to thematics. She sees him as providing a way around the classic form/content opposition by considering the discursive work a text does:

> *[With Foucault w]e can read the text in question as a classificatory performance within a larger cultural-historical project. From this perspective things are not "about" a reality that is already in place outside the text. Rather, themes constitute the world we actually inhabit, as they divide it, for example, into inside and outside, subject and object, self and other, male and female, public and private, as well as into the official media, genres, and disciplines of knowledge. Indeed, the story of* Surveiller et Punir *(1975) can be read as the story of a theme, of how discipline transformed itself from a residual cultural formation into the master theme of modern culture. The story indicates that as it underwent this transformation, discipline became virtually indistinguishable from order, or "form," itself. (39)*

If we follow Armstrong's reading, we see the thematic as crucial to Foucault, at least in his "genealogical" writings, not because the workings of power-knowledge can be understood thematically, but because they function thematically. In a more traditional narratological analysis of a text, the "theme" serves, as Gerald Prince says, as a "semantic macrostructural category or frame extractable from (or allowing for the unification of) distinct (and discontinuous) textual elements which (are taken to) illustrate it and expressing the more general and abstract entities (ideas, thoughts, etc.) that a text or part thereof is (or may be considered to be) about" (97). The difference in Foucault's way of reading has less to do with the objects of his study—discursive formations and institutions versus narrative texts—than with the fact that his thematic has a constitutive rather than macrostructural relation to the meanings read. Foucauldian knowledge—with all of its categorizing power—would be, according to Armstrong's reading, a knowledge-effect, produced by thematics.[4]

Without pursuing the validity of this analysis for an understanding of the theme in Foucault, I will venture that what Armstrong says of Foucault pertains to Sedgwick's Foucauldian-inflected use of thematics. In *Epistemology of the Closet* it is precisely the "closet" that is constitutive of a vast array of meanings that structure modern Western civilization. For Sedgwick, the closet is a site of generalized cultural anxiety produced by a society that is at once pervasively homoerotic and intensely homophobic. In the last century, in particular, she sees that anxiety intensified in the homophobic structuring of male homosocial bonds:

> *Because the paths of male entitlement, especially in the nineteenth century, required certain intense male bonds that were not readily distinguishable from the most reprobated bonds, an endemic and ineradicable state of what I am calling male homosexual panic became the normal condition of male heterosexual entitlement. (185)*

What continually nurtures and sustains this panic is "closetedness," a "performance initiated as such by the speech act of a silence—not a particular silence, but a silence that accrues particularity by fits and starts, in relation to the discourse that surrounds and differentially constitutes it" (3). The silence of the closet is one of power; it produces "ignorance effects" that coerce by forcing meanings into their field, much as the ignorance of one interlocutor will determine the limits of discursive exchange (3–5). It is Sedgwick's hypothesis— which she supports with readings of a number of texts—that the definition of homo/heterosexual, with its closet relations of known and unknown, explicit and implicit, has been "a presiding master term of the past century, one that has the same, primary importance for all modern Western identity and social organization . . . as do the more traditionally visible cruxes of gender, class, and race" (11). Sedgwick goes on to list more than twenty "definitional nodes" marked by homo/heterosexual. Cast as binarisms, they range from the expected (secrecy/disclosure, knowledge/ignorance) to the provocative (discipline/terrorism, utopia/apocalypse).

If, as Armstrong says, *Discipline and Punish* can be read as the story of how "discipline transformed itself from a residual cultural formation into the master theme of modern culture" (39), *Epistemology of the Closet* tells the story of a closet that is at once "internal and marginal to the culture" (56), at once the truth of a small shadowy group of people and that of a whole society. For the culture caught in the double bind of the homophobic and homoerotic does not know—cannot make up its mind—whether same-sex desire is limited to a restricted group of homosexuals or whether it inhabits all persons. It is this "radical and irreducible incoherence" (85) that Sedgwick finds so central to a range of social formations and meanings since the last century and thus so productive for critical theory.

To do full justice to Sedgwick's thematics, one would have to give careful consideration to her use of critical concepts such as speech acts, the performative, and reader relations, all central to the way she approaches texts. For my purposes—in order to consider the relations between Sedgwick's thematics and sexual difference—I will look at just one trait of the Sedgwick theme: its fullness. In Sedgwick's work the theme is always full and plentious, even when it speaks of silence, ignorance, and absence. This can and does yield exceptional readings, which is why Sedgwick has been so successful. What the superabundance of meaning, the explosion of signification *cannot* make room for is a certain sexual difference that cannot be read through discursive thematics.

The sexual difference I refer to is clearly not the essential maleness and femaleness so richly mobilized throughout Western culture, but rather the difference of Woman that cannot, as Luce Irigaray says, be spoken within the thematics of the symbolic order. I refer, then, to the sexual difference theorized through—and specific to—psychoanalytic and deconstructive readings.

What interests me is not the adequacy or inadequacy of discursive versus psychoanalytic or deconstructive criticism. It is a reading's *limit* I want to look at, in this case, the limit of a full thematics. I suggest that sexual difference is a limit—the limit?—of discourse-based criticism, and as such marks the limit of the extent to which discursive, psychoanalytic, and deconstructive reading strategies can be said to intersect.

It is useful for this discussion to remember what the thematic looks like in deconstruction and psychoanalysis. It is a thematics everywhere present but never fully present. Rather, it appears in the form of an evacuated or anti-thematics. For Jacques Derrida, the lure of the thematic is the lure of metaphysics, and in "The Double Session" he suggests both the seductiveness and limit of thematics by considering Jean-Pierre Richard's reading of Mallarmé's poetry. What is striking for Derrida is Richard's persistence in finding an inexhaustible thematic plenitude in Mallarmé, even with the recognition that the poet's language produces its meanings through diacritical gaps (Derrida 245–50). In Jonathan Culler's words, Derrida suggests that "the inexhaustibility identified [in Richard's reading of Mallarmé] . . . is not that of richness, depth, complexity of an essence, but rather the inexhaustibility of a certain poverty" (209). And for Derrida, the fact that nothing in the Mallarméan text blocks Richard's access to a fullness of meaning attests to the power of thematicism's metaphysical project.

Psychoanalysis has a somewhat different but related objection to a thematics of full presence. Nicolas Abraham sets out the problem:[5]

> *The condition sine qua non of the relation to self, the space that separates the "I" from the "me," necessarily escapes reflexive thematization. It is in this space, in the nonpresence of the self to itself— the very condition of reflexivity—that phenomenologists unwittingly place their foothold in order to scrutinize, from this terra incognita, the sole horizon visible to them, the inhabited continents. But psychoanalysis stakes out its domain precisely on this* unthought *ground of phenomenology. To say this is already to designate, if not to resolve, the problem facing us: how to include in a discourse—in any one whatever—the very thing which, being the precondition of discourse, fundamentally escapes it? (84)*

How is non-presence to be made to speak? By the very particular language of psychoanalysis:

> *The language of psychoanalysis no longer follows the twists and turns (tropoi) of customary speech and writing. Pleasure, Id, Ego, Economic, Dynamic, are not metaphors, metonymies, synecdoches, catachreses; they are, by dint of discourse, products of designification*

> *and constitute new figures, absent from rhetorical treatises. These*
> *figures of antisemantics, inasmuch as they signify no more than the*
> *action of moving up toward the source of their customary meaning,*
> *require a denomination properly indicative of their status and*
> *which—for want of something better—I shall propose to designate by*
> *the neologism* anasemia. *(85)[6]*

What links deconstruction and psychoanalysis is their way of reading the structural against the semantic in the workings of signification. Neither pretends to function outside the semantic, but both work to resist its power. Derrida's project in "The Double Session" and elsewhere is to displace (as Barbara Johnson says in another context) an "ontological semantics" with an "undecidable syntax," thematics (that macrostructural category of semantics) with articulation (Johnson, Introduction xxviii). And if deconstruction is concerned with the articulation of signification and language, psychoanalysis looks to the multiple articulations of signification, the psychic, and the somatic. Psychoanalysis's very theorizing of unconscious operations is a reading against the self-evident. As Daniel Lagache says in his introduction to *The Language of Psychoanalysis*, "ordinary language has no words to evoke mental structures and tendencies that do not exist for common sense" (vii).

It is this linking of deconstruction and psychoanalysis that Irigaray, the best known of the sexual difference theorists, brings to her efforts to produce a specificity of Woman that is not already subsumed by the generalized thematics of male and not-male. "Real" sexual difference, the difference of Woman, is foreclosed by the economy of presence which underwrites the symbolic order, the order of the "demonstrable, the thematizable, the formalizable" (99).[7] For her, only a reading against the symbolic order can open a space for Woman.

Returning to Sedgwick, we see a very different approach to thematics. Sedgwick's project relies neither on the anasemia of psychoanalysis nor on the inexhaustible poverty of deconstructive thematics; it has its interest precisely in the sedimented thematic operations of meaning. Deconstruction, Sedgwick argues, might expose the "opposition" of heterosexuality/homosexuality as "irresolvably unstable" (10), psychoanalysis might provide some insights,[8] but the work is in seeing how the "'common sense' of this epistemologically cloven culture" (12) is continually shored up and produced.

At stake are different theoretical projects and very different ways of reading. Sedgwick makes her preference particularly explicit in her chapter on Herman Melville's *Billy Budd*. In her discussion of the novel's enigmatic master-at-arms, John Claggart, and of the riddle of his "hidden nature," she makes it clear why she is drawn to the character, why he is a prime candidate for closet epistemology: "the answer to the riddle [of Claggart] seems to involve not the substitution of semantically more satisfying alternatives to the epithet 'hidden' but merely a series of intensifications of it" (94). In evoking the way the enigmatic works in the text, she cites approvingly Barbara Johnson's deconstructive reading of Claggart as a "pure *epistemological essence*," as, in Johnson's words, "a personification of ambiguity and ambivalence, of the distance between signifier and signified, of the separation between being and doing . . . [a properly] ironic reader, who, assuming the sign to be arbitrary and unmotivated, reverses the value signs of appearances . . . " (*Critical* 85; qtd. in *Epistemology* 96).

While Sedgwick endorses this reading, however, she is unwilling to stop there. She is interested in looking at the textual encounter of, on the one hand, the abstract epistemology embodied by Claggart and, on the other, the fruitless diagnoses made of his depravity by doctors, lawyers, and clergy. This encounter she names as a "rhetorical impaction . . . between a thematically evacuated abstraction of knowledge and a theoretically jejune empiricism of taxonomy effects," a crossing of epistemology with thematics that "can be effected only through a distinctive *reader*-relation imposed by text and narrator" (96–97). This crossing works, according to Sedgwick, because the reader identifies with the modes of categorizing of a text and narrator although, or because, the knowing of that knowledge is undercut:

> The inexplicit compact by which novel-readers voluntarily plunge into worlds that strip them, however temporarily, of the painfully acquired cognitive maps of their ordinary lives . . . on condition of an invisibility that promises cognitive exemption and eventual privilege, creates, especially at the beginning of books, a space of high anxiety and dependence. In this space a reader's identification with modes of categorization ascribed to her by a narrator may be almost vindictively eager. Any appeal, for instance, to or beyond "knowledge of the world" depends for its enormous novelistic force on the anxious surplus of this early overidentification with the novel's organizing eye. (97)

Because Sedgwick's analysis leans more to the anxious novel-reader than to Johnson's "ironic reader," because Sedgwick is interested in that reader's "overidentification with the novel's organizing eye," the thematically evacuated epistemology exposed by Johnson is incomplete for her without the rich semantic associations of the readerly text.

This, then, is the reading practice which, with its rich semantic associations and its full thematics, enables Sedgwick to read sexuality as the "most meaning-intensive of human actions" in modern Western culture (5). This is also the reading practice which does not allow for the anti-thematic reading that sexual difference requires. And yet, it is not to Sedgwick's text that I will look to see how sexual difference functions as the limit of thematics. How, indeed, does one show the absence of something that cannot be read through a critic's critical discourse? The only way one might do this is through a kind of symptomatic reading of a text that somehow speaks its exclusion of sexual difference. To attempt this I will turn to a work that is both unlike *Epistemology of the Closet* and yet congruent with it: D. A. Miller's *Bringing Out Roland Barthes*. Unlike Sedgwick's book, Miller's is an essay on a single focussed topic; like *Epistemology*, it addresses, within its own terms, the familiar questions of homophobia, closetedness, the separation of sexuality and gender, and the fullness of thematics.[9] No less theorized than Sedgwick's book, Miller's essay eschews explicit theorizing (implicitly drawing on Miller's earlier work) as well as the scholarly apparatus. Perhaps for those reasons, *Bringing Out Roland Barthes* is less guarded, less protected than *Epistemology of the Closet*, and as such offers the reader a vivid staging of its own reading practice, including the cost of that practice for sexual difference.

Roland Barthes by D. A. Miller

The title of D. A. Miller's essay, *Bringing Out Roland Barthes*, is provocative. Why Barthes? Why the writer whose very project was that of eluding the name and who, especially in his later works, displayed his sexuality for all to read? The essay itself both dispels and sustains the provocation, the scandal, of the title. It asserts a pressing need: "To refuse to bring Barthes out consents to a homophobic reception of his work"(17), while acknowledging a difficulty: "In a culture that without ever ceasing to proliferate homosexual meaning knows how to confine it to a kind of false consciousness . . . there is hardly a procedure for bringing out this meaning that doesn't itself look or feel like just more police entrapment" (18). To negotiate both the need and the risk, Miller proposes a very particular encounter with Barthes:

> . . . *there is hardly a procedure for bringing out this meaning that doesn't itself look or feel like just more police entrapment. (Unless such, perhaps, were a* folie à deux—*where "two" stands for the possibility of community—that would bring it out in as subtle and flattering a fashion as, say, the color of a garment is said to bring out a complexion.) (18)*

The proposal is Barthesian in its inspiration, not in the glimpse it offers of what R. B. might look like in leather, but in its promise to detach Barthes from Barthes, to help us to see him afresh by seeing him differently.

Miller's essay begins by appropriately inscribing itself in the interests of desire and writing, of desire-as-writing. In the opening pages, Miller indicates why he wants a shared "gayness" with Barthes and what that imaginary relation might enable him to do. The *why* inclines toward desire: "why, after all, had it come to interest me that Barthes—or any man for that matter—was gay, except for the reason that such information broached to fantasy the possibility of alleviating *an erotic pessimism* by producing with him, against him, a sexuality that had become 'ours'?" (6–7). *What* Miller wants from his encounter with Barthes has to do with writing: "This essay proposes an album of moments . . . responses to a handful of names, phrases, images, themes (whether or not strictly written by Barthes, all inscribed in his *text*) that happened to provide me occasions for assessing 'between us' particular problems that must, as well as particular projects that might, inform a gay writing position" (7).

Miller is true to his word that the encounter will not be exempt from the "usual vicissitudes of adulation, aggression, ambivalence" (8). After all, as we learn at the start, he has long been inhabited by Barthes and any transformation from inhabitation to encounter is bound to be vexing. Consider, for example, the engaging story of Barthes, Miller, and Miller's first trip to Japan. As he is preparing for a trip on which he intends to sample Japanese sexual delights, Miller is determined to take his leave from one of his literary points of departure, *The Empire of Signs*, Barthes's book on Japan. Now sexually enlightened, Miller has come to see the book as that of just an armchair intellectual whose few words of Japanese included none of the crucial ones and whose sexuality seemed hopelessly repressed in any case. Imagine, Miller says, his "fury" at discovering in a rereading of Barthes's text something that had been there all the time: in a sketch illustrating the street directions Tokyoans give to strangers, a map of "gay Tokyo" (4–5).

There are other such encounters where Miller reads Barthes's way of speaking to gay men of another time and place. In "Two Bodies," for instance, he suggests that Barthes's body, so different from the gay male gym-body, nonetheless can be seen to share something in common with it. The beautifully developed gym-body presents itself as something to be desired; it sets itself off from the heterosexual male body by its availability. Barthes's availability is of a very different sort. It is something Miller quite strikingly reads in the way Barthes, whose love for his mother was intense, unapologetically "proffers and 'assumes' this evidence of the body's id," as in every photo of him which "materially reinscribes his mother in the characteristically dejected posture of his body, always ducking and drooping, as though always wanting, but never any longer able, to drop into her arms" (33). What Barthes shares with the gay "clone": "this common refusal: of the desirability, even the possibility, of the male body's *autonomy*" (33).

But there are also more aggressive moments where the encounter between Miller and Barthes is a confrontation between two theories of writing and two theories of desire. On the one side is Barthes's theory of the writerly text, of a writing which in order to live must elude coagulated meaning, received ideas, *doxa*: "Like a watchful cook," one reads in *Roland Barthes by Roland Barthes*, "he makes sure that language does not thicken, that it doesn't stick" (162). On the other is Miller's theory of salutary, even urgently salutary naming. "The Goddess H," a topic heading in both *Roland Barthes* and *Bringing Out Roland Barthes*, is the site for such an encounter. Barthes writes:

> *The pleasure potential of a perversion (in this case, that of the two H.'s: homosexuality and hashish) is always underestimated. Law, Science, the* Doxa *refuse to understand that perversion, quite simply, makes happy; or, to be more specific, it produces a* more*: I am more sensitive, more perceptive, more loquacious, more amused, etc.—and in this* more *is where we find the difference (and consequently, the Text of life, life-as-text). Henceforth, it is a goddess, a figure that can be invoked, a means of intercession. (63–64)*

For Miller, Barthes's persistent preference for the letter over the name[10] speaks not of the "purity" of the unencumbered signifier but of the "promiscuity" of the "evacuated" letter that cannot rid itself of its semantic associations. We know from an illustration in *Roland Barthes* of notes made in preparation for the book, that "la Déesse H" was originally "la Déesse Homo" or "Homosexualité" (75). And we know from virtually the whole Barthesian text that this is Barthes's modus operandi, the move from full meaning to the fragment which opens the space, which quickens the pulse. For Miller, however, homosexuality is not just one more theme of the text, nor is it just one perversion among many. What is at stake here for Miller is a symptomatic diminishment: "In the movement from the Name (as meaning *that name*) to the Letter (as meaning, only possibly, that name *among others*)—more accurately, in the oblique but observable *proffering* of the movement—consists the whole figured relation of Barthes's writing to his homosexuality" (23).

What enables Miller to read Barthes against Barthes is his own critical theory in which the "open secret" figures prominently. In Miller's book, *The Novel and the Police*, he exposes the machinery of the Victorian novel by which the character's secret inside, as opposed to the social outside, is always in some sense an open secret to readers who in turn derive their readerly pleasure from forgetting what they know in order better to enjoy the novel's suspense. Extending this structure of open secrecy and pleasure to a more general cultural habit, Miller goes on: "In this light, it becomes clear that the social function of secrecy—isomorphic with its novelistic function—is not to conceal knowledge, so much as to conceal the knowledge of the knowledge" (206).

It is when Miller's reading is further extended to the question of subjectivity that his argument takes on its full force. Asking what takes secrecy for its field of operations, he writes:

> *In a world where the explicit exposure of the subject would manifest how thoroughly he has been inscribed within a socially given totality, secrecy would be the spiritual exercise by which the subject is allowed to conceive of himself as a resistance: a friction in the smooth functioning of the social order, a margin to which its far-reaching discourse does not reach. Secrecy would thus be the subjective practice in which the oppositions of private/public, inside/outside, subject/object are established, and the sanctity of their first term kept inviolate. And the phenomenon of the "open secret" does not, as one might think, bring about the collapse of those binarisms and their ideological effects, but rather attests to their fantasmatic recovery. In a mecha-*

*nism of Freudian disavowal, we know perfectly well that the secret is
known, but nonetheless we must persist, however ineptly, in guarding
it. The paradox of the open secret registers the subject's accommodation to a totalizing system that has obliterated the difference he would
make—the difference he does make, in the imaginary denial of this
system "even so." (207)*

This argument gives us more insight into Miller's project to bring out
Barthes, his contempt for "evacuated" meaning, and his concern with the
secret as cultural thematics.[11] Yet there is a paradox here. Despite the vigor
with which he points to Barthes's phobic retreat from his own homosexuality,
Miller persists in *desiring Barthes's desire.* One of Miller's reasons for writing
the essay, it will be remembered, is his fantasy of "alleviating an erotic
pessimism" by producing with Barthes a common sexuality. Those who have
seen the edition of *Bringing Out Roland Barthes* will know that the fantasy is
somewhat materialized in the packaging of the handsome book along with its
companion volume, a translation by Richard Howard of Barthes's *Incidents.* The
two volumes have the same jacket design featuring on the front cover repro-
ductions of two rooms of the artist Bernard Faucon, with the difference being
that on Miller's cover is "The First Room of Love," where two male lovers lie,
while on Barthes's is "The Thirteenth Room of Love," where the sheets on the
floor lie empty. And on the back cover are close-up photographs of the two
authors' faces, featuring the eyes.

Incidents is crucial to Miller's essay because it contains writings of
Barthes's that remained unpublished at his death in 1980 (to be first collected
and published under the title "Incidents" in 1987) in which he writes about his
sexual life with a degree of explicitness not found in his published writings. In
the last section of the slim volume, "Soirées de Paris," Barthes writes (six
months before his death at the age of 65) of his despair at realizing that the
young boys he desires no longer desire him and that nothing is left for him but
the hustlers: "But then what would I do when I go out? I keep noticing young
men, immediately wanting to be in love with them. What will the spectacle of
my world come to be?" (73).

Miller sees "Soirées de Paris" as the point at which the "(poignant,
exasperating) hysteria" that characterizes Barthes's "phobic" attitude toward
his sexuality, collapses into despair (28). He knows that Barthes's real dilemma

is whether his own desire can survive this blow so soon after the death of his mother (54), and he knows that Barthes's passion has never been sex but desire, born at the always deferred meeting of sex and meaning. Desire for Barthes is what is produced by the gap between meaning and its loss, the point at which "the death of language is glimpsed," just as the most erotic part of the body is "where the garment gapes" (*Pleasure* 6,9).

Thus, the naming that Miller demands is the very thing that kills desire for Barthes, and yet it is this same desire that Miller looks to in the hope that it might alleviate a certain erotic pessimism, this same desire that might have something to say to the young gay "clone" who suffers from an "all-effecting depression by the devastation of his once flourishing culture" (33). The desire which in Miller's reading produces only a "phobic" and "censorious" pleasure of the text is the very desire that never fails Barthes, at least not—perhaps—until the end.

Evoking death, Miller writes: "Death is doubled when, after the decease of someone I love, I suddenly comprehend that the person to whom in my grief I have thought of turning . . . is the very person who has just died" (53). For this reason, among others, Miller dreams of bringing Barthes back.

It is as if "silence is death" had taken on a double, undecidable life of its own in Miller's text: at once the theorized silence that impels him to bring out Barthes, and the final silence of Barthes's desire which makes him yearn to bring him back.

There is at least one other aggressive encounter in Miller's essay. In the very first section, "La Zambinella," just after the opening pages, Miller refers to what he calls "evidence of hedging and infighting in the resistance to the modern gender system" (12). He is speaking of "female-inflected homophobia" and "gay-inflected misogyny," and the context is a brief commentary on three moments in Honoré de Balzac's *Sarrasine,* the subject of Barthes's *S/Z.* By a liberal reading of *Sarrasine*—which I will not recount here—Miller produces a feminist and anti-homophobic look at the way the regimes of gender are displayed in Balzac's text. The position of the woman is revealed as that of the double bind (she must be, cannot be a woman, patriarchy constituting femininity as always already castrated); that of the gay man is seen as a double double bind ("he must be, can't be a man; he must be, can't be a

woman") (10–11). The problem with the "gay man" and the woman in question—the castrato, la Zambinella, and the marquise to whom the narrator tells
la Zambinella's story—is that neither fully understands the "other" position;
hence the misogyny and homophobia.

In the next section, "Neuter," Miller registers his disappointment at
Barthes's neglect of the full implications of *Sarrasine*, of his failure to "recognize the pertinence of what in any case the spirit of his analysis would tend to
dismiss as a mere homosexual thematics" (12). In Miller's analysis the neuter,
which goes on to play a large role in Barthes's work, is never freed of its
Zambinellian origins. As the gender of the castrato, it can never be ungendered
or unsexed, never neutral, no matter how much Barthes hopes for the possibility of "active/passive, of possessor/possessed, buggerer/buggeree" coming to
know a neutral (*neutre*) term where meaning and sex will be "liberated from
the binary prison" (*Roland* 133). No matter how much Barthes wants to elide
the bind of the gay man into what Miller calls the "general problematic" of the
sexual utopia, for Miller this neuter "does not register a *general* deprivation of
gender but the specifically *male* experience of such deprivation; still more
important, neither does it restrict this deprivation to a loss of 'masculinity,' that
is to the dread castration by which the general imagination of the neuter is
usually monopolized, but makes no less definitive of itself a man's barred
access to 'femininity'" (14–15).[12]

It is then that Miller makes the following surprising charge:

> *Precisely when the discreet but discernible gay specificity of Barthes's*
> *text is ignored does this text present the most propitious occasion for*
> *rehearsing an antigay doxology. For in the guarding of that Open*
> *Secret which is still the mode of producing, transmitting, and receiv-*
> *ing most discourse around homosexuality, the knowledge that plays*
> *dumb is exactly what permits the abuses of an ignorance that in fact*
> *knows full well what it is doing. Recognizing this logic must greatly*
> *diminish the persuasiveness of recent accounts (embraced by critics of*
> *both sexes, though—predictably—under the rules of a single sexual-*
> *ity) that equate the Barthesian neuter with a ruse for submerging,*
> *under general sexual indeterminacy, the specificity of women.*
> *Although such critics are demonstrably aware both of Barthes's*
> *gayness and of gay readings of Barthes's work, they see no reason to*
> *mediate their critique through articulation or even acknowledgment*

of the gender aporia that makes the social symbolic space allotted to
gay men as impossible, as impassible, as perspective in Escher.
However much in evidence, no other sexual difference in Barthes
receives notice but the "good" kind he is charged with eliding. (16–17)

Miller does not agree or deny that Barthes effaces sexual difference; the charge remains to be proven, he goes on to say, but if it is true, such a charge by what Miller calls the "gender police" cannot but contribute to the stereotyping of the homosexual ("il n'aime pas les femmes") (17).

Because Miller provides no citational information, one has to assume that the criticism he is referring to includes essays such as Stephen Heath's "Barthes on Love," and Naomi Schor's "Dreaming Dissymmmetry: Barthes, Foucault, and Sexual Difference." Even if he is not referring to these critics, they would nonetheless fall into the category of the guilty. As Schor says, the sexual difference of man/woman is not simply displaced in Barthes; to "displacement" she prefers the term "clinamen," or swerve:

I prefer this term to the more common displacement, because displace-
ment implies taking a concept or word and transporting it over to
another conceptual field, thereby creating a new and startling
configuration. Whereas displacement denotes a shift, *the clinamen as I*
am using it here denotes a shift away from; *whereas in displacement*
the two paradigms coexist, in the Barthesian clinamen one paradigm
is literally effaced by the other. (51)

Miller's invective is surprising because the essay does not prepare for it. Even the allusion to gay-inflected misogyny and female-inflected homophobia does not prepare for the moment when the latter is indicted by an almost parodic performance of the former. The outburst surprises also because it occurs immediately after Miller *himself* has just argued that the Barthesian neuter can only ever be male and that Barthes's paradise of indeterminacy "can hardly be thought of as an indeterminate paradise" (16). Not even a style as animated and distinctive as Miller's can account for this textual *excess.*

The impression of excess is reinforced by Miller's next comment: "To refuse to bring Barthes out consents to a homophobic reception of his work" (17). This tautology—the choice is no choice: Miller theorizes the closet *as* homophobia—turns out to be, if we attend to the voice of passion as well as to rhetorical placement, *the* reason for bringing out Roland Barthes. To bring out

Barthes is to perform a kind of apotropaic gesture that will shield him from the homophobic reception of the gender police. It is not surprising that homophobia makes frequent appearances in Miller's essay, but it is startling that neither the homosexual panic (to use Sedgwick's term) of some readers, nor Barthes's own "phobia" is assigned the rhetorically privileged place of responsibility; it is, rather, feminism's concern for the specificity of women that draws the most anger.

I do not think Miller is misogynist, nor do I think his complaint is without merit. "Sexual difference" is a difficult term and it can benefit from the kind of critical pressure Miller puts on it. Moreover, what Miller is calling for is not that far from what Schor wants. Both are troubled by a certain indeterminacy of sexual difference in Barthes. When Barthes writes of an indeterminate utopian sex, Schor reads him as rendering the difference of man/woman invisible, unreadable. Miller sees Barthes doing the same thing with male homosexuality in his tendency to render it either one thing among many (homosexuality, hashish), or to subsume it by a seemingly larger problematic (the Text, utopian sexuality). Why, then, the angry tone of the passage? The fact that both critics, for very different reasons, can be troubled by the same Barthesian effacement is not something that need *necessarily* lead to vituperation.

I suggest simply that the excessiveness of the passage is symptomatic of the problem that "sexual difference" does in fact present for any critical work on sexuality—and I use the term now in its classic sense of not only male/female, but also man/woman. It is the problem of sexual difference that ineluctably plunges men and women back into the "enmeshments of gender," as Sedgwick says (30). And it is the problem of sexual difference that makes Barthes return always to the couple sex-and-meaning, that Oedipal scene of epistemology.

Miller's formulation of the double bind (the woman who must be, can't be a woman) and the double double bind (the gay man who must be, can't be a man and who must be, can't be a woman) is not unproductive; it can open up some blind spots. But it opens up nothing for a reading of sexual difference; indeed, it shuts down some insights that have been crucial to feminism. If we are to take seriously any of the work of the last decades which reads the phallic logic underpinning our symbolic order, we have to recognize that the barring of femininity to women is of a *different* theoretical register from the barring of masculinity and femininity to gay men. Miller collapses the category "man/woman" and the category "straight or lesbian woman/gay man" onto the single category "woman/gay man." To do this is to efface the psychoanalytic category of man/woman where the theorizing of the phallus has its greatest purchase. As Joan Copjec reminds us, phallic logic for Lacan renders the woman's relationship to the symbolic order as one of *impossibility* and the man's as one of *prohibition* (41). These positionings work in different ways and require different theorizations of the trajectory of woman's desire (wherever it goes) and man's desire (wherever it goes). A similar argument can be made when articulating psychoanalytic theory with questions of ethnic or racialized subjectivity: the analysis that looks at the man/woman split is of one register; that which looks at the (racializing) twists and turns of the subject's desire in the symbolic field is of another. The point is that sexual difference theorized psychoanalytically is *different* from other differences; the fact that psychoanalysis in general has been dismally inadequate in its thinking about practices other than the heterosexual, and about subjects other than those of the Anglo-European middle class, does not change that point or its potential effectiveness as a theoretical formulation (see Copjec 32–35).[13]

One argues to retain the psychoanalytic specificity of sexual difference not, to borrow a phrase, because it is right—the theory that wants to be fully adequate to its object can only speak its nostalgia for metaphysics—but because it works. That is, it yields readings about signification and gaps in signification; about desire, repetition, and interpellation; and about the insistent cultural reproduction of fetishistic structures—all of which help us to understand the power and violence of the culture, and all of which are produced by reading something *other* than the already known, the already legible.[14]

To argue to retain this reading of sexual difference is not to suggest that conflicting theories should be rendered congruent or somehow accountable to one another;[15] it is, rather, to note with Schor that displacement can easily become effacement. The salutary politicization of criticism during the last two decades has had as one of its risks the temptation to discard whatever theory is seen to have blocked the new more "liberatory" reading. That is not Sedgwick's or Miller's declared project. Yet the effacement of "gender"—which had already displaced "sexual difference" in dominant feminist criticism in the U.S.—has had its effects. With its strong thematics of epistemology, legibility, and illegibility, Foucauldian-inflected queer criticism tends to subsume—when it does not overtly repudiate—the different registers of illegibility theorized by deconstruction and psychoanalysis. Deconstruction reads, as Johnson says, the "difference within," the difference between a text and itself that is not reducible to the semantic.[16] (It was Johnson's brilliant reading of *S/Z* which showed that even Barthes, always anxious to preserve the play of meaning, nonetheless pins it down by naming in *S/Z* what the text of *Sarrasine* could not name: castration [*Critical* 3–12].) Psychoanalysis, too, as noted earlier, theorizes a structural rather than a semantic illegibility. Copjec elucidates:

> *[It is misleading] to imply that sex is something that is beyond language, something that language forever fails to grasp. . . . When we speak of language's failure with respect to sex, we speak not of its falling short of a prediscursive object, but of its falling into contradiction with itself. Sex coincides with this* failure, *this inevitable contradiction. Sex is, then, the impossibility of completing meaning, not . . . a meaning that is incomplete, unstable. (20)[17]*

The risk, then, is that the cleavage of sexuality and gender in some queer criticism will—has already—rendered the difference of sexual difference *once again* unreadable. It is to be hoped that in the future the encounter of feminist and queer theories will entail as much rereading as new reading. If in twenty-five years of feminist criticism "women" has been displaced by "Woman," only to be displaced in turn by (a different) "women," which now must once again confront "Woman," who knows what the future might bring.

Reading On

In the spirit of rereading, it seems appropriate to point to another way of figuring legibility and illegibility that is neither strictly deconstructive nor strictly psychoanalytic but very Barthesian, and that is Barthes's notion of the body. The "body" is what he calls a "mana-word," never "*pigeonholed*, always atopic" (*Roland* 129). The body is the cogito but also everything that escapes the cogito; it is the work of the psychosomatic, where the "anarchic foam of tastes and distastes is located" (117). Noting that his struggle against received ideas is as often as not a struggle with himself ("often what he must oppose is not the banality of common opinion but his own"), he writes:

> *Suppose he is to describe his situation in a Tangier bar—what he first manages to say is that the place is the site of an "interior language": a fine discovery! He then attempts to get rid of this importuning banality and to fish out of it some fragment of an idea with which he might have some relation of desire: the Sentence! Once this object is named,*

everything is saved; whatever he writes (this is not a question of performance), it will always be a vested discourse, in which the body will make its appearance (banality is discourse without body). (137)

Under the aegis, then, of Barthes's body, I will close with a fragment of his that offers a different look at thematics:[18]

The Theme

Thematic criticism has come under a certain suspicion in recent years. Yet we must not abandon this critical notion too readily. The theme is a useful notion to designate that site of discourse where the body advances under its own responsibility, *and thereby thwarts the sign: the "gnarled" (rugueux), for instance, is neither signifier nor signified, or both at once: it pins down here and at the same time refers farther away. In order to make the theme into a structural concept, a certain etymological delirium is necessary: as the structural units are in one case or another "morphemes," "phonemes," "monemes," "gustemes," "vestemes," "erotemes," "biographemes," etc. Let us imagine, according to the same formulation, that the "theme" is the structural unit of the thesis (ideal discourse): what is posited, outlined, advanced by the utterance, and remains as* the availability of the meaning *(before being, occasionally, its fossil). (178)*

Thanks to Christina Crosby for her good criticism of the paper, and to Naomi Schor and Joan W. Scott for their helpful comments.

Notes

1   Sedgwick does take up the term "queer" in *Tendencies*. My later use of the term in relation to Miller's work is not authorized.

2   In recent years gender has lost some of its privilege. See Butler and Braidotti who argue very differently for a non-Cartesian embodied gender (Butler) and a non-Cartesian embodied sexual difference (Braidotti).

3   "The thread unraveled by Ariadne, cut by the Fates, woven by Penelope, is a peculiarly feminine attribute, a metonym for femininity" (5). In bringing out this feminized thematics, Schor cautions that however strong the work of a thematic reading, the new thematics are to be restricted, not to go beyond the framework of the individual text (28). As we shall see, Sedgwick's thematics are of a very different sort.

4   See some interesting convergences in Richard's discussion of thematics: "Any thematics will thus derive both from cybernetics and from systematics. Within this active system, the themes will tend to organize themselves as in any living structure: they will combine into flexible groupings governed by the law of isomorphism and by the search for the best possible equilibrium. This notion of equilibrium, which first arises out of the physical sciences but whose crucial importance in sociology and psychology has been demonstrated by Claude Lévi-Strauss and Jean Piaget, seems to us to be of considerable utility in the understanding of the realms of the imaginary. One can indeed observe how themes arrange themselves into antithetical pairs, or, in a more complex manner, into multiple compensating systems" (26; qtd. in Derrida 246–47).

5   In Culler's discussion of thematics he refers both to "The Double Session" and to Abraham's discussion of "Psychoanalysis as Antisemantics" in the essay "The Shell and the Kernel" in the volume of that name. See Culler 206–10.

6   In his April 1994 lecture at Johns Hopkins, "Psychoanalysis Is Not a Hermeneutic," Laplanche argued that from a clinical perspective the most productive Freudian text is the least hermeneutic. Among the most useful texts for him are Freud's early readings before associations are "shut down" by symbolic formulations such as castration: "When symbolism speaks, associations are silent."

7   See the interview with Irigaray entitled "The Power of Discourse and the Subordination of the Feminine" (*This Sex* 68–85).

8   See "The Beast in the Closet" (*Epistemology* 182–212) for an interesting twist on the Oedipal story. For Sedgwick's condensed assessment of the general inadequacy of deconstruction and psychoanalysis to her project, see *Epistemology* 23–24.

9   Miller's and Sedgwick's critical concerns are very closely related, of course, throughout the 1980s.

10   A preference shared in part, at least, by a writer who signs "D. A. Miller."

11   We understand too his mistrust of connotation—that term which has a considerable role in Barthes's repertoire—which for Miller is "the dominant signifying practice of homophobia" ("Anal" 125).

12 That Barthes is referring to men in the passage Miller cites (with its "buggerer and buggeree") can never be in doubt. There are other, less gendered fragments evoking sexual utopias, such as the one entitled "Plural, difference, conflict": "Who knows if this insistence on the plural is not a way of denying sexual duality? The opposition of the sexes must not be a law of Nature; therefore, the confrontations and paradigms must be dissolved, both the meanings and the sexes be pluralized; meaning will tend toward its multiplication, its dispersion (in the theory of the Text), and sex will be taken into no typology (there will be, for example, only *homosexualities*, whose plural will baffle any constituted, centered discourse, to the point where it seems to him virtually pointless to talk about it)" (69).

13 Copjec's essay is a critical reading of Butler's *Gender Trouble*; I cite it out of that context. This is not the place to assess Copjec's critique of Butler or her arguments with deconstruction.

14 It is perhaps necessary to restate that the symbolic order theorized by Lacan and Irigaray is historically specific to the Enlightenment and post-Enlightenment era of the subject. In their writing, the theorization of the subject is always the theorization of the relationality of the subject and the social field. The two terms are historically constitutive of each other.

15 See Ellen Rooney's argument for the necessary incongruence of critical theories in her *Seductive Reasoning.*

16 See Johnson's introduction to Derrida's *Dissemination* (vii–xxxiii).

17 It is in this foreclosure that Irigaray situates a cultural anxiety about matter which is displaced onto women and which expulses women from the thematics of the symbolic order.

18 One might call it a "restricted thematics."

Works Cited

Abraham, Nicolas. "The Shell and the Kernel: The Scope and Originality of Freudian Psychoanalysis." Abraham and Torok 79–98.

Abraham, Nicolas and Maria Torok. *The Shell and the Kernel.* Ed. and trans. Nicholas T. Rand. Chicago: U of Chicago P, 1994.

Armstrong, Nancy. "A Brief Genealogy of Theme." *The Return of Thematic Criticism.* Sollors, *Return* 38–45.

Barthes, Roland. *Incidents*. Trans. Richard Howard. Berkeley: U of California P, 1992.

——. *The Pleasure of the Text*. Trans. Richard Miller. New York: Hill and Wang, 1975.

——. *Roland Barthes by Roland Barthes*. Trans. Richard Howard. New York: Hill and Wang, 1977.

——. *S/Z*. Trans. Richard Miller. New York: Hill and Wang, 1974.

Braidotti, Rosi. *Patterns of Dissonance: A Study of Women in Contemporary Philosophy*. Trans. Elizabeth Guild. New York: Routledge, 1991.

Butler, Judith. *Gender Trouble: Feminism and the Subversion of Identity*. New York: Routledge, 1990.

Copjec, Joan. "Sex and the Euthanasia of Reason." *Supposing the Subject*. Ed. Joan Copjec. London: Verso, 1994. 16–44.

Culler, Jonathan. *On Deconstruction: Theory and Criticism after Structuralism*. Ithaca: Cornell UP, 1982.

Derrida, Jacques. *Dissemination*. Ed. and trans. Barbara Johnson. Chicago: U of Chicago P, 1981.

Heath, Stephen. "Barthes on Love." *Sub-Stance* 37–38 (1983): 100–106.

Irigaray, Luce. *This Sex Which Is Not One*. Trans. Catherine Porter. Ithaca: Cornell UP, 1985.

Johnson, Barbara. *The Critical Difference*. Baltimore: Johns Hopkins UP, 1980.

——. Introduction. Derrida vii–xxxiii.

LaGache, Daniel. Introduction. Laplanche and Pontalis vii–ix.

Laplanche, Jean. "Psychoanalysis Is Not a Hermeneutic." Johns Hopkins University. Baltimore, April 1994.

Laplanche, Jean, and Jean-Bertrand Pontalis. *The Language of Psychoanalysis*. Trans. Donald Nicolson-Smith. New York: Norton, 1973.

Miller, D. A. "Anal Rope." *Inside/Out: Lesbian Theories, Gay Theories*. Ed. and intro. Diana Fuss. New York: Routledge, 1991. 119–41.

——. *Bringing Out Roland Barthes*. Berkeley: U of California P, 1992.

——. *The Novel and the Police*. Berkeley: U of California P, 1988.

Prince, Gerald. *Dictionary of Narratology*. Lincoln: U of Nebraska P, 1987.

Richard, Jean-Pierre. *L'Univers imaginaire de Mallarmé*. Paris: Seuil, 1961.

Rooney, Ellen. *Seductive Reasoning: Pluralism as the Problematic of Contemporary Literary Theory*. Ithaca: Cornell UP, 1989.

Rubin, Gayle. "Thinking Sex: Notes for a Radical Theory of the Politics of Sexuality." *Pleasure and Danger: Exploring Female Sexuality*. Ed. Carole S. Vance. Boston: Routledge, 1984. 267–319.

——. "The Traffic in Women: Notes on the 'Political Economy' of Sex." *Toward An Anthropology of Women*. Ed. Rayna R. Reiter. New York: Monthly Review, 1975. 157–210.

Schor, Naomi. "Dreaming Dissymmetry: Barthes, Foucault, and Sexual Difference." *Coming to Terms: Feminism, Theory, Politics*. Ed. and intro. Elizabeth Weed. New York: Routledge, 1989. 47–58.

——. "For a Restricted Thematics: Writing, Speech, and Difference in *Madame Bovary*." Trans. Harriet Stone. *Breaking the Chain: Women, Theory, and French Realist Fiction*. New York: Columbia UP, 1985. 3–28.

Sedgwick, Eve. *Epistemology of the Closet*. Berkeley: U of California P, 1990.

——. *Tendencies*. Durham: Duke UP, 1993.

Sollors, Werner. Introduction. Sollors, *Return* ii–xxiii.

Sollors, Werner, ed. *The Return of Thematic Criticism*. Cambridge: Harvard UP, 1993.

The Labors of Love. Analyzing Perverse Desire:
An Interrogation of Teresa de Lauretis's
The Practice of Love

Beyond Phallic Desire

*T*he recent publication of Teresa de Lauretis's long-awaited book, *The Practice of Love: Lesbian Sexuality and Perverse Desire*, provides an ideal occasion to reflect on the impact of gay, lesbian, and queer theory on the ways in which psychoanalysis is currently politically utilized, and on the troubled and troubling relations between sexually transgressive practices and the practices of theoretical production. De Lauretis's text can be seen as the culmination and point of intersection of the feminist fascination with psycho-analytic theory which emerged twenty years ago, and the more recent politi-cal eruption of queer politics in the 1990s. This book allows many crucial questions to be framed and asked with the increasing urgency they deserve. In this paper I will focus primarily on the methodological and theoretical relationship between psychoanalysis and feminist and lesbian theory as this is arguably the most intense site for feminist theory in its confrontation with the specificities of lesbian (as well as working class, indigenous, and third world) subjects.

The Practice of Love is an attempt—perhaps the final one[1]—to bring psychoanalysis to account for its own most strategic and vulnerable blind spots, its points of greatest elision or repression: its by now well-recognized failure to account for, to explain, or to acknowledge the existence of an active and explicitly sexual female desire, and, more particularly, the active and sexual female desire for other women that defines lesbianism. This book is a call for psychoanalysis to be accountable to a lesbian constituency for both its (hitherto inadequate) characterizations of female and lesbian desire and for its potential to problematize and to surpass itself and thereby provide the raw materials for a better account. At the same time, it is also a call to attention for lesbians, and especially those who have disdained or avoided psychoanalytic theory for its presumptions about women. It shows that in ignoring the contributions of psychoanalysis to thinking desire, especially lesbian desire, women have abandoned the preeminent cultural discourse of desire.

There is a cluster of psychoanalytic terms that have proven to be a thorn in the side of all feminists, dating from the inception of psychoanalysis itself: the Oedipus complex, the castration complex, penis-envy, the status of the phallus, the paternal metaphor or Name of the Father, the symbolic order, and so on. The question facing feminists who are in some way still attracted to or fascinated by psychoanalytic theory is whether to accept these terms as they stand, and to explain them in political and social terms—thus providing as an acceptable description the (perpetual re-)installation of patriarchal values which such terms imply and produce—or whether to challenge, problematize, and abandon these terms altogether, either replacing them with more accept- able alternatives or moving beyond them; or, more recently, and with more sophistication, to do both together, bringing out the tension between them and the paradoxes, aporias, and points of contradiction that such a tension may generate. At stake here is more than the value—provisional or long-term—of psychoanalytic theory, that is, the question of whether feminists should or should not abandon a discourse that paints so bleak a picture of women's containment within the psychical norms of masculinity. It also affects the intellectual and political status of feminist theory itself.

Is it a reading practice, a practice of interpreting patriarchal texts differently, affirming the capacity of every text (however phallocentric or patriarchal it may be) to be read otherwise? Or is it a practice of the production of alternative or different knowledges, whose goal may be either the produc- tion or revelation of "new" objects using given investigative procedures[2] or the development of different methodological procedures? These key political and ethical questions remain crucially alive and in need of continual affirmation if feminist theory is to develop and transform itself productively through the proliferation of "identities" and "subject-positions," the plethora of "speaking subjects" and "multiple perspectives," through the fragmentation and ques- tioning of its basic goals and assumptions raised by the emergence and insistence of its "others"—lesbians, women of color, working class women, neocolonial subjects.

If psychoanalysis has been so useful for feminist theory and its particular concerns, can it remain so for lesbian theory and its distinctive, if sometimes overlapping, interests? Can theoretical frameworks which have been instrumental in the development of present-day feminist theory be presumed to be of the same or similar interest to lesbian theory? At stake here is an assessment of the overlap—or lack of it—between the interests of feminism and those of lesbianism. Indeed for too long there has been a presumption that feminist interests incorporate and include those of lesbians, that feminism is a more general and generic category representing the interests of all women, and that lesbian interests are a more specific and local sub-category of feminist concerns. Such a model assumes a fundamental continuity between feminism and lesbianism, a relation of general to particular that overly homogenizes their relations and is incapable of understanding the dissimilarities, the space of separation and difference, that divide them. Such a model assumes an inclusive and encompassing feminism, a feminism representative of, or at least capable of representing the interests of all women, a feminism that is strictly speaking impossible. For a feminist position to be equally inclusive of all women is to insist on a feminism of bland generality, a banalized or vulgar feminism, which includes all but speaks to no one group in its particularity, a muted and depoliticized feminism. If feminism no longer represents itself as the privileged discourse of and for all women but instead openly acknowledges and affirms its particularities, its representation of the values and commitments of some groups but not all, then the sometimes complex and intricate negotiations between (white, middle class, heterosexual) feminism and its equally particular others, including lesbians, can begin.

Lesbian Desire in a Psychoanalytic Frame

The relationship between psychoanalysis and feminism has always been fraught with complications, qualifications, hesitancies. From Juliet Mitchell's and Luce Irigaray's earliest feminist investigations of the relevance of psychoanalysis to understanding the experiences and structures governing women's psychical and sexual lives, it has been well recognized that there are major hurdles to be overcome, and explanations to be developed regarding those elements of psychoanalytic theory that were unassimilable to feminist concerns. While the more sexually neutral propositions Freud developed (those regarding the unconscious, the notion of infantile development, the typology of disorders, his understanding of psychical agencies, etc.) seemed to be easily incorporable into a feminist framework without too much political conflict, there were a number of unpalatable assertions many feminists found difficult to swallow, those which characterized women only in terms of their complementary and supporting role regarding the privileged and (pseudo-)autonomous position accorded to men and masculinity, the presumption of a teleologically copulative and reproductive sexual ideal, and the assertion that women's most gratifying source of sexual satisfaction is the compensatory relation to a child. In short, the problem was, and remains, the structure of the containment of women in categories and concepts relevant to men. The structure which de Lauretis, following and modifying Irigaray, describes as a regime or system of "sexual indifference" is one which can only view women insofar as they are comparable to or commensurable with men; it is such indifference that refuses to grant female sexuality or female genitality any authority, agency, or activity, any form or coherence or desire of its own. It consequently reduces female sexuality and genitality to the status of castration, lacking the very organ that is given presence in men. Woman is man minus the phallus, and thus without the benefit of its consequences; she lacks the capacity to initiate, to activate.

It is no surprise that in such a model lesbianism must be either reduced to the terms which govern heterosexuality, with the lesbian lover assimilated to a masculine norm (Freud's hypothesis of the masculinity complex as a constitutive ingredient in the life histories of his lesbian patients), or the lesbian relation must be regarded in desexualized terms, as a regression to the mother-infant relation or a relation of narcissistic mirroring. Lesbianism has been left largely unexplained by psychoanalytic theory (and, for that matter, all the other male discourses that have influenced the questions explored in feminist theory). And it seems as if this area of obscurity is not simply contingently or accidentally obscured through oversight or neglect, but rather, as if this blind spot is constitutive of the psychoanalytic project. If psychoanalysis has problems in its accounts of (heterosexual) women and ("normal") femininity, these problems are amplified and consolidate a point of constitutive incoherence and confusion when it is the topic of lesbianism and not just (heterosexual) female sexuality that is being addressed.

These problems have been well-recognized, even among Freud's most fervent supporters. This recognition has not resulted in the abandonment of psychoanalytic theory as irrelevant to theorizing lesbianism however; on the contrary, it has led to renewed attempts to make psychoanalysis more amenable to such a project. Psychoanalysis has remained the preferred, though certainly not the exclusive or monopolistic, discourse of sexual pleasure and sexual desire within lesbian theorizing.[3] It is now time, I believe, that certain epistemological and political questions be asked: Why do we need psychoanalysis to think lesbian desire? What are the limits of its explanatory power regarding subjectivity and desire, the points beyond which it risks incoherence and contradiction? And who are the subjects it is unable to fit into its explanatory schemas? What is at stake in trying to include what was previously excluded, to place at the center what was marginalized, to explain and analyze what was inexplicable and unanalyzable? Is it to try to recuperate a theoretical or epistemophilic (libidinal) commitment in the light of psychoanalytic theory's manifest inadequacies? Is it an attempt to stretch psychoanalysis beyond its limits of toleration? Is it an attempt to legitimize lesbian practices, to ensure that they are amenable to some kind of analysis and explication, even if that is beyond the usual terms provided by psychoanalysis? Is it to broaden the notion of desire to open it up to the appropriation and use of women, and particularly, lesbians? To broaden the notion of desire such that perversity instead of normalization becomes its explanatory framework? Or is it to shore up and support a discourse whose time has come, an attempt to resurrect a theoretical paradigm facing its limits? The question which needs to be asked here is: Does de Lauretis function to provide a political rationale and credibility for psychoanalysis as it lies dying? Does she, and do other lesbian theorists who have tried to appropriate psychoanalysis for lesbian projects, serve to prolong the agony of this dying discourse, giving it hope for remission when in fact it should be buried?

De Lauretis's book clearly demonstrates that the feminist and lesbian fascination with psychoanalysis is not only understandable, but has provided both with a number of insights unavailable anywhere else, a series of key questions, methods of analysis, and concepts which have become integral to much work being written within feminist and lesbian circles. She is able to bring these feminist and lesbian issues to bear on psychoanalytic discourse, and while her book does not aim to convince lesbians and others that they should be interested in psychoanalysis, she does assume that psychoanalysis has provided and should perhaps continue to provide an understanding of intricacies of the subjective psyche, the structure of fantasy, and the modalities of desire and sexual pleasure. Most significantly, psychoanalysis can be linked to larger social, cultural, and political issues. As long as a psychoanalytic account of lesbian desire avoids certain theoretical temptations and pitfalls, de Lauretis maintains that it can be of great value in understanding the personal passions and the psychical structuring that constitute lesbianism.

Some of her hesitations and suggestions can help provide criteria by which to judge the success or failure of various explanations and accounts of lesbian desire in its different forms and types. For example, de Lauretis quite rightly resists the tendency to romanticism and utopianism in much writing about lesbians and lesbian desire which leads to a nostalgia for the lost (pre-Oedipal) mother-child relation or the fantasy of an imaginary symbiosis with the mother.[4] In insisting on the necessity of an Oedipalized rather than a pre-Oedipal or imaginary structuring to lesbian desire, de Lauretis insists on the fundamentally adult, genital, and sexual nature of lesbianism, against a tendency to see lesbianism as a non-sexualized woman-loving. In emphasizing the post-Oedipal or mature nature of lesbianism, in refusing to accord the idea of psychical or libidinal regression to pre-Oedipal forms of loving, de Lauretis is not suggesting that the pre-Oedipal or imaginary is unimportant or irrelevant but merely that it must be symbolically or Oedipally overcoded, that our access to the pre-Oedipal is always mediated, indeed produced, only through the Oedipal. Moreover, in insisting on the adult, genital nature of lesbian desire, de Lauretis problematizes the notion of the "lesbian continuum" first developed by Adrienne Rich, a concept of the fundamental continuity between lesbian relations and the (non-sexual or non-genital) relations between all women which has been used by some, usually heterosexual, feminists to elide the very real political, social, economic, and sexual differences between lesbians and non-lesbians. In insisting on the distinctively erotic and genital relations between women that characterize the structure of lesbian sexual desire, de Lauretis refuses models of desire proposed by psychoanalytic theory which see female sexual desire as active only according to the notion of the masculinity complex and its correlative conception of penis-envy. Such models can, at best, and highly problematically, explain masculinized or "butch" lesbian sexuality, but are unable to account for the non-masculine or "femme" lesbian.[5] In characterizing lesbianism as the active sexual desire of a woman for another woman, de Lauretis questions the usefulness of any model which reduces or explains away women's desire in male terms, or sees lesbianism as a mode of imitation or emulation of heterosexual role models. But in refusing to masculinize women's desire for other women, de Lauretis does not lurch into the position which tries to reject psychoanalysis in its entirety because it reduces women to either passivity or masculinity. She represents psychoanalysis as still the most viable discourse of desire, the most potent account of subjectivization.

In order to understand de Lauretis's claims regarding psychoanalysis, two pivotal terms in her very detailed and elaborate argument need some explanation: the notion of perverse desire, and the notion of the lesbian fetish (which in many ways feeds into and elaborates the metaphor of the lesbian phallus put forward in Judith Butler's analysis and in my analysis of lesbian fetishism developed in the pages of *differences*).[6]

De Lauretis's explicit goal is the development of a "formal model of perverse desire" (xiii), by which I understand her to mean a general model capable of adequately explaining all the various modalities of lesbian desire (whether "butch" or "femme," "top" or "bottom," sadomasochistic or "vanilla," whether the "real life" experiences of subjects, or the filmic, theatrical, poetic, or literary representations, a model whose particular details need to be filled in and modified according to the subject's particularity). In order to develop such a formal model, de Lauretis needs to specify what she means by the notion of "perverse desire," and how this is related to and differs from the normatively heterosexual understanding of sexuality and desire that pervades the practice of psychoanalysis. There is already a tension in Freud's writings between an acceptance of the teleology of heterosexual copulation and reproduction, and the perpetual undermining of the naturalness or inevitability of this sexual teleology through his understanding of the constitutive function of the deviations or vicissitudes of sexual aims, objects, and sources of erotic pleasure.[7]

In reading Freud through the work of Jacques Lacan, Jean Laplanche, and a number of feminist theorists, de Lauretis proposes a "negative theory of the perversions," a theory of sexuality as inherently perverse, non-normative, impossible to definitively separate from either normality or neurosis. If perversion is, as Freud suggests, a deviation from an instinctual activity, the insinuation of a gap between a drive and its aims and objects, then *all* sexuality is a deviation, all desire perverse, all pleasure an amalgam of heterogeneous component drives which refuse any simple subordination to genital and reproductive functions. Heterosexual genital and reproductive sexuality are only the tenuous results of the repression and reordering of the heterogeneity of drive

impulses. If one emphasizes the perverse side of Freud's unresolved ambivalences regarding the nature of human sexuality, as de Lauretis, following
Laplanche, proposes, then the peculiarities of heterosexual normality are
thrown into stark relief. If, instead, one emphasizes Freud's normative understanding, then clearly it is the perversions, and particularly homosexuality,
which are in need of explanation:

> *Thus perversion, and homosexuality in particular, has a peculiarly*
> *paradoxical status in Freud: both central and yet disruptive; neces-*
> *sary and yet objectionable; a "deviation" from the norm and yet more*
> *compatible with positive social goals; degrading of human relation-*
> *ship and yet more pleasurable than "civilized" sexuality; regressive or*
> *involuntary and yet expressive of an originary intensity of being. (25)*

What is both interesting and puzzling about de Lauretis's speculations
on the "negative trace of the perversions" (28) is her claim that such a negative
theory of the perversions will prove as useful an explanatory model for homosexual desire as the positive or normative theory is useful for explaining
heterosexual desire.[8] In short, her presumption is that the ambivalence surrounding Freud's two contradictory understandings of sexuality can be to some
extent resolved by separating the two models—the normative, heterosexual
model, from this theory of desire as perversion—so that one can explain
perverse desire and the other "normal" desire. This tends to mute the cutting
edge of Laplanche's extrapolation from Freud that the deviation is what both
enables and undermines the norm, that the perversions are also capable of
characterizing *all* forms of (human) sexuality and *all* forms of desire. Laplanche
claims that the sexual drive per se is instituted by way of a (deviant) retracing
of psychical and biological processes mapped initially by biological or instinc-
tive processes. Where instincts require a real object for satisfaction and for the
material maintenance of life, the drive insinuates a fantasy object in place of
the instinct's real object, a fantasy object whose powers of attraction rapidly
outstrip and incorporate the real. Sexuality is in itself a deviation, a departure
from the real, from biology, from necessity, into the meandering detours of
fantasy. On the other hand, this separation is what is necessary for de Lauretis
to accept as relevant the formal structures Freud proposes—the Oedipal scenario, the notion of castration, and the phallus—while transforming the way
they operate and how they are commonly understood. This is necessary for her

to differentiate her account of lesbian desire from Laplanche's more general understanding of the perversity of all desire. This separation of the normative from the perverse is the condition for de Lauretis's project for rethinking the sexual specificity of lesbian desire; but at the same time, it involves unravelling precisely the process of self-undoing Freud's two accounts of sexuality set up for each other. And thus it involves unravelling precisely the tension that has so attracted feminists and others to psychoanalytic discourse.

Splitting at the Seams

I cannot hope to adequately cover much of de Lauretis's highly intricate arguments regarding the structure of perverse desire. Instead, I will focus on what I believe is the most distinctive and contentious of her claims, her linking of lesbian desire to the structure of fetishism. De Lauretis develops as convincing an analysis of the genesis and structure of lesbian desire using the psychoanalytic framework as has been yet attempted. If *she* is unable to accommodate lesbian desire within this framework, then it seems unlikely that it can be done. In a sense, her text is a test or limit case for psychoanalysis. Given that the standard Freudian account of the Oedipus complex and penis-envy are not able adequately to explain lesbian desire, can a modified, transformed, or selectively rewritten version, one, for example, which replaces the privileged role of repression as the mechanism of defence which most ably resolves the Oedipus complex, fare better as a mode of explanation?

This is de Lauretis's gamble, her wager: that if psychoanalysis is to remain relevant to understanding lesbian desire, its foundation in male and heterocentric privilege must be overcome, and alternatives, devised from within its frame, put forward. If these or similar transformations are to succeed, then psychoanalysis may be able to retain its political relevance in the face of the political dispersion that "postmodern culture" effects. If, on the other hand, it must be either so drastically modified as to become a different theory, no longer recognizably that psychoanalysis based on the privilege of masculinity, the phallus, or heterosexual coupling, then perhaps it is time that the amount of energy and effort feminists, lesbians, and gays have invested in psychoanalysis might be better invested in other theoretical approaches and intellectual endeavors.

De Lauretis develops her analysis of lesbian fetishism from a detailed reading of Radclyffe Hall's *The Well of Loneliness* and Cherríe Moraga's *Giving*

Up the Ghost. It is on her rereading, or rather, her revision of the status and nature of the concepts so carefully tied together in an apparently inextricable cluster in Freud's account of Oedipalization—the notion of castration, the paternal phallus, the concept of penis-envy, and the masculinity complex. It is clear that these concepts must either be abandoned (and if they are, psycho-analysis as a whole must go with them insofar as the Oedipus complex is not only the nucleus of the neuroses, but also the center of a knot which ties together Freud's understanding of sexuality with his understanding of the unconscious), or they must be stretched and contorted so as to be able to accommodate female, or lesbian, desire. This latter is precisely the task de Lauretis sets for herself: how to take one strand of Freud's ambivalent asser-tions and leave the alternative.

For example, it is significant that the notion of castration is composed of two strands: the notion of the (potential or actual) amputation of the child's genital organs as punishment for sexual transgression (a notion which must be disturbing to feminists, whether the disturbance is directed to Freud's theory or the patriarchal culture it purports to describe), and a notion of the prohibition and abandonment of the pre-Oedipal, incestuous attachment of the child to the mother. In more orthodox readings of Freud's work, these two claims are intricately linked: the prohibition on desiring the mother has force and effect only because the (boy?) child is threatened with castration, that is, with feminization. De Lauretis tries to extricate these two strands from each other, to think a notion of castration in which the child's desire is disentangled from the desire of the mother (while still remaining linked to it), as Freud suggests, but where amputation does not necessarily entail the privileging of the penis or of masculinity as the only active form of desire. Unlike some lesbian theorists who wish to displace, to move beyond, the notion of castration (or to read it in linguistic rather than corporeal terms), de Lauretis maintains that some notion of castration must be retained, and that some notion of phallus needs to be developed. But these can no longer be simply linked to the presence or absence of the penis, as Freud suggests, and Lacan, in spite of his denials, also affirms.[9]

Coupled with her disentanglement of the primacy of the penis (and particularly the paternal penis) from the castration complex is de Lauretis's attempt to explain the notion of lesbian desire, not in the terms most suited for discussing neurosis[10]—repression—but in those which may be more appropri-ate for perverse pleasure: disavowal and fetishism. Following the work of Leo

Bersani and Ulysse Dutoit, she suggests that perhaps the very structure of desire itself—all desire—might be characterized as fetishistic, insofar as it both affirms and denies a founding primal object of desire while creating a substitute for it. That substitute is the series of (endless) objects that are taken, in Lacanian parlance, as the "cause" of desire, its motivation or trigger. Like de Lauretis, Bersani and Dutoit want to distinguish the fetish from the phallus, or rather, from the penis that the mother is assumed to have had, and lost, and that the father is demonstrated as possessing. They claim that the fetishist does not see the fetish as the missing (maternal) penis but as something separate and different, a sign or talisman or, perhaps better, a metonym related to the penis but in no way resembling it.[11] The fetish is not a replacement penis; rather, it is a "fantasy-phallus" (225), an object/sign invested in fantasy with the status of phallus (=object of desire). It does not replace, resemble, or compensate for the missing penis, which is irrevocably "gone," a function of the castration of women's narcissism and body-image rather than anatomy. Rather it functions only on the recognition, the affirmation, of castration. It is only if the subject's desire is detached from its first libidinal objects that the perverse freedom of desire to range over all manner of objects with a great variety of sexual aims becomes possible. In this sense, castration is the condition of perversion as much as of neurosis or normality.

De Lauretis needs to disinvest the notion of castration from the amputation of bodily organs, and to see perverse desire in terms of disavowal rather than repression in order to explain how the phallus can be detached from the father and paternity, and to be able to provide an account of lesbian desire beyond the masculinity complex. Where disavowal is also clearly involved in Freud's account of the masculinity complex (in which the girl disavows her castration and clings to the belief that one day the stunted clitoris [or little penis] will grow), it is a question of *what* is disavowed. In the case of the masculinity complex, it seems, the girl disavows her own castrated condition and retains a competitive, "masculine" relation to activity. In the case of the lesbian, however, it is not her castration that she disavows (the lesbian accepts that she is a woman who desires a woman, not a woman who desires to be a man). It is rather the absence or loss of *another woman's* body (in the first instance, the mother's body)—the separation of mother and child that is part of the nexus of terms constituting castration—she must disavow and displace onto a fetishistic substitute (236), a sign that qualifies or modifies a woman's body, which constitutes for her the lure of lesbianism:

> . . . *what the lesbian desires in a woman . . . is indeed not a penis but a part or perhaps the whole of the female body, or something metonymically related to it, such as physical, intellectual, or emotional attributes, stance, attitudes, appearance, self-presentation—and hence the importance of clothing, costume, performance, etc. in lesbian subcultures. She knows full well she is not a man, she does not have the paternal phallus (nor would her lover want it), but that does not preclude the signification of her desire: the fetish is at once what signifies her desire and what her lover desires in her. . . . In short, the lesbian fetish is any object, any sign whatsoever, that marks the difference and the desire between the lovers: say, "the erotic signal of her hair at the nape of her neck, touching the shirt collar" or, as Joan Nestle also suggests, "big-hipped, wide-assed women's bodies." It could be the masquerade of masculinity and femininity of the North American butch-femme lesbian subculture. . . . (228–29)*

De Lauretis does not deny the notion of castration—for to do so, she claims, is to abandon the right to symbolic and signifying efficacity and genital or orgasmic maturity. What is castrated, what is both lost and disavowed, covered over and displaced, is a lovable or desirable *female body*. Here de Lauretis, as others before her have done, locates the (retrospective?) effect of castration on the earlier narcissistic self-representation that accomplishes an ego and ego-ideal for the subject. Castration does not so much sever the girl from a genital organ of her own as transcribe or rewrite an earlier loss, the loss of a female body (her own, or that of the mother). In the case of Stephen Gordon, for example, it is the mother's incapacity to desire Stephen's body, her failure to find it feminine that performs a wound or castration of Stephen's (imaginary) body-image. In de Lauretis's reading, the narcissistic problem for Stephen is not that her body is phallically castrated; her body is *too phallic*, too masculine to be desired.[12] What she mourns is the lost female body. What lures and attracts her are the fetish replacements of this lost body (which may, but need not be understood as the maternal body; the body lost in Stephen's case is her own female body), the irresistible attraction of mannish clothing, and the conventions governing masculine bodily gait and habit within her culture. These are among her particular lesbian fetishes. The fetish is a displacement of the bodily dispossession that constitutes the castration that the girl suffers.[13] This fetish cannot be identified with the object of lesbian desire (the woman) but is the subject's means of access to and mode of attraction for the love-object. And ideally, the fetish is what in turn induces an interest from the love-object. No doubt there are a potentially infinite number of signs, traits, gestures, mannerisms that pose the lure Lacan attributed to the *objet petit a*. These "strange attractors" which signal the inducements of the erotic object to a desiring subject are those special details that attract a woman to a woman.[14]

Significantly — and this is a measure of the improvement de Lauretis's model of lesbian desire has over competing models — she is able to explain both the similarities and the differences between "butch" and "femme" sexual positions using her account of lesbian fetishism. In the case of the "butch" lesbian, paradigmatically represented by the figure of Stephen Gordon, de Lauretis suggests that the lure of mannish clothing and the trappings of masculinity are hardly surprising given that it is the signification of masculinity which, in our culture, most readily and directly represents active sexual desire for the female body:

> The reason seems too obvious to belabor: not only is masculinity associated with sexual activity and desire, imaged in the erect penis and its symbolic or ritual representation in the phallus; but, more to my immediate point, in a cultural tradition pervasively homophobic, masculinity alone carries a strong connotation of sexual desire for the female body. That is the lure of the mannish lesbian—a lure for her and for her lover. The fetish of masculinity is what both lures and signifies her desire for the female body, and what in her lures her lover, what her lover desires in her and with her. (243)

The "butch" lesbian does not desire to be a man, or envy what it is that men have (the penis) but rather takes as her own signifiers of desire that have helped characterize men's desire.[15] Her model of lesbian fetishism is also capable of qualifying the position of the "femme" as well, for just as the mannish woman is able to take the signs of masculinity as fetish-objects, so too the "femme" takes the signs of femininity, sometimes in parodied form, as a fetish, as both her mode of attractiveness for another and as what provides her with satisfaction. De Lauretis sees this femininity as a hyper-femininity, a mode of reclamation and restaging of the loss and recovery of the female body:

> *The exaggerated display of femininity in the masquerade of the femme performs the sexual power and seductiveness of the female body when offered to the butch for mutual narcissistic empowerment. (264)*

The same can be said for all the various scenarios of lesbian desire, whatever particular forms it may take. In lesbian sadomasochism too, it is the question of the status, value, and control of the female body that is at stake, and the implements of sexual desire which serve as fetishes. What lesbians share in common, de Lauretis suggests, is that "in all these cases perverse desire is sustained on fantasy scenarios that restage the loss and recovery of a fantasmatic female body" (265). The fantasy scenarios within which the fetish functions are always, or "structurally," a restaging of the loss or abandonment of the female body. This is what distinguishes lesbian, or perverse, desire from the structures and desires which mark stereotyped heterosexuality: a kind of primal scene of dispossession by which lesbianism is structured as both compensation and resistance.[16]

Lines of Flight

There is no doubt that *The Practice of Love* is a significant book. It represents an intriguing last-ditch effort to preserve psychoanalytic theory, to retain the critical and radical edge that theory achieved when first taken up by feminists as the discourse of subjectivity and desire. I am not convinced that de Lauretis has succeeded, although I suspect that those perhaps less disillusioned with the political and theoretical implications of too heavy a reliance on psychoanalytic theory would find the project more appealing and quite convincing. My concerns are not about the quality of de Lauretis's work but more about the capacity of the framework of psychoanalysis to explain precisely that which it must exclude in order to constitute itself as a mode of knowledge.

One of the major strategies of the 1970s and 1980s in feminist theory has been the impressive capacity of some feminists to extend one model of power, particularly a masculinist text, so that it covers domains and objects hitherto left out or unthought, which thus constitute a point of blindness or vulnerability for that model (domestic labor for marxism, lesbian desire for psychoanalysis, feminine modes of discipline or ethical self-regulation for

Foucault). While an immense amount of (sometimes productive and reward-ing) feminist thought, ingenuity, and labor has gone into this project of stretching or extending the tolerable boundaries of male discourses so that they may be made useful for or amenable to feminist projects, it is not clear what the long-term benefits are of continuing to prop up or support a discourse which has well-recognized problems. Perhaps the major drawback of such an approach is the claim that the objects or concepts neglected or excluded by these male discourses are *not* simply (passively) forgotten through a kind of oversight. Domestic labor, lesbian desire, female discipline are actively ex-cluded concepts, concepts whose exclusion conditions the field in which they function as blind spots. These concepts that are literally unthinkable in their given frameworks involve either a contradiction in the theoretical model involved, or a space incapable of being theoretically colonized by that frame-work. Attempts to fit women, or in de Lauretis's case lesbians, into these frameworks is bound to be intellectually profitable—one learns an immense amount about these frameworks, and their limits in the process—but in the long run, they prove impossible.

In order to take on and productively utilize Freudian and Lacanian discourses in a context where they not only have manifest shortcomings but also a systematic commitment to these shortcomings for theoretical coherence, de Lauretis must both face and expose what is problematic about psychoana-lytic discourses, and then show that these problems are not so overwhelming that they entail the abandonment of its frame. Her critical endeavor of chal-lenging the various uses of psychoanalytic theory by other feminists, lesbian, or gay theorists—which I believe is the most powerful part of her book—is necessarily bound up with (an implicit) recuperative project, that of insulating psychoanalysis from the implications of feminist and lesbian criticisms, keep-ing it propped up when it is only with major transformations, transformations which have unclear and ambiguous effects, that it can maintain its explanatory power in the case of its excluded others.

Her utilization of psychoanalysis has been ingenious, and I believe that her account of "fetishism" (which for me is not really adequately separated from a Lacanian notion of the phallus as mobile, not tied to either the penis or masculinity) provides a complex and quite plausible model for explaining some of the styles and orientations of lesbian desire; but this explanation is built at considerable cost, both to theories of lesbian desire and to psychoanalysis. While I do not have an alternative account of lesbian desire to offer in place of the labor of love she undertook in producing this book and in devising a theory of lesbian desire based on a "rereading" (but actually a reworking) of psychoanalysis, what I can offer is some (sympathetic) criticism, proffered in the spirit of one committed to a broadly similar project.

My most general concerns are precisely about the status of psychoanalytic discourse (in its various permutations), and de Lauretis's reliance on it as the sole explanatory framework in her account of the structuring of lesbian desire. It is a similar concern I have for other feminist projects that take psychoanalytic explanations as the paradigm or norm for what constitutes an explanation. It seems to me that one must be aware of a certain "ethics" of reading, an ethics of the appropriation and use of discourses. One cannot simply buy into a theoretical system (especially one as complex and as systematically conceived, in spite of its inconsistencies, as psychoanalysis) without at the same time accepting its basic implications and founding assumptions. I am not here suggesting that one must always read Freud with the view to accepting it all, but rather, that when one uses a discourse for one's own purposes it is never entirely clear which of its implications or assumptions are incompatible with one's own. Problematic implications cannot be contained and prevented from infiltrating those considered unproblematic. It is not clear, more specifically, that one can utilize a whole range of Freud's concepts (about fantasy, desire, pleasure, sexuality, etc.) without accepting that which underlies and links them—the castration complex, the primacy of the phallus, the relations of presence and absence governing the sexes. This is what de Lauretis's strategy seems to be, and, ironically, it is this wish both to have one's cake and eat it, both to "castrate" and preserve psychoanalysis, which characterizes the fetishist's use of disavowal.

De Lauretis's revisionism is aimed at three target concepts: the notion of castration, the centrality of repression and the concept of the masculinity complex, a cluster of concepts which deserve rigorous interrogation. It remains unclear to me how one can claim to accept the framework of Oedipalization, the notion of the paternal phallus, the concept of castration and yet locate "castration" as a mirror-stage or imaginary bodily dispossession. This, even in Freud's terms, cannot be a castration, even if it anticipates and makes castration possible, even if castration retrospectively inflects its meaning and status. And it remains unclear how, in claiming that it is the psychical structure of disavowal rather than repression which characterizes lesbian desire, what implications this has, for example, with respect to the notion of the unconscious for lesbians. Or is it that disavowal exists alongside of repression? In this case, why is the dispossession of a female body the object of disavowal rather than repression, and why is this one object of disavowal alone significant for lesbians? While I certainly agree with de Lauretis that the masculinity complex is not an adequate model for understanding lesbianism because it subsumes women under phallic norms, it is unclear that the fetish is any less phallic in its structure and implications. Her model of the fetish, which she openly relates to Butler's use of the notion of "lesbian phallus," entails an attempt to detach the phallus from its metonymic connections with the penis, to detach the phallus from paternity and authority and thus to render it more mobile.[17] But if the fetish is just as implicated in masculinity as the phallus, then a theory which displaces the masculinity complex with fetishism does not necessarily leave lesbianism any better off. This is something she seems to recognize, at least in her discussion of Naomi Schor's account of female fetishism (269), where she admires Schor's intellectual honesty in both positing female fetishism and at the same time questioning its political and strategic value as a disruptive term within the psychoanalytic corpus.

Perhaps more disconcerting than her revisionist use of psychoanalysis is the potential effect of using psychoanalysis for theorizing lesbian desire itself. De Lauretis seems to be proposing the possibility of a specific "lesbian psychology," an aetiology of lesbianism that distinguishes the structure of lesbian desire from the structures of heterosexuality not simply in terms of a distinction between love-objects but also in terms of different body-images and representations, and thus a different symbolic and imaginary. If this is the case, then she is (implicitly) committed to a concept of a "lesbian psychology." But here we must ask if indeed there is a systematic difference of the kind de Lauretis suggests—a common dispossession of a female body and the desire to (re)attain it—which separates lesbians from heterosexuals. If there is such a difference, moreover, this seems to problematize the position of those women who "become" lesbians, which, ironically, is how she characterizes herself (xix). Just as the feminine lesbian constitutes a point of blindness for both orthodox psychoanalysis and some lesbian appropriations of it,[18] de Lauretis seems to have difficulty accounting for those lesbians who have *become* lesbians. Do these lesbians undergo a change in psychology (a transfer from repression to disavowal)? Or are they simply repressed lesbians who had to await their chance for sexual pleasure and desire (while suffering under heterocentric ideology)? But if one is to grant such women an accepted status as lesbians, then how can de Lauretis account for the apparent mobility of (perverse) desire? How is it that not only can heterosexual women sometimes convert to lesbians, but the converse is also true: some women "become" heterosexual. Do these women, or those who label themselves as "bisexual" change their psychologies and the structure of their desire while in lesbian relationships? If there is a systematic difference in the structure of desire between lesbians and heterosexual women, how can such mobility be accounted for? Unless there is a common structure of desire—or at least a very broad continuum on which both lesbian and heterosexual women's desires can be located—the openendedness of desire in its aims, objects, and practices cannot be adequately explained.

Moreover, while I can see the strategic value of focussing on "butch"-"femme" relations as those which, when lived out by women's bodies, constitute a transgression of the naturalizing effects of heterosexual "gender roles," and while I can see how her analysis of the mannish woman is pivotal in de Lauretis's challenge to the model of the masculinity complex, I remain worried about models of lesbian sexuality and desire that focus primarily on these relations at the expense of others. I have similar reservations about the strategic value of a notion like the "lesbian phallus," "lesbian dildos," and virile display; while they do have the effect of unsettling or disquieting presumptions about the "natural" alignment of the penis with social power and value, they do so only by attempting to appropriate what has been denied to women and to that extent remain tied (as we all are) to heterocentric and masculine privilege. Such modalities remain reactive, compensatory. This is more or less the presumption that must be drawn from de Lauretis's ascription of an inadequate mirroring of the female body by the mother. The fetish is compensation for this lost female body, making sexual access to (other) women's bodies possible.

I do not want to suggest that de Lauretis's project is a useless one or a waste of time. On the contrary, it is an immensely important project which needs to be pushed further and further to its very limits, as de Lauretis has herself pushed psychoanalysis to its limits of toleration—the limits of *knowing sex* or *knowing desire* which Foucault investigated in terms of its links to power and knowledge and modes of subjectivization. Her work has enabled this question to be placed on the political agenda: What is the (political) value and function of rigorously understanding, theorizing, lesbian desire and lesbian psychology? While clearly it may be, as de Lauretis claims, a mode of rethinking one's own fantasies, of understanding oneself better (xiv), of understanding oneself in terms other than those which confirm the majoritarian heterosexist conception of desire, pleasure, and power, it must also be recognized that by placing lesbian desire under the microscope of intellectual, scientific, or discursive investigation, it is thereby increasingly invested with a will to know that may be part of the very taming and normalization (even if not hetero-sexualization) of that desire.[19] This depends to a large extent on the status and effects of the discourses one uses. Perhaps now is the time to rethink which discourses these should be.

Notes

1   This will be my major argument in this paper—that psychoanalysis is incapable of providing an account of female sexual desire and that this failure is constitutive.

2   For example, the extension by marxist-feminism of a marxist framework of productive labor onto the domain of domestic labor, or the extension by psychoanalytic feminism of (Freudian, Lacanian, Kleinian, etc.) psychoanalysis onto the domain of female or lesbian sexuality.

3   In addition to de Lauretis's work, the writings of Judith Butler and Judith Roof must be mentioned as relevant.

4   Such a fantasy of wholeness, harmony, and completion in the imaginary mother-child dyad is a rewriting of the major sources of tension and bodily upheaval that characterize the infant's earliest relations with the mother. In describing this as a period of corporeal fragmentation and incapacity, and in linking the structure of the imaginary order to frustration and aggressivity, Lacan provides a necessarily sobering counterbalance to this retrospective idealization.

5   "... with regard to lesbianism, the masculinity complex has little or no explanatory power, for it fails to account for the non-masculine lesbian, that particular figure that since the nineteenth century has baffled sexologists and psychoanalysts, and that Havelock Ellis named 'the womanly woman,' the feminine invert" (de Lauretis, xiii).

6   See Butler and Grosz.

7   "Freud's equivocation with regard to this issue—whether a normal sexual instinct, phylogenetically inherited, preexists its possible deviations (in psychoneurotic individu-als) or whether instinctual life is but a set of transformations, some of which are then

defined as normal, i.e., non-pathogenic and socially desirable or admissible—is a source of continued but ultimately insoluble debate" (10).

8   "What if one set out to pursue a theory of sexuality along the negative trace of the perversions—let us say, fetishism? Such theory might not, perhaps, account for the majority of people, but then the positive theory of sexuality does not either; and then again, the notion of 'the majority of people' is as troubled as the notion of 'the normal' . . . " (28).

9   Her question is posed under the rubric of the "negative theory of the perversions":

"What if, then, one were to reframe the question of the phallus and the fantasy of castration in this other perspective provided by Freud's negative theory, so to speak, of the perversions? . . . [T]he two lesbian texts under discussion [Hall's and Moraga's] speak fantasies of castration; but they also, and very effectively, speak desire; and thus they are fully in the symbolic, in signification. Yet the desire they speak is not masculine, nor *simply* phallic. But again, if the phallus is both the mark of castration and the signifier of desire, then the question is, What acts as the phallus in these lesbian fantasies?" (222).

10   Which de Lauretis rather mysteriously distinguishes from hysteria, although hysteria can only be understood as a particular form or type of neurosis.

11   De Lauretis quotes a crucial passage from Bersani and Dutoit's analysis:

"The crucial point—which makes the fetishistic object different from the phallic symbol—is that the success of the fetish depends on its being seen as authentically different from the missing penis. With a phallic symbol, we may not be consciously aware of what it stands for, but it attracts us because, consciously or unconsciously, we perceive it *as* the phallus. In fetishism, however, the refusal to see the fetish as a penis-substitute may not be simply an effect of repression. The fetishist has displaced the missing penis from the woman's genitals to, say, her underclothing, but we suggest that if he doesn't care about the underclothing resembling a penis it is because: (1) he knows that it is not a penis; (2) he doesn't want it to be only a penis; and (3) he also knows that nothing can replace the lack to which in fact he has resigned himself" (Bersani and Dutoit, 68–69; qtd. in de Lauretis, 224).

12   De Lauretis claims that Stephen's revulsion of her own body image, captured in a kind of "primal scene" in viewing her own body in a mirror, is too phallic a body, rather than, as classical psychoanalysis would represent her, a woman under the sway of the masculinity complex, a woman envious of the penis:

"What Stephen sees in the mirror (the image that establishes the ego) is the image of a phallic body [de Lauretis claims], which the narrator has taken pains to tell us was so from a very young age, a body Stephen's mother found 'repulsive.' Thus, since 'the other person' who serves as model of bodily desirability is Stephen's mother, the image of herself that Stephen sees in the mirror does not accomplish 'the amorous captivation of the subject' or offer her a 'fundamentally narcissistic experience,' but on the contrary inflicts a narcissistic wound: that phallic body-image, and thus the ego, cannot be loved, cannot be narcissistically invested *because* it is *phallic*" (240–41).

One with a more orthodox psychoanalytic bent might perhaps respond by claiming that the problem for Stephen's representation is that, while her body may be imaged or signified as *virile*, nonetheless, what it lacks, what prevents it from attaining the status of the phallic body is the absence of the very signifier (the imaginary, detachable penis) that signals her female status. Her personal misery comes, in her own eyes, from her being neither properly feminine nor properly masculine, from her lacking the signifiers of femininity (as de Lauretis affirms) *and* the signifiers of masculinity (the phallus).

13   In her characterization of this sense of bodily dispossession, de Lauretis lurches perilously close to implying that it is the mother who is in a sense responsible for the daughter's sense of bodily dispossession. This is clear in her discussion of the genesis of Stephen Gordon's body-image, and in her more general characterization of what it is that the girl disavows. Such an implication is disturbing insofar as it leaves the father out of the account of the "origin" of lesbian desire, when it seems clear that the father's position must have some effect on the psychology of the daughter, whether she becomes heterosexual or a lesbian. And it is problematic insofar as any model which "blames" the mother (although her position is not as crude as attributing straightforward blame) must itself explain the mother's position as well, and how it is that she is unable to narcissistically validate the daughter's embodiment: "Failing the mother's narcissistic validation of the subject's body-image, which constitutes the imaginary matrix or first outline of the ego, the subject is threatened with a loss of body-ego, a lack of being" (262).

Moreover, if this dispossession occurs in the imaginary or pre-Oedipal orders, if it is a consequence of the mother's relation to the infant daughter's body, we must ask if this implies there is such a thing as a distinctively lesbian ego or lesbian body image.

14   It remains unclear why this highly suggestive model, not necessarily of lesbian *desire* as de Lauretis claims, but more of lesbian attraction, is not as appropriate for men and heterosexual women as it is for lesbians. That strange elusive "thing" that attracts one person to another (whether the attraction culminates in a sexual relation or not) could be thought in terms of this very specific notion of fetish that de Lauretis develops.

15   "If the lesbian fetishes are often, though certainly not exclusively, objects or signs with connotations of masculinity, it is not because they stand in for the missing penis but because such signs are most strongly precoded to convey, both to the subject and to others, the cultural meaning of sexual (genital) activity and yearning toward women. Such signs

can also most effectively deny the female body (in the subject) and at the same time resignify (her desire for) it through the very signification of its prohibition" (263).

16 De Lauretis claims an inherent political status to lesbian sexualities, and particularly for the fetish of masculinity which seems to me rather disturbing and problematic:

"... the signs of masculinity are the most visually explicit and strongly coded by dominant discourses to signify sexual desire toward women, and hence their greater visibility in cultural representations of lesbianism, which correlates to their greater effectivity in a political use of reverse discourse" (264).

While I do not want to deny that in specific contexts lesbianism, and particularly the adoption of the signs of masculinity, may perform a transgressive function, there seems to be nothing inherently transgressive about any particular sexualities or desires. It is not clear whether de Lauretis wants to claim that greater visibility constitutes greater political effectivity (which seems a rather dubious principle) or whether she wants to suggest that women's adoption of precisely *those* sexual positions is transgressive here and now. This again seems to me conditional on the context: where the butch lesbian may certainly transgress the expectations of a straight community, in the context of lesbian social life, it is clearly a mode of conformity to a set of shared images or fetishes.

17 "We need not just to refuse to anchor ourselves *firmly* on one or the other side of the paternal phallus, but to loosen ourselves from it altogether, and to really follow through the idea of a mobility of fetishistic or perverse desire by giving up the convenience of notions such as oscillation and undecidability" (269).

18 Including my own earlier attempts ("Lesbian"), as de Lauretis correctly argues.

19 I develop this argument in considerably more detail in a paper presented to the MLA in 1992 ("Experimental Desire"). A longer version of this paper is forthcoming in *The Subject*, a volume edited by Joan Copjec.

Works Cited

Bersani, Leo, and Ulysse Dutoit. *The Forms of Violence: Narrative in Assyrian Art and Modern Culture.* New York: Schocken, 1985.

Butler, Judith. "The Lesbian Phallus and the Morphological Imaginary." *differences: A Journal of Feminist Cultural Studies* 4.1 (1992): 133–70.

de Lauretis, Teresa. *The Practice of Love: Lesbian Sexuality and Perverse Desire*. Bloomington: Indiana UP, 1994.

Grosz, Elizabeth. "Experimental Desire: Bodies and Pleasures in Queer Theory." *The Subject*. Ed. Joan Copjec. London: Verso, forthcoming.

——. "Lesbian Fetishism?" *differences: A Journal of Feminist Cultural Studies* 3.2 (1991): 39–54.

Rich, Adrienne. "Compulsory Heterosexuality and Lesbian Existence." *Blood, Bread and Poetry: Selected Prose 1979–1985*. New York: Norton, 1986. 23–75.

TERESA DE LAURETIS

Habit Changes. *Response*

> *It is true that, so far as we know, no*
> *psychical apparatus exists which*
> *possesses a primary process only and*
> *that such an apparatus is to that extent a*
> *theoretical fiction. But this much is a*
> *fact: the primary processes are present*
> *in the mental apparatus from the first,*
> *while it is only during the course of life*
> *that the secondary processes unfold, and*
> *come to inhibit and overlay the primary*
> *ones.* (Freud, *Interpretation* 603)

*I*t is not the purpose of this article to engage with the terms of debate set forth in the title of this special issue. I have indeed written on all three— gender, feminism, and queer theory—in the pages of this journal and else- where, but the theory I want to meet here is (forgive the presumption) my own: a theory of sexuality, and in particular lesbian sexuality and desire, as outlined in my recent book *The Practice of Love.* The occasion for this article and the reason for its appearance in this issue of *differences* are Elizabeth Grosz's review essay, also published here, and the opportunity it offered me for reflection, retrospection, and reconsideration of the ideas I developed in the book.[1] What *is* the book about? What did I want to accomplish in it? What are its presumptions and conceptual limits, its unresolved or enabling questions, its contribution to a contemporary understanding of sexuality and desire?

Unlike some of my other works, *The Practice of Love* is not concerned with feminist theory, except insofar as feminist theory has concerned itself with lesbian sexuality. I say this not in order to distance myself from feminist theory, but rather to distance myself from the marketing trend that labels "feminist theory" any speculative work authored by a woman, whatever its critical approach, disciplinary framework, and political commitment. As for "queer theory," my insistent specification *lesbian* may well be taken as a taking of distance from what, since I proposed it as a working hypothesis for lesbian and gay studies in this very journal (*differences* 3.2), has quickly become a conceptually vacuous creature of the publishing industry. I will add, therefore, that *The Practice of Love* is not about feminist theory or queer theory; it is a study of sexuality or, if you will (though it does sound pretentious), a theory of sexuality. But if it can be considered a work of feminist theory it is because my practice of critical writing, the form of address and the rhetorical strategies I chose, including what I call the politics of reference, are consistent with the practice of feminist theory as I see it.

For example, while I read Freud's theory as the elaboration of a passionate fiction, I do not claim otherwise of my own writing: I acknowledge that the impulse for this work comes from my own fantasies and experiential history, and I locate it in my particular socio-geographical and intellectual formation. Even more important, perhaps, I build my argumentation with reference to and in dialogue with works by other lesbians and feminists which I engage directly, sometimes critically, often painstakingly, and always explicitly because I want to acknowledge that the writings of these women—be they theorists or poets, novelists or critics—constitute the epistemological terrain of my own thinking no less than do the more prestigious writings of Freud, Lacan, or Foucault.

My practice of grounding arguments in particular texts, whether literary, filmic, or critical, is a deliberate and at times risky intellectual practice, a resistance to the institutional demands that would have me, the "author," be the sole and unique point of origin of my discourse. In other words, it is a manner of practicing what one preaches, so to speak, an effort to convey at once an intellectual attitude and a set of theoretical assumptions in the very *form* of one's writing, to instantiate or inscribe in that form the theoretical assumption that discourse—and thus, too, anyone's discourse, speech, writing, and thought itself—is constructed from other discourses; which does not mean that discourse is merely repetitious, mimetic, univocally predetermined or finally contained in an unchanging Symbolic order. On the contrary, it is the very constructedness of discourse, its overdetermination, and its slipperiness that allow for what Judith Butler calls "a reiterative or rearticulatory practice" (15).

Put another way: it is precisely the intrinsically dialogic and situated character of discourse that makes it possible to intervene in the symbolic order through practices of reappropriation or resignification which affect and to some extent alter the symbolic and which, I argue, affect and alter the imaginary as well.

In this context, the project of *The Practice of Love* is a rereading of Freudian psychoanalysis in order to rethink lesbian sexuality both within and against its epistemological and conceptual framework. But this *thinking within and against* should not be equated with some simple, voluntaristic notion of subversive or transgressive theoretical practice (the recent history of the world should have cured us of the illusions of the sixties and seventies). *Thinking within and against* is the condition of all critical thinking. Mine is no exception.

There are two main theoretical objectives or critical directions in the book. One is the reevaluation of the concept of perversion in Freud, as distinct from the pathological, and its resignification in what I call perverse desire, a type of desire fetishistic in a general sense and specifically homosexual or lesbian. The other is the effort to theorize what Foucault calls the "implantation of perversion" in the subject, to analyze the mechanisms social and psychic by which the subject is produced at once as a social and a sexual subject through her solicitation by and active participation in various discourses, representations, and practices of sex. These sexual-representational practices, I argue, both overdetermine and continually inflect sexual structuring. I will come back to this term, this awkward gerund-phrase, and why I use it. But first let me give you, briefly, a sense of my argument.

The constitutive ambiguity of Freud's discourse on sexuality from the *Three Essays on the Theory of Sexuality* of 1905 to the posthumous works on fetishism makes it possible to read two theories of sexuality in his work: one is explicit and affirmative, a positive theory of "normal" sexuality that goes from the infantile stage of polymorphous perversity to a successfully Oedipalized, normal, heterosexual adulthood. The other, I contend, is implicit and negative, appearing as the nether side or clinical underground of the first: it consists of two modalities, perversion and neurosis, depending on the presence and degree of repression (there can of course be repression or neurosis with/in perversion—the two are not mutually exclusive). In this theory, what is called "normal" sexuality is not an innate disposition or configuration of the sexual instinct, but rather the result of particular negotiations that a subject manages to achieve between the internal pressures of the drives, the various component instincts or partial drives, and the external, parental and societal pressures.

This latter theory follows from Freud's radical insight that the relation between an instinct or drive [*Trieb*] and its object [*Objekt*] is not natural, preordained by "biology," fixed, or even stable. The sexual instinct, he wrote, is "in the first instance independent of its object" (*Three* 147–48), and later added:

> *The object of an instinct is the thing in regard to which or through which the instinct is able to achieve its aim. It is what is most variable about an instinct and* is not originally connected with it, but becomes assigned to it only in consequence of being peculiarly fitted to make satisfaction possible. *("Instincts" 122; emphasis added)*

In this sense, perversion is not a distortion of "nature," a deviation from a biologically determined law that assigns one and only one type of object to the sexual drive, but is rather an inherent way of being of the drive itself, which continuously seeks out the objects best fitted to its aim of pleasure and satisfaction. Thus, if the drive is independent of its object, and the object is variable and chosen for its ability to satisfy, then the concept of perversion loses its meaning of deviation from nature (and hence loses the common connotation of pathology) and takes on the meaning of deviation from a socially constituted norm. This norm is precisely "normal" sexuality, which psychoanalysis itself, ironically, proves to be nothing more than a projection, a presumed default, an imaginary mode of being of sexuality that is in fact contradicted by psychoanalysis's own clinical evidence. Perversion, in this sense, is virtually the opposite of pathology, as it is formally the opposite (the positive, Freud said) of neurosis: perversion is the very mode of being of *sexuality* as such, while the projected norm, in so-called normal sexuality, is a requirement of social *reproduction*, both reproduction of the species and reproduction of the social system. Now, the conflation, the imbrication, of sexuality with reproduction in Western history has been shown by Foucault to come about through what he called "the technology of sex" and has been analyzed by feminist theory in the concept of compulsory heterosexuality. And it is, obviously, still central to hegemonic discourses. But my point is that the specific character of *sexuality* (as distinct from *reproduction*), the empirically manifested form of sexuality, as far as psychoanalysis knows it, is perversion, with its negative or repressed form, neurosis.

Following up in this perspective, the second part of my study undertakes the elaboration of what I call perverse desire. Rereading the classic studies on female homosexuality, the case histories written in the 1920s and 1930s by Freud himself, Jeanne Lampl-de Groot, Helene Deutsch, and Ernest Jones, in conjunction with the classic novel of female inversion, Radclyffe Hall's *The Well of Loneliness* (also of 1928), and with contemporary lesbian literary and filmic texts of the 1980s by Cherríe Moraga, Adrienne Rich, and Sheila McLaughlin, among others, I delineate a type of desire whose signifier is not the phallus but something (object or sign) more akin to a fetish; that is to say, in the texts I analyze, the object-choices of a lesbian subject appear to be ruled, as in fetishism, by the psychic mechanism of disavowal [*Verleugnung*], which is at once the denial and the acceptance of castration.[2] All my texts exhibit an unmistakable fantasy of castration or dispossession.

To articulate such a desire into a formal model (a model with general validity), I undertake a reconsideration of the fantasy of castration in relation to a female body. The reconsideration is necessary because the threat of castration can only work in relation to what Freud calls a bodily ego or body-ego (*Ego* 26–27); in other words, in order to be effective, the threat of castration must mean the possible loss of something on which the subject has bodily aims, something which is a source of sensations, pain and pleasure. I argue, therefore, that the threat that confronts the female subject (and that is disavowed by the formation of a fetish) is not the lack or loss of a penis but the lack or loss of a libidinally invested body-image, a body that can be narcissistically loved, and that loss of a bodily ego is tantamount to a loss of being, or a loss *in* being. Thus the fantasmatic "lost object" of perverse desire is neither the mother's body nor the paternal phallus; it is the subject's own lost body, which can be recovered in fantasy, in sexual practice, only *in and with* another woman. This perverse desire is not based on the masculinity complex (the denial of sexual difference), nor is it based on a regressive attachment to the mother (a regression to the pre-Oedipal or the phallic phase). It is based on the post-Oedipal disavowal of that loss—the loss of one's body-ego, the loss of being.

Finally, then, what I call perverse desire is a form of female (lesbian) desire that *passes through* the Oedipus complex but, contrary to all psychoanalytic accounts, including feminist ones, does not remain caught in its binary terms and moves on to other objects. These fetish-objects sustain and represent the subject's desire, her possibility of *being-in-desire*; in Freud's terms, they would engage at once both object-libido and ego-libido. But how do particular objects or signs become cathected or invested by the drives?

Perhaps the most ambitious part of my project is the effort to delineate the paths by which the drives select and invest their objects, and thus the paths through which psychic reality interacts with external reality. The drives, for Freud, are innate, but sexuality is not. As we understand it since and from Freud, sexuality is neither innate nor *simply* acquired, but is constructed or dynamically structured by psychic processes and forms of fantasy—conscious and unconscious; subjective, parental, and social; private and public—which are culturally available and historically specific. Fantasies, in Laplanche and Pontalis's famous phrase, are the scenarios (scripts or stage settings) of the subject's desire, and sexuality itself is constituted in the field of fantasy. It seems to me that if desire is dependent on the fantasy scenario that the object evokes and helps to restage, then it is in that restaging that an object—any object—acquires the fantasmatic value of object of desire. So now the question to ask is, how do objects become attached to a desiring fantasy?

Reading Freud with Peirce, I speculate that sexuality is a particular instance of semiosis, the general process of sign and meaning formation, a process which articulates and enjoins subjectivity to social signification and material reality. How objects become assigned to instincts, in Freud's words, can be conceptualized through Peirce as a semiosic process in which objects and bodies are displaced from external to internal or psychic reality (from dynamic object to immediate object in Peirce, from real body to fantasmatic body in Freud) through a chain of significate effects or interpretants, habits, and habit-changes. With the concept of habit, in particular, I emphasize the material, embodied component of desire as a psychic activity whose effects in the subject constitute a sort of knowledge of the body, what the body "knows" or comes to know about its instinctual aims. The somatic, material, and historical dimensions that the Peircian notions of *habit* and *habit-change* inscribe in the subject reconfigure sexuality as a *sexual structuring*, a process overdetermined by both internal and external forces and constraints.

I use this awkward gerund-phrase, *sexual structuring*, instead of more familiar ones like sexuality or sexual identity because the gerund form conveys, both etymologically and performatively, the sense of an activity, a dynamic and interactive process: *gerund* comes from the Latin *gerere*, to carry, and the gerund form carries the meaning of the verb, makes the verb work in its meaning, its signifying, or makes that meaning a working, an activity. This is not conveyed in the term *identity*, or *sexuality*, nor is it clearly conveyed in the term *sexuation*, used in Romance languages, the noun form of which also suggests something solid, definitive, the outcome of a process but still an outcome, a result, something achieved, done with, or final. By *sexual structuring* I want to designate the constructedness of sex, as well as of the sexual subject, its being a process, an accumulation of effects that do not rest on an originary materiality of the body, that do not modify or attach to an essence, matter or form—whether corporeal or existential—prior to the process itself. In other words, neither the body nor the subject is prior to the process of sexuation; both come into being in that continuous and life-long process in which the subject is, as it were, permanently under construction.[5]

Several years ago I argued the same apropos of gender; I wrote that the subject is effectively en-gendered in an interactive subjection to what I called the technology of gender. I wrote *en-gendered* with a hyphen (it was in the mid-eighties, a time when word punning by diacritical marks like hyphens, parentheses, slashes, etc. was becoming very popular). The subject is *en-gendered*, I wrote—that is, produced or constructed, and constructed-as-gendered—in the process of assuming, taking on, identifying with the positionalities and meaning effects specified by a particular society's gender system (*Technologies* 1–30). Recently, Judith Butler has elaborated on the concepts of assumption and identification in her book *Bodies That Matter*; she argues that the assumption of or identification with the norms of sex (or of gender) on the part of a subject is a reiteration of the symbolic law, a kind of "citationality," a citing of the law, and thus a performativity (12–14), which does not preclude agency in subjectivation (what a few lines above I called *interactive subjection*, borrowing the term from video games, one of the latest social technologies). Butler also argues, however, paradoxically, that agency or subjectivation "in no way presupposes a choosing subject" and must be seen rather as "a reiterative or rearticulatory practice, immanent to power" (15), without an agent or a subject who acts. "There is not power that acts," she states, but only a reiterated acting that is power in its persistence and instability" (9). Power has no subject, Butler insists; and if we think of power as having a subject, it is purely an effect of grammar and of the humanist discourse that places the human subject or, in his stead, power, at the origin of activity and agency.

To be sure, this early-Foucauldian argument is still a powerful critique of the Cartesian subject, who appears to be alive and thriving in some circles, in spite of Freud, Nietzsche, Foucault himself, deconstruction, postmodernism, and so on. But in Butler's book, the radical delegitimation of the subject lives uncomfortably with a "progressive," or redemptive, political project; namely, the reinscription of excluded, abjected, queer bodies into the body politic by a "resignification of the symbolic domain" (22) and thus their revaluation, inclusion, or legitimation as bodies that matter. For me, Butler's argument and her project live uncomfortably together because it is difficult to imagine how symbolic resignification is to occur, and to result in such revaluation and legitimation of the abjected bodies, without agents or subjects of those practices of reiteration, citation, and reappropriation that Butler identifies in, for example, drag, passing, and renaming.

For the purposes of my study of sexuality, it is not only bodies that matter; the subjects, each of them constructed and constrained through a bodily boundary, must also matter; for me they are indispensable in a theory of sexuality, queer theory, or any other. For, if sexual structuring, sexuation or subjectivation, is an accumulation of effects that does not accrue to a preexisting subjectivity or to a primal, original materiality of the body, nevertheless the process takes place in and for a bodily ego; and moreover, a body-ego that is constituted, literally comes into being, through what Freud calls *Urphantasien*, primal or original fantasies, which are also fantasies of origin.[4]

What is this subject, then? In my reading of Freud, the subject is a body-ego, a projected perceptual boundary that does not merely delimit or contain the imaginary morphology of an individual self, but actually enables the access to the symbolic: in my reading of Freud, the body-ego is a permeable boundary—an open border, so to speak—a site of incessant material negotiations between the external world, the domain of the real, comprising other people, social institutions, etc., and, on the other side, the internal world of the psyche with its instinctual drives and mechanisms of defense—disavowal, repression, and so forth. To map those negotiations, which is one of the objectives of *The Practice of Love* and of my practice of theory, I try to bring together three unwonted bedfellows: Freud, Peirce, and Foucault—not only the Foucault of the technology of sex but also and especially the Foucault of the practices of the self.

For my study of perverse desire, although more concerned with intrapsychic than with institutional mechanisms, is premised on a conception of the sexual that is actually closer to Foucault than to Freud, namely that individual sexual structuring is both an effect and a condition of the social construction of sexuality. While Foucault's first volume of the *History of Sexuality* describes the discursive practices and institutional mechanisms that implant sexuality in the social subject, Freudian psychoanalytic theory describes the subjective or psychic mechanisms through which the implantation takes, as it were, producing the subject as a sexual subject.

I suggest that Peirce's notions of interpretant and habit-change may serve as the juncture or point of theoretical articulation of Freud's psychosexual view of the internal world with Foucault's sociosexual view: the chain of interpretants and its resulting habit may serve as a model of the semiosic process in which objects and bodies are displaced from external to psychic reality—from dynamic object to immediate object in Peirce, and from real body to fantasmatic body in Freud. In each set, the objects and the bodies are contiguous but displaced in relation to the real; and the displacement occurs through a series of significate effects, habits or habit-changes. The site of this displacement is what I call the subject: that is to say, the subject is the place in which, the body in whom, the significate effects of signs take hold and are contingently and continuously real-ized.

When, reading one of Foucault's last published works which outlines his projected study of the "Technologies of the Self," I encountered the term *self-analysis* in relation to the introspective exercises and the writing of self that, according to him, defined a new experience of the self in Greco-Roman thought of the first two centuries A.D., the coincidence of that term, *self-analysis*, with Peirce's "self-analyzing habit" could hardly fail to strike me. Could Foucault be reconciled with Peirce? I propose that, yes, this may be more than a coincidence. You may be skeptical, but hear me out.

In volumes 2 and 3 of his *History*, as Foucault's research shifts from the macro-history of modern sexuality in the West to the micro-history of localized practices and discourses on one type of sexuality (that between men and boys), his focus, too, shifts from the social to the subjective, from the technology of sex to the "technologies of the self," the discursive practices and techniques of the individual's construction of self. As he describes it retrospectively, his project was

> *a history of the experience of sexuality, where experience is under-*
> *stood as the correlation between fields of knowledge, types of nor-*
> *mativity, and forms of subjectivity in a particular culture. . . . But*
> *when I came to study the modes according to which individuals are*
> *given to recognize themselves as sexual subjects, the problems were*
> *much greater . . . it seemed to me that one could not very well analyze*
> *the formation and development of the experience of sexuality from the*

eighteenth century onward, without doing a historical and critical
study dealing with desire and the desiring subject. . . . Thus, in order
to understand how the modern individual could experience himself as
a subject of a "sexuality," it was essential first to determine how, for
centuries, Western man had been brought to recognize himself as a
subject of desire. . . . It seemed appropriate to look for the forms and
modalities of the relation to self by which the individual constitutes
*and recognizes himself qua subject. (*Use 4–6*)*

In the introductory volume, Foucault had indicted psychoanalysis as complicit
with the dominant power-knowledge apparati of the modern era. Here, even as
he speaks of the subject of desire, he pointedly sidesteps the psychoanalytic
knowledge on that subject, looking instead for another approach. The whole
first part of volume 3, for example, is devoted to Artemidorus's *Interpretation of
Dreams* without a single reference to Freud, whose homonymous text also
marked the starting point and first elaboration of his theory of desire on the
basis, as we know, of his *self-analysis*. (And indeed Freud refers to Artemidorus's
Oneirocritica in his *Traumdeutung* [98–99].)

Now, it is impossible to imagine that Foucault missed these obvious
analogies; on the contrary, he must have purposely implied them to emphasize
the distance between Freud's scientific project, if based on his personal,
Oedipal fantasy, and Foucault's own critical genealogy of desire. But neither his
pointed taking of distance from psychoanalysis nor his much greater historical
distance from his materials and sources can altogether erase the effective
presence of an enabling fantasy, though not an Oedipal one, in Foucault's
authorial subject of desire. The care with which the erotic relations between
men and boys are examined, described, and pursued from Greece to Rome,
through modifications in sexual ethics, to the development of "an art of
existence" and the constitution of the self "as the ethical subject of one's sexual
behavior" (*Care* 238–40), more than suggests the presence of both a *self-
analysis* and an enabling fantasy in Foucault's theory. While the enabling
fantasy of Freud's theory is admittedly Oedipal, Foucault's is the fantasy of a
non-Oedipal world, beyond the Fall, perversion, repression, or Judeo-Christian
self-renunciation, a world sustained instead by a productively austere, openly
homoerotic, virile ethics and practice of existence.

It is in the context of this genealogical project, effectively a genealogy of man-desiring man, that Foucault speaks of self-analysis. In describing the "new experience of self" derived from introspection, from taking care of oneself, and from the practice of writing about oneself that was prominent in the second century A.D., he highlights Marcus Aurelius's "meticulous concern with daily life, with the movements of the spirit, with self-analysis" ("Technologies" 28). This latter term, *self-analysis*, together with *self-exercise* (27) and other techniques "which permit individuals to effect by their own means or with the help of others a certain number of operations on their own bodies and souls, thoughts, conduct, and way of being" (18), seems to me altogether convergent with Peirce's notion of habit as final interpretant: the "*deliberately formed, self-analyzing* habit—self-analyzing because formed by the aid of analysis of the *exercises* that nourished it" (5.491; emphasis added). This, for Peirce, is the "living" effect of semiosis. In short, the new *experience* of self that Foucault describes is, in effect, a habit-change.

I don't know yet what significance to find in the fact that the works of Freud's and of Foucault's I drew on in this last section of the book are works they wrote as they were approaching death. Perhaps the conceptual limits of my project—the wild attempt to map a space between heterogeneous theoretical domains by means of analogies, tropes, word associations; and the presumption to account for a kind of desire that I have lived in the terms of a conceptual universe, that of Freud's psychoanalysis, in which it is not understood or contemplated but through which I nevertheless do think—perhaps these limits have something to do with the limit that is imposed by a growing awareness of death. As I get older, time gets shorter every day, one needs to hurry.

Questions have been raised in several quarters regarding my working through psychoanalysis (which I think of rather as a working-through of psychoanalysis). The most frequent is, why look to psychoanalysis for an account of female—let alone lesbian—desire, when Freud himself finally gave up, saying it could only be asked of poets? Or, why buy into a conceptual system that altogether precludes the possibility of a female desire, as Elizabeth Grosz rephrases that question in her thoughtful "interrogation" of *The Practice of Love* in this issue? Moreover, Grosz states, psychoanalysis is "a discourse whose time has come," a "dying discourse," and would best be buried. Yet she proceeds to take issue with my improper or unorthodox use of psychoanalytic concepts: if one insists in seeking understanding through psychoanalysis, then one should accept its founding assumptions and rigorously employ its concepts—e.g., castration—and not wilfully stretch them to the point of theoretical incoherence. Can the fetish, for example, ever be anything but a morphological inflection of the phallus?

Further, Grosz suspects that my attempt to take psychoanalytic theory where none of its adepts has gone before implies a revisionist project; in other words, my book is not the funeral ode to psychoanalysis that she would auspicate, but an implicit (surreptitious) attempt to prop it up or resuscitate it by the infusion of a seemingly progressive problematic, the lesbian question. It thus appears to her as a recuperative project aimed at insulating psychoanalysis from the criticisms of those social subjects whom psychoanalysis does not contemplate and therefore, it is alleged, excludes. Conversely (perversely), however, Grosz also argues that my elaboration of a model that distinguishes between lesbian and heterosexual female desire can be seen as an *anti*-psychoanalytic move, a covert attempt to create a lesbian *psychology*, leading to a particular, unchanging, fixed, or reified configuration of (lesbian) subjectivity. And finally, she asks, why would one want to "know" lesbian desire? to make lesbian desire the object of "intellectual, scientific or discursive investigation," to subject it to the will to know? Isn't a formal model of lesbian desire tantamount to normalizing lesbianism and taming desire? These are harsh questions, coming from one who is supposed to know.

Other readers have given me the benefit of the doubt, suggesting that it is as a feminist scholar of literature and film that I can inhabit "the radical edge of psychoanalytic thinking" in a country where psychoanalysts still secretly believe that homosexuality is an illness (Benjamin); or that my reading of "a subversive Freud" succeeds in moving lesbian sexuality "out of its ghetto within the academy and into the spotlight of twentieth-century Euro-western discourses," and seeks to settle the score for "decades of, at the very least, mental abuse that we lesbians have suffered from psychoanalytic and feminist theorists" (Brinks). Needless to say, I tend to agree with them.

With regard to the second critical direction of my project, the reading of Freud with Peirce to find a linkage between Freud's privatized view of the sexual subject and Foucault's eminently social view of sexuality—a reading which I consider just as theoretically risktaking as the theorizing of a perverse desire—no one has yet, to my knowledge, commented or questioned it.[5] And the silence may be more ominous that the harsh criticisms. But because the notion of a perverse lesbian desire and what in the book I call the seductions of lesbianism to a feminist imaginary appear to be more immediately catching, I will now take up some of the issues that have been raised concerning that part of my project.

In fact, I have posed some of those questions myself, in the book. It is possible, I suggested, that what I call perverse desire can account for other forms of sexuality than those represented in the texts I analyze, that my work can enable thinking about other so-called "perversions" or other forms of female sexuality that are ostensibly heterosexual. It is even possible that my notion of perverse desire may be productive toward a theorizing of male homosexuality, and all these possibilities are most welcome to me. But that was not the project of *this* book: masochism, female heterosexuality, bisexuality, and male homosexuality are not within my competence and not my fantasy. Or they are not at this moment.

I did, however, spend some time addressing the question, why psychoanalysis, why Freud, what can they contribute to an understanding of lesbian desire? For one thing, since sexuality is "the essential contribution of psychoanalysis to contemporary thought," as Laplanche put it (*Life* 27), we cannot think the sexual outside of psychoanalytic categories or, much more often, outside of psychoanalytic myths and reductive vulgarizations of those categories. Second, it is true that psychoanalysis was developed within the apparati of power-knowledge that one class, the bourgeoisie, deployed in the nineteenth century to ensure its own reproduction and survival as a class, as Foucault argues, but he also adds:

> in the great family of technologies of sex, which goes so far back into
> the history of the Christian West, of all those institutions that set out in
> the nineteenth century to medicalize sex, [psychoanalysis] was the one
> that, up to the decade of the [nineteen] forties, rigorously opposed the
> political and institutional effects of the perversion-heredity-
> degenerescence system. (History 119)

This is an important factor in one's choice of understanding lesbian sexuality through psychoanalysis, and as distinct from heterosexual female sexuality, precisely because the perversion-degeneracy system (and some version of heredity, now possibly heredity-as-nurture) is still operative, if not explicitly invoked, in mainstream views of lesbianism as contrasted to a healthy, maternally inclined, female *hetero*sexuality; and that psychoanalytic tradition—just now one hundred years old—of political opposition to the medicalization of perversion, homosexuality in particular, can be reactivated and rearticulated, if need be against the psychoanalytic clinical establishment.

There is still, however, the issue of theoretical coherence. How far can a notion like castration be stretched or resignified before it loses its structural value and epistemological effectivity? I have suggested that the texts I analyze are thematically centered on a fantasy of dispossession, which can be read as a fantasy of castration *because* of its structural role in the formation of a fetish. That fetish, which in some (but only some) of my texts appears as variously coded signs of masculinity,[6] is not the *paternal* phallus, although it retains its structural function of signifier of desire. In Freud's account, the fetish is a substitute for the maternal penis that the male child expects to see in the mother's body but finds missing; his apperception of a body without penis produces castration anxiety, which is relieved by the fetish. By the same account, no fetishism is possible for women since the castration complex is produced quite otherwise in the female, namely, by her seeing a body with penis, a male body, and not the mother's body, which is said to be "like" her own. But is it *like* her own?

I proposed that, for the female subjects of my texts, the castration complex rewrites in the symbolic—and therefore in the terms of (hetero)sexual difference, penis, no-penis—a prior or concurrent perception: the perception, or rather the non-perception, of no-body; that is to say, the perception that her own body is precisely *not like* the mother's, and hence not desirable, not lovable, a no-body. This threat of castration as non-being is based on a non-perception (a fantasy), just as the threat of castration for the male fetishist is based on the non-perception of the (missing) maternal penis. In other words, there is a clear homology, at least in this theoretical speculation, between the male's fetish in the classic theory of fetishism and the female's fetish in my formulation, although they are based on two distinct corporeal morphologies, both of which are of course fantasmatic. In the two cases, the fetish stands to disavow the lack or loss, to represent the object that is missing but narcis-sistically wished for: the penis/phallus in one case, the female body in the other. In both instances, the fetish, in its various and contingent forms, is nothing but the signifier of desire.

It seems to me that this formulation of female fetishistic or perverse desire is, if anything, too structurally coherent with the psychoanalytic model (one might say that it is truly a case of fearful symmetry), and may be too coherent for our own good. Thus, if incoherence is charged, may it not be out of adherence to the *letter* of the law, and a wish to uphold the *paternal* phallus above all? For what I have suggested is that the fetish in perverse desire takes on the function of the phallus as signifier of desire, but leaves behind the paternal function of the phallus, its role in physical and sociosymbolic repro-duction. In other words, the fetish releases *sexuality* from its embeddedness in *reproduction*, and thus demonstrates that reproduction is not a feature of sexuality as such, but rather an effect of the construction of sexuality in modern Western cultures.

Now, I do not think that such a project is revisionist in the sense of a conservative move to restore psychoanalysis as good object and protect it from the criticisms of those for whom it is or has become a bad one. It is, I think, a critical reading, an effort to work through critically—to work with and against—the concepts and the rhetorical and conceptual ambiguities of Freud, in order to remobilize their potential for resistance. It is true that Freudian psycho-analysis cannot envisage female homosexuality—not even as a perversion—and can only assimilate it to either female heterosexuality or male homosexu-ality. And yet Freud's own project, as Sander Gilman argues in *The Case of Sigmund Freud*, was not only marked but also enabled by his "racial differ-ence," his "racial" inscription as a Jew, and the struggle with scientific para-digms which cast him, a doctor, as primitive, degenerate, and diseased. For, in an actual instance of poetic justice, the theory of psychoanalysis enabled Freud to resignify those categories as the very stuff civilization is made of, and thus to transform the conditions of representability and the paradigms of knowledge of his time. That is one of the lessons I would draw from Freud: that no science and no theory is an immutable decalogue written in stone, and, therefore, if he could not imagine such a thing as lesbian desire, while others can, then it is for those others to attempt to resignify the categories of his theory from the location of their own difference and for their own time.

To conclude, I would like to say something about one of the questions that remains unresolved in the book, and unresolved for me, namely, the relation of fetishism to narcissism in perverse desire; that is to say, whether the particular form of primary narcissism that is involved in perverse desire can be related to the secondary narcissism that Freud said to be specifically feminine. The narcissistic dimension in perverse desire, I argue, is related to primary narcissism and infantile autoeroticism because it is the loss of a narcissistically invested body-image that threatens the ego with a loss of being and prompts the defense process of disavowal. For this reason, I propose, that threat is equivalent to the threat of castration in the male subject: both are narcissistic wounds that threaten the ego—the respective body-egos—with a loss of being. However, secondary narcissism, too, is an effect of the castration complex in women, according to Freud. He describes it as a sort of reimbursement that femininity demands for the loss of the penis, and says that it can stand in the way of object-cathexes, as in the case of "narcissistic women," who love only themselves "with an intensity comparable to that of the man's love for them" ("Narcissism" 88–89).

In my notion of perverse desire, primary and secondary narcissism cannot be distinguished as clearly as in Freud's metapsychological essay. However, as I pointed out, Freud is characteristically ambiguous in his theory of narcissism, which he bases on a distinction between ego-libido and object-libido (or ego-instincts and sexual instincts): at times the distinction is given as an opposition, while at other times they are said to coexist side by side. Taking the latter hypothesis—let us give Freud the benefit of his own uncertainties—it may be the case that so-called feminine narcissism is in fact coextensive or homologous to the ego-enhancing, autoerotic primary narcissism. This was the view held by Lou Andreas-Salomé, one of Freud's closest interlocutors. As Biddy Martin remarks in *Woman and Modernity*, Salomé challenged "the privilege Freud seem[ed] to accord to object-libido over narcissism" (207) and argued for primary narcissism as an indeed primal, original "connection with All," which she associated explicitly with femininity and with an autotelic development of the feminine psyche (205). According to Martin, Salomé believed that this original, innate narcissism was particularly strong in women, as well as creative artists and (male) homosexuals, and hence her notion of "a fundamental bisexuality" of women (211).

But this notion, now popular among feminist theorists, much like Freud's postulate of a latent or potential homosexuality in all human beings, cannot finally account for why or how particular object-choices are made by each individual. It seems to me that the distinction—not an opposition, but a distinction between two psychic forces that can coexist with one another—between ego-libido or narcissistic disposition and the object-choice component of sexual desire is usefully maintained when one is concerned to articulate the sexual difference between lesbian and heterosexual female desire. The question of bisexuality, if it is a question, should be addressed not before but after the modalities of such sexual dispositions have been understood. To posit an a priori, potential or latent bisexuality, as Freud and Salomé did, goes a very short way toward illuminating the psychic forms and socio-sexual practices of homosexuality, heterosexuality, or even actual bisexuality itself.[7]

Distinguishing between these socio-sexual practices and supposing that they entail and produce distinct socio-symbolic forms of subjectivity are not at all the same as saying that one and only one structure of desire can exist for any one subject, are not the same as saying that subjectivity is necessarily fixed, stable, or unchanging over the course of an individual's life. I coined the awkward term *sexual structuring* precisely to designate the permanently-under-construction character of sociosexual subjectivity in its ongoing, over-determined relation to fantasies and representations that are both intra- and inter-subjective. It is only by disregarding this part of my project that one can see in it a reification of lesbian sexuality or the creation of a lesbian "psychology" as the product of a will to knowledge that would spell out and normalize the makeup of a lesbian identity. Especially since the question of *identity* is not one of the questions asked in *The Practice of Love*.

I will end by saying that my book is not intended to revise or improve psychoanalysis but to displace the limits of the conceptual categories through which I, and not I alone, can think the sexual. So I would like my readers to think of this work as a series of hypotheses, speculations, contentions, dialogues, and reflections for the staging of a theoretical fiction that addresses itself not *to* psychoanalysis but *through* psychoanalysis . . . to whom it may concern.

Notes

1 An earlier version of this paper was presented in a plenary session at the 1994 meeting of the Society for Phenomenology and Existential Philosophy in Seattle.

2 Both disavowal and repression are defense mechanisms and both are operative in sexuality, in perversion and neurosis (see Bass 321).

3 See note 7 below.

4 Richard Wollheim discusses Freud's notion of the bodily ego in relation to mental and corporeal representations or internal and external realities. Drawing on Melanie Klein, his discussion of internalization (introjection) in relation to the unconscious fantasy of

incorporation is necessarily tied to the notion of developmental (progressive) stages; his argument is limited to and by a developmental perspective. My reading of the bodily ego draws on Jean Laplanche, who links fantasy to Freud's *Nachträglichkeit* (deferred action or, as Laplanche translates it, "afterwardness"), which makes the notion of fantasy more supple and conducive to a dynamic view of sexuality or sexual structuring (see Laplanche, "Freud").

5   With the exception of Anne Freadman, an Australian Peirce scholar, to whom I express my gratitude for her careful reading and generous suggestions in a personal communication.

6   In others, the fetish is a writing hand, a femme's masquerade of femininity, a flower, or even a whole fantasy scenario—none of which makes reference to masculinity.

7   A similar point is argued in Whitney Davis's *Drawing the Dream of the Wolves*, a study of homosexuality and visual interpretation in Freud's "Wolf Man" case. I am indebted to Davis for the trope of the subject as permanently under construction.

Works Cited

Bass, Alan. "Fetishism, Reality, and 'The Snow Man.'" *American Imago* 48 (1991): 295–328.

Benjamin, Jessica. "The Other Woman." *New York Times Book Review* 4 September 1994: 15.

Brinks, Ellen. "The Awesome Pull of Desire." *Lambda Book Report* July-August 1994: 19.

Butler, Judith. *Bodies That Matter: On the Discursive Limits of "Sex."* New York: Routledge, 1993.

Davis, Whitney. *Drawing the Dream of the Wolves: Homosexuality, Interpretation, and Freud's "Wolf Man" Case.* Bloomington: Indiana UP, 1995.

de Lauretis, Teresa. *The Practice of Love: Lesbian Sexuality and Perverse Desire.* Bloomington: Indiana UP, 1994.

———. *Technologies of Gender: Essays on Theory, Film, and Fiction.* Bloomington: Indiana UP, 1987.

Foucault, Michel. *The Care of the Self.* Trans. Robert Hurley. New York: Random House, 1986. Vol. 3 of *The History of Sexuality.* 3 vols. 1978–86.

———. *The History of Sexuality: An Introduction.* Trans. Robert Hurley. New York: Pantheon, 1978. Vol. 1 of *The History of Sexuality.* 3 vols. 1978–86.

——. "Technologies of the Self." *Technologies of the Self: A Seminar with Michel Foucault.* Ed. Luther H. Martin, Huck Gutman, and Patrick H. Hutton. Amherst: U Massachusetts P, 1988. 16–49.

——. *The Use of Pleasure.* Trans. Robert Hurley. New York: Random House, 1985. Vol. 2 of *The History of Sexuality.* 3 vols. 1978–86.

Freud, Sigmund. *The Ego and the Id.* 1923. *The Standard Edition of the Complete Psychological Works of Sigmund Freud.* Trans. and ed. James Strachey. Vol. 19. London: Hogarth, 1961. 1–66. 24 vols. 1953–74.

——. "Instincts and Their Vicissitudes." 1915. *The Standard Edition.* Vol. 14. 1957. 109–140.

——. *The Interpretation of Dreams.* 1900. *The Standard Edition.* Vol. 4–5. 1953. 1–628.

——. "On Narcissism: An Introduction." 1914. *The Standard Edition.* Vol. 14. 1957. 67–104.

——. *Three Essays on the Theory of Sexuality.* 1905. *The Standard Edition.* Vol. 7. 1953. 123–246.

Gilman, Sander. *The Case of Sigmund Freud: Medicine and Identity at the Fin de Siècle.* Baltimore: Johns Hopkins UP, 1993.

Laplanche, Jean. "The Freud Museum Seminar." *Seduction, Translation, Drives.* Ed. John Fletcher and Martin Stanton. London: Institute of Contemporary Arts, 1992. 41–63.

——. *Life and Death in Psychoanalysis.* Trans. Jeffrey Mehlman. Baltimore: Johns Hopkins UP, 1976.

Laplanche, Jean, and Jean-Bertrand Pontalis. "Fantasy and the Origins of Sexuality." *Formations of Fantasy.* Ed. Victor Burgin, James Donald, and Cora Kaplan. London: Methuen, 1986. 5–34.

Martin, Biddy. *Woman and Modernity: The (Life)Styles of Lou Andreas-Salomé.* Ithaca: Cornell UP, 1991.

Peirce, Charles Sanders. *Collected Papers.* 8 vols. Cambridge: Harvard UP, 1931–1958.

Wollheim, Richard. "The Bodily Ego." *Philosophical Essays on Freud.* Ed. Richard Wollheim and James Hopkins. Cambridge: Cambridge UP, 1982. 124–38.

Notes on Contributors

R O S I   B R A I D O T T I is Professor and Chair of Women's Studies at the University of Utrecht in the Netherlands.

J U D I T H   B U T L E R is Chancellor's Professor in the departments of Rhetoric and Comparative Literature at the University of California, Berkeley. Her recent books are *Gender Trouble: Feminism and the Subversion of Identity* and *Bodies That Matter: On the Discursive Limits of "Sex."* She also co-edited, with Joan W. Scott, *Feminists Theorize the Political.* Her forthcoming books include *The Psychic Life of Power: Essays in Subjection* and *Excitable Speech: A Politics of the Performative.*

T E R E S A   D E   L A U R E T I S is Professor of the History of Consciousness at the University of California, Santa Cruz. She guest-edited *differences* 3.2 (1991), the "Queer Theory: Lesbian and Gay Sexualities" issue. Her most recent book in English is *The Practice of Love: Lesbian Sexuality and Perverse Desire.*

E L I Z A B E T H   G R O S Z holds a Personal Chair in Critical Theory and Philosophy at Monash University in Victoria, Australia. She is the author of *Sexual Subversions: Three French Feminists* and *Space, Time and Perversion.* She is currently working, with Vicki Kirby, on a book on the posthuman.

E V E L Y N N   H A M M O N D S is an Assistant Professor of the History of Science in the Program in Science, Technology, and Society at MIT. She is currently working on a book on the history of the concept of race in biology and medicine.

T R E V O R   H O P E is a PhD candidate in Comparative Literature at Cornell University. He has recently published in *Diacritics* and has completed a dissertation currently entitled "Articulating the Social Body: Psychoanalysis, Sexual Difference, and Queer Sexualities."

B I D D Y   M A R T I N is Associate Professor of German Studies and Women's Studies and Associate Dean of the College of Arts and Sciences at Cornell University. She has recently completed a book of essays on constructions of lesbianism at the intersections of feminist and queer theory entitled *Femininity Played Straight.*

K I M   M I C H A S I W teaches eighteenth-century English literature and psychoanalytic theory at York University. He is working on a book on popular aesthetics and has recently published an edition of Charlotte Dacre's *Zofloya, or The Moor* (1806).

G A Y L E   R U B I N currently teaches Women's Studies at the University of California, Santa Cruz.

C A R O L E - A N N E   T Y L E R is an Associate Professor of English at the University of California, Riverside, and the author of *Female Impersonation*.

E L I Z A B E T H   W E E D is Associate Director of The Pembroke Center for Teaching and Research on Women at Brown University and editor of *Coming to Terms: Feminism, Theory, Politics*.

Index

A

Abelove, Henry: *The Lesbian and Gay Studies Reader*, 3–4, 6, 11, 23, 26n3, 26n5, 137–38

Abraham, Nicolas, 273–74, 288n5

Alarcón, Norma, 8

Allison, Dorothy, 10

Alonso, Ana Maria, 138

Althusser, Louis, 70, 71, 89, 236

Andreas-Salomé, Lou, 330

Armstrong, Nancy, 270, 272

B

Balzac, Honoré de, 281–82

Barale, Michèle: *The Lesbian and Gay Studies Reader*, 3–4, 6, 11, 23, 26n3, 26n5, 137–38

Barbin, Herculine, 249–50, 253, 257–59

Barney, Natalie, 90

Barthes, Roland: Miller's essay on, 276–86, 288n11, 289n12; on photographs, 231, 239–40, 260n3; thematics in, 269, 287

Baudrillard, J., 192

Bazin, André, 231

Beauvoir, Simone de, 42, 50, 52, 56

Bell, Andy, 162

Benhabib, Seyla, 235

Benjamin, Walter, 47

Bentson, Kimberly, 229

Berlant, Lauren, xiiin3, 237

Bersani, Leo: on camp, 157, 160, 172–75, 182n11; and desire, 169, 302; on fetishism and the phallic symbol, 311n11

Bérubé, Allan, 96

Bhabha, Homi, 35, 241, 251, 255

Bloch, Iwan, 88

Bock, Gisela, 40

Boothby, Richard, 261n7

Borch-Jacobsen, Mikkel, 190, 211n8

Borghi, Liana, 40

Bourdieu, Pierre, 71

Braidotti, Rosi, xi, xii, 223–26; on anti-racism, 39; on difference, 49–51; on Eurocentrism and women's studies, 35–38; on the European Union, 31–33, 35–36, 49; on gender, 20, 40–43, 48–49; on the German Movement, 41–42; on the homosocial contract, 208; on multiculturalism, 38; on nationalism, 39–40; on new subjects, 61; on patriarchy's demise, 188–93, 198; on queer theory, 54–55; on sexual difference theory, 19, 41, 42–47, 49, 51–54, 57–58, 60–62, 287n2; on the symbolic, 59–63; on Wittig's lesbian authorship, 53–57; on women's studies in Europe, 33–34

Bronfen, Elisabeth, 112, 173

Brown, Elsa Barkley, 153n3

Bryant, Anita, 72

Burke, Kenneth, 158, 159

Butler, Judith, xi; on the constructedness of discourse, 316–17; on the delegitimization of the subject, 321–22; on Eurocentrism, 3–35, 37; on Foucault's analysis of the hermaphrodite, 249–50, 253–54, 258, 259; and the gender/sex distinction, viii, 287n2; *Gender Trouble*, 2, 133n2, 289n13; on kinship, 72, 74, 94; on patriarchy, 255; on politics and gender, 47–48; on queer thematics, ix, xiiin5, 237; on sexual difference theory, 42–43, 51, 53–54, 58, 73–76; on the symbolic and the social, 60, 62; on white and black women's power relations, 141; on Wittig's lesbian authorship, 57

C

Cacciari, Massimo, 35

Carby, Hazel, 152n1

Castel, Robert, 189

Cixous, Hélène, 40, 52, 56, 57, 64n12

Clarke, Cheryl, 146, 150

Collins, Patricia Hill, 146

Copjec, Joan, 285, 286, 289n13

Core, Philip, 163

Cornell, Drucilla, 22

Corrigan, Maureen, 181n2

Crenshaw, Kimberlé, 144

Crimp, Douglas, 167, 178

Culler, Jonathan, 273, 288n5

D

Davis, Madeline, 96

Davis, Whitney, 332n7

de Lauretis, Teresa, xi, xii, 28 n11, 137; on the castration complex, 301–303, 307; on female homosexualities, 146; on lesbian desire, 148, 297, 300, 303–309, 312n13; on lesbian fetishism, 300–305, 307–309, 311n11, 312n15; on the masculinity complex, 302–303, 308, 309, 311n12, 313n16; on per-